THE CAMBRIDGE COMPANION TO
SHAKESPEARE ON FILM

Second edition

Film adaptations of Shakespeare's plays are increasingly popular and now figure prominently in the study of his work and its reception. This lively *Companion* is a collection of critical and historical essays on the films adapted from, and inspired by, Shakespeare's plays. An international team of leading scholars discuss Shakespearean films from a variety of perspectives: as works of art in their own right; as products of the international movie industry; in terms of cinematic and theatrical genres; and as the work of particular directors from Laurence Olivier and Orson Welles to Franco Zeffirelli and Kenneth Branagh. They also consider specific issues such as the portrayal of Shakespeare's women and the supernatural. The emphasis is on feature films for cinema, rather than television, with strong coverage of *Hamlet*, *Richard III*, *Macbeth*, *King Lear* and *Romeo and Juliet*. A guide to further reading and a useful filmography are also provided.

RUSSELL JACKSON is Allardyce Nicoll Professor of Drama and Theatre Studies in the University of Birmingham. He has worked as a textual adviser on several feature films including *Shakespeare in Love* and Kenneth Branagh's *Henry V*, *Much Ado About Nothing*, *Hamlet*, *Love's Labour's Lost* and *As You Like It*. He is co-editor of *Shakespeare: An Illustrated Stage History* (1996) and two volumes in the *Players of Shakespeare* series.

THE CAMBRIDGE
COMPANION TO

SHAKESPEARE ON FILM

Second edition

THE CAMBRIDGE
COMPANION TO
SHAKESPEARE
ON FILM

Second edition

EDITED BY
RUSSELL JACKSON

CAMBRIDGE UNIVERSITY PRESS
Cambridge, New York, Melbourne, Madrid, Cape Town, Singapore, São Paulo

CAMBRIDGE UNIVERSITY PRESS
The Edinburgh Building, Cambridge CB2 8RU, UK

Published in the United States of America by Cambridge University Press, New York

www.cambridge.org
Information on this title: www.cambridge.org/9780521685016

First published 2000
Second edition 2007

Printed in the United Kingdom at the University Press, Cambridge

A catalogue record for this book is available from the British Library

ISBN 978-0-521-86600-2 hardback
ISBN 978-0-521-68501-6 paperback

CONTENTS

CONTENTS

CONTRIBUTORS

DEBORAH CARTMELL, De Montfort University

SAMUEL CROWL, Ohio University

H. R. COURSEN, University of Maine, Augusta

ANTHONY DAVIES, Stratford-upon-Avon

NEIL FORSYTH, Université de Lausanne

BARBARA FREEDMAN, Tufts University

MICHAEL HATTAWAY, University of Sheffield

TONY HOWARD, University of Warwick

RUSSELL JACKSON, University of Birmingham

J. LAWRENCE GUNTNER, Technische Universität, Braunschweig

HARRY KEYISHIAN, Fairleigh Dickinson University

PAMELA MASON, Wroxton College

CAROL CHILLINGTON RUTTER, University of Warwick

MARK SOKOLYANSKY, University of Odessa

NEIL TAYLOR, Roehampton University

PATRICIA TATSPAUGH, London

MICHÈLE WILLEMS, Université de Rouen

PREFACE

As the medium enters its second century, the cinematic repertoire has accumulated a fair number of films derived from (or inspired by) Shakespeare's works, and 'Shakespeare on Film' figures prominently in academic study of the dramatist's work and its reception. The essays in this *Companion* represent a diversity of approaches and responses to this lively topic. The primary emphasis is on feature films – made on celluloid stock and intended primarily for theatrical distribution – rather than expressly for television or video productions. The films are considered as artistic achievements in themselves; in terms of the economics of the entertainment industry; in relation to film and dramatic genre; in the context of studies of the director as *auteur*; and with regard to broader issues of cultural politics. In this *Companion* several films and plays are considered by different contributors from different points of view: in particular, the various films of *Hamlet*, *Richard III*, *Macbeth* and *Romeo and Juliet* reappear in a variety of contexts.

As 'text adviser' I myself have had a hand or (in the words of the Elizabethan playwright Thomas Heywood) at least a main finger in a number of recent Shakespeare films, particularly those of Kenneth Branagh. As editor of this volume, I have not attempted to influence or alter the contributors' responses to them. This second edition of the *Companion* has afforded the opportunity to take account – as appropriate – of films released since its first publication in 2000, and to correct some errors. The filmography (which is not exhaustive, but lists films referred to in the text) has been revised and the bibliography has been brought up to date.

R.J., Birmingham
March, 2006

A NOTE ON REFERENCES

Unless otherwise indicated, references to Shakespeare's plays are to the one-volume *Complete Works* edited by Stanley Wells and Gary Taylor (Compact Edition, Oxford, 1988).

RUSSELL JACKSON

Introduction: Shakespeare, films and the marketplace

The romantic comedy *Shakespeare in Love* (1998) wittily puts the dramatist into the world of show business. Shakespeare's relationship with the theatre manager, Henslowe – and through him with 'the money' – is the occasion for a multitude of jokes referring to the entertainment industry of late sixteenth-century London in terms of its equivalent four hundred years later. In one moment of crisis Henslowe is even on the point of giving birth to a great cliché. 'The show must . . .' he starts, and Shakespeare completes the phrase by urging him impatiently to 'Go on.' The moment passes, unnoticed by either of them. The tension between the artist and the marketplace has always been a good source of humour in drama and fiction and on film, and by situating a parody of it in Shakespeare's time, the film probably makes it seem less harmful than it really is. The story is usually told in terms of the crassness of the producers and the crushed idealism of the 'creative' department. To quote Pauline Kael, 'There's a natural war in Hollywood between the business men and the artists. It's based on drives that may go deeper than politics or religion: on the need for status, and warring dreams.'[1]

On a less personal and anecdotal level, analysts of culture have often been reluctant to allow that commercial films can be effectively radical. In *Big-Time Shakespeare* (1996), Michael Bristol ruefully observes that 'the cultural authority of corporate Shakespeare has nothing to do with ideas of any description'. Perhaps one might argue that if 'ideas' are defined less restrictively, the tension between 'Shakespeare', ideas and big business has yielded an engaging variety of cinematic results. In *Shakespeare and Modern Popular Culture* (2002) Douglas Lanier takes a wary but less dismissive view of what his title's 'and' conveys: 'a sense of simultaneous attraction and tension between Shakespeare and popular culture, and the cultural constituencies they represent'.[2]

The chapters in this *Companion* reflect the variety of ways in which Shakespeare's unique status – both as a complex of poetic and theatrical materials and a cultural icon – has been married to the equally complex phenomenon of the cinema. Shakespearean films are discussed in this volume from different points of view and in different contexts: as reflections of the business and craft of film-making; in terms of cinematic and theatrical genres; as the work of particular directors; and in relation to wider issues of cultural politics. Themselves part of the history of the reception of Shakespeare's plays, the films also have a significance in any account of the aims and effects of the cinema.

In fact the number of films made from Shakespeare's plays is relatively small, although the 'Shakespeare factor' in cinema has been enhanced by the numerous 'offshoots' – films, like *Shakespeare in Love*, that draw on Shakespearean material without claiming to perform any one of the plays. In the first century of moving pictures, Shakespeare's plays played an honourable but hardly dominant role in the development of the medium. Some fifty sound films have been made of Shakespearean plays to date, but it has been estimated that during the 'silent' era – before synchronised dialogue complicated the business of adapting poetic drama for the screen – there were more than 400 films on Shakespearean subjects. These took their place in an international market unrestricted by considerations of language and (consequently) untroubled by the relatively archaic dialogue of the originals. Like the films of other 'classics', they conferred respectability on their makers and distributors, while providing an easily transportable rival to the pictorial, melodramatic mode of popular theatre. As a working definition of the 'classic' in this context, it is hard to better that provided by an American trade paper, the *Nickelodeon*, in 1911:

> 'Classic' is here used in a rather loose and unrestricted sense, as it generally is used by adherents of the photoplay, meaning vaguely a kind of piece that is laid in a bygone era and one which aims to evoke some kind of poetic and idealistic illusion differing from that illusion of mere reality with which photoplays are ordinarily concerned. 'Costume play,' 'historical piece,' 'poetic drama,' variously convey a similar idea.

The story will be familiar and drawn from fiction, poetry, drama, history or the Bible, and such 'photoplays' will be costly, requiring 'an expensive outlay of costumes and scenic effects' and 'deep and careful research into the manners and customs of the era depicted'. Above all they call for a 'producer' with 'the eye of an artist and the mind of a poet'.[3] When this was written Shakespeare was more firmly embedded in popular culture than he is some nine decades later. The plays (or at least a few of them), heavily adapted to accommodate lavish realistic staging and show off the star actors' performances in leading roles, were a staple of actor-managers' theatre. Painters in the persistently popular narrative mode could confidently exhibit and sell works based on favourite characters, scenes and situations, and illustrated editions of the *Works* had their place on family bookshelves. At the same time a more earnest, less richly upholstered Shakespearean experience could be found in the touring activities of idealistic

companies such as those of F. R. Benson and Ben Greet, or in the many annotated and more or less scholastic editions marketed for the general reader and the
schoolroom. Many silent Shakespeare films claim either to replicate or at least
represent stage performances: such are the fragment showing Sir Herbert
Beerbohm-Tree in *King John* and the 1911 film of F. R. Benson's company on
stage at Stratford-upon-Avon in scenes from *Richard III*.[4] Some films either
emulate theatrical values while offering more convincing (or at least more
portable) equivalents of stage productions, or combine both aims with a more
sensitive use of the new medium: subtler acting and the use of locations in the
1913 British *Hamlet*, with Sir Johnston Forbes-Robertson, offer a case in point.
Perhaps the decisive moment in the development of Shakespeare films is reached
when film-makers cease to rely on the audience's prior knowledge of plays
(or even specific performances) or such extra-filmic devices as a narrator or lec-
turer. Luke McKernan suggests 1916 as a watershed year, citing the production
of a *King Lear* (produced by Edwin Thanhouser) and a lost *Macbeth*, both made
in the USA.[5] This increased confidence may also be reflected in the greater
freedoms taken by a group of German-produced films which combine
Shakespearean material with elements not to be found in the plays: Svend Gade's
remarkable *Hamlet* of 1920, Dmitri Buchowetski's *Othello* (1922) with Emil
Jannings and Werner Krauss and Peter Paul Felner's version of *The Merchant of
Venice* (1923).[6]

Nevertheless, Shakespearean films and other 'classics' were hardly a staple of
the new and burgeoning cinema business: it was comedy, melodrama, the Western
and the exotic historical romance that were regarded as bankable. By the 1920s
the making and selling of films entailed increasingly high outlays and corre-
spondingly high risks, and there was already an 'undeclared' trade war between
the United States and Europe.[7] It was their prestige value or the power of a particular personality that recommended Shakespearean projects to film companies,
or at least overcame their reluctance. None of the first wave of Shakespearean
sound films was a financial success. The 1935 Warner Brothers' *A Midsummer
Night's Dream* was announced as inaugurating a series to be made with its distinguished co-director, Max Reinhardt, but after its failure at the box-office
nothing came of these plans. The opulent *Romeo and Juliet* directed by George
Cukor and produced by Irving Thalberg at MGM was an expensive showcase for
Thalberg's wife, Norma Shearer. Paul Czinner's British production of *As You
Like It*, starring Elisabeth Bergner and Laurence Olivier, with sets by Lazare
Meerson and music by William Walton, was no more of a success, for all its
lavish production values. Olivier's wartime *Henry V*, released in 1944, came as an
early glimmer of one of the false dawns that recur in the history of the British
film industry's presence in the worldwide market. The appeal of classic material performed by British (and therefore 'authentic') talent was undoubtedly

overestimated. The same director's *Hamlet* (1948) was a successful 'prestige' undertaking for the producer J. Arthur Rank, but after *Richard III* in 1956 the proposed *Macbeth* was stopped in its tracks by Rank's accountants.[8] Roger Manvell, reviewing *Hamlet* on its appearance, summed up the limitations of a film that – like many others of the time – might well be a *succès d'estime*, but would never make good money outside Britain (and perhaps not even there):

> Like other major British pictures, this film to a certain extent labours under the weight of a calculated technique, and so loses the heart and the sweat of passionate feeling. Months of planning become too evident; everything seems too meticulous. Nevertheless, there is a nobility in the production, a desire to give everything that the studio can muster to make Shakespeare effective on the screen at a cost of half a million pounds.[9]

Less earnest, less self-consciously 'classic' Shakespeare films might stand a chance, but it would be a decade before they arrived.

The breakthrough seemed to come with Franco Zeffirelli's *The Taming of the Shrew* (1966) and *Romeo and Juliet* (1968). Shakespeare was established in the context of popular international cinema and potentially impressive profit: in the USA alone *Romeo and Juliet* earned fourteen times its negative costs. (One yardstick of box-office success is that a film should make at least two-and-a-half times the cost of making the master negative.)[10] The success of Kenneth Branagh's modestly financed *Henry V* ($5m. negative cost) in 1989 appears to have inaugurated a new wave of confidence in Shakespearean projects, enhanced by the same director's *Much Ado About Nothing* (1994), which cost only $8m. to make and grossed over $22m. in the USA on its initial theatrical release. The films following immediately in the wake of these two seem not to have fared so well. Branagh's four-hour, full-length *Hamlet*, made for $18m., earned little more than $4.4m. in its first release in the US domestic market, which remains a crude but reliable index of the financial fortunes of English-language films. (Zeffirelli's 1991 *Hamlet* grossed approximately $20.7m.)[11] By June 1999 *A Midsummer Night's Dream* (directed by Michael Hoffman) and an 'offshoot' of *The Taming of the Shrew* (*Ten Things I Hate About You*) had recently been released, and a number of other feature-film versions of Shakespeare soon followed, none of them with period settings that would deter an audience hostile to 'traditional' Shakespeare but none achieving more than modest box-office returns: Kenneth Branagh's *Love's Labour's Lost* is a pastiche of 1930s musical, Julie Taymor's *Titus* (1999) is set in an eclectic (or post-modern) 'Rome' and Michael Almereyda's *Hamlet* (2000) is a story of corporate and familial politics in modern Manhattan. Branagh had also announced his intention of filming *Macbeth* and *As You Like It* in the near future: at the time of writing (Spring 2006) only the comedy has been filmed – it is set in nineteenth-century Japan.

The Merchant of Venice, directed by Michael Radford with Al Pacino as Shylock (2004), opts – unusually – for sixteenth-century Venice.

The general wisdom – or fervent hope – of 1999 seemed to be that the phenomenal successes of Baz Luhrmann's *Romeo + Juliet* (1996) and John Madden's romantic comedy *Shakespeare in Love* (1998) would enhance audience interest in the works of the playwright. The former was held to appeal to teenagers, the latter had a wider target audience but by all accounts included them too. In May 1999, Fox Searchlight, the distributors of Hoffman's *A Midsummer Night's Dream*, were reported to be targeting 'mature females' in its initial US theatrical release, hoping that their own 'romantic comedy' would benefit from that audience's lack of interest in the much-hyped *Star Wars* 'prequel'.[12] What is always hoped for though is the all-important shift from one section of the market to another, the crossover that can move a Shakespeare film out of the 'niche' or (worse) art-house sector. If a project has cost relatively little to produce (as has been the case with most Shakespeare films) but turns out to have the broad appeal that justifies increased distribution, the investors have been blessed with good fortune. Luhrmann's *Romeo + Juliet*, with its youth appeal and Leonardo DiCaprio as Romeo, must have seemed like a winner from an early stage. Although its budget was a relatively modest $14.5m., it was given the 'wide' opening regularly employed with much bigger films: the distributors opened it on 1,276 screens in the USA, taking over $11m. out of its $46,351,345 first-run gross in the first weekend. (In the same season Branagh's *Hamlet* opened on three screens initially, and made only $148,000 in its first weekend, although more cinemas showed it and more money was made in subsequent weeks.) If the money spent on a film has been commensurate with even a modest degree of box-office success – over $10m., say – and it still remains stubbornly in its niche, no one will be made rich by it, but nor will they be surprised. The sums quoted above should be put in the perspective of the really big earners and spenders: setting aside really 'high concept' and 'summer blockbuster' films, a popular comedy might reach nine figures on its first release (*Mrs Doubtfire*, $219,195,051) and an earnest, 'quality' drama can edge into the same league (*Schindler's List*, $96,060,353). A blockbuster of the late 1990s, *Titanic* (1997), earned over $600m. in the USA alone. Revenue from DVD and video rentals and sales, which now provides the greater part of a film's profits, is of course significant – Shakespeare films have a long shelf-life at least in the educational market – but the credit in the industry that accrues to cast, director and producers may be more valuable than any monetary returns.[13]

Some unusual angle on the material, and attractive or quirky casting – usually combining Hollywood stars with actors of recognised 'classical' theatre background – seem indispensable for an acceptable degree of success with Shakespeare in the popular cinema. But modest budgets do bring with them a welcome freedom from the industry's grosser absurdities and constraints. As one American actor remarked to me while working on a Shakespeare film, 'It's nice to know that no one in an office somewhere is going to say, "Hey, this is boring. Let's blow up a building."' At the same time, these films (like any others) are likely to be dependent on international funding, and consequently answerable to the suggestions, if not diktats, of producers with an eye on the US market. The 'independent' distributors in Hollywood, such as Miramax, invest mainly in relatively low-budget films, often made outside the USA. The movies are typified by their 'attention to theme, character relationships and social relevance' and targeted at a market somewhere between the art-house and the 'mainstream'. They set themselves apart from the simplifications and marketing orientation of the 'high concept' film.[14] Release for home viewing provides one element of a film's revenue, but it is the initial theatrical release in the USA – the attraction of a large cinema-going audience, often on the first weekend – that provides the reviews and is usually taken as indicative of a film's financial success. The situation is not necessarily or indeed usually one of conflict between writers or directors and dollar-hungry 'suits': the makers of films want to have their work seen by as many people as possible, and the producers may have artistically valid suggestions to make. However, given William Goldmann's adage that in Hollywood 'NOBODY KNOWS ANYTHING', it is really one informed guess that is being pitted against another.[15] Compromise in the direction of sentimentality (especially in the ending) and characterisation (only certain kinds of complexity being thought acceptable at a given time) can entail a film's being refashioned to an overall pattern known to find favour. 'Buddy' movies, tales of personal triumph over adversity and heart-warming celebrations of a vaguely defined sense of communality, are more likely than searching analysis of any kind.

Participation in the marketplace entails a degree of compromise with what the potential purchaser is known to want. Trevor Nunn, listing in the published screenplay (1996) the alterations he was obliged to make to his *Twelfth Night* at the behest of the distributors and in the light of test screenings, 'confesses' the sins of omission and commission that included the writing of a voice-over prologue in verse to clarify further the 'story so far' – 'I resisted, I wept, I tampered.' Definitions of the viable commercial film have usually been in terms of character, story and duration: attractive, interesting people will encounter difficulties and overcome them, probably making allies and fending off adversaries, and take something less than two hours to do so. Although the gurus of mainstream screenplay-writing vary in their recommended strategies, there is general agreement that what sell best in the USA (and consequently in most markets worldwide) are stories containing ideas rather than ideas turned into stories.[16] Shakespeare films – even of the tragedies – are not immune to the cruder Hollywood imperatives. The title character – a producer – in Robert Altman's satire *The Player* (1992) provides a list: 'Certain elements we need to market a film successfully . . . Suspense, laughter, violence, hope, heart, nudity, sex, happy endings – mainly happy endings.' In the academic study of Shakespeare happy endings, together with anything else that might smooth the path of the plays' characters, have long been out of favour. (So that Branagh's *Much Ado*, for example, consigns its characters to happiness more readily than most recent critical readings or stage productions of the play have done.) Moreover, dramatic 'character', constructed on a psychologising basis in the manner of Stanislavsky and his heirs, has been treated with suspicion as an unhistorical imposition from the popular theatre and cinema. Publicity statements about characters and their 'journey' through the play/film tend to be cast in terms of modern self-improvement literature. Michele Pfeiffer, for example, observes in a note to the script of Michael Hoffman's *A Midsummer Night's Dream* (1999) that Titania's affair with Oberon is 'somewhat tempestuous', and that 'a relationship with Bottom is very liberating in its simplicity' – an analysis innocent (like the film itself) of the darker imaginings that have haunted academic criticism and many stage productions at least since 1964, when the English translation of Jan Kott's *Shakespeare our Contemporary* was published.[17] Even when the writer of a Shakespearean screenplay is not being threatened by the front office with the formulas of plot and characterisation prized by Hollywood and its leading players (both actors and producers), he or she is more likely to be constructing than deconstructing.

It is in advertising that the Shakespeare film is likely to present itself most stridently in terms of the broadest attractions. Publicists (over whom the director usually has limited influence) have often striven to depict Shakespearean films as products of a familiar – and therefore welcome – kind. Thus, the campaign book for the 1956 British release of Orson Welles's *Othello* includes these proposals for advertising headlines:

THE MIGHTY STORY OF THE TRAGIC MOOR
RECREATED BY ORSON WELLES IN ALL ITS SPLENDOUR!
THE STORY OF LOVE . . .
OF ONE WHO LOVED NOT WISELY BUT TOO WELL!
SPECTACULAR DRAMA OF JEALOUSY . . . MURDER . . . RETRIBUTION!
POWERFUL . . . MAGNIFICENT . . . ELECTRIFYING . . . SPELLBINDER!
BRILLIANT . . . . FABULOUS . . . DRAMATIC SENSATION

In a similar vein, and printing selected words from the reviews in extra large type, a flyer for the British release of Richard Loncraine and Ian McKellen's *Richard III* in 1996 promised an 'EXCITING . . . ADVENTUROUS . . . THRILLER' (a description not far removed from its makers' aims).

The tactics adopted for an appeal to a more sophisticated audience are subtler. In 1935 the US campaign book for Max Reinhardt's *A Midsummer Night's*

Dream offered a strategy 'designed exclusively for premiere engagements' suggesting ways in which the film could be turned into a social and cultural event: 'The exploitation of THE DREAM should follow the same unfailing Reinhardt formula. Get the best people interested. Socialites and cultural leaders gladly lend the prestige of their names to promote Reinhardt and Shakespeare.'

Cinema managers were urged to 'SELL ENTERTAINMENT by direct advertising and publicity. SELL CULTURE by under-cover propaganda, personal sales work and indirect and inferential advertising and publicity.' The British publicity office also made much of the star-power of the film and its lavish production values, and urged the headlining of Reinhardt and Shakespeare, 'the greatest money-names of the theatre'. This theatrical pedigree was duly emphasised in the advertising together with the listing of the stars and the usual disclosure of behind-the-scenes facts ('More than 600,000 yards of cellophane were used for the ballets; Titania's train required 90,000 yards of gossamer strands alone').[18]

Similar material, with varying degrees of stridency, could be cited for most of the Shakespearean films. The sums invested are relatively small and, as with distribution, no great outlay is hazarded unless a film looks as though it might 'cross over'. These are films that it is hard to label as sequels (no one has yet attempted a *Wars of the Roses* sequence of feature films) or to advertise in the terms used for *Lethal Weapon IV* on its British release in 1998: 'The faces you love, the action you expect.' At different stages in its progress from preparation to studio floor, and through post-production to its audience, a film has to be presented to a succession of potential buyers: first to the major distributors, then by them to the distributors in different territories, who in turn must sell it to their own clients, the exhibitors. The promotional films used for this then give way to trailers for theatrical use, which are put together from available footage by editors and directors who have no connection with the original work. Direct reference is less likely to be made now than in the 1930s to the high cultural status of Shakespeare or of the period the film is set in. The identity of the principal actors and the scale of the production are usually the main selling points. Love interest (or sex) and action may be emphasised, and the film's director may even have to argue strongly for the exclusion of particular images or scenes that would take away the element of surprise when the movie itself is shown.

Films made from Shakespeare's plays exist at a meeting-point between conflicting cultural assumptions, rival theories and practices of performance, and – at the most basic level – the uneasy and overlapping systems of theatre and cinema. As Manfred Pfister points out in *The Theory and Analysis of Drama*, film partakes of the nature of narrative as well as dramatic texts.[19] Beyond this, the dramatic form of the originals favours metadramatic devices, makes use of techniques akin to (and absorbed in) post-Brechtian 'alienation', and returns theatre to a presentational mode that predates most of the sophisticated literary narratives that cinema emulates. There will always be a conflict of techniques as well as of value systems when these Renaissance plays form the pretext for movies.

The relationship between Shakespearean films aimed at the mass market and the academic study of the plays has always been tense. In the early decades of the century, film-makers anticipated the accusation of desecrating what were routinely treated as secular scriptures. More recently, the interrogation of the cultural functions of the plays themselves and their interpretation has resulted in some directors being taken to task for harnessing one hegemony (Shakespeare as a figurehead of conservative anglocentric culture) to another (international big business). An academic disinclination to celebrate harmonies and resolutions has made the unifying efforts of mainstream cinema suspect and stimulated sympathy for the determinedly *avant-garde*. To this can be joined the long-established distrust of the cultural politics of mass entertainment films as powerful generators of false consciousness. This suspicion extends in some cases into a fundamental suspicion of the medium itself: Walter Benjamin's indictment of the film as a factor in 'distraction' of the viewer has been particularly influential.[20] Consequently, many commentators have favoured the Shakespearean films of such directors as Derek Jarman (*The Tempest*, 1979) or Christine Edzard (*As You Like It*, 1992; *The Children's 'A Midsummer Night's Dream'*, 2001), who have refused to make commercial success a priority. Orson Welles's problematic relationship with the established formulas of filming and the business practices of the industry has resulted in his being posthumously recruited as an early postmodernist. Kenneth Branagh's whole-hearted participation in the marketplace has probably contributed to a tendency for his films to be discussed in terms of their cultural politics as much as (or rather than) according to any technical or aesthetic measure. Alternative sources of finance, often including government grants (in Europe but not in the USA) or co-production deals with television 'arts' producers, have supported such projects as *Prospero's Books* (1991) by a director (Peter Greenaway) who professes no interest in the popular cinema. There is also an 'alternative' world of Shakespeare on film beyond even the art-houses, inhabited by what Richard Burt identifies as 'queer' Shakespeare.[21]

For better or worse, Shakespearean films continue to appear in the multiplexes and on the shelves of the video stores. Since the early 1980s the revolution in home video has made most (if not all) of the sound-era Shakespeare films widely available, not least to the scholars who used to hunt down showings in film clubs and revival houses, or arrange to watch them in the study rooms of libraries and archives.

It is probably as much of a mistake to ask whether 'film' can do justice to 'Shakespeare' as to reproach 'Shakespeare' with being inappropriate material for 'film'. Neither are stable entities, reducible to a simple set of definitions, but two bundles of techniques and opportunities that may be mixed together with more or less enjoyable and impressive results. We can no more pronounce that *Hamlet* (for example) essentially means one thing or another, and that a particular film fails to capture this quality, than we can object that Shakespearean drama jeopardises essentially filmic virtues. Nor are 'film' and 'Shakespeare' the same in every 'territory' mapped out by distributors. Moreover, a director, actor or film might be ignored in one country and revered in another, just as a play may have a resonance in (say) Russia, that it lacks elsewhere. On the other hand, we can identify the intentions of writers and directors or the behaviour of larger groups (production companies, their publicists, audiences) by reference to the texts they started from and the congruence of the results with interpretations in circulation when the film was made. The audiences appealed to or implied in the films are an important object of study, but the same arguments turn up in widely different social and political contexts. Few would argue with a director who declares 'If you're making a Shakespeare film for a contemporary audience, you have to make sure that they don't get bored.' Many would have echoed the anxiety of a prospective producer offered a *Merchant of Venice* project: 'It is impossible to use Shakespeare's exact words in a film that will be two hours long. It is ridiculous and absurd and will at best end up as nothing but a literary experiment. Such experiments are impossible now, when we can make at best only forty-two films a year.' The first of these statements is by Richard Loncraine, co-director of a *Richard III* set in the context of 1930s fascism, and the second by Dr Josef Goebbels, responding in 1944 to a proposal by the director Veit Harlan.[22]

The producers and directors of Shakespeare films – like any others – gamble on their sense of what the viewing public is used to, and what (all being well) it will find a welcome surprise. This is as true of the varieties of 'alternative' cinema as of the mainstream. There will always be movies that address their audience by saying 'You thought Shakespeare was like this – well, he is and we've captured it on film.' There are also, at the beginning of cinema's second century, plenty that say 'You didn't think Shakespeare could be like this, did you?'

NOTES

1 On the business of Hollywood in the 'classic' period, see Thomas Cripps, *Hollywood's High Noon. Moviemaking and Society before Television* (Baltimore, 1997), which includes an invaluable 'Bibliographical Essay', and Tino Balio, *Grand Design. Hollywood as a Modern Business Enterprise, 1930–1939* (Berkeley, Los Angeles and London, 1993). An incisive recent account of the screenwriter's way of life is John Gregory Dunne, *Monster. Living off the Big Screen* (New York, 1997). Pauline Kael's article 'On the Future of the Movies' (1974) is in her *Reeling. Film Writings 1972–1975* (London, 1977), pp. 309–31, 315.

2 Michael Bristol, *Big-Time Shakespeare* (London, 1996), p. 101 (the context is a discussion of the reception of Kenneth Branagh's *Henry V*); Douglas Lanier, *Shakespeare*

and *Popular Modern Culture* (Oxford, 2002), p. 4. See also Barbara Hodgdon, *The Shakespeare Trade. Performances and Appropriations* (Philadelphia, 1998).

3 Quoted by William Uricchio and Roberta E. Pearson, *Reframing Culture, the Case of the Vitagraph Quality Films* (Princeton, New Jersey, 1993), p. 50. See also the works by Robert Hamilton Ball and John Collick listed in 'Further reading', pp. 324–7 below.

4 In 1999 The British Film Institute released *Silent Shakespeare*, a video transfer of eight early films in its collection: a DVD, with an iuformative commentary by Judith Buchanan, followed in 2005. See below, 'Filmography', p. 328.

5 Luke McKernan and Olwen Terris, eds., *Walking Shadows. Shakespeare in the National Film and Television Archive* (London, 1994), p. 5.

6 Gade's *Hamlet* has been widely discussed: see Ann Thompson's essay in Lynda E. Boose and Richard Burt, eds., *Shakespeare, the Movie. Popularising the Plays on Film, TV and Video* (London, 1998), and J. Lawrence Guntner's chapter below. On the other films the best sources are Robert Hamilton Ball, *Shakespeare on Silent Film* (London, 1986) and the notes in Kenneth S. Rothwell and Annabelle Henkin Melzer's *Shakespeare on Screen: an International Filmography and Videography* (London, 1990). *Othello* is currently available on DVD in a badly hacked version (at least thirty minutes appear to have been cut from the original running time) but this may be all that survives.

7 See David Puttnam, with Neil Watson, *The Undeclared War. The Struggle for Control of the World's Film Industry* (London, 1997). On the British film industry in relation to the world markets see also James Park, *British Cinema. The Lights That Failed* (London, 1990), and Alexander Walker, *Hollywood, England. The British Film Industry in the 1960s* (London, 1974).

8 On *Macbeth* see Laurence Olivier, *On Acting* (London, 1986), pp. 213–14, and Charles Drazin, *The Finest Years: British Cinema of the 1940s* (London, 1998), who relates it to the history of Two Cities Films and Olivier's earlier projects (p. 39). The company's major films had averaged a cost of £200,000–300,000, with *Henry V* breaking a record at £350,000. Dallas Bower, a prime mover in the making of *Henry V*, discusses the financing of this and other films in Brian McFarlane, ed., *An Autobiography of British Cinema* (London, 1997), pp. 80–4.

9 Roger Manvell, 'The Film of *Hamlet*', *The Penguin Film Review*, 8 (1949), 16–24; p. 24.

10 Zeffirelli claims that *The Taming of the Shrew* 'made' $1m., and *Romeo and Juliet* cost $1.5m. and grossed more than $48m. (*Zeffirelli. The Autobiography of Franco Zeffirelli* (London, 1986), p. 242). Walker (*Hollywood, England*, pp. 397–400) repeats the figure of $1.5m. for *Romeo and Juliet* and quotes *Variety* to the effect that it grossed $14.5m. in the United States.

11 Box-office figures here and in the following paragraphs from website: www.boxofficeguru.com.

12 Report on *A Midsummer Night's Dream* targeting from www.boxofficeguru.com/weekend.htm (14 May 1999).

13 On 'niche' markets, and the configuration of the film business in the 1990s, see Martin Dale, *The Movie Game. The Film Business in Britain, Europe and America* (London, 1997), Justin Wyatt, *High Concept. Movies and Marketing in Hollywood* (Austin, Texas, 1994) and Steve Neale and Murray Smith, eds., *Contemporary Hollywood Cinema* (London, 1998). Edward Jay Epstein's *The Big Picture. Money and Power in Hollywood* (New York, 2005) is a readable and informative account of the current

state of the industry, and suggests forcefully that DVD sales (and other, newer forms of delivery, such as the internet) are likely to take over to the point where a film's theatrical grosses become significant more for its advertising than as indicators of its real financial profitability. In 2003, showings in cinemas accounted for a mere 18 per cent of revenues for major studios (Epstein, pp. 19–20).

14 Definition of the independents' policy and films is from Wyatt, *High Concept*, p. 96. A racy and revealing account of the Miramax phenomenon and its impact on the 'indie' and foreign film sector, is Peter Byskind's *Down and Dirty Movies* (New York, 2003). See also Geoff King's *New Hollywood Cinema. An Introduction* (London, 2003), which describes the 'new' Hollywood of the postwar decades, and Epstein's *The Big Picture* (note 13, above).

15 William Goldmann, *Adventures in the Screen Trade. A Personal View of Hollywood and Screenwriting* (1983; paperback edn, London, 1985), p. 38: 'the single most important fact, perhaps, of the entire movie industry'.

16 See Syd Field, *The Screenwriter's Problem Solver* (New York, 1998) p. 5. For a different but also influential view of commercial screenwriting, see Andrew Horton, *Writing the Character-Centred Screenplay* (Berkeley, CA, 1994). The introduction to Trevor Nunn's *Twelfth Night* screenplay, cited above, instances a number of the changes the medium required, and then enumerates those called for after he thought he had done his work (London, 1996: unnumbered pages).

17 *William Shakespeare's A Midsummer Night's Dream Adapted for the Screen and Directed by Michael Hoffman* (London, 1999), p. 80. Peter Brook's 1970 production of the play for the Royal Shakespeare Company was one of the first to draw on and acknowledge Jan Kott's influence: see Jay L. Halio, *Shakespeare in Performance: A Midsummer Night's Dream* (Manchester, 1994), pp. 55ff., and J. L. Styan, *The Shakespeare Revolution* (Cambridge, 1977), ch. 11.

18 Campaign books for Welles's *Othello* and the Reinhardt–Dieterle *Midsummer Night's Dream*, Birmingham Shakespeare Library.

19 Manfred Pfister, *The Theory and Analysis of Drama*, translated by John Halliday (Cambridge, 1988), pp. 23–5.

20 Walter Benjamin, 'The Work of Art in the Age of Mechanical Reproduction', in *Illuminations*, ed. with an Introduction by Hannah Arendt, trans. by Harry Zohn (New York, 1968; London, 1973). The essay was first printed in German in 1936.

21 Richard Burt, *Unspeakable Shaxxxspeares: Queer Theory and American Kiddie Culture* (New York, 1998).

22 Richard Loncraine in 'Shakespeare in the Cinema: a Directors' Forum', *Cinéaste*, 24.1 (1998), 48–55; p. 48. Goebbels quoted by David Culbert, '*Kolberg* (Germany, 1945): the Goebbels Diaries and Poland's Kolobrzeg today', in John Whiteclay Chambers II and David Culbert, eds., *World War II. Film and History* (New York, 1996), pp. 67–83; p. 72.

PART I

Adaptation and its contexts

I

RUSSELL JACKSON

From play-script to screenplay

In fashioning their theatrical raw material into screenplays the makers of Shakespearean films have adopted strategies as diverse as the impulses behind their various projects. The wish to convey faithfully some of the perceived qualities of the chosen play has led to the adoption or rejection in varying degrees of the original's dramatic structure, language and character relationships. The Introduction to this *Companion* has already suggested some ways in which commercial considerations might not only influence the way a Shakespeare film is promoted, but stipulate outlines to which characterisation and narrative may conform. The example, for better or worse, of what has already been sold successfully is reflected in the affinities with film genre that Harry Keyishian discusses below (chapter 4). As Geoffrey O'Brien observed in February 1997 – when another flurry of new Shakespeare films had just been released – 'singular opportunities have been created, not to recapitulate, but to invent'.[1]

In the study of film techniques a broad distinction can be made between films in which story-telling is effected by the montage of images, and which foreground the means by which this is done; and others which conceal the art which places dramatic scenes before the camera with an illusion of unobstructed and privileged access for the audience. Identified in particular with Hollywood before the 1960s, this latter style of 'continuity editing' came to be accepted as a norm of mainstream cinema.[2] However, audiences quickly become habituated to innovation, and since the 1960s films perceived as mainstream have tended to combine both approaches. The films of Orson Welles are remarkable for the simultaneous use of both montage and continuity editing, which partly explains the tension between the sense of radical disruption and a coherence that might (in an ideal world, with the right materials) be restored before the films reach their audience.[3] In filmic terms, the most conservative Shakespeare films are those which adopt as many features of a given play's structure and language as possible, while adapting them to the accepted rules of mainstream cinema in continuity editing, clarity of character and story, and intelligibility of speech. The most radical seek to achieve the play's ends by using as fully as possible the medium's ability to

15

juxtapose images and narrative elements, to superimpose one element of the narrative upon another, shift point of view and register, and disrupt the sense of a coherent world seen clearly. In such films the original's form and methods are not respected, but replaced. The more 'mainstream' group includes such apparently straightforward adaptations as Joseph L. Mankiewicz's *Julius Caesar* (1953), which makes very modest use of techniques only available to or associated with the cinema. Among the most radical versions are Peter Greenaway's *Prospero's Books* (1991) or films derived more or less directly from Shakespearean originals but not seeking to replicate their effects. (See Tony Howard's discussion of 'Offshoots' in chapter 17.)[4] Between these extremes there is much blurring of boundaries. Nor can the presence of elements of avant-garde technique be assumed to indicate radicalism in the cultural values implicit in a film. *Prospero's Books*, for example, for all its elaborate visual effects and self-conscious theatricality (framed in turn by cinematic self-consciousness) includes the original play, spoken almost entirely by Sir John Gielgud. In the director's own words, this provides 'a still centre around which everything revolves'.[5] Akira Kurosawa's 1957 *Macbeth* adaptation, *Kumonosu-djo* (commonly known in English as *Throne of Blood*), includes none of the original play's words but can be said to adopt (and indeed enhance) the play's fusion of psychology, superstition and politics. A feature of this, and of Kurosawa's later *King Lear* film, *Ran* (1985) is the infusion of elements of Noh theatre, so that an elevated, aristocratic theatrical form with an eloquent repertoire of archetypes is married with elements of the Western and of Shakespeare. In the West, this director's adventurous mixing of conventions has been more widely admired than in his own country. [6]

Cinemagoers with a prior interest in Shakespeare – a significant but not dominant portion of a film's anticipated public – tend to begin by assessing the degree of a screen version's divergence from the published (and edited) dramatic text. Even if the ultimate measure of a film's worth is not its degree of fidelity to the words and structure of the original, understanding of the relationship between the two is an important element in the viewer's perception of what a given film is doing. An examination of some ways the mainstream film adaptations have used the texts of their originals also offers a means of assessing more insistently radical work.

Speech, action and poetry

The most obvious difference between a screenplay and the text of an Elizabethan play is the number of spoken words. In writing for the mainstream cinema it is axiomatic that dialogue should be kept to a minimum. What happens in a scene – as the director's traditional command indicates – is 'action'. Syd Field, an influential teacher of screenwriting skills, insists that 'a screenplay is a story told in pictures, and there will always be some kind of problem when you tell the story through words, and not pictures'. His definition of 'the real dynamic of good screenwriting' offers an encapsulated definition of successful mainstream work: 'strong and active characters, combined with a unique, stylized visual narrative that constantly moves the story forward'.[7]

Aiming for the 'ideal' running time of less than two hours, most Shakespeare films have used no more than 25–30 per cent of the original text, and it has been shown that Welles (again, a good example of the most adventurous use of an original) consistently uses fewer words for each transaction between characters.[8] Kenneth Branagh's Shakespeare films and Trevor Nunn's *Twelfth Night* probably reflect the specific theatrical experience of their makers by following the common stage practice of cutting within speeches and scenes, making the dialogue leaner but (mostly) preserving the scene's original shape. In each of these cases there is some reordering of the play's scenes, as in the opening of Nunn's *Twelfth Night*, the 'watch' scenes of *Much Ado* and, more extensively, in the more radically adapted text of *Love's Labour's Lost*. In these and in *The Merchant of Venice* (Michael Radford, 2004), there is also some transposition and cutting of entire scenes, but the narrative outline of the original is more or less adhered to and theatrical practice and priorities are acknowledged although not slavishly followed.

In July 1935, when Max Reinhardt returned to Vienna after filming *A Midsummer Night's Dream* in Hollywood, he expressed his delight that the sound film would allow an immense audience to appreciate the subtleties of the most intimate conversation: the cinema now had the potential to become *Kammerspiele für die Massen* ('chamber theatre for the masses').[9] The opportunity, unfashionable as it may seem, continues to attract. Geoffrey O'Brien, in the essay quoted above, argues passionately for attention to the plays' language in film versions. In the films by Branagh and the theatre directors Trevor Nunn and Adrian Noble (*A Midsummer Night's Dream*, 1996), as well as those by Olivier and Mankiewicz (the 1953 *Julius Caesar*), dialogue retains its theatrical role as a dominant vehicle for characterisation and for the conducting of business between the persons of the play. This has resulted in some notable clashes between the habitual technique of actors and what the camera needs. A classic account of a stage-trained Shakespearean's encounter with acting for the camera is that of Micheál Macliammóir, enlisted by Welles to play Iago to his Othello. Macliammóir wrote in his diary:

> Find what I have long suspected: (a) that one's first job is to forget every single lesson one ever learned on the stage: all projection of personality, build-up of a speech, and sustaining for more than a few seconds of an emotion are not only unnecessary but superfluous, and (b) that the ability to express oneself just below the rate of normal behaviour is a primal necessity . . .[10]

Since the 1950s the distance seems to have diminished between the speaking of Shakespeare's language in the theatre and on screen, if only because few theatre actors make their living by acting Shakespeare in large spaces, and forceful projection and self-conscious rhetorical mannerisms are consequently less prevalent.

Films, however, have their own non-verbal means of denoting transactions between characters. Some have their equivalent in the theatre, such as the construction of spatial relationships between characters. Others are specific to cinema, notably the choice of camera angles and the rhythm of shots in the edited film. Musical emphasis under dialogue is also more common and more readily accepted than it is in the theatre. In the bustling world of Zeffirelli's *Taming of the Shrew* the intimacy of the looks they exchange and the moments of silent understanding they share – underlined by the orchestral score – suggest the inevitability of eventual union between Kate and Petruchio. A striking example of film's aptitude for revealing intimate feelings occurs early in Joseph L. Mankiewicz's *Julius Caesar* (1953): when Caesar, on his way to celebrate the feast of Lupercal, asks Antony (Marlon Brando) to touch Calpurnia after the foot-race, because she is barren. A glance from Brando, seen in medium close-up, suggests a response of sympathy for the dictator's wife. The staging of the forum scene in the same film makes effective use of the large studio set, with moments when Antony and Brutus are seen against an expanse of steep steps or in juxtaposition with the crowd. But there is little in the direction that seems uniquely cinematic – except, that is, for the glimpses the camera affords of Antony's eyes, and the sense they give of his intentions and feelings. Typically, it is Welles who furnishes the greatest abundance of examples of emotionally charged camera angles and staging. In *Chimes at Midnight*, for example, Hal's encounters with John Gielgud's starchily morose Bolingbroke take place in what seems to be an empty cathedral, a cold, stony environment with the camera positions emphasising the distance between the two and the elevation of the king. The tavern world inhabited by Falstaff is characterised not only by low ceilings, wood furniture and half-timbering, but also by the habitual proximity of one person to another. Laurence Olivier is less dynamic (or disruptive) than Welles in his editing and staging, and more theatrical in the way he stages scenes for the camera. Comparison of the two directors' work suggests the range of techniques available. The stylised mode of Olivier's *Richard III* encompasses not only the frankly artificial studio sets but also the emblematic and quasi-theatrical placing of figures within them, notably in the two coronations. In the first – that of Edward – Olivier stage-manages a ceremony that constitutes a formal statement of relationships between the three brothers and the rest of the court; in the second, Richard's, the throne is elevated on a high dais and vertiginous camera-angles suggesting the usurper's point of view help to convey an atmosphere of fear and confusion.

The manipulation of the audience's sense of time and place, and the perception of action in them, is one of the fundamental elements of cinematic narrative. In the cinema, shifts in time can be represented in ways that range from the subliminal to the ostentatious. If a character sees a face at a window, then goes to look closer, in continuity editing it is not necessary – or usually desirable – to show the move made across the room to the window. If days, months or years are to pass, the images suggesting that may be compressed into a few seconds of screen time by the use of montage (the crudest means include such devices as inserts of calendars with pages torn off). In the texts written for the Elizabethan theatre's unlocalised and daylit stage, changes of place and time are accomplished by the simplest of means: statements in the dialogue, accompanied if necessary by clearance of the stage. It has been customary to regard it as an imperative in film that there should be movement among locations, which involves 'opening out' a stage script. A useful comparison can be made with the adaptation of plays written for the realistic, scenic theatre, such as those of Wilde or Shaw. Here the difficulty is more acute, because an organising principle of the original is that as many significant turns of event as possible should take place in a limited number of locations within a given period of time.

Elizabethan dramatic texts invite more latitude, and adapters are more likely not only to abbreviate dialogue, but to use it outside the framework provided by the original. The beginning of Welles's *Othello* exemplifies this, as do the opening sequences in Michael Hoffmann's 1999 *A Midsummer Night's Dream*, in which we are shown several dimensions of Theseus (estate owner, prospective bridegroom and dispenser of the 'Athenian' law) together with different aspects of the domain he presides over. *The Merchant of Venice* (2004) sets up the historical situation regarding the Jews in Venice – and the Ghetto – then opens with a public display of Venetian anti-semitism in which a mob, urged on by a 'new' character, a hectoring monk, grab a Jew and throw him off the Rialto Bridge into the canal. Encountering him among the crowd, Antonio takes the opportunity to void his rheum on Shylock. Another instance is the first court scene in *Hamlet*, as treated by three recent directors. Kenneth Branagh's 'full-text' version (1996) shows Claudius's first speech delivered in full to a massed audience of courtiers. Kozintsev (1964) and Zeffirelli (1990) both employ a selection of the lines to give a more varied picture of the king's power at work, including (in both films) public and private contexts.

The modification of the text of the theatrical original in this way is not so much an unavoidable and regrettable consequence of filming, as an opportunity the director forgoes at his or her peril. The film-maker is able to enjoy greater freedom in showing the words and deeds of characters in relation to the environment created for them. The *mise en scène* of a film is in fact a vital element of the cinematic experience – in all its definitions and varieties – and in Shakespearean films it retains this importance, rather than becoming a reprehensible competitor with the spoken word.

The milieu – 'production values' vs. 'poetry'

From its early days, the narrative cinema proclaimed its ability to show a dramatic action's physical surroundings more vividly, spaciously and accurately than the illusionist theatre. This capacity for delivering 'reality' was established alongside the capacity for depicting fantasy – establishing the now-familiar dialogue between the Lumière and Méliès aspects of the medium.[11] Some early Shakespeare films (such as the Vitagraph *Julius Caesar* of 1908 or the 1911 film of Benson's company in *Richard III*) were effectively a series of animated tableaux, corresponding at once to the pictorial aesthetic of contemporary Shakespeare productions, and to the tradition in the graphic arts of illustrating key moments from the plays. Others, such as the American film of *Richard III* with the actor Frederick Warde (1910) and the *Hamlet* featuring the actor-manager Sir Johnston Forbes-Robertson (1913), were more concerned to convey the narrative shape of the play and the quality of the actor's performance, but also took advantage of the opportunity to 'illustrate' to a degree not possible in the theatre, sometimes by using open-air shooting. From the commercial point of view, relatively spacious and historically authentic settings and appropriate costume designs were 'production values' that both mimicked and challenged the popular theatre.[12] What silent films lacked, of course, was dialogue, and with it not merely its function in conveying character and transactions, but also the presence within the film of poetic description and evocation to rival the milieu shown by the film-maker. Paradoxically, the advent of the 'talkies' made it more difficult to film Shakespeare's plays. The theory and practice of staging Shakespeare in the theatre had moved radically away from pictorialism, symphonic music around and during speeches and the wholesale cutting of the text.[13] Now it seemed that the cinema was reinstating these habits of the actor-manager's theatre.

The reception accorded the Warner Brothers' *A Midsummer Night's Dream* in 1935 demonstrates the ways in which sound crystallised the problem of poetry. This film married the glamour of movies – costly production values, big stars – to 'high' European culture, represented not only by William Shakespeare but also by Max Reinhardt, one of the greatest and most versatile theatrical directors of his time. Its promotion in these terms has been mentioned already (Introduction, p. 7). Beyond the 'trade' press (where exhibitors' anxiety about audience resistance dominated) the reviewers tended to focus on a new element of suspense, as to whether the movies could handle Shakespeare at his most 'poetic'. The anonymous reviewer in *The Times* (17 October 1935) posed the question with a degree of condescension: 'No doubt it was too much to expect an adequate performance of a play by Shakespeare in a film, though there does not seem to be any real reason why it should not be attempted, and the result might be extremely exciting . . .' Reinhardt's version 'has all the faults that grandiose stage productions of Shakespeare once committed but have now happily outgrown'. The *Daily Express*, under the headline 'It Should Never Have Been Filmed', admonished the producers: 'Shakespeare is not, and never will be, film material. You will never make screen entertainment out of blank verse. It has nothing to do with cinema, which is primarily a visual form' (11 October 1935).

MGM's *Romeo and Juliet*, with Norma Shearer and Leslie Howard, released a year later, was treated by many critics as yet another test for the cinema – or at least, the sound film – and the publicity was clearly designed to meet objections half-way. Audiences were given to understand that the whole thing had been approached conscientiously. Shakespeare's wishes were being fulfilled to a degree beyond the capacity of his own stage. (This was an argument familiar in the days of the Victorian and Edwardian actor-managers.) In the published 'scenario' the literary adviser, Professor William Strunk, Jr., wrote that the advantages of the screen lay 'in continuity, in control of tempo, and in portrayal of background'.[14] The burden of this fell on such lavish set pieces as the spectacular opening sequence, with the rival factions processing to church on a Sunday morning in Verona, or the 'noisy, brightly colored pageant of fifteenth-century Italian life under blue skies in spring weather' that provided the setting for Shakespeare's Act 2 scene 2. Such scenes could be enlisted in support of Strunk's claim that the film 'does not merely tell a story of individuals; it gives a picture of the life of a great epoch, and in so doing illuminates the story'.[15]

Writing in the *Spectator*, Graham Greene found himself 'less than ever convinced that there is an aesthetic justification for filming Shakespeare at all'. He observed of Cukor's film of *Romeo and Juliet* that 'the effect of even the best scenes is to distract, much in the same way as the old Tree productions distracted'. Perhaps the poetry could only be served if 'we abjure all the liberties the huge sets and extras condemn us to. Something like Dreyer's *Passion of Jeanne d'Arc*, the white-washed walls and the slow stream of faces, might preserve a little more of the poetry than this commercial splendour.'[16] Harley Granville Barker, whose own practice and theory had done much to discredit the pictorialism of the old lavishly pictorial staging of Shakespeare – particularly as practised by Sir Herbert Beerbohm-Tree in the 1900s – denounced both the new *Romeo and Juliet* and Reinhardt's *Dream*. The film-maker's concern, he wrote, 'was not with the integrity of Shakespeare's play but with the making of pictures, as many and as good pictures as possible'. The lesson was that the two art forms did not mix: 'if we intrude scenery when [Shakespeare] thought he needed none . . . we wrong his art'. The following week a rejoinder from Alfred Hitchcock praised the dramatist for having 'almost the scenario writer's gift for keeping the story moving from setting to setting'.[17]

The English-language Shakespeare films of the 1940s and early 1950s – with the exception of Castellani's 1954 *Romeo and Juliet* – all use milieu in a more or less symbolic, stylised manner. This has more in common with contemporary stage production of the plays than with the habitual production values of the commercial cinema. None of Olivier's three films is conventionally realistic either in production design or in camerawork. *Henry V* (1944) moves from a depiction of Elizabethan London in realistic mode to stylised settings based on the Duc de Berri's Book of Hours.[18] For *Hamlet* (1948) the production designer Roger Furse created Elsinore as a castle of the mind, and Olivier himself remarked that he first imagined the film as a series of engravings. In *Richard III* (1955), also with Furse as designer, Olivier uses a sparsely decorated, apparently interconnected series of locations in a medieval London that has something of the style but none of the prettiness of the tableaux in *Henry V*. Here milieu can assume symbolic significance with relatively little support from cinematography or editing. In both *Henry V* and *Richard III* the move to a genuine outdoor location for the climactic battle comes as a shock.

Orson Welles's *Macbeth* (1948), with its deliberate sense of confinement, and frankly (and cheaply) 'studio' settings, has been read as either deliberate exercise in the manner of 1920s German Expressionism, or a failure to achieve a realistic milieu. The former is consistent with Welles's other work, where 'real' locations (as in *Othello* and *Chimes at Midnight*) are used expressively, either by photography or editing. As Pauline Kael observed of *Chimes at Midnight*, 'Welles, avoiding the naturalistic use of the outdoors in which Shakespeare's dialogue sounds more stagey than on stage, has photographically stylized the Spanish locations, creating a theatrically darkened, slightly unrealistic world of angles and low beams and silhouettes.'[19] Peter Hall's *A Midsummer Night's Dream* (1968) uses locations, with a deliberate 'alienation technique' in the daytime world ('Athens' appears aggressively as a title over an opening shot of the inescapably English house at Compton Verney in Warwickshire) and a chaos of filters and accordingly disruptive editing devices in the night-time woods. For many reviewers the woodland remained obstinately earthy. 'Nature' (wrote Eric Rhode in the *Listener*), 'a complex concept in the text, becomes visible, concrete, specific: we move back, as it were, from the workings of the poet's mind to the possible source of his inspiration.' Another reviewer complained that Hall had 'lost all touch with unreality'.[20]

Peter Brook once declared that 'the power of a Shakespeare play on stage stems from the fact that it happens "nowhere". A Shakespeare play has no setting. Every attempt, whether supported by aesthetic or political reasons, to try to build a frame round a Shakespeare play is an imposition which runs the risk of reducing the play: it can only sing, live and breathe in an empty space.'[21] Brook's own film of *King Lear* (1971) does not create a 'nowhere' and does build a frame round the play, but the wintry civilisation, the sense that nature is a constant threat against which furred gowns and huddled encampments are a fragile defence, might be considered a symbolic rather than 'real' milieu. Kozintsev, working in a comparable manner in his 1970 *King Lear*, displays the structures of a society more forcefully than Brook. The opening shots depict the slow progress across a barren heath of what becomes a large crowd of peasants. They assemble silently on the ridges overlooking what we presently learn is Lear's castle. As Sergei Yutkevitch observed, 'the whole film begins remarkably, not as an incident within the walls of a castle, but as an event with repercussions far beyond. It is not only the characters of the drama who are involved but an important new hero: the people.'[22] Kenneth Tynan hailed the same director's earlier *Hamlet* (1964) for populating Elsinore – normally deserted in the theatre, 'apart from the characters with names and a few extras to tote halberds, serve drinks and express shock when people of rank are insulted or slaughtered'. Kozintsev 'never let the audience forget that a royal castle is like a vast hotel which somebody has to run'.[23]

Akira Kurosawa's *Kumonosu-djo* (*Spider's Web Castle*) is more symbolic than realist: the Spider's Web Forest – the equivalent of Birnam Wood – is its governing metaphor, and the wood's defiance of the laws of nature reflects the hero's own subversion of the moral order.[24] The only signs of benign nature in the film are the peaceful fields (with toiling peasants) through which Tsuzuki's (Duncan's) entourage approaches Washizu's (Macbeth's) castle. Architecture and domestic settings may be historically correct (at one point in the published screenplay the 'black' style of castle building is referred to), but as in the same director's later *Ran* (1985) they are equally charged with symbolic significance. The interiors, with their classical Japanese proportions, elegant sparseness and sliding walls, are made to isolate the figures as though on a Noh stage, placing them in symbolic rather than realistic relation to each other and to such emblems of status as a sword or a wall-hanging.[25]

In comparison, the medieval milieu of Roman Polanski's *Macbeth* (1971) is fashioned in a commonplace if accomplished 'realistic' historical mode but remains neutral – except when the weather turns bad or the killing begins. The matter-of-(medieval)-fact world created by Polanski is part of a strategy, what one reviewer identified as his being a 'gothic realist' whose 'murderous carnivals have an everyday look'.[26] Polanski creates an unremarkable, if meticulously realised milieu in which extraordinary events will take place and unconventional thought will be given utterance. The setting is not itself a privileged speaker, as in Brook or Kurosawa, nor does it carry the social significance that Kozintsev makes it provide. Of the films set and partly filmed in Venice – the *Othellos* of Welles and Parker, and Radford's *Merchant of Venice* – only Welles and, to a lesser degree, Parker, capitalise on the potential of the location's unique 'found' environment for mystery or glamour: the benchmark has probably been set by Luchino Visconti's lyrical *Death in Venice* (1971) and Nicholas Roeg's semi-supernatural thriller *Don't Look Now* (1973).

This brief survey of milieu in a handful of films reflects one important development in the reception of Shakespeare on film: the setting gradually receives its due as an element of the poetic vocabulary of film and, consequently, as an active element in the process of adaptation, as significant as the cutting or reordering of the spoken words. Although projects (such as André Bazin's) to formulate a phenomenology of cinema rightly make distinction between dialogue in the theatre and on film, it is the nature of the space shown to the viewer, and the way it is shown, that dominates. As Bazin observes, 'the screen is not a frame like that of a picture but a mask which allows only a part of the action to be seen'.[27] The deployment of scenic space, the creation of a world before the lens and the implication of one beyond its field of vision, are central to the narrative cinema. This dimension of the films' work as interpretations of the original text is crucial to any assessment of them. At the same time, it should be remembered that – quite apart from the milieu depicted and the sense we are given of the actors' relationship to it (and to each other within it) – films also manipulate the audience's relationship to the space in which action unfolds. Overhearing scenes, often of great complexity and sophistication on Shakespeare's stage, are particularly difficult to transfer to the screen. In the theatre we see the whole of the playing area, and we can choose (even if the director takes steps to influence us) whom to attend to when Othello overhears Cassio with Iago and Bianca, or when Benedick and Beatrice overhear the allegations of their love for each other. The effect is intensified in scenes with greater numbers of on-stage observers. When *Hamlet* is performed on stage we see all the witnesses of the 'Mousetrap' at once; in *Love's Labour's Lost* we see the concealed Berowne – somewhere 'above' on the stage – observing the King, Longaville and Dumaine in turn, and watch each newly arrived (and newly concealed) Lord as they observe the others. In the cinema our view of the observers and the observed in such scenes is controlled, and its quality altered. We are all shown the same selection of images and sounds, and we are obliged to see and hear each person's reactions serially rather than simultaneously. The members of a theatre audience (themselves diversely placed) may pick and choose to diverse effect: here the cinema, at least in its conventional form, has the effect of limiting the audience's options and with them, arguably, the scope of its reactions.[28]

Showing, telling and thinking

Many critics, though, particularly in the earlier decades of sound, were influenced in their response by the fact that in the theatre Shakespeare had only recently been emancipated from the scenic display that in the theatre as now in the cinema had come to represent commercial vulgarisation. This anxiety about the visualised image usurping the spoken word's legitimate function has often dominated commentary on filmed Shakespeare. A notable example is the reception by literary critics of Polanski's *Macbeth*, where the director's professed aim was to 'visualise' as much as possible. Apart from its role in the treatment of the supernatural (discussed by Neil Forsyth in chapter 16), this practice produced occasional over-deliberate enactment of imagery. At the feast after Macbeth's installation as king a bear is baited. The bear is first seen in its cage in the courtyard during preparations for the feast, and Lady Macbeth hails it as 'our chiefest guest'. Later, before we (via the camera's eye) enter the banqueting hall, the carcass of the bear and one of its assailants are dragged past the camera down a corridor, leaving a vivid bloody smear on the floor. Towards the end of the film, as he receives reports of the enemy's advance, Macbeth notices the pillar to which the bear had been tied, and much later, as he faces his first assailant, he sees the same pillar, ring and chain. This time he speaks the line 'They have tied me to the stake.' Frank Kermode, declaring that 'the film mustn't spoil [Shakespeare's] astonishing effects of language'[29] complained that these were lost in Polanski's film: one might observe that the visual effects created by the director were a transposition of imagery into another medium. Against this we can set one of the most fulsome defences of a Shakespeare film against such objections: Robert Cowie's assertion that in Welles's *Othello*, 'Far from being attenuated, the play reveals under [his] direction that restless, brooding aspect that lies hidden in the folds of Shakespeare's verse.'[30]

Another point of coincidence or collision between the spoken word and the shown image in Shakespearean film is the soliloquy. The theatrical convention, allowing access to a character's 'private' thoughts, depends on that character's ability to address the audience directly. With the tragic heroes in particular this conventional means of access to their interiority has been essential to a critical tradition celebrating the plays as studies in psychology. The speeches are perceived both as technical tests, and as a measure of the performer's emotional (even spiritual) range and capability in the role.

Film has other means of access to the characters' interiority, to which speech may even be a hindrance, and has little (or at least, very selective) use for direct address to the audience. Welles deprives Iago of his soliloquies, but this does not seem to diminish the impact of Macliammóir's performance, and Kurosawa's Washizu (Toshiro Mifune) is no less effective for being a Macbeth whose thoughts are given no words. When a character in a film does speak directly to camera, the effect is a radical disruption of the sense of fictional space – the intimation of a whole world beyond the camera's range, of which we are being shown a part – and is potentially far more momentous (and alienating) than direct address to a live audience from an actor on stage. Usually, when a film character must be seen to reflect, she or he will look to the left or right of camera, the eye-line depending on the demands of continuity and with respect to what is understood to be in the space 'off'. Speaking to the lens has a distinctive effect and has to be used sparingly and strategically.

This important element of the plays' theatrical conventions may, however, be modified to advantage, in that soliloquy can be elided with the 'aside'. In Polanski's *Macbeth* both Macbeth and Lady Macbeth move in and out of 'spoken' and 'thought' soliloquy, usually speaking only one phrase or sentence out loud. Their thoughts can now be juxtaposed with other action, and the characters do not have to be alone – to be given, as it were, a stage to themselves – for the thinking to take place. Lady Macbeth (Francesca Annis) reads her husband's letter in voice-over, but speaks some phrases out loud. We see preparations for Duncan's arrival as her voice is heard ('Hie thee hither, that I may pour my spirits in thy ear') and her invocation to the 'spirits, that tend on mortal thoughts' is spoken as she watches Duncan's arrival. She 'thinks' her invitation to night as she comes down into the courtyard, and a speech that on stage could hardly be spoken without a passionate display of commitment to evil, is here juxtaposed with Lady Macbeth's outward composure. The medium's capacity for placing the protagonists' passages of reflection in, or at least beside, the world around them has been diversely articulated in the different *Hamlet* films. Hamlet's first, bitter soliloquy, is a case in point. Olivier (1948) isolates Hamlet on his chair in the now empty, shadowy council chamber, a setting expressionistically appropriate for his state of mind. Kozintsev (1964) has Hamlet 'thinking' as he makes his way through a throng of fawning courtiers, a grave and isolated intellectual amid a politically dangerous chattering class. Branagh (1996) splits the difference by having Hamlet pace, bursting with angry vocal energy, through the vast, brilliantly lit but now deserted hall. Ethan Hawke, in Almereyda's 1999 film, distances himself from the corrupt business world of his uncle with as many video-making and editing devices as he can muster, and ponders the effects of 'thinking too precisely on th'event' as he wanders through the 'action' section of a Blockbuster video store.

The various filmic adaptations of the soliloquy convention permits the protagonists to go about other business while we hear them think, and often (though not inevitably) suggests a corresponding psychological trait: Macbeth or Hamlet can seem like men who frequently think but don't have to stop to do so. Because the camera can keep close to him, Olivier is able to allow Henry V a moment of thoughtfulness 'aside' on the line 'And how Thou pleasest, God, direct the day' after he has defied the French herald before the battle of Agincourt. Polanski's camera is always catching Jon Finch's Macbeth in moments of reflection, even when we cannot hear his thoughts, and he is no less a man of action for all his troubled imagination. In any case, Polanski gives us privileged access to the visions that trouble Macbeth's imagination. Towards the end of the film, as the usurper's regime disintegrates, we see Lady Macbeth's hands from her point of view, stained with illusory stigmata. In a play where visions are of paramount importance, Polanski's camera insists on a degree of complicity in the viewer that would not be available to the theatre spectator.

Additional narrative: pictures telling stories

Scenes not represented in action in Shakespeare's theatre but added by screen-writers have sometimes been thought an undesirable challenge to the supremacy of poetic description. This is clearly the case when an incident described in the dialogue is enacted for the camera. Outstanding examples occur in Olivier's *Hamlet*, when we see the scene of Hamlet's distraught visit to Ophelia's closet; in both films of *Henry V*, which show us the death of Falstaff to illustrate Mistress Quickly's words; in Branagh's *Henry V*, when flashbacks clarify the former relationship of Henry with Falstaff and his tavern companions; and on several occasions in Branagh's *Hamlet*. A notable 'double dose' of illustration occurs when Olivier accompanies Gertrude's description of Ophelia's drown-ing with a scene imitating Millais's painting of the same subject. In these cases the director has had to decide between the desire to take his audience with him, and the fear of distracting from what is being said (and how it is expressed) rather than illuminating some necessary question of the play. Examples of divergent approaches to the problem can be found within Branagh's *Hamlet*: we are not shown Hamlet's visit to Ophelia's closet, and the image of her drowned face is seen after, not during, the scene in which Gertrude describes her death. On the other hand, there are many other 'illustrations', ranging in seriousness from Hamlet and Ophelia in bed together to images of Priam and Hecuba *in extremis* to accompany references in the player's speech.[31] In Almereyda's 2000 modern Manhattan *Hamlet* we are shown Hamlet's visit to Ophelia's closet – in fact her Soho loft apartment where she is working in her photographic dark room. By the red working light they embrace warmly, and we see him offer her the crumpled paper on which he has been composing his love-poem, but her father arrives (with a cake-box and two party balloons) and Hamlet rushes off, leaving the paper for Polonius to find. The sequence is without audible dialogue, as the camera is some feet away and the couple are behind a glass partition, and there is non-diegetic music to accompany it. Almereyda is able to show the depth of their affection, and also to save Ophelia the trouble of telling her father what has happened - if indeed she would have any desire to in this version, where the generational oppositions are very strong. As for the death of Ophelia, this film reduces Gertrude's description to a two-word voice-over ('Drowned, drowned') as the camera looks down from a height at the body of Ophelia, floating, surrounded by what seem to be her 'remembrances' (photographs) in the fountain where she and Hamlet met after the news conference of the first 'court' scene. (This location, on the plaza beneath the World Trade Center towers, was destroyed in the terrorist attack of 11 September 2001.) These episodes replace or effectively abridge elements of the play, as well as providing additional opportunities to show rather than tell. More problematic are images which illustrate (and perhaps implicitly validate) what a character imagines – such as those in Oliver Parker's *Othello* where the hero visualises Desdemona in bed with Cassio. The effect is anticipated (more decorously) in the German silent film of 1922, but there Othello cannot speak of his imaginings, and they have to be shown.

Additional sequences are more certain of being welcome when they advance or amplify the narrative rather than duplicate or expand on information already expressed verbally. There is a clear correspondence here with the Elizabethan stage conventions of prologues, choruses and other framing devices. Olivier's *Henry V* is remarkable for its use of a 'play within a film' structure to facilitate the shifting of the historical events into an aestheticised past, a process which effects a negotiation between the conflicting 'realist' and 'escapist' modes of wartime cinema. Once the Elizabethan playhouse and the London it is set in have been established, the film proceeds for some time by framing the lines from the original play in a 'historical' performance mode, rather than by adding new lines and sequences. In Olivier's epic the ideological dimension of this 'prologue' is strong, but is not explicit. (In what was at the time a powerful contrast to the drab, war-damaged London of 1944, Shakespeare's city is shown as idyllic, and its theatre as ideally democratic, colourful and lively, which seems to confer a particular validity and relevance on the dramatic fare presented there.)[32] Branagh, by contrast, focuses on the medium itself by opening 'backstage' in a film studio (in the first drafts of his script this was to be a theatre) before moving to a scene of conspiracy between the two clerics: cinema, he implies, can make us privy to the secret workings of the state. In other films framing devices direct the audience more explicitly to a point of view from which the ensuing events should be contemplated: Olivier's *Hamlet*, Kurosawa's *Macbeth* version and Welles's *Othello* accomplish this with, respectively, a sequence foreshadowing the final scene and including a legend read by a voice-over (Olivier himself); a chanted chorus as a pillar bearing an inscription is first revealed, then enfolded in mists which clear to reveal the castle that has since vanished; and an elaborate episode anticipating the conclusion of the film by showing the funerals of Othello and Desdemona, with Iago hanged in his cage.

Films of the history plays might be thought to require even more by way of preparation, not so much in terms of attitude, but rather of information required for comprehension of what is to follow. Thus, Olivier's *Richard III* begins with a rolling title, emblazoned on an illuminated parchment, which indicates that what is to follow is one of the legends attached to the crown – establishing the latter as a recurrent symbol – and then moves into a rearranged and augmented version of the play's opening scene, designed to clarify the allegiances and background of the principal characters. Olivier is following a venerable stage tradition, but it is notable that Welles, having worked for some years on his stage version of the Falstaff material, frames his *Chimes at Midnight* with passages from Holinshed (spoken in voice-over by Ralph Richardson) and at one stage intended to open further back in the story, with sequences depicting the death of Richard II and Bolingbroke's reception of the corpse.[33] Although Branagh decided (at a late stage) to include the Falstaff flashbacks in his *Henry V*, on the grounds that they were essential to an audience's understanding of the film, he decided against a prologue because it would not have been directly useful to the narrative. Included in the original script, this was to have shown a young man (subsequently identified as the king) gazing mournfully out to sea while a voice-over recited lines from *Richard II*: 'For God's sake let us sit upon the ground / And tell sad stories of the death of kings . . .' Branagh felt that it indicated an attitude rather than helping to tell the story.[34] Scene- and mood-setting devices in the same director's *Much Ado about Nothing* form a bridge between the messenger's announcement that 'Don Pedro is approached' and the arrival of the prince and his retinue in the villa courtyard: the main titles are superimposed on scenes of frenzied preparations, frankly sexual anticipation and broad comedy. This is effectively a delayed prologue, sanctioned by the filmic custom of pre-title sequences designed to engage attention and launch the story. (The first section, with the words of 'Sigh no more' shown on screen and declaimed by Beatrice perhaps counts as a pre-prologue, so that by the time Don Pedro's entourage approaches we are into what is effectively a third opening sequence.)

Less clearly capable of integration with the rest of the script, but answering a perceived need for exposition and stage-setting, was the preliminary sequence drafted (but not filmed) for Reinhardt's *A Midsummer Night's Dream*, which would have shown the war between the Amazons and the Athenians, and Theseus's hand-to-hand combat with his future bride.[35] Nunn's *Twelfth Night*, like some theatrical productions of the play, begins with a spectacularly staged storm, but it goes beyond a mere transposition of the two opening scenes, to include evidence of the resemblance between Viola and her brother and also to strike the first note of the recurring theme of sexual confusion. Here, as with

Branagh's *Much Ado*, exposition is already moving beyond narrative into interpretation. In Derek Jarman's *Tempest* (1979) a storm at sea (footage shown in a
blue filter) is represented as being 'dreamt' by Prospero and Miranda before the
dialogue tells us it is also 'real', a device which shows the director's responsiveness to the medium he is adapting from and his imaginative readiness to use film's
capability to go beyond it.

In Kozintsev's *Hamlet* the opening title sequence shows a torch against a stone
wall as a bell tolls, with Shostakovitch's plangent score cutting in as the camera
pans left to reveal the sea. This establishes elemental metaphorical material
(water, earth, fire) for what is to come. It is followed by a rapid sequence of shots
showing the protagonist galloping across landscape on his way to Elsinore,
rushing into the courtyard, up a flight of steps and along a corridor to meet
Gertrude. This momentum is then arrested by the raising of a castle drawbridge
and the slow obliteration of the daylight reflected in the well beneath: Denmark's
a prison indeed. One might contrast this in terms of technique (allowing for the
self-evident distinction of mood) with the mysterious but clearly momentous
movement of the mass of poor people through a bleak landscape that opens the
same director's *King Lear*. This has no direct participation in the narrative development of the film: as well as establishing milieu it functions as a prologue, and
directs us to consider what follows in a particular light. Both Adrian Noble in
his film of *A Midsummer Night's Dream* (1996) and Julie Taymor in *Titus* (1999)
add more radical sequences that amount to new framing devices. Both feature a
child, whose view of – and participation in – the action serves to complicate the
viewers' responses.

These examples are of films adding to the play in order to indicate a point of
view, provide background information, establish mood and scene or announce
a theme. In Kenneth Branagh's *Love's Labour's Lost* a 'frame' of pastiche newsreel footage (and some genuine material), together with a commentator whose
jaunty tone evoked the genre in the 1930s, were added at a late stage of production – after a lukewarm reception at a preview had made it clear that the
audience did not know quite how seriously they should take the film's characters or their situation. In the case of Noble and Taymor, the additional material adds a puzzling and challenging frame whose purpose is to enhance the
thematic content of the film, respectively psychologising the *Dream* and politicising war-games for Titus. These might be described as additions to or
enhancements of the film's narrative work. It is also common for 'showing' to
replace rather than supplement 'telling' at a less sophisticated level: audiences
have come to see, rather than hear about, events. This is especially noticeable
when an important event that occurs off-stage in the play is either a vital plot
point (in Branagh's *Much Ado* we are shown Margaret's impersonation of
Hero) or because a large-scale event can hardly be expected to take place 'off-

screen' or be represented by a few alarums and excursions (the battles in Olivier's *Henry V* and in *Chimes at Midnight* are the most remarkable examples). Not infrequently, however, scenes and sequences of the original may be cut because the rhythm of the stage play does not accord with the pace thought desirable in a film: for this reason (it appears) Mankiewicz shot but omitted the murder of Cinna the poet in *Julius Caesar*, and at a late stage Branagh's *Much Ado* lost the equivalent of the scene with the women on the morning of the wedding (Act 3 scene 4). It has been said that for a director there are three films: the film you imagine and script, the one you shoot and the one you edit. At any stage in this process elements may be removed, and during the shooting stage some may even be added.

The opening and closing sections of the plays seem to be most problematic, and even those adapters who otherwise stick to the structure of the original worry about the ways in which the central business of the play is approached and how it is left. In the opening sequences forceful establishment of the principal characters, indications of milieu and the springboard of the story are essential, and in the last scenes time seems the major problem. Because the screen versions of *Romeo and Juliet* have tended to follow the narrative shape of the original play, their treatment of events after Romeo's banishment offers particularly useful illustrations of what can happen at a point (around Act Four of a five-act text) where some compression is called for without seeming to be merely 'cutting to the chase'. In Zeffirelli's *Romeo and Juliet* (1968) the incidents are set out more or less in the order of the play, but with some notable expansions and compressions.

The most remarkable compression in the incidents of the play comes towards the end. In a brave – and apparently late – decision by the director to slide over a major plot point, Romeo is not seen obtaining the poison, and it is not identified as such until Juliet remarks 'poison, I see, hath been thy timeless end' on discovering his body.[36] In Luhrmann's *Romeo+Juliet* (1996) the corresponding scene with Crusty (the pusher) is more easily accommodated, partly because of a faster-paced, rougher-cut style, partly because the pool-hall and its owner are central to the film's depiction of a subculture.

Events in the tomb are simplified by Zeffirelli: Paris does not appear, Romeo sends Benvolio away but does not threaten him, and gains entry by smashing the door with a stone – no mattock and wrenching iron – and there is little sense that the expedition is dangerous. The watchmen are only heard in the distance as Friar Laurence tries to persuade Juliet to leave. (Luhrmann's police pursuit of the banished Montague leaves no doubt that Romeo is in danger.) Milo O'Shea repeating 'I dare not stay' emphasises his fear and confusion as he exits. Luhrmann's script allows the friar to stay at Juliet's side: her suicide with the revolver takes him by surprise.[37]

None of these strategies are unknown in stage productions of the play: during its theatrical career for diverse reasons the play's text has been trimmed and parts of it reshuffled – particularly in the final two acts.[38] Within their respective parameters, both Luhrmann and Zeffirelli deal in similar ways with the business to be got through in the grander sequences. Zeffirelli's film is operatic, but in the manner of his own naturalistic opera stagings: it offers what will seem natural settings and behaviour to accompany expansive emotional utterance. Once Romeo is into the cathedral (not a private tomb), Luhrmann stages a scene from the grandest of operas – or perhaps Broadway musicals – ending in an aerial shot of the lovers surrounded by a sea of candles. For Zeffirelli, the play's very last lines can be replaced with an abbreviated version of the Prince's speech. Luhrmann, concluding not with a funeral and reconciliation but with the media absorption of the story, makes a similar selection of the available lines.

One crude but persistent truth about making films out of these Elizabethan plays seems to reassert itself in both films: the ending needs to show, rather than promise, something to the audience. Even in Luhrmann's film, going hence to talk of these sad things will not be enough on its own, and he is able to end with a reminder of the medium (broadcast news) in which events are apprehended nowadays. *Romeo+Juliet* has a stylised sense of actuality and modernity, but it is no less romantic at heart and pictorial in values than Zeffirelli's film – or than Olivier's *Henry V*, for that matter. Perhaps we should remind ourselves of a remark made by Alfred Hitchcock during the debate arising from the new sound films of Shakespeare's plays in the mid-1930s: 'The cinema . . . has seen stage directions in Shakespeare's poetry where decades of theatrical craftsmen have seen only words.'[39] For the good of the cinema, Shakespeare films have to end – as well as begin – in shows.

NOTES

1 Geoffrey O'Brien, 'The Ghost at the Feast', in George Plimpton, ed., *The Best American Movie Writing* (New York, 1998), pp. 199–215; p. 202. The essay first appeared in the *New York Review of Books* on 2 February 1997.

2 For an account of film history emphasising 'continuity editing', see David Bordwell, *On the History of Film Style* (Cambridge, MA, 1997) and David Bordwell, Janet Staiger and Kristine Thompson, *The Classical Hollywood Cinema. Film Style and Mode of Production to 1960* (London, 1985).

3 See Michael Anderegg, *Orson Welles, Shakespeare and Popular Culture* (New York, 1999). André Bazin suggested that 'As in the films of Orson Welles and in spite of conflicts of style, neorealism tends to give back to the cinema a sense of the ambiguity of reality' (André Bazin, *What is Cinema?* selected and translated by Hugh Gray, 2 vols. (Berkeley, CA, 1967), vol. I, p. 37).

4 On alternatives to the (then) 'canonical' Shakespeare films, see Graham Holderness,

'Shakespeare Rewound', *Shakespeare Survey, 45: 'Hamlet' and its Afterlife* (1982), 63–74.

5 Peter Greenaway, interviewed in Brian McFarlane, ed., *An Autobiography of British Cinema* (London, 1997), p. 241.

6 See Ann Thompson, 'Kurosawa's *Ran*: Reception and Interpretation', *East–West Film Journal*, 3/2 (June 1989), 1–13, and also Robert Hapgood's essay in Anthony Davies and Stanley Wells, eds., *Shakespeare and the Moving Image. The Plays on Film and Television* (Cambridge, 1994).

7 Syd Field, *The Screenwriter's Problem Solver* (New York, 1998), pp. 56, 78.

8 A systematic analysis of Welles's treatment of the text is provided by François Thomas, 'Orson Welles et le rémodellage du texte Shakespearien', in Patricia Dorval, ed., *Shakespeare et le Cinéma* (Paris, 1998), pp. 171–82.

9 Interview in the *Neues Wiener Journal* (28 July 1935): reprinted in Edda Fuhrich and Gisela Prossnitz, eds., *Max Reinhardt. Die Träume des Magiers* (Vienna, 1993), p. 175. A similar point was made by Allardyce Nicoll in a response to Reinhardt's film: see Charles Eckert, *Focus on Shakespeare on Film* (Englewood Cliffs, NJ, 1972), pp. 43–7; p. 46.

10 Micheál Macliammóir, *Put Money in Thy Purse. The Making of Orson Welles's Othello* (London, 1952), pp. 96–7.

11 On the Méliès/Lumière or fantasy/reality dichotomy in the historiography of film, see Neil Forsyth, chapter 16 below.

12 On the relationship between the early cinema and the pictorial stage, see Ben Brewster and Lea Jacobs, *Theatre and Cinema: Stage Pictorialism and the Early Feature Film* (New York, 1997). The pioneering study by Nicholas Vardac, *From Stage to Screen* (New York, 1949; repr. 1968), remains stimulating and informative.

13 On developments in Shakespearean staging see J. L. Styan, *The Shakespeare Revolution* (Cambridge, 1977) and Dennis Kennedy, *Looking at Shakespeare* (Cambridge, 1996). On other consequences of the advent of sound, see Barbara Freedman, chapter 3 below.

14 '*Romeo and Juliet*' . . . *A Motion Picture Edition* . . . *Arranged for the Screen by Talbot Jennings* (New York, 1936), pp. 13, 20.

15 *Ibid.*, p. 21.

16 Graham Greene, *The Pleasure Dome. Collected Film Criticism, 1935–40*, ed. John Russell Taylor (Oxford, 1980), p. 111.

17 Alfred Hitchcock, The *Listener* (10 March 1937). Granville Barker's article appeared on 3 March.

18 On Olivier's *Henry V* and its connotations as an 'art' film, see Dudley Andrew, *Film in the Aura of Art* (Princeton, NJ, 1984), chapter 8: 'Realism, Rhetoric and the Painting of History in *Henry V*'.

19 Pauline Kael, *The New Republic* (24 June 1967): quoted in Bridget Gellert Lyons, ed. *Chimes at Midnight* (New Brunswick, NJ, and London, 1988), pp. 298–300; p. 298.

20 The *Listener* (6 February 1969); *Observer* (2 February 1969).

21 Peter Brook, *The Shifting Point: Forty Years of Theatrical Experience, 1946–1987* (London, 1988), p. 191. Brook was speaking at a conference in 1977.

22 Sergei Yutkevitch, 'The Conscience of the King', *Sight and Sound* (October 1971), 192–6; p. 194. (Translation from an article in *Isskustvo Kino*.)

23 Reprinted in Kenneth Tynan, *Tynan Right and Left* (London, 1967) pp. 208–9; p. 208.

24 J. Blumenthal, '*Macbeth* into *Throne of Blood*', *Sight and Sound*, 34/4 (Autumn 1965), 190–5; p. 191.

25 Donald Ritchie, *The Films of Akira Kurosawa* (3rd edn, Berkeley, CA, 1996) p. 123. See also the interview with the director in Roger Manvell's *Shakespeare and the Film* (1971; revised edn, London, 1979), p. 104.

26 *New Yorker* (5 February 1972).

27 André Bazin, *What is Cinema?* vol. 1, p. 105. See also chapter 1, 'Cinematic and Theatrical Space', in Anthony Davies, *Filming Shakespeare's Plays* (Cambridge, 1988).

28 I am indebted to Peter Holland for this important point in relation to the plays' stage-craft and the audiences of the different media. On the overhearing scenes in comedies, particularly Branagh's *Much Ado* and Nunn's *Twelfth Night*, see Michael Hattaway, chapter 5 below.

29 Frank Kermode, 'Shakespeare in the Movies', *New York Review of Books* (4 May 1972), 18–21; p. 21.

30 Robert Cowie, *The Cinema of Orson Welles* (London, 1965) pp. 104–5. See also Bazin's remark, quoted in note 3 above.

31 For a detailed discussion of these additions, see David Kennedy Sauer, ' "Suiting the Word to the Action." Kenneth Branagh's Interpolations in *Hamlet*', in Holger Klein and Dimiter Daphinoff, eds., *Hamlet on Screen, Shakespeare Yearbook*, vol. VIII (Lampeter, 1997), pp. 349–69.

32 See my 'Two Films of *Henry V*: Frames and Stories' in François Laroque, ed., *Astrea, No 4: The Show Within . . . Proceedings of the International Conference held in Montpellier . . . 1990* (Paris, 1991), pp. 181–98.

33 Lyons, ed. *Chimes at Midnight*, p. 269: the information is in an interview with Keith Baxter, who played Hal.

34 The sequence was included in the script used for the first read-through, but was never filmed (personal information from Kenneth Branagh and David Parfitt).

35 I have discussed the 'missing' scenes in the 1935 *Dream* in 'A Shooting Script for the Reinhardt–Dieterle *Dream*', *Shakespeare Bulletin*, 16/4 (Fall 1998) 39–41.

36 It seems that the fight with Paris was filmed, but not the 'Apothecary' scene. (Personal communication from Leonard Whiting.)

37 Craig Pearce and Baz Luhrmann, *William Shakespeare's Romeo and Juliet* (London, 1997), p. 160.

38 On the theatrical fortunes of the play, see Levenson, *Romeo and Juliet*, chapter 2 ('Early Revivals') and 3 (on Brook's 1947 production); and Patricia Tatspaugh, chapter 8 below.

39 The *Listener* (10 March 1937).

2

MICHÈLE WILLEMS

Video and its paradoxes

Videotapes or DVDs, whether they represent a Shakespeare film, a made-for-television production or a transfer of a theatrical version, have become the means by which most academics and students study a Shakespeare play. To anyone interested in performances of *Hamlet* for instance, the RSC shops and catalogues now offer, alongside the expected videos of Olivier's, Zeffirelli's or Branagh's films, videos of live stage performances, from Tony Richardson's 1969 production of the play with Nicol Williamson, to John Gielgud's 1964 New York *mise-en-scène* with Richard Burton.[1] Until 2005 when the BBC Shakespeare series was finally re-issued on DVD, the catalogue of available videos of the play included few versions actually designed for the small screen, but the would-be viewer could always fall back on the half-hour-long cartoons provided by *The Animated Tales*, a very successful series of videos (complete with study guides), geared to the needs of teenagers confronted with a Shakespeare play on their exam syllabus. This series, which recalls Charles and Mary Lamb's similar enterprise of popularisation of Shakespeare's *Tales* for a public of readers, has so far been translated into thirty-seven languages.[2]

Even such a rapid survey is sufficient to indicate that Shakespeare multimedia is alive and well. Thanks largely to the vogue of new technologies and of video and DVD recordings, it is gradually taking over a good part of the Shakespeare industry, which now rests upon a very active educational market. Back in the 1980s, the production of a complete televised Shakespeare by the BBC was already motivated (and financially supported) by the possibility of providing video-libraries of the Shakespeare canon to universities (particularly in America) supposedly deprived of the real thing in the theatre. The 10 May 1986 issue of the *Times Literary Supplement* greeted the completion of the most ambitious project of its kind with the headline: 'The Canon in the Can'. The tapes of the first series were sold, mainly to institutions, at the high price of £300–£400 for each play, and were distributed for broadcast in forty-two countries. In non-anglophone countries they were either dubbed (e.g. Germany) or subtitled (e.g. France.) By 1987 a dozen titles were retailed in Great Britain at £99 each, and later the more popular were distributed at regular video prices, eventually reaching the £5 level by the mid-1990s. With the release of the series on DVD, at first as boxed sets according to genre, then individually, prices settled in 2005 around the £12 level. Nowadays, teaching aids of all types rely on spin-off products from film by way of video, from the 'interactive guides' which include extracts of film versions, to the CDRoms which accompany some scholarly editions.[3] Beyond these media, following the development of the Internet, stills and video-clips are being collected to create a world-wide Shakespeare web which scholars like Michael Mullin enrich by taping their own recordings of Shakespeare performances in other cultures.

Strictly speaking, video cannot be considered as a medium in its own right, but rather as a vehicle for other media. It thus appears as a very loose category, a label which, on its own, is of little taxonomic value. The risk even exists that it may nurture a multitude of theoretical confusions affecting teaching as well as research. Students of *Macbeth*, for instance, can be offered a large variety of videotapes to support their readings of the play: these range from Welles's or Polanski's well-known films (1948 and 1971 respectively), to Jack Gold's 1983 television production for the BBC series; they also include Trevor Nunn's famous version, originally presented in 1976 at The Other Place in Stratford, then rethought for television and recorded in a Thames Television studio in 1978. A student's immediate reaction will often be to refer to any of these as *a* video, or even *the* video of *Macbeth*. It is too easy for students to forget the original medium for which what they are watching was designed: 35 mm films are so often shown on a television screen that squinting to follow panning or travelling shots has become second nature; conversely, the availability of projector screens and video-projectors may create unexpected viewing conditions in which close-ups, originally planned for smaller screens, find themselves suddenly blown up to unforeseen proportions.

For a variety of reasons, videotapes are hybrid products, since they result from transfers from film to television or from crossovers between stage and film. Rothwell and Melzer's very useful filmography and videography introduces differentiating labels to classify this large variety of Shakespearean products: Polanski's film is listed as *motion picture/adaptation*, Gold's TV film as *video/teleplay* and Trevor Nunn's *Macbeth* as *video/interpretation*.[4] This is a first step towards distinguishing between Shakespeare-on-film, Shakespeare-on-television and Shakespeare-on-the-stage, and a necessary one, since the fast development of video as a medium for media tends constantly to disrupt received ideas on each medium: when performances of all types and origins are disseminated and studied through video, borderlines and definitions become blurred and the specific codes of each medium may find themselves occluded.

All sorts of other displacements are liable to occur when a performance is deflected from its original aims and audience. The blurbs on the boxes of Shakespeare videos categorise their contents like other commercial products: Parker's *Othello* is 'a classic tale of love, passion, jealousy and betrayal' and Loncraine's *Richard III* becomes 'kidnap, seduction, betrayal and bloody murder . . . the bloodbath [Richard] unleashes takes its terrible toll on family and friends . . .' The advertisement for Branagh's *Hamlet* also resorts to sensationalism, at the same time reducing the plot to a family affair: 'Hamlet (Branagh), the Prince of Denmark, is thrown into despair when his recently widowed mother, Gertrude (Julie Christie) marries his father's brother Claudius (Derek Jacobi). A terrifying confrontation with his father's ghost reveals to Hamlet that his father was murdered by Claudius, who by his actions won both the throne of Denmark and Hamlet's mother.' Videos being destined to 'private domestic viewing' (and sometimes declared, like Loncraine's film, 'suitable only for persons of 15 years and over'), it is not surprising to find political and cosmic conflicts shrinking into domestic confrontations. This corresponds to the scaling down expected on television and seems designed for the intimacy of the living-room. At the same time, the arguments used to attract customers (passion, suspense, blood, sensation) are characteristic of the priorities of commercial cinema, whose main features the video magnifies, thus making them more perceptible. Although it is usual for the distributors to control the publicity for both film and video, the promotion of cinema-films is transitory – few remember it – while videos carry it on their boxes permanently. Videos give films a relative permanence, being less subject to the vagaries of distribution and the gradual degradation of prints.

Now that plays taped live on the stage or recorded in a studio cohabit with film and TV versions in our video-libraries, it may be useful to remind ourselves that each medium is governed by its own codes, and that the languages used to translate a Shakespeare play into a stage production or into a film or teleplay cannot be studied with the same grammar. A clear illustration emerges by comparing the way in which a cinema film (Polanski's *Macbeth*), a TV programme (Gold's version of the play for the BBC) and filmed theatre (the studio-recorded production of Trevor Nunn's critically acclaimed *mise-en-scène* for The Other Place) render Banquo and Macbeth's reactions to the news that the latter has been made Thane of Cawdor. This is the end of Act 1 scene 3, a passage which alternates dialogue, monologue and asides in true theatrical fashion. Now, it is a commonplace to say that the translation to the screen of a text written for the theatre implies transcoding strategies which, though they necessarily vary from the large screen to the small screen, can by and large be defined, after Kosintzev, as shifting the stress from the aural to the visual.[5]

In order to involve the spectator in the story, Polanski relies on spatial strategies much more than on speech. Unlike a rival video of the same play, his film cannot pride itself on being 'authentically set in eleventh-century England',[6] but it *was* filmed on location in Wales, and the heath through which Macbeth (Jon Finch) and Banquo (Martin Shaw) are riding while exchanging carefree echoing banter ('Your children shall be kings', 'You shall be king') persuades us that it is Scottish. Cinema is expected to be more realistic than television and in a case like this, the big screen works like 'the fourth wall' on a naturalistic stage: it opens on to a world of total illusion. A following shot discovers Macbeth lying in his tent and speaking in voice-over four lines displaced from his earlier dialogue with the witches ('The Thane of Cawdor lives . . .'); the spectator is invited to penetrate the hero's inner thoughts as well as to understand that some time has elapsed. Next, Macbeth is discovered outside his tent, by the edge of a stream, and his attitudes (stretching out, pulling up his trousers, spitting) realistically suggest that he is waking up the next morning. The camera picks up two riders in the distance; no word is spoken until Ross and Angus have joined Macbeth to deliver the brief message of his promotion. Throughout the scene, the text is not only considerably shortened, it is also drawn out in time and space and often disconnected from what is shown on the screen: Banquo's words of warning about 'the instruments of darkness' (Macbeth has gone back to his tent and Banquo is delivering his speech from the door) are accompanied by a close-up of the sandals which Macbeth is busily putting on; the hero's inner meditation (which only begins at 1.3.129, 'This supernatural soliciting . . .') is delivered in voice-over while he is getting ready for a journey, looking around for, then picking up, his sword, throwing a rug over his shoulders, etc. The voice-over delivery, used for this soliloquy as for the earlier aside ('Glamis, and Thane of Cawdor: / The greatest is behind') is only interrupted when he proclaims aloud: 'I am Thane of Cawdor' while donning his chain of office, a reminder of his recent nomination; a subsequent silent shot catches Ross's meaningful look as he registers that Macbeth is wearing it. In spite of a few significant text-supporting pictures of this type, the audience is more often treated as a privileged peeping Tom than as a partner in the task of exploring a difficult text, if only because the actors never speak straight to the camera.

Things are very different elsewhere. On television, words carry more weight than they do in the cinema, because of the phatic function of the medium. Besides, the small screen is, after all, small, and television cannot count on the film's financial resources. This is particularly striking in the case of the limited-budget studio sets which, in Gold's teleplay, do their best to suggest a heath totally unlike the real-life landscape of Polanski's film. Yet, in spite of restricted means, many BBC directors felt that they had to opt for a cinematographic language whose realistic priorities are traditionally – sometimes unduly – associated with the small screen, with sets and costumes striving to provide plausible replicas of reality. Camera-movements, however, are mostly limited to the ping-pong which the cinema only resorts to for dialogue. But the main characteristic of the medium is that, instead of filming in long takes, a television camera will move in close to concentrate on the characters, who are thus often reduced to faces, or to heads and shoulders.

Philip Casson, the television director for Nunn's production, covered the studio-space with four cameras; but after that space had been initially visualised as a ritual circle which each actor, waiting on the outside, entered on cue, it soon merged into the screen-space allocated to the characters. The viewer, like the theatre spectator before him, discovers Macbeth (Ian McKellen) and Banquo (John Woodvine) in a bare, undetermined setting, the feeling of surreality being increased when these two soldiers in armour are joined by Ross and Angus looking like contemporary civil servants in black clothes complete with attaché-cases. But even the ambience created by the proximity of the actors at The Other Place could not approximate the feeling of claustrophobia induced by this succession of close-ups on faces with hardly any depth of field or against a blurred background. Thus the group constituted by Banquo and the messengers is alternately in and out of focus when Macbeth is delivering his soliloquy. With minimal visual or sound effects (no background music, no pauses), the spoken word becomes prominent and seems to be restored to what Christian Metz, the French film theoretician, describes as its sovereignty on the stage in opposition to its auxiliary function in the cinema.[7]

Some viewers considered the intensification provided by television in Nunn's *Macbeth* too oppressive: 'I could not watch it,' Jack Gold told me in an interview in the course of a conversation on the influences of precedents on his own tele-play.[8] In Gold's version, as in Nunn's studio-recorded performance, the soliloquies are spoken aloud and played to camera. But whereas Ian McKellen speaks the aside over his shoulder, relying on the convention of the camera-as-audience, in the BBC film Nicol Williamson delivers it in voice-over, another short-lived concession to cinematographic conventions. Yet, in both performances, the small screen offers an effective verbal and aural support which the actors exploit by speaking their lines, facing the camera, or sometimes into it. This initiates a privileged relationship between viewer and protagonist which becomes closer as the soliloquy develops. The camera focuses on McKellen's face, and the following shot includes his hands, which are beginning to shake. The close-up on Williamson becomes tighter as his voice becomes more rasping to signal that evil is gradually taking possession of the character. This is probably why this actor never talks to the camera but looks through it or round it, particularly when he speaks the couplet 'Come what come may, / Time and the hour runs through the roughest day' (1.3. 145–6). The contrast between his newly discovered inner voice and his public tones appears strikingly for the first time when he turns to the other three characters with an enigmatic apology ('my dull brain was wrought / With things forgotten'), after the camera has revolved to include them all in the shot. This sort of pedagogy of the text is rarely offered in the film medium, which more often dilutes the spoken word in space. Reaction shots, which serve the same effect, are also scarcer on the large screen. In all three performances, the camera records Macbeth's, and sometimes Banquo's, reaction to the news that the first prediction has come true; but in Nunn's production, it also catches McKellen's knowing look when Angus reminds him of Cawdor's treachery, and in Gold's tele-play it never leaves Williamson's face until he speaks the aside. The audience are enrolled as partners and accomplices in the camera's exploration of the text.

The status of the spoken word thus appears as the main variable in the transcoding of a play for the cinema or for television. Trevor Nunn, a renowned practitioner of all forms of transcriptions, describes the discipline he used for television as 'shooting the text', as opposed to the necessity of 'shooting the action' for the cinema.[9] Polanski's film does not offer an extreme example of translation from the verbal to the visual; it rather strikes a middle course between faithful translation of the original and adaptation which may go as far as re-writing and drastic transposition. Orson Welles's *Macbeth* takes more liberties with the text than Polanski's, and Kurosawa's *Kumonosu-djo* (*Throne of Blood*, 1957) uses the conventions of the Noh and of Samurai films to render the spirit rather than the letter of Shakespeare's play. Each director has his own way of solving the tension between the Shakespearean text and cinematographic visuals, which Roger Manvell notably referred to as 'oil and water'.[10]

But once again, the change in marketing (resulting from the dissemination of films and teleplays for home viewing) complicates matters and entails a re-evaluation of the problems of reception and spectatorship normally associated with each medium. Take, for instance, the BBC Complete Shakespeare which was originally meant for domestic consumption as a series of TV films, sold from the start to forty-two countries, but aiming at a second life as video-cassettes on the educational market. Even at the time, it struck me that the initial brief of per-forming unabridged plays, set in periods 'which Shakespeare could recognize' (a policy which later suffered some fluctuations), catered for the needs of the aca-demic public more than for the tastes of the general viewer.[11] With the benefit of hindsight and with a clearer vision of the implications of video, I now suspect that if the most ambitious project in the history of television (as it was called) sometimes failed to convince, it was because it fell between two stools, a victim to its own divided aims: although video-cassettes and TV films use the same screen, they do not, *in this case*, aim at the same target. And as the problem was neither identified nor discussed, each director was thrown on to his own devices to meet the challenge of making both the classroom and the living-room swallow a Shakespearean play straight and whole: some drew on the naturalistic resources which were supposed to meet the average viewer on his own cinematographic grounds, while others resorted to pictorial references or visual quotations probably more adapted to an informed audience.

Because spectatorship normally conditions interpretive choices and sometimes decisions of transposition, its context is an essential parameter in the analysis of a film, TV film or video. No one would dream of studying Laurence Olivier's *Henry V*, released in 1944, without taking into account the fact that it was dedicated (even though after the completion of principal photography) to the paratroops who had landed in Normandy. At the other end of the scale, *The Animated Tales* have to be appreciated in their context of contemporary youth culture, with its comic strips which reduce the text to speech bubbles, its cartoons and video-clips. This is taken as the common denominator of the audience for which the product is marketed, that is, the average British teenager compelled by his curriculum to read a Shakespeare play, although he is suspected of being unable to concentrate for more than half an hour.[12] It is symptomatic of the prevalence of pictures over the written word in our media culture that, whereas his parents were fed on digests, this young person should be coaxed with 'comic book' versions of the plays or with cartoons. In the case of *The Animated Tales*, these draw on the East European animation tradition (especially the stop-frame puppets, reminiscent of the Czech *Dream* done in 1958 and issued in Britain with dubbing by Burton and others) to provide a worthy equivalent, on the visual front, to the Lambs' *Tales*, their ancestor in the reading field.

Factors of appreciation become more complex when the original performance, already submitted to one transcoding, is again diverted from its initial public and medium once it has been released on video. When film directors put together their Hollywood-style movies, they now have to think of the video which plays a major part in the financing of a film and will, six months later, take over from it. A couple of people sitting in a living-room are going to watch, on their electronic square, pictures which were originally intended for a cinema audience gathered in front of a large screen in a dark auditorium. A film director cannot be thinking of the television screen when he sinks *Titanic*, or when he explodes old Hamlet's ghost into a series of special effects. On the other hand, a videotape of Branagh's *Hamlet* may do more justice than the film to its mostly unabridged text. But some might argue that these distinctions between the effects of the small and big screens will soon be obsolete: new technologies such as laserdiscs, Dolby Pro Logic sound and digitised images, added to the wider use of 16/9 screens, will blot out the differences between auditoriums and home cinemas. Our theoretical cards have to be reshuffled all the time, as the borderline between media constantly fluctuates.

The main mutation, however, remains that which affects theatrical performances. These can now be preserved in a variety of forms: some have been recorded by a single camera for archives (as is the case with productions of the

RSC or of the Shakespeare Festival at Stratford, Ontario) or for live broadcasts after a stage success. One early example of this was the BBC version of the Royal Shakespeare Company *Wars of the Roses*, shot on stage at Stratford in 1964 without an audience, and only available today in the RSC archive as all this took place before the advent of video. Similar recordings were later to be commercialised as video-cassettes: Tony Richardson's *Hamlet*, filmed in the space where it was performed as a live theatrical event; or Michael Bogdanov's English Shakespeare Company *Wars of the Roses*, similarly recorded; or, more recently, Deborah Warner's National Theatre *Richard II*, with Fiona Shaw, broadcast on BBC2 before becoming available on video. Sometimes television producers attempt to recontextualise their broadcasts by assertion: the Renaissance Classics or the Renaissance Theatre series, the latter advertised as 'a night in the theatre' (e.g. Branagh's *Twelfth Night*, 'captured by Thames TV' with its original cast in 1988) or Miller's National Theatre production of *The Merchant of Venice* with Laurence Olivier, filmed by ATV for Renaissance Classics in 1973). Such recordings were all shot from what André Bazin described as the vantage-point of the spectator sitting in the stalls.[13] But not every crossover between stage and TV film has been taped live on stage. Some of the most effective videos originate from successful stage-shows (like Trevor Nunn's 1974 *Antony and Cleopatra*, first directed for the Main House at Stratford, or his 1976 *Macbeth* and 1990 *Othello*, both popular first at The Other Place) which are then rethought for television and filmed in a studio.[14] To this wide range of filmed performances must now be added video transfers of long lost productions such as the New York 1964 *Hamlet* with Richard Burton. One might be tempted to conclude that the video, as it claims to be doing for the cinema (even a 'lost film' like Welles's *Othello* can now be reissued),[15] is gradually becoming the theatre's memory.

Such a claim could not go without qualifications and reservations, though. As André Bazin also explains, in any type of film, the screen will mask part of the scene; a film audience or a television viewer are only shown what the director has chosen to select. Whatever the conditions in which a play has been filmed, whatever the number of cameras used, what is off-camera will remain outside the scope of his vision. The visual selection which is unavoidable on a screen excludes the simultaneous perception which is possible in the theatre. This is a reason why plays-within-the-play are one of the main casualties in conversions from play to film or television film: the camera shows less than the spectator's eye would see; too often it focuses on the actors and on their audience successively, whereas, on a stage, they would be seen concurrently. We could of course argue that the camera always finds itself where the action is, or that close shots and close-ups clarify what we have to know or see. But, as a result, the reorganisation of signs that normally occurs in the theatre is considerably limited on the screen. Consequently, instead of remaining open, the meaning of a performance is given, sealed as it were, once and for all.

With videos trying to encapsulate stage productions, we reach the height of paradox, since a live performance, which is something essentially ephemeral and fluid, is suddenly frozen, immobilised, preserved for endless repetition, although the singularity of a theatrical experience can never be recaptured. Ceremonies and celebrations, like performances, have lost their immediacy and unicity now that everyone has started playing around with a video-camera: available for repeated showings, they have become both present and absent, projected into a virtual world meant to be visited again and again. To which must be added the possibility given to a video-viewer of controlling his viewing. We have yet to appreciate the full effects on spectatorship of the displacement of the conventions of representation ascribed to each medium. The same spectator who is traditionally described as passive in the cinema while he is supposed to be both involved and detached in the theatre, now finds himself, thanks to his remote control, invested with the power of interrupting the performance, of making it move faster or slower, forward or backward, in short, of pulling it to pieces.

One consequence is that the convenience of studying Shakespeare-on-videotape is gradually displacing performance-analysis from the auditorium to the small screen. The video has opened up new fields of research by providing critics with an ideal object of study: a videotaped play which can be viewed repeatedly and studied in precise detail. Live performances recorded on video can be analysed with an accuracy and confidence which spectators sitting in an auditorium could never rival, even if they attended the show on several consecutive evenings. Given the possibility of repeated viewings of the same scene, of pausing to concentrate on a crux, or of moving it forward or backward at a touch of the remote control, the critical viewing of a performance has become very similar to the critical reading of a page. Another advantage is the possibility of comparing various productions of a given play on the same medium or on different media. Such comparisons will make it tangible that every performance construes the blanks in the text in its own way, and that it is based on a number of choices (of setting, casting, acting, etc.) which exclude other choices.

The flexibility of Shakespeare-on-video (and the viewer's ability to move around a programme on a DVD) is the positive counterpart to the finality of its recorded performances, a dialectical relationship which may be usefully borne in mind, particularly where teaching is concerned. Canned Shakespeare is an irreplaceable teaching aid. While Shakespeare-on-film is a means of generating popular interest for the Bard, Shakespeare-on-video (which does, in theory, make Shakespeare available to all), is in fact essentially exploited as material for teaching and for academic study. But as a teaching aid, Shakespeare-on-video is again double-edged. Canned Shakespeare runs the risk of being assimilated to canonic

Shakespeare. Because it can be endlessly repeated, split up into sections, interrupted and taken up again, a video performance is charged with a permanence and an authority which the initial film or teleplay did not carry when viewed in the conditions for which it had originally been conceived. Paradoxically, it is the very flexibility of video which encourages perception of it as a permanent object.

But the same video which has made of Welles's film of *Macbeth* a classic or of Trevor Nunn's production a model, also transforms them into documents which soon become dated, sitting as they do on the same library shelf as a collection of other taped performances. The risk of finding the meaning of a scene fixed once and for all in the minds and imaginations of students can easily be corrected by the possibility of showing several versions and even, as in some teaching experiments, of making a class act and tape their own version of that same scene. It will then be obvious that a given performance is neither *a* video nor *the* video of a play, but the result of conditions of production which all contribute to the final construct.

In effect, with the advent of Shakespeare-on-videotape, the Bard has lost as much as maintained his canonical status. For one thing, the dissemination of his plays in a variety of forms by way of video most probably played its part in the questioning of the canon which has marked the last decades of Shakespearian criticism. By relaying films as well as teleplays and theatre performances, videos have made audiences familiar with such directorial interventions as transcoding, transposing or adapting which have come to be taken as a matter of course. The original text is then naturally received as an essentially unstable entity, something to be rewritten from one performance to the next. The supposedly definitive performance of a play is a thing of the past. Beyond some impossible readings, which may be used positively in teaching (students who have been shown Polanski's savage screen murder of Duncan will more readily understand the specific rapport induced with the murderer in Shakespeare's play where the so-called 'murder scene' sets the murder off-stage), an infinite range of possible interpretations can be seen to surface, depending on audiences and contexts of production.

The text can thus be approached like a musical score to be interpreted by each director in accordance with his or her own choices. This is only one of the fields opened up for research, teaching or even personal reflection, through the variety of Shakespearean performances made available on video. More traditional ones may include comparisons between the different types of transcodings imposed by the various media, or the connection between spectatorship and the kind of transposition chosen. As video-libraries and theatre archives multiply, videotapes will become part of a play's theatrical history, visual and aural testimonies to the unending changes in Shakespearean performance, whether on film, television or on the stage. At the same time, the wide distribution of all these through video develops a Shakespearean media culture which in turn nurtures an interactive relationship between theatre and film. This also conditions the expectations of spectators and critics in the theatre. Michael Billington's reaction to Stéphane Braunschweig's 1997 production of *Measure for Measure* for the Edinburgh Festival is a case in point: 'it lacks the cinematic fluency we expect in modern Shakespeare. Rather than melt into each other, scenes are divided up by the onward march of the revolve', he wrote in the *Guardian* (24 August 1997). It is significant that such a seasoned theatre critic should object to the choice of a specifically theatrical device, now dismissed as too artificial and too slow for audiences bred on cinema.

And other questions will follow: how far does growing familiarity with Shakespearean 'author' films (like Welles's, Olivier's and now Branagh's) encourage a director's appropriation of the play in live performance? How far does it influence horizons of expectations and lead spectators to accept and expect intertextual (or intermedia) references in new representations of Shakespeare? Could we go as far as to say that postmodern re-presentation of Shakespeare, with its self-referential system of echoes, allusions or even visual quotations, is in part at least the product of our new video culture? These must remain open questions for the time being. Shakespeare-on-video is here to stay and we have yet to appreciate all its implications.

NOTES

1 A film of this had been shot at the Lunt-Fontanne Theatre to be shown at a few cinemas across the USA; it was restored in 1995 'for domestic and home viewing'. Tony Richardson's *Hamlet* was filmed in the Round House in London in 1969, shown on television in the USA and in cinemas in the United Kingdom in 1969–70 and then marketed as a video in 1991. (The early history of the relationship between televised and theatrically exhibited Shakespeare films is further discussed by Barbara Freedman, chapter 3 below.)

2 Six plays were first marketed in cartoon form (*Macbeth, Romeo and Juliet, A Midsummer Night's Dream, Twelfth Night, The Tempest* and *Hamlet*). They were followed by six more, after the initial success (*Julius Caesar, Richard III, The Winter's Tale, The Taming of the Shrew* and *Othello*).

3 Stephen Greenblatt's *The Norton Shakespeare* was launched in the spring of 1997 with a demo disk containing materials on *A Midsummer Night's Dream* and heralding 'The Norton Shakespeare Workshop' which will offer similar materials on six plays.

4 Kenneth S. Rothwell and Annabelle Henkin Melzer, eds., *Shakespeare on Screen: an International Filmography and Videography* (London, 1990). *Cahiers élisabéthains*, 53 (April 1998) publishes an updated videography which unfortunately does not mention the origin (theatrical or otherwise) of the videos listed: 'Shakespeare on Video', compiled by Patricia Dorval, pp. 53–75. *Shakespeare, The Movie*, Lynda E. Boose and Richard Burt, eds. (London and New York, 1997), is among the first publications to take into account the manifestations and effects of video culture, as its subtitle (*Popularising the Plays on Film, TV and Video*) indicates.

5 Quoted by Jack J. Jorgens in *Shakespeare on Film* (Bloomington, IN, 1977), p. 10.

6 This particular *Macbeth*, described on the video box as 'winner of the 30th US film and video festival', was directed by Jeremy Freeston, with Jason Connery in the title-role.

7 'Le verbe du théâtre est souverain . . . alors que la parole du film est sujette.' Christian Metz, *Essais sur la signification au cinéma*, 2 vols. (Paris, 1972), vol. I, p. 60.

8 See *Shakespeare à la télévision, analyses et interviews présentées par Michèle Willems* (Rouen, 1987), p. 49.

9 See his interview about his recent film of *Twelfth Night*, in *Cahiers élisabéthains*, 52 (October 1997), 89.

10 Roger Manvell, *Shakespeare and the Film* (London, 1971), p. 15.

11 See my article 'Verbal-Visual, Verbal-Pictorial or Textual-Televisual? Reflections on the BBC Shakespeare Series', first published in *Shakespeare Survey*, 39 (1989), 91–102, then reprinted in Anthony Davies and Stanley Wells, eds., *Shakespeare and the Moving Image* (Cambridge, 1994), pp. 69–85.

12 On this subject, see Laurie E. Osborne's essay 'Poetry in Motion: Animating Shakespeare', in Boose and Burt, eds., *Shakespeare, The Movie*, pp. 103–18.

13 'Le point de vue du monsieur de l'orchestre'. See the chapter entitled 'Théâtre et cinéma', in André Bazin, *Qu'est-ce que le cinéma* (Paris, 1958), pp. 130–78.

14 In an enlightening article, Michael Mullin studies how Trevor Nunn transformed the excellences of his theatre production in order to preserve them through television: 'Stage and Screen: The Trevor Nunn *Macbeth*', *Shakespeare Quarterly,* 38 (Autumn 1987), 350–9; reprinted in J. C. Bulman and H. R. Coursen, eds., *Shakespeare on Television* (Hanover, NH, and London, 1988), pp. 107–15.

15 Whereas in the past films could acquire a peculiar status through their unavailability ('classics' to be seen only in film-libraries, or at the annual showings of Olivier's films at the Academy Cinema in London), suddenly almost everything is accessible. This is similar to what is happening on the CD market, in which all the backlists are becoming available while there seems to be a crisis in record production, and not enough new classical CDs are being recorded.

3

BARBARA FREEDMAN

Critical junctures in Shakespeare screen history: the case of *Richard III*

As we mark the opening of the second century of Shakespeare films, we might also mark out new directions for their study. Chief among them is an approach to Shakespeare films in the context of a rigorous historicising and politicising of media configurations, and a theoretical model capable of generating new approaches based upon them. The model suggested here would not be new to historians: to explore the effects upon Shakespearean actors and productions of critical junctures in media history, when the use of emerging, competing and dormant technologies reflects situations of crisis, defence, reciprocal influence, commercial interdependency and realignments among various branches of the entertainment industry. Such an approach, based on the assumption that no Shakespeare film can be studied apart from changes in other media, opens up research into productions and performances that were caught on the cusp of what we typically refer to as technological change.[1] The phrase 'critical junctures' here replaces 'technological change' both to avoid implications of technological autonomy or determinism and to emphasise the reintroduction of technologies as a strategic and competitive practice, inseparable from specific political, economic and social interests. For the sake of brevity, these media configurations will be approached through the experiences of Shakespearean actors and directors as they succeeded or failed to adapt to them.

Three film productions and one filmed segment of *Richard III* will best serve as a test of this approach: the recently rediscovered Keane 1912/13 silent *Richard III* starring Frederick Warde – the earliest extant American full feature; the 1929 Warner Brothers' *Show of Shows* – one of the first Hollywood talkies to feature Shakespeare, in which John Barrymore delivers a soliloquy from his stage production of the play; Olivier's 1955 production, the first feature film to première on American television directly before its theatrical release; and the 1996 Loncraine/McKellen *Richard III*, starring cinema itself. Each film, historically significant in its own right, exemplifies the problems posed to Shakespearean actors as they attempted to adapt their stage performances to shifting media configurations: for Warde, the perception of silent cinema as a threatening double;

for Barrymore – who serves here as the exception to the rule – the urgent problem of elocution and mike training posed by the talkies; for Olivier, the mid-century insection and confusion of stage, cinematic and televisual influences; and for McKellen, the *fin de siècle* use of computer technology to radically reconstruct his stage and screenplay originals – to displace the word with the image and the image with the simulacra – the copy of the original that never existed.

Robert Hamilton Ball, the world-renowned expert on silent Shakespeare films, never lived to see the Keane/Warde *Richard III*. Yet Ball not only managed to unearth an enormous amount of material about its history, but also to predict something of its future that has not been adequately acknowledged: Warde's performance of *Richard III* has not, in fact, been fully recovered. Following up on newspaper reviews, Ball discovered a performance that the American Film Institute could never capture: 'Mr Warde offers five reels of moving pictures, depicting the great play, *King Richard III*. While the eyes rest in the intermissions between the showing of the reels, Mr Warde entertains the audience with a dramatic recital of famous passages in the play, elucidating them at the same time. During the showing of the pictures he explains the situations.'[2] Yet if Warde, the eminent tragedian, was offering his audiences the real thing, the public who confronted this odd doubling understandably responded with a sense of amazement. Reviewers duly noted the film's educational value; but of far greatest interest was the novelty of the literal 'sideshow' of Warde and his Travelling Image: 'Although it is announced that Edison is ready to make motion pictures talk . . . Frederick Warde's wonderful photographic masterpiece of himself in *Richard III* . . . illustrates that Mr Warde has anticipated the great Wizard of electricity.'[3]

When Warde took the film on tour, he himself was on tour as a live performer.[4] The American Film Institute knew that Warde would recite from Shakespeare before the film, and appropriately prefaced its October 1996 screening with a rare 1921 film short, in which Warde recited his poetry. But Warde's recitals before, in between and even during the reels were not preserved. And to theatre scholars, this is an important piece of performance history, if not an epochal moment in the relation of stage and screen. For film historians the recovery of this *Richard III* is significant because it was preserved intact, no reel missing; for performance historians, the missing real is Warde himself.

That Warde not only lectured before the film and recited between reels but apparently recited along with the film betrayed his hope that the public still needed and wanted the body of the actor, much as Warde, the actor, still wanted and needed a live audience. He did not leave the stage by choice. By adding his well-trained voice and body to the silent film, Warde had discovered a unique means of countering what the silent film had truncated, distorted and silenced. Whereas touring with films was not uncommon, it was uncommon for the star to do so, and to do it this extensively. By travelling with the film, not only in New York but through a host of Southern cities, Warde could remind the audience of what it was missing. Unable to confine himself to intermissions, Warde's unusual performance aptly conveys the peculiar relation of the Shakespearean stage actor to silent films: the sense of the inadequacy of cinematic Shakespeare, the competition which the cinema posed to the stage and the supplementary relation of the body to the silent image. By travelling from city to city, following his screen double as if he could reclaim or control it, Warde was also *acting out* a new and uneasy relationship to his image.

In an interview designed to advertise the film, 'Warde Likes Pictures: Shakespearean Actor is Enthusiastic Over Production of *Richard III*!', Warde praised films as an educational force. Yet he couldn't help but confide his discomfort in adjusting from stage to screen: 'The director of the company simply told the other actors what to do, telling them when to look glad or sorry, when to shout and when to fight, without telling them why they did any of these things. It was another matter for me. I simply couldn't act without saying my lines, and I had to suppress all sense of the ridiculous to go through with the thing in such surroundings.'[5] Warde's response was not uncommon. Sir Herbert Beerbohm Tree was notorious for the difficulties he posed on the Hollywood set of *Macbeth*. He not only had difficulty staying within camera lines; he was unable to confine himself to the lines of the script. An ingenious cameraman finally succeeded by fooling Tree into delivering his full part to an empty camera; when Tree had concluded his impassioned speeches, the real camera shot the silent film.[6] The distinguished Shakespearean Sir Johnston Forbes-Robertson found silent acting especially odd. When viewing rushes, his director notes, he 'invariably greeted . . . [his] own appearance in black and white with shrieks of laughter'.[7]

Warde was no Forbes-Robertson. But he had been a well-known 'second-rate' tragedian in his day, and his theatrical credits were impressive. As he proudly recounts in his memoirs, in 1874 he had been invited by managers Jarrett and Palmer to join the company at Booth's repossessed New York theatre.[8] He had played against or in supporting roles with Charlotte Cushman, Adelaide Nelson and John McCullough. He had even supported Edwin Booth on a two-year tour after the president's assassination. And now Warde was to be directed by a virtual unknown, to play to an empty stage, to play silenced. With no alternatives but Chautauqua lecturing, the ageing Shakespearean forced himself to adapt to the new medium: 'I found the action of the camera necessitated entirely different methods of acting from the stage. Spontaneity had to be replaced by deliberation and concentrated expression take the place of words. I had much to learn and considerable to unlearn.'[9] Like Forbes-Robertson, he continued in the trade.

Warde adapted slowly. Despite the film's pageantry, its lush sets, its cutaways – however limited – and general fidelity to stage versions of the Shakespeare/

Cibber text, the film's major flaw is Warde himself. Unlike the film's other actors, Warde carries the weight of stage gestures that were long out of date. He enacts the wooing of Anne in the much despised seesaw manner, revives the long-attacked characterisation of Richard as such an open and obvious hypocrite that the character's dignity and intelligence is sacrificed, and he punctuates his assigned sequenced movement of plotting, acting and exulting through such gestures as heartily slapping his raised knee and grinning while circling the index finger of his upraised hand to signal victory. Whereas silent film often depended upon stage business, outdated bits such as these limited the film's appeal.

For the tricentennial of Shakespeare's death in 1916, Edwin Thanhouser featured a far better Warde in *King Lear*. The film begins with a typical Méliès trick dissolve: Warde, reading *King Lear*, dissolves, or 'morphs' into King Lear. The technique was far more common to silents than has been recognised, and reminds us that cinematic techniques which present a threat to the integrity of the film actor's body are far from postmodern. But it is only at this time that this technique actually mirrors actors' experiences of their bodies in the very *process* of being filmed. Beerbohm Tree described his experience of acting before the camera as if he had taken a mild hallucinogen: 'Well . . . one throws oneself into the thing as one goes into a submarine. You take a dive – a plunge as it were – into the unknown, and calmly await the result. It was a strange experience for me, I admit . . . Before the film was finished I wondered if I had not deteriorated.'[10] Pirandello put it more poignantly: 'The film actor feels as if in exile – exiled not only from the stage but also from himself. With a vague sense of discomfort he feels inexplicable emptiness: his body loses its corporeality, it evaporates, it is deprived of reality, life, voice, and the noises caused by his moving about, in order to be changed into a mute image, flickering an instant on the screen, then vanishing into silence . . . The projector will play with his shadow before the public, and he himself must be content to play before the camera.'[11]

The actor's body in the age of mechanical reproduction was further threatened with the introduction of commercial radio in the 1920s; more accurately, the voice displaced the body. By 1919, the Radio Corporation of America (RCA) had been established, and in the following years, many feared radio would hurt theatre profits. A 1925 editorial explained it well: 'Motion picture theatre owners are lying awake nights worrying about the effect of radio on box office receipts.'[12] Yet the film industry was deaf to innovators who offered sound technology, due to previous disasters. Even the frontrunner, Warner Brothers, had to be convinced of the edge which sound technology offered, adopted it solely for music and only to compete with other studios. The 1920s saw a variety of experimental film techniques which were not revived until cinema was truly threatened, in part by television, at mid-century. These included two-colour Technicolor and 3D, first introduced in 1922, and widescreen, introduced in 1926. Technicolor alone remained popular. By 1925, Warners began work on sound films and broadcast from its first radio station. With the success of its first Vitaphone production in 1926, and Fox's first Movietone newsreels in 1927, the other studios followed suit. By 1928, Warners offered the first Hollywood full feature talkie – although it used title cards for transitions – and both Warners and Fox began preparing their theatres for sound. By 1930, most American cinemas were wired for sound. But if the cinemas were ready, the actors were not.

The uncanny experience which silent, or silenced, actors had described was replaced by sheer frustration with the conditions of the early talking pictures. Some actors lacked the voice to make the transition; others had trouble with the mike or the cumbersome set. Both Douglas Fairbanks – who was actually discovered by Frederick Warde and who joined his company out of high school – and Mary Pickford, international silent screen star, experienced various annoyances on the set of Sam Taylor's 1929 long undervalued *The Taming of the Shrew*.[13] Fairbanks spoke with such gusto into the microphone that he shattered a valve in the recording room.[14] And according to Laurence Irving, nephew of the great Sir Henry Irving – arguably the most interesting and significant stage Richard at the turn of the century – Fairbanks 'hated the sight of the padded cell which the embryonic sound studio had become. ' "Laurence," he said, "the romance of film-making ends here." '[15] Pickford fought with the director and her husband, hated the film and wanted to have it destroyed.

Before the *Taming of the Shrew* was released, two Hollywood studio showcases featuring Shakespeare had already premiered. 'Firsts' are always difficult to establish, and the relation of premieres to releases and of Hollywood to New York further complicates the matter. The latest 'first' talkie in English was a 1927 ten-minute version of the trial scene from *The Merchant of Venice*.[16] And as noted below, the first segment of an English-speaking Shakespeare film to appear on television was as early as 1936. But although these studio premieres do not appear to have been followed up by general releases until after *The Taming of the Shrew*, they were significant: the only successful appearances of Shakespeare in early talkies were segments within gala variety shows designed to showcase studio talents. In the midst of all-star casts performing songs, dance and bits of Vaudeville humour, a brief Shakespeare scene would be inserted not only to lend an air of prestige and respectability to the film but to signal the versatility of the studio's players. The best known among them is MGM's *Hollywood Revue of 1929*, which included the well-known preview of *Romeo and Juliet* with Norma Shearer and the renowned screen lover, John Gilbert. The choice of Gilbert made good sense – John Gilbert and Greta Garbo were widely considered the greatest lovers of the silent screen. Ironically, the question of the day – 'Can Garbo talk?' – was displaced by amusement that Gilbert could not.[17] But John Barrymore's highly-trained voice was perfectly suited for the talkies.

The high point of Warner Brothers' *Show of Shows* was John Barrymore's performance of Richard in a soliloquy drawn from *3 Henry VI*, which had been featured at the beginning of his five-hour long 1920 Broadway production of *Richard III*. Reviews of his surprisingly successful stage production had singled out this soliloquy as the actor's finest, and he therefore repeated it, in various venues, when a short speech was required of him. But for screen fans who had never heard the great voice, and there were many, the thrill was extraordinary. This was not simply a Shakespeare segment; this was a silent screen idol whose vocal abilities surpassed any known to his audience. When the film premiered in New York, the critics were equally impressed – and their reviews repeated the praise of Barrymore that he received after his first Broadway performance.[18] Given that the soliloquy was sandwiched between a comic sketch and a performance by Rin Tin Tin, this may carry less weight, but the New York critics had been harsh on Barrymore at other times.

One of the greatest English-speaking stage Richards, it was said of Barrymore in 1923 that his transformation should be titled 'The Story of a Voice'.[19] Twenty years later, Warner Brothers released *The Voice that Thrilled the World* – a documentary on the history of sound film which featured Barrymore, and included this soliloquy. But the voice that thrilled the world required the help of Margaret Carrington, who not only was responsible for aiding Barrymore in his characterisation, but, as Michael Morrison documents, who retrained and recreated Barrymore's voice.[20] Earlier, the voice had been criticised by his family, by reviewers, even by Barrymore himself. 'I wish something could be done for my nephew's diction and his voice', complained his uncle, John Drew; 'It's a disgrace to the family.'[21] Arthur Hopkins, the brilliant stage director of *Richard III*, was more charitable: 'It was characteristic of Jack to know that he had to find a new voice.'[22] Barrymore himself was aware that something had to be done, and done quickly: 'My voice had a high, nasal tone and I recited "A horse, a horse, my kingdom for a horse!" like a terrified tenor trying to escape from a couple of blondes.'[23]

For Barrymore, the problem was not that of a silent actor faced with the challenge of moving into the talkies, nor that of a stage actor faced with adapting to films, but something more complex. With stage credits as early as 1903, and silent films credits by 1913, he was a stage star and screen idol when he turned to Shakespeare in 1920. Despite his ample experience both on stage and screen, his initial plans to star in a Shakespearean production were met with scepticism. He had played comedic parts in both mediums, but it was not until the late teens that his versatility was acknowledged. As a silent screen star he was adored; reviews of his appearances on the stage, however, were met with criticisms of his voice. Attuned to the criticism, Barrymore anticipated the silent screen actor's retraining by working with elocutionists and finally with Margaret Carrington in a backbreaking preparation for his five-hour bravura 1920 performance of *Richard III*, and again for his extraordinary 1922 performance in *Hamlet*. Carrington helped him not only to change his voice but the conception of the roles and of verse delivery, and in the process paved the way for the modern Shakespeare. It was her idea to have Richard turn to the audience after the wooing of Anne: 'I suggested that Barrymore throw the speech right into the auditorium. The effect was startling and at this point . . . he got a tremendous reaction from the audience by prolonged applause.'[24] Both Olivier and Loncraine have since followed suit, without giving credit to Barrymore, let alone to Carrington.

But the voice Carrington helped to create could not recreate Barrymore. The voice became drunk, ornery and unreliable. It became separated from its memory. It relied upon cue cards to function. Barrymore's ill health, breakdowns and alcoholism prevented him from continuing on-stage. It might be said that performing Shakespeare on stage both made him and broke him for the stage, as the traumatic experiences of so quickly reconstructing his voice, and of approaching his performances as only a perfectionist daunted by Shakespeare would, in addition to his numerous personal problems, contributed to break-downs and a return, in 1925, to the silent screen. Urged to return to the stage, he attempted and planned numerous aborted come-backs. The silent screen was safer. Barrymore was in the midst of making his last silent when news of the talkies broke. He contacted his agent at once: 'Will you try to think of some more movies for me, ones where the talking device might possibly be used? It seems to be coming in, and apparently now is the time for me to make a killing in it.'[25] The response was the *Show of Shows*. Barrymore's work in the talkies was problematic. Efforts in 1933 and 1934 to capture his theatrical genius in film versions of his 1922 theatrical production of *Hamlet* failed terribly, and in addition to relying on cue cards, he was nearly impossible to work with in his role as Mercutio on the set of the 1936 *Romeo and Juliet*.

Radio now provided the safest solution. Competition between American radio stations was fierce; in 1937, when NBC learned that CBS radio would broadcast a summer series of Shakespeare on Mondays from 9 to 10 p.m., it announced its own Streamlined Shakespeare series for Mondays from 9.30 to 10.30. Barrymore delivered six Shakespeare performances through NBC that summer to mixed reviews; his *Richard III* was one of his best. Silent screen actors moved in the other direction, and sought experience in radio to train their voices for the talkies. An early 1929 *Variety* headline, 'Film People Seeking Radio Dates as Mike Training for Voices' highlighted the pressure which actors faced almost overnight.[26] Radio stars adapted more quickly to the talkies than either film or stage actors. The problem of elocution, which faced any stage actor, was heightened by the need to adjust to the changes in the mechanically magnified voice;

the phrase 'mike fright' entered common usage. Responding with excitement to the issue in 1936, George Bernard Shaw explained: 'I should go so far as to say that you can do things with the microphone that you cannot do on the ordinary stage. I want again to emphasize the fact that you are dealing with a new instrument and that in speaking on the screen you can employ nuances and delicacies of expression which would be of no use spoken by an actor on the ordinary stage in the ordinary way.'[27]

Shaw's lecture was of importance nationally as well. Hollywood had been importing British stars not only for Shakespeare but for the talkies in general. Now the British were going to have their revenge – with the first full-length British Shakespeare film and, surprisingly, the first Shakespeare segment on television. Those who complained, like Basil Dean, that the problem with Shakespeare on film was Hollywood were in for a rude surprise. The greatest problem with director Paul Czinner's *As You Like It* was the miscasting of his wife Elisabeth Bergner as Rosalind; its greatest interest is in the casting of Olivier as Orlando. But the film is important historically.

In *The Times* listing for 26 August 1936, under the headlines 'First Television Broadcast. Demonstration at Radio Show. To-day's Programme' one is first impressed by the opening sentence: 'The first organized television programme in this country will be broadcast today.' One is loath to move on through the actual listings – yet among the Baird system listings for that day are film excerpts, and at 12.49 and 5.19 the film listed is *As You Like It*, with Elisabeth Bergner. That Olivier was not even mentioned is rather extraordinary; that Shakespeare is not mentioned is also surprising. But the excitement over the broadcast overshadowed what, for us, is a historic moment: the first Shakespeare film clip on television – a fact that has not been acknowledged in any of the Shakespeare filmographies.[28]

The famous series of Shakespeare scenes broadcast by the BBC began in 1937. Following up, perhaps, on the film, an eleven-minute scene from *As You Like It* inaugurated the distinguished series; Richard's wooing of Anne was chosen for the eighteen-minute *Richard III*. By September 1939, over 20,000 television sets were estimated to have been in use in London when war intervened and programming came to a halt, not to resume until 1946.[29] Commercial programming in America took much longer to develop, largely due to in-fighting, litigation, high prices and FCC rulings. But American television viewers had no love affair with Shakespeare, despite the arguments of Shakespeareans.

There were at least three factors that help to explain the role of Shakespeare on American television: limited programming options in the early years, threats from the Federal Communications Commission of non-renewal of licences if educational fare was not offered and specially sponsored programmes such as Hallmark. In the late 1940s and early 1950s, when television was based in New

York and the networks had all too much time to fill, cultural programming was enormously convenient. When coaxial cables were set up which enabled broadcasting from the East coast to the Midwest in 1949, and then to the all important West coast in 1951, programming changed. Variety shows, situation comedies and television playhouses with contemporary plays and Hollywood film stars met American tastes more suitably than New York cultural programming. It is all too easy to look at lists of Shakespeare plays on television without considering either the length of the segment, or the time slot. However limited the various Trendex and Neilson ratings were, they easily establish that Americans wanted contemporary drama over Shakespearean drama, and that even when they tuned in, they soon tuned out.

Hallmark's *Hall of Fame* commercial interests kept great Shakespeare productions alive. Of all the Shakespeare productions, Hallmark did send the very best. It could afford to. As Merrill Panitt in his editorial to the *TV Guide* explains, 'Since 1951, when it started *Hall of Fame* on television, the company's gross income has increased from an estimated $45,000,000 a year to $90,000,000 – 100 percent. So, Hallmark isn't too impressed by the ratings, which indicate how many people watch its shows.'[30] But Hallmark relied upon the best stars, and for these stars, the move to television was unexpectedly difficult. One of the most widely advertised Shakespeare productions on television featured Broadway star Maurice Evans in the Hallmark 1953 *Hamlet*. Advertised by NBC as two hours in length – although, with constant commercials, it was closer to ninety minutes – the event was highly anticipated. Evans was less positive about its outcome. In an essay he wrote, published in the *New York Times*, he mused: 'Haunted by the minute hand, surrounded by fearful booms and cameras and microphones, by sealed-up engineers, monitors, and unidentified wigwaggers, I approach this afternoon's ordeal with mixed emotions . . . Whatever the verdict . . . I am convinced that frequent TV performances can only dissipate the actor.'[31]

Evans could not anticipate the production, which was filled with more mishaps than most. But his response to the exigencies of adapting his performance from the large stage to the close-shots of mid-century television was typical: 'Accustomed to playing *Hamlet* in the wide spaces of the theater, I found it excruciatingly difficult to deliver certain passages with the requisite vehemence without looking ridiculous at such close quarters.'[32] And so he did. He could not forget the moment when a camera mercilessly closed in on a tight shot of him blinking rather obviously into the lights while portraying a dead Hamlet.[33] That would never happen again. Evans took to making cut-outs to fit his face as it would be seen on small screen, and shared them with his performers: 'In rehearsal, we found the best way to scale the performance down to TV proportion was to have an assistant hold a piece of cardboard before the actors' faces.

This represented the exact size of the image which would appear on the screen. This device helped me enormously.'[34] Hallmark and television playhouses were themselves a mixed medium, caught between stage and screen. 'Whenever we think of early TV drama,' Kenneth Rothwell reminds us, 'we must re-position ourselves in history and remember that these productions were broadcast "live", with all the perils pertaining thereto. They were closer to live theatre than modern television.'[35]

To counter the massive exodus of viewers from cinema to television, the American film studios initiated a revolution which redefined the cinema as a radically new perceptual experience, based on huge wrap-around and curved wide screens, brilliant colour and stereophonic sound. The widespread adoption of CinemaScope, due to one of the most aggressive marketing schemes in cinema, resulted in wide screens up to 64 by 24 feet. Having adjusted to extreme close-ups on small-screen television, Shakespearean actors now had to adjust to larger than life images of themselves on huge screens. Getting smaller, getting larger – perhaps Beerbohm Tree was right after all; the actors facing such media configurations must have felt caught in a fantasy devised by Lewis Carroll.

Yet if ever there were a master media shifter, it was Laurence Olivier. His ability to move deftly back and forth between stage, screen and television as early as 1937, his predilection to do so within a given year, and to weather the changes within each medium throughout a lengthy career, was nothing short of extraordinary. After a bad first experience in film, he announced: 'I don't believe in Shakespeare on screen.'[36] Yet as he continued to star under directors such as Hitchcock and Wyler, he caught the disease of movie madness: 'How I loved the medium! Wyler's medium, mine, William Shakespeare's.'[37] That Olivier was fascinated by film, more than half in love in with it, is wonderfully evident in his *Henry V* and *Hamlet*, and amply described in his two autobiographies. But his 1955 *Richard III* is a very different affair. That it sits uneasily on the cusp of stage and screen, and leans far more heavily on a prior stage production than any of his other films is common knowledge. Less often acknowledged are the ways in which both the production of the film and Olivier's performance are imbricated within the complex and changing relations of stage, screen and television in the mid-1950s. More specifically, as the first feature film to premiere on American television before appearing in the prestige theatre houses, his *Richard III* became a major source of public controversy on the role of American television and its future.

No one doubts that Olivier's *Richard III* is essentially a performance film. Despite the occasional claim for its complex cinematic design, the film was neither planned nor praised for cinematic virtuosity.[38] According to his new cinematographer, Otto Heller, Olivier's first words to him were: 'Don't try to win yourself an Oscar.'[39] Examples of Olivier's blatant lack of concern over the technical aspects of the film are rife; the details of how he handicapped Heller by failing to provide him with the necessary equipment, even in the first scenes to be shot, are shocking. But they confirm Olivier's interest, as repeatedly conveyed to Heller, in using film to capture his stage performance, and in doing so as easily and quickly as possible. The 1944 stage production of *Richard III*, directed by John Burrell, had been enormously successful, and had toured as recently as 1948 before it was revived in London the following year. The production was so set in Olivier's mind that he asked Heller to shoot scenes so that they might appear exactly as they had in the theatre. 'For Sir John Gielgud's scene in the cell', Heller explained to interviewer Harold Benson, 'he described his effect of near-darkness in his stage production and said he'd like me to try to imitate it.'[40] Heller had to prove to Olivier why it wouldn't work by shooting the scene twice: first Olivier's way, and then his own. Only then could he make the simplest of points obvious.

What had changed since Olivier's last foray in Shakespearean films was a new reliance on experimental techniques to combat the popularity of television and to resuscitate an ailing film industry. A smooth adaptation of a theatrical performance to film, which would have been viable before the cinematic revolution, required knowledge of the equipment installed in the American theatres and of current and emergent widescreen technologies. Olivier's difficulties with the VistaVision format he chose, his interest in speed over technical mastery, and his attitude towards adjusting his stage performance for cinema, help to explain the limitations of *Richard III*.

Olivier's choice of Paramount's VistaVision was a brilliant one, but it militated against an easy translation of performance to film. As Roger Manvell explains:

> Sir Laurence said he liked the screen ratio [of VistaVision], which made a well-shaped picture, and the improved picture quality. But he had much trouble with the 500ft. reels, which necessitated reloading after 5 minutes' shooting. Special spools had had to be made for one scene, which required 5¼ minutes' continuous shooting. Reloading broke the atmosphere, and often involved practically re-lighting the whole set before shooting could proceed. There was hardly a scene when reloading did not have to be done after each take.[41]

A large rather than widescreen format, with height to width ratio of 1:66.1, VistaVision had many advantages over CinemaScope: sharper images, superb clarity and depth of field, as well as ease of flexibility with other formats. Despite studio recommendations for costly equipment for maximum effect, VistaVision could be inexpensively projected on to a huge CinemaScope screen with a far superior picture.[42] Paramount was the only studio to release this format, and offered it for free. But the American studios had joined together around the inferior CinemaScope process, with a true widescreen ratio of 1:2.35, forcing managers to renovate their theatres and purchase the expensive screens for its exclusive use. Accordingly, VistaVision threatened the studios' monopoly. At the same time that Olivier was contemplating screen formats, American Mike Todd was preparing to film with superior Todd-A.O., which remedied the problems Olivier was to have with VistaVision. Olivier had Heller ready to go to study the first such film in the making when he changed his mind. Although flexible, the process was extremely costly.

Olivier's desire for a speedy shooting and editing schedule militated against the artistry and technical mastery Heller offered. Despite the time spent in both shooting the film through VistaVision and the massive post-production headaches that Heller faced, Olivier finished *Richard III* in a rushed seventeen weeks. Olivier knew that this was 'exceptionally short for this type of picture', and boasted: 'I was one half day under schedule when I finished the whole film.'[43] If this included the date by which Heller completed the laborious editing and colour matching, and also compensated for the lack of adequate equipment for the first scheduled scenes of the battle sequence, the pace was quite extraordinary.

But Olivier's interest in speed over technique may help to explain why this was the first of his films not to be graced with an Academy Award. In an interview with Peter Brinson at the completion of the film, Olivier presented his approach as a bold experiment: 'This rapid approach to such a complicated and large-scale subject is a new attitude towards directing which came to me partly through former experience and partly as a new experiment.'[44] 'Olivier achieved great tempo of production,' Brinson explains, 'by refusing to dwell on tiny or imaginary imperfections at the cost of the pace and mood of the action and characters.'[45] Yet the phrases 'new attitude' and 'new experiment' were no more than euphemisms for a rush job – an unusual lack of interest in expertly adapting the production to cinema and in post-production editing.

Finally, Olivier was surprisingly cavalier about the adaptation of his performance to the screen; he also used stage blocking at times when a cinematic strategy was more suitable. He boasted that he toned down his stage performance for the film within two weeks.[46] Directly after the film's completion, he claimed: 'I think there is much less difference between film acting and stage acting than people think – much less. If you are a long way off in the dress circle you are really no further away than in a long shot.'[47] Olivier's acting cannot be faulted. But the film's mixture of stage blocking and shooting style is not always successful. When Olivier used the camera voyeuristically, so that audiences see characters at a distance through Richard's eyes, the effect is cinematic. Moreover, Olivier's plan to flirt with the camera as a seated audience was a brilliant move: 'Richard would be flirting with the camera – sometimes only inches from his eyes – and would lay his head on the camera's bosom if he could.'[48] But for Olivier, flirting included a good deal of distance, and here stage performance does not translate into a successful cinematic strategy. When he identified the camera's look with a seated audience, and insists on a form of stage blocking whereby Richard is often at great distances from the camera, as in his opening soliloquy, the effect is peculiar, and theatrical. And here, of course, is the problem. Stage blocking, upon which Olivier relies all too often, is no substitute for camera movement; was Olivier acting for the cinema or the stage?

On the other hand, audiences were shocked and delighted by Olivier's use of a direct address to the camera; it continues to rivet audience attention today. Relevant here is a shrewd comment on televised Shakespeare by Robert E. Wood: 'I would suggest that we are far more prepared . . . to accept the Elizabethan stage conventions of direct address as members of a television audience than we would be as members of a film audience, accustomed as we are to direct address by the face on the small screen.'[49] The personal address to the camera was perceived by film reviewers at the time as a brilliant revival of a technique long considered *déclassé*. Yet it was perfectly comprehended by a mid-1950s television audience. Although Shakespeareans still debate *Richard III* in terms of the relation of theatre to cinema, Olivier himself supplies the missing third term: 'Richard talks to the audience all the time . . . This is absolute audience approach, not meditation. When I do it in the film I talk to the camera, and take the camera into my confidence . . . I treated the camera as a person . . . It's nothing new really: *people are seeing it on television all the time.*'[50] When Richard addresses the camera directly, the effect is of a fortuitous confluence of theatrical, filmic and televisual styles. Olivier's set design further underlines the televisual influence. Roger Manvell explains: 'For this film the technique derives much from television. In the manner of television production at the time, the key sets (the Palace, the Westminster area, the Tower of London) are made physically contiguous, so that a few paces move the cast from one location to another.'[51] Olivier's attribution to television of his direct address to the camera, coupled with his use of a set derived from television, suggests a significant media crossover.

But the relationship to television was both more direct and more controversial. *Richard III* made American television history. It was the first feature film to premiere on American television directly before its theatrical release – Alexander Korda's comedy, *The Constant Husband*, preceded it but was labelled by the industry a 'turkey', lacking market potential. The news was announced on the front page of the *New York Times*.[52] After its television premiere on Sunday afternoon, 11 March 1956, *Richard III* was to be screened at an Actors' Fund gala event that evening; the film opened to the public the next day. Stills from the film were featured on covers of major trade journals and popular magazines alike. No one at the time with any interest in media could miss its significance. No one would suppose that by the turn of the twentieth century, all the major Shakespearean filmographies would refer to the *simultaneous* screening of *Richard III* on television and cinema.

Six months before the December 1955 London world premiere of *Richard III*, NBC was completing negotiations to screen the film on American television.[53] For Olivier, the deal was problematic in that the film's largest and widest audience would see it in a medium which militated against its adequate reception. For media executives, the deal was problematic due to the stand-off between American television and the film industry. Since the major studios had resisted selling or renting films to the networks, up to 1955 feature films were either B quality films from defunct studios, or from Great Britain, whose industry still suffered from mismanagement and from government efforts to keep it afloat. Studio compliance with the Supreme Court Paramount decree requiring that the studios sell off their theatre chains, based on an anti-trust suit, had been stalled, given the argument that the studios could not get fair price for their theatres. But when Howard Hughes sold the RKO library to television in 1955, a new and profitable avenue had opened up. In 1956, Warner Brothers and MGM followed suit but with more profitable packages. The television industry, which still relegated films to the slots least likely to interfere with its own programming, now faced increased public demand as well as internal fears that the medium would become a conduit for feature films. This was the context in which Olivier's film premiered on television.

News that the television premiere of *Richard III* would *precede* its cinematic release and that NBC would receive a considerable percentage of the box-office receipts suggested a new alternative, and a viable model for the future. Network insiders opposed the trial with titles such as 'NBC's 3-Hour *Richard III* Premiere Not Likely to Set a TV Pattern.'[54] Veteran reviewer Gilbert Seldes, who acknowledged the possible limits of the film as a test case, speculated – as did most every review – that should the screening hurt the film's box-office takings, at least one consequence to consider was that 'the now merging lines of television and Hollywood will diverge. We will return to the status of some years ago – competition.'[55] Even Jack Gould, the sceptic of the *New York Times*, voiced the common refrain: 'If the receipts [of Olivier's film at the box-office] are not adversely affected, a new era in film distribution may be here or at least just around the corner. If they are adversely affected, the present liaison between the TV and movie industries may be strained.'[56] Both camps ignored the fact that Shakespeare films had rarely, if ever, been sufficiently successful at box-offices to make up for their costs. One of the few sane voices in the wilderness was Henry Hart, editor of *Films in Review*, who pointedly remarked: 'The longhairs who see Olivier's *Richard III* on tiny t.v. screens in black-and-white may be inspired to go to see it in VistaVision and Technicolor in a theatre. But what about the crew-cuts?'[57] To pin one's hopes and fears on the future relations of television to film to the fate of a single film appears illogical enough; to do so with a Shakespeare film, ridiculous. Yet for those who were aware of the rapid changes which the industry was undergoing in America during these crucial years, *Richard III*'s television premiere provided ample reason for cultural anxiety regarding the uncharted territory that lay ahead.

Olivier's response to the television screening, voiced in hindsight, reveals the inestimable costs to a director whose work is trapped in the wrong medium. His fascination with clarity of image and long distance shots did not translate to the new medium, and characters' facial expressions in such scenes were indecipherable. Only a small percentage of television viewers had colour television sets, and the reception of colour transmission by black and white sets was especially poor. The loss of Roger Furse's colour-coded costumes, intended to help audiences identify characters, further complicated an already complex plot. Years later, Olivier tried to explain his approval of the fiasco: 'I think the temptation behind this deal, which was made by Robert Dowling and which I must say was very strongly deplored by me, was that by obtaining whatever the figure was from television he would have already achieved the equivalent of the first million dollars at the box office. This idea was too heady a one to resist, I suppose, and there it was. But in my opinion, it did the film great damage . . . I would have said then and I would say now that to show any film initally through the medium of television would be disastrous, though it may well be that now, fifteen years after the event, the position would be different.'[58]

Olivier's argument still makes sense, but the prescience of Dowling's strategy cannot be denied. His rethinking of the relation of exhibition to production and distribution provided a model for financing films of Shakespeare and other classic texts. Olivier's retrospective complaint was recorded close to the premiere of Peter Hall's 1968 production of *A Midsummer Night's Dream*, shown on television in the United States (but theatrically in Great Britain). Ironically, Hall's producer, Michael Birkett, described the same strategy Dowling employed as a recent trend:

> As for the deal-making, financial, aspects of Shakespearean films, there's no doubt that television has made a great deal of difference. Films are regularly financed today by including the eventual television residuals in the deal . . . also, several films have been made for showing first on television and thereafter in cinemas. The usual pattern of distribution (achieve a reputation in the cinemas, then sell to TV) is not necessarily the only pattern. It may be possible to show a film *first* on television, achieving a considerable amount of publicity and a very wide audience, and *then* show it in cinemas so that those who missed it, those who want to see it again, and those who merely heard about it, can go and add to the revenue. This scheme has only arisen because of 'the classics'; obviously it would not apply to a normal

feature film. The feeling is that a film of Shakespeare will not date; the sheer newness of the film is not as big a commercial factor as usual.'[59]

Looking back upon Birkett's reasoning, what most surprises is the speed with which it became obsolete. By 1976, under ten years after his remark, home video systems and cable television were introduced; by 1985, both proved more popular than American theatre rentals; and the surprise of the 1990s has been the popularity of film versions of the classics. But that popularity has had its costs, as evidenced in the account by Ian McKellen of his role in the 1996 film *Richard III*, written in collaboration with film director Richard Loncraine.

Like Olivier, McKellen's major impetus in making a film of *Richard III* was primarily to capture and popularise a theatre production – in this case, his 1990 stage performance in the Royal National Theatre production, directed by Richard Eyre. Unlike Olivier, who was continually moving back and forth between media, starring in and directing film, television and stage productions, McKellen is first and foremost a stage actor, despite occasional forays into other media. He knew virtually nothing about film when writing his first screenplay. Yet although Eyre and stage designer Bob Crowley, among many others, helped McKellen enormously with the screenplay before he approached Loncraine, McKellen had difficulty seeing cinematically. And as much as McKellen tried to prepare himself for film acting, he was not prepared for the speed with which Loncraine shot and edited the film.

Both as an actor and as an author, then, McKellen's transition to the world of the cinema was especially difficult. Since he had had so little experience in this area, McKellen quickly made a number of films, taking bit parts to get the experience that he needed. Nothing prepared him, however, for what was to occur. Recounting the first day of shooting he admits: 'Everyone assumed I must be excited to be filming at last. I only realised that this was unlike any other job when at Steamtown I saw the scale of the enterprise . . . and all because three years ago I wanted to go on playing Richard III!'[60] But it was not the scale of the enterprise, nor first-day jitters alone, that posed the real problem. Although he enjoyed the opportunity to review shots on the video monitor, and explains, 'I always monitored my progress in this way', he found it 'unnerving to realise that a performance is basically fixed once the director is satisfied and decides to move to the next set-up'.[61] As a renowned Shakespearean actor who is used to rehearsing and perfecting his performance, the loss of control must have been horrifying.

The loss of control over editing may explain the discrepancy between McKellen's perception and film audiences' perception of the character of Richard himself. Interviews in a website press kit advertising the film reveal McKellen's confidence that audiences will identify with Richard, sympathise with him and hope for his success. 'You're not suggesting', asks the interviewer, 'that the audience should have sympathy for him?' McKellen responds: 'I'm not suggesting that they do anything, but if they don't I'd be very disappointed. He's very engaging . . . He is undoubtedly an attractive figure and that's why Lady Anne is momentarily seduced by him.'[62] With restraint, the interviewer responds: 'Yes. I find that rather hard to believe', only to be assured by McKellen, 'You find it hard to believe on the stage but you won't when you see it on the screen . . . Basically, she believes him when he says he loves her.' The audience, he imagines, will also be won over: 'I hope, when the film is over, they will remember how much they wanted Richard to succeed.' Although a range of responses towards Richard is possible, McKellen's confidence regarding a fixed audience response to his character underlines his innocence regarding the control of the camera over performance. One can only guess that he gauged audience response to his film performance in relation to his far less sympathetic stage portrayal, and so imagined a warmer audience identification than in fact he received.

The same interview establishes McKellen's problems as a screenwriter. Despite the massive help he received from Eyre and Loncraine, among others, McKellen had trouble seeing in filmic terms, as demonstrated in the press kit interviews. When he is asked what he saw as cinematic about *Richard III*, McKellen waffles. 'At what moment did you decide that you wanted to make a film of *Richard III*?' the interviewer asks, 'What was it that you saw as essentially cinematic?'[63] 'This was an immensely successful production with audiences throughout the world', McKellen explains. 'They all responded to it and as usual I was thinking "why can't we reach an even larger audience? Why can't we film it? Why can't we put it on television, or something?" . . . Now it was clear that I was looking for what in Shakespeare was cinematic or was not cinematic.' The interviewer, encouraged, returns to the question: 'What is cinematic about the play?' But again McKellen fails to respond adequately; he repeats the old saw that 'one scene follows on from another in Shakespeare with the alacrity of a cinema "cut"', observes that 'The setting of the 1930s could be immensely photogenic', since 'there is a lot of Thirties London which is still left' and concludes: 'The costumes, too, would be very good to look at and very clear.' That none of these answers responds to the question of what could be or is cinematic about the play *Richard III* is surprising.

Much as Olivier was to pay for conceding to the screening of his film on American television, so McKellen had to pay for his ambition to make an internationally popular film. In selling his screenplay, McKellen had to face the problem of popularising Shakespeare on cinema for an international audience and at the same time remaining true to the text. He solved his moral dilemma with a specious form of chop-logic that one is more accustomed to finding at the conclusion of a Shakespearean soliloquy:

it's my duty to make sure that what they [spectators] are excited by is not just another action movie, not just another political intrigue thriller, not just another play about sex and family betrayals and a cruel tyrant with a lot of blood spattered on the screen – but to point out that these were inventions, not of the cinema, but of Shakespeare. Cinema has adopted so much of the melodrama, the excitement and the thrills which Shakespeare first brought to life 400 years ago and the vital link is Shakespeare's words. So I will not betray Shakespeare and I don't have to betray Shakespeare because one could say he invented many of the clichés of cinema and many of the things that people find exciting in the cinema.[64]

Now that Shakespeare was redefined as the source of cinema's appeal, now that Shakespeare was, in fact, a fellow screenwriter, McKellen's guilt was assuaged: 'This project took off because film people got excited about the script. Whether they realised it or not, the person who excited United Artists was Shakespeare. I'm happy to be his agent.'[65]

But McKellen's role was far more difficult in taking on the responsibility of preserving Shakespeare's verse in a popular film. If Loncraine and McKellen did get along, as McKellen claims, they had a major problem on their hands, since the question of how to join the verbal and the visual is compounded by the problem of how to do justice to the richness of Shakespeare's language in what is essentially a visual medium. Even Olivier argued, at the completion of *Richard III*, and despite Roger Manvell's complaints, that 'very, very good writing like Shakespeare's does not really suit so completely visual a medium as the screen'.[66]

After a lecture at MGM's British studios by a well-known screen elocutionist in 1936, the same questions with which each Shakespearean film director struggles today were posed most succinctly by Sydney Carroll to Bernard Shaw: 'Is it possible to do justice to Shakespear's [sic] verse as verse through the medium of screen?'; 'Dont [sic] all these [filmic] devices in themselves constitute an interruption of the verse, the rhythm, the sweep of the verse?'[67] Neither Shaw nor anyone since has adequately answered Carroll's questions – although Peter Hall's solution to the problem in his televised *Midsummer Night's Dream* by cutting on the verse is among the more interesting. Rather, many have since seconded Carroll's conclusion: 'The main function of the screen is to relate the stories in terms of moving images. Strictly speaking, speech should be secondary, whereas on the stage speech is primary.'[68] Despite brilliant translations, it may be that foreign language Shakespeare films appear to transfer more fully to a cinematic medium for precisely this reason.

In contrasting cinema and theatre, McKellen observes: 'A theatre audience, by definition, ought to listen before it looks.'[69] But Richard Eyre, director of the National Theatre production of *Richard III*, is aware that it is not that simple, and he has addressed the question of the relation of sight and sound in film as well as theatre most perceptively.[70] Trained in theatre, he had worked in television and radio drama before his directorship of the Royal National Theatre. Eyre is in many ways closer to Olivier in his ability to move back and forth between film, television drama and theatre, and to excel in all three. The similarities and differences between the media are always in his mind. As a result, in working with designer Bob Crowley, he was uniquely prepared to direct Shakespeare's *Richard III* for a primarily visual audience and to force them to hear – to deploy the visual so that it enhanced rather than overcame the speech.

Loncraine was under no such constraints. For him, the visual is primary; the film director is already working with problems in cinema and comes to a given screenplay with those questions and problems intact. Among a number of strategies that Loncraine developed to satisfy popular audience interest and McKellen's insistence on Shakespeare's text, two are most obvious. The first is closest to a technique of the earliest talkies – a separation of action from speech. As Frederic Thrasher explains it: 'The camera focused on action – then on speech; never on the two together. Audiences were satisfied at first because they were so fascinated by the sound actually coming out of an actor's mouth. They . . . would have felt cheated if the camera had strayed away from the open mouth.'[71] The amount of time before a single word is spoken in this film is extraordinary; it is not simply a matter of identifying characters, but of drawing the audience in through lush visuals and cinematic inter-referentiality. Action often takes place in a leisurely but silent fashion. Lord Rivers's death is a high point of the film for viewers; no listening is required. Any number of scenes exist to please or fascinate the viewer, not the listener.

The film would not have succeeded without McKellen's screenplay, his extraordinary performance, and, for English-speaking countries, his insistence on preserving what he could of Shakespeare's verse. If one listens to *Richard III* with one's eyes shut, one might say he succeeded. Yet if one opens one's eyes, Shakespearean verse is undercut by the film's intensely visual language, including visual quoting of other films, a join of real and computer-generated places and a decidedly hyper-real look. Although for McKellen, Shakespeare's words are the ultimate origin and reference point, verbal referentiality is here undercut by visual intertextuality, and referentiality itself undermined by hyper-reality.

What helps to account for this film's popular appeal to a depoliticised American and Americanised international youth market is how seamlessly McKellen's impeccable acting is integrated into what is widely perceived as an enjoyable postmodern film. The comfort level of this work depends upon the way in which well-known actors associated with roles from other films, and scenes from popular commercials, films and rock videos are so carefully interwoven with *Richard III*. Audiences who neither know the play nor the horrors of twentieth-century history happily leave the cinema with their sense of Shakespeare intact. A master of the arts of market research, award-winning film director

Loncraine and his cinematographer, Oscar-winning Peter Biziou, were responsible for literally hundreds of commercials. Both knew how to appeal to wide segments of an audience in record time. In the first ten minutes of *Richard III* they managed to draw in fans of action films, period drama, musicals and even, with the entrance of Robert Downey, Jr., light comedy, in addition to longstanding fans of their star actors. That all the targeted audiences were kept satisfied as the film progressed was a major cause of its popularity. For such audiences, the allusions to popular films are obvious – Richard's heavy breathing in a Darth Vader mask, the action film's *Rambo*-like bold red letter title and opening scene, scenarios from *Sophie's Choice* to *Bladerunner*. But much of the visual quoting is indirect and merely evocative. The shot of a man eating dinner by the fire, his dog at the hearth, the camera panning to a photograph on his desk of a beautiful woman, the close-up of the wine, leisurely poured into a glass, and one feels – without being able to place it – all the comfort of a well done Christmas commercial. One is already guessing that this might be a 'Gallo moment', if not the slightly less comfortable scene in which a woman opens a Christmas present of a watch and slowly meets the expectant eyes of her young man with pouty disappointment: 'I was expecting a Longines.'

None of us expected a *Richard III* that would come alive for us – not because we didn't know English history but because we had forgotten the sources of our own memory-traces. It is no news that we deposit our deepest emotions in visual and aural objects of popular culture – that a song evokes a memory, or that an old photograph may even create one. What is new here is not only that our filmmakers are past masters at commercials and rock videos – nor simply that they are using techniques from them. What is revolutionary is that the audience doesn't know when it is seeing *Richard III* and when it is seeing a commercial. The difference has been erased.

At least one secret of the collaboration between Loncraine and McKellen is that Loncraine agreed to keep McKellen's performance relatively pure, unchanged and real – but only to paste it within a computer-generated hyper-reality. He explains: 'We've created a completely fictitious world . . . Our palace is St Pancras Station, a London railway station which, with the help of computer technology, we will set on the banks of the Thames. Our royal country retreat, the Brighton Pavilion, in reality located in the heart of town, becomes a beach front property.'[72] Although Loncraine is relatively silent about McKellen, he makes his point bluntly: 'I want the acting to be very real and the imagery to be very unreal.'[73] What could have been a fiasco – a collaboration between a master of inventive, strong postmodern cinematic language and a master of Shakespearean acting and verse delivery was turned to an advantage by Loncraine. In many ways this was the hardest matching of all, comparable to Loncraine's joining of multiple realities to create a British past that never existed.

The strategy worked: the real Shakespearean who is past master at real Shakespearean verse stars in a hyper-real postmodern film. McKellen's accomplished performance both emerges and yet is displaced by postmodern cinematic strategies.[74]

In this sense the film exemplifies the radical shift in the conditions to which the Shakespearean film actor's performance was submitted at the end of the twentieth century. With the computer revolution and the digitisation of cinema, a basic representational shift has occurred in the relation of the actor and the spectator to the image. The generation of places that never were and never could be merge with realistic characters, and unreal characters inhabit everyday recognisable places; advertisements for the would-be blend with the never-has-been to form a concrete real. Computer hackers are the new film editors, and can reconfigure and disfigure McKellen's voice, face and action at will. To what degree Shakespearean actors in film will have control over their craft, their images and their voices in the next century is the real question; a loss of control in computer-generated reproductions, as well as a backlash against them, has already begun.

Just as important to turn of the century Richards is the displacement of the dictator who is seen on media with the invisible role of media as dictator. In a lighthanded, almost imperceptible fashion, Loncraine's film points to some of the political uses of media in the 1930s, and by extension, calls into question our relationship to media today. At first it all seems of passing interest – from the use of teletype in Edward's headquarters, to the development of pictures in Clarence's darkroom, and through to Clarence's numerous family photographs. When the singer is replaced at the microphone by Richard, however, the tone changes, and the demonic image of the close-up of his mouth as he speaks suggests that more is at stake. Richard's acceptance speech is delivered into multiple microphones, and he is later seen in his private cinema room, watching newsreels of his own propaganda. If we are attuned to this pattern, it repositions us in the cinema watching this film. If we don't catch on, we are in the position of Anne, drugged, as the newsreel rolls on. Or worse, we are in the position of Clarence. McKellen explains that 'RL [Richard Loncraine], who collects cameras, decided Clarence should be an amateur photographer, recording his surroundings without noticing what is going on until it is too late.'[75] But we are either taking pictures or watching pictures and equally unaware. The parodic laughter of Richard at the end of the film, and the music of Al Jolson – known for the first American talkie – suggest that the joke is on us. And it is treated as a joke. And that, perhaps, is the difference.

Or is it? In 1927, after seeing Mussolini in the Movietone *Voices of Italy*, Shaw wrote to Britain's first Labour Prime Minister, Ramsey MacDonald: 'The audience both sees and hears Mussolini ten times more distinctly and impressively than any audience has ever seen and heard us; and the political party that wakes up to the possibilities of this method of lecturing will, if it has money enough, sweep the floor with its opponents.' [76] In the previous year, when Mary Pickford and Douglas Fairbanks were on their European tour, Fairbanks confided to Mussolini, 'I have seen you often in the movies, but I like you better in real life.'[77]

NOTES

1 To date, the only book-length treatment of a Shakespearean play from the standpoint of comparative media is Bernice W. Kliman's *Hamlet: Film, Television, and Audio Performance* (Cranbury, NJ, 1988).

2 Robert Hamilton Ball, *Shakespeare on Silent Film: a Strange Eventful History* (New York, 1968), p. 159, quoting the *Charleston News and Courier* (12 January 1913). For Ball's considerable research on this film, see pp. 155–62 and p. 342. For information regarding the rediscovery, redating, and restoration of this film, I am grateful to Ken Wlaschin, Director of Creative Affairs and Vice Chair of the National Center for Film and Video Preservation at the American Film Institute.

3 Ball, *Silent Film* 156; his source he admits is unreliable, but Edison's talkies dates the review close to January 1913. A selection of Edison's sound films was screened for a New York audience on 12 February 1913; among his collection was the argument between Cassius and Brutus from Act 4 of *Julius Caesar*. The kinetophone was not yet perfected, however, and the audiences were soon disenchanted with out-of-sync speech and acting.

4 In England as early as 1912, Eric Williams showed/performed his photoplays, excerpted scenes from Shakespeare which he accompanied with dramatic delivery.

5 *New York Dramatic Mirror* (13 November 1912) p. 35.

6 Constance Collier, *Harlequinade: The Story of My Life* (London, 1929), p. 245.

7 E. H. Plumb, 'A Peep Behind the Scenes', *Kinematograph and Lantern Weekly* (4 December 1913), as cited in Ball, *Silent Film*, p. 190.

8 Frederick Warde, *Fifty Years of Make-Believe* (New York, 1920).

9 *Ibid.*, p. 306.

10 Herbert Beerbohm Tree, in an interview with Low Warren, *The Film Game* (London, 1937), pp. 60–1, cited in Ball, *Silent Film*, p. 82.

11 Luigi Pirandello, *Si Gira*, cited by Walter Benjamin, 'The Work of Art in the Age of Mechanical Reproduction' (1936) in *Illuminations*, ed. Hannah Arendt, trans. Harry Zohn (1970; rept. London, 1992), p. 223.

12 James R. Quirk, 'Editorial', *Photoplay* (March 1925), 1.

13 Warde, *Fifty Years of Make-Believe*, pp. 269–70. Although Fairbanks often referred to Warde as his mentor, he apparently only stayed with the actor's company for two years.

14 Alexander Walker, *The Shattered Silents* (London, 1978), p. 148.

15 Roger Manvell, *Shakespeare and the Film* (London, 1971), p. 25, as privately conveyed to Manvell by Laurence Irving, one of the designers for the film.

16 The first published note of this early film is in Luke McKernan and Olwen Terris, eds., *Walking Shadows: Shakespeare in the National Film and Television Archives* (London, 1994), pp. 105–6.

17 On the controversy over whether Gilbert's voice was simply bad, or whether its discrepancy from his screen roles caused audience laughter, see Alexander Walker, *The Shattered Silents*, pp. 171–2.

18 See Michael A. Morrison, *John Barrymore, Shakespearean Actor* (Cambridge, 1997), p. 269. I am indebted in this section to Morrison's work on Barrymore in Hollywood, pp. 259–96.

19 Heywood Brown, 'Mr Shakespeare, Meet Mr Tyson', *Vanity Fair* (February 1923), 33.

20 See Michael A. Morrison, 'The Voice Teacher as Shakespearean Collaborator: Margaret Carrington and John Barrymore', *Theatre Survey*, 38.2 (November 1997), 129–58. (Reprinted with changes in his *John Barrymore, Shakespearean Actor*.)

21 Gene Fowler, *Good Night, Sweet Prince: The Life of John Barrymore* (New York, 1944), p. 191.

22 *Ibid.*, p. 190.

23 *Ibid.*, p. 117.

24 *Ibid.*, p. 196.

25 Eric Wollencott Barnes, *The Man Who Lived Twice* (New York, 1956), p. 237.

26 *Variety* (6 March 1929) p. 9.

27 Bernard Shaw, 'The Art of Talking for the Talkies', *World Film News* (November 1936), in Bernard F. Dukore, ed., *Bernard Shaw on Cinema* (Carbondale/Edwardsville, IL, 1997), p. 117.

28 Michael Ritchie, *Please Stand By: A Prehistory of Television* (New York, 1994), observes: 'The first BBC drama of the electronic era was a film clip of Laurence Olivier in *As You Like It*' (p. 75). Because Ritchie offers no source or date I was led to the newspapers: see *The Times* (26 August 1936).

29 Television broadcasting on a regular basis began on 2 November 1936. Asa Briggs cites estimates that by August 1939 20,000–25,000 sets were in use. (*A History of Broadcasting in the United Kingdom, vol II: The Golden Age of Wireless* (London 1965), pp. 594, 620.)

30 Merrill Panitt, 'Editorial: As We See It', *TV Guide*, 8.8 (20 February 1960), 3.

31 Maurice Evans, 'An Actor Discusses his TV Debut', *New York Times* (26 April 1953), section ii, p. 11, col. 3.

32 NBC Files, Maurice Evans, 'Hallmark Hall of Fame', as cited by Frank Sturcken, *Live Television: The Golden Age of 1946–1958 in New York* (Jefferson, NC/London, 1990), p. 58.

33 As recounted by Marvin Rosenberg, 'Shakespeare on TV: An Optimistic Survey', *The Quarterly of Film, Radio, and Television*, 9.2 (Winter 1954), 166–74; rpt. in J. C. Bulman and H. R. Coursen, eds., *Shakespeare on Television: An Anthology of Essays and Reviews* (Hanover, NH, and London, 1988), p. 88.

34 Evans, cited by Sturcken, *Live Television*, p. 58.

35 Kenneth Rothwell, in Kenneth S. Rothwell and Annabelle Henkin Melzer, eds., *Shakespeare on Screen: an International Filmography and Videography* (London, 1990), p. 116.

36 Laurence Olivier, *On Acting* (New York, 1986), p. 253.

37 *Ibid.*, p. 269.

38 Anthony Davies, *Filming Shakespeare's Plays* (Cambridge, 1988) offers a defence of the film's visual complexity (pp. 65–82).

39 Otto Heller, in an interview with Harold Benson, in Benson, 'Shakespeare in VistaVision', *American Cinematographer*, 37 (February 1956), 94.

40 *Ibid.*, 119.

41 Roger Manvell, 'Laurence Olivier on Filming Shakespeare', *Journal of the British Film Academy* (Autumn 1955), 3.

42 1954 Paramount Pictures Corporation Brochure on VistaVision/HTML
Transcription, The American Widescreen Museum; Peter Donaldson kindly alerted
me to this material.

43 Manvell, 'Laurence Olivier on Filming Shakespeare', 3.

44 Olivier, in an interview with Peter Brinson, in Brinson, 'The Real Interpreter', *Films
and Filming*, 1 (April 1955), 4.

45 *Ibid.*, p. 5.

46 Olivier, *On Acting*, p. 297.

47 Manvell, 'Laurence Olivier on Filming Shakespeare', 3.

48 Olivier, *On Acting*, p. 297.

49 Robert E. Wood, 'Cooling the Comedy: Television as a Medium for Shakespeare's
Comedy of Errors', *Literature/Film Quarterly*, 14.4 (1986), 195–202, rpt. in Bulman
and Coursen, eds. *Shakespeare on Television*, p. 202.

50 Manvell, 'Laurence Olivier on Filming Shakespeare', 3, 5 (italics mine).

51 Roger Manvell, 'Shakespeare on Film', in Levi Fox, ed., *The Shakespeare Handbook*
(Boston, 1987), p. 243.

52 Bosley Crowther, '*Richard III* Has U.S. Premiere On Television and at Bijou Here',
New York Times (12 March 1956) p. 1, col. 4.

53 Bernice W. Kliman (in *Hamlet: Film, Television, and Audio Performance*) is one of the
few to note the negotiations; she refers to the film as 'partly financed by arrangements
to show it on television coincident with its theatrical release and thus filmed with television in mind' (p. 119). I can find no evidence that the financial backing was available
by the time the film was completed, in January 1954, but there is every reason to
suppose that Olivier was following up on the practices of Alexander Korda and that
the *New York Times* report of the negotiations marked the completion of a lengthier
process.

54 George Rosen, 'NBC's 3–Hour *Richard*', *Variety* (14 March 1956), 33.

55 Gilbert Seldes, 'Sir Laurence Olivier and the Bard: TV Comments', *Saturday Review*
(10 March 1956), 28.

56 Jack Gould, 'TV: Another Milestone', *New York Times* (12 March 1956), 49, col. 3.

57 Henry Hart, '*Richard III*', *Films in Review*, 7.3 (March 1956), 126.

58 Olivier cited by Roger Manvell, *Shakespeare and the Film*, pp. 131–2, n. 3.

59 Michael Birkett, from an interview with Roger Manvell in *The Journal of the Society
of Film and Television Arts*, 37 (1969), cited in Manvell, *Shakespeare and the Film*,
p. 120.

60 Ian McKellen, *William Shakespeare's 'Richard III': A Screenplay Written by Ian
McKellen and Richard Loncraine, Annotated and Introduced by Ian McKellen* (New
York, 1996), p. 242.

61 *Ibid.*, p. 260.

62 'Interview with Sir Ian McKellen', Richard III Society Homepage, Mayfair
Entertainment International Ltd. Press Kit, HTML Transcription, p. 6 for all quotations in this paragraph.

63 *Ibid.*, p. 2; for McKellen's first response, see pp. 2–3, and p. 3 for all following quotations in this paragraph.

64 *Ibid.*, pp. 3–4.

65 'McKellen Shakespeare Film, Production Notes', Richard III Society Homepage,
Mayfair Entertainment International Ltd. Press Kit, HTML Transcription, p. 4.

66 Manvell, 'Laurence Olivier on Filming Shakespeare', 3.

67 Bernard Shaw, 'The Art of Talking for the Talkies', in Dukore, ed., *Bernard Shaw*, pp. 117, 119.

68 *Ibid.*, p. 120.

69 Ian McKellen, *William Shakespeare's 'Richard III'*, p. 16.

70 Richard Eyre, *Utopia and Other Places* (London, 1993), pp. 162–3.

71 Frederic Thrasher, *OK for Sound . . . How the Screen Found Its Voice* (New York, 1946), p. 79.

72 'McKellen Shakespeare Film, Production Notes', Richard III Society Homepage, Mayfair Entertainment International Ltd. Press Kit, HTML Transcription, p. 2.

73 *Ibid.*

74 Barbara Hodgdon's 'Replicating Richard: Body Doubles, Body Politics', *Theater Journal*, 50 (May 1988), 207–26, surveys an array of recent stage and screen Richards, exploring how Loncraine deploys popular culture to displace McKellen's performance.

75 Ian McKellen, *William Shakespeare's 'Richard III'*, p. 68.

76 Bernard Shaw to J. Ramsay MacDonald, Holograph Post Card, 26 November 1927, in Dukore, ed., *Bernard Shaw*, p. 52.

77 'Film Stars see Mussolini', *New York Times* (11 May 1926), p. 29, col. 7.

4

HARRY KEYISHIAN

Shakespeare and movie genre: the case of *Hamlet*

Film historians have tended, naturally enough, to think of movies based on Shakespeare's works as forming a distinct genre. Such films use his words, characters and plots; they are part of performance history of his plays; their rich language stands apart from standard Hollywood dialogue; and they were, at least back in the days of the studio system, perceived as 'prestige' works, distinct from the standard mass-market film product. It has often seemed, in Geoffrey O'Brien's words, as if 'there are regular movies, and then there are Shakespeare movies'.[1]

Recent Shakespeare films have so openly and conspicuously embraced traditional film forms that the distinction has become quite obviously untenable. But even Lynda E. Boose and Richard Burt, who applaud this development, speak of a past era of 'direct' or 'straight Shakespeare', a model they associate with the efforts of Olivier and Welles (and whose last gasp they identify as Stuart Burge's 1970 *Julius Caesar*), which has been succeeded by a period they celebrate, in which the playwright couples creatively with popular culture.[2]

In fact, however, it is doubtful there ever has been such a thing as 'direct' Shakespeare (even in his own day the same playtext might be produced in very different circumstances, outdoors, indoors, on the road and abroad); and, I would argue, even the films that Boose and Burt so designate cannot be understood outside of Hollywood genres. It is very hard, without reference to movie history, to make useful generalisations that will cover productions as different from each other as Reinhardt and Dieterle's *A Midsummer Night's Dream*, Laurence Olivier's *Hamlet* and Trevor Nunn's *Twelfth Night* – or, for that matter, the *Romeo and Juliet*s of George Cukor, Franco Zeffirelli and Baz Lurhmann. We need to encounter Shakespeare films in the context of movie history and, in particular, film genre. We need to ask of any 'Shakespeare film', 'what kind of *movie* is this?'

It was one of the achievements of Jack J. Jorgens's groundbreaking *Shakespeare on Film*[3] to fully acknowledge cinematic forms in his analyses: he characterises Orson Welles's *Macbeth* (1948) as an example of Expressionist film; Joseph Mankiewicz's *Julius Caesar* (1953) as gangster movie in the mould of *Little Caesar*; Reinhardt and Dieterle's *A Midsummer Night's Dream* (1935) as a combination of 'ornate escapist fantasy and dark vision' suffused with 'expressionist images'; George Cukor's ornate 1936 *Romeo and Juliet* as a typical Hollywood 'period' film; the acting in Welles's *Othello* (1952) as suggestive of formalist works like *The Cabinet of Dr Caligari* and *Ivan the Terrible*; and he remarks on the similarity of Olivier's *Richard III* to the festive, carnival mode of Vincente Minelli's *Meet Me in St Louis* (!).

Unfortunately, books by film historians on genres and their evolution have tended to omit works based on Shakespearean texts. Despite the obvious connection of Laurence Olivier's *Hamlet* (1948) with *film noir*, most film books on the genre do not think to mention it. I propose, therefore, to write these films into the histories of the genres of which they are examples. Only by placing them in the cinematic traditions that make their production possible and that shape and inform their meaning can we engage the actual film product before us, rather than our preconceptions, based on knowledge of the Shakespeare text and its critical and performance traditions.

When 'Shakespeare' meets 'The Movies', two mighty entities converge. And while Shakespeare's texts are conceptually and linguistically powerful, and carry with them a tremendous weight of critical commentary and literary/theatrical tradition, their force is matched, and perhaps exceeded, by the power of film – its aesthetic, social and commercial power – to create and convey meanings. I think it can be said that when his plays are made into movies, Shakespeare adapts to the authority of film more than film adapts to the authority of Shakespeare; and this is not necessarily a bad thing.

In stressing the importance of genre I do not mean to slight the *auteur* theory, which identifies the individual vision of particularly strong directors as the most important element shaping their productions; or the influence of studios, which (when they reigned) produced and financed movies according to definite artistic and corporate philosophies; or the importance of movie stars, whose entire careers might be built upon the repeated depiction of particular character types that appeal powerfully to the public.

On the contrary, the Shakespeare projects of Orson Welles, evocative as they may be of German Expressionist film and the Russian epic, are probably best explained in terms of his personal body of work and his interest in personality and power. And it seems clear that when Warner Brothers elected to produce *A Midsummer Night's Dream* in 1935, it deliberately installed popular American actors like James Cagney and Mickey Rooney to occupy a realm previously reserved for 'classical' performers: indeed, Kenneth Rothwell says, the film was *about* 'the "Americanization" of Shakespeare by way of German

Expressionism'.[4] MGM brought its own brand of spectacle and star power to the casting and production of *Romeo and Juliet* in 1936, in which the mature Norma Shearer and Leslie Howard played the teenage lovers.

Recent films have moved even closer to Hollywood forms. Franco Zeffirelli's *Hamlet* is, among other things, a Mel Gibson movie, with discernable connections to his earlier films. (The director has said that he cast Gibson in the role after seeing his character contemplate suicide in the first *Lethal Weapon* film.) Baz Luhrmann's *William Shakespeare's Romeo+Juliet* is a Leonardo DiCaprio vehicle, which was followed by another tale of great and doomed love, *Titanic*. From a critical perspective, coherent analysis can follow from setting the Shakespearean ventures of these actors into the context of their other films.

It is true, of course, that Shakespeare texts are themselves genre products. Whether seen on stage or purchased as books, plays are thought of as belonging to specific 'types', and are scarcely to be understood outside the conventions of genre. Genre establishes particular areas of understanding – specific subject matters and settings, recurrent narrative patterns and themes, characteristic techniques and tone. We speak of the novel – and then we speak of sentimental novels, crime novels, novels of manners and so forth; we speak of film; and then of Westerns, screwball comedies, horror movies and so forth. Different films' genres suggest different settings: the drawing-room, the seedy office, the dusty street, the country estate, the haunted castle; and we expect certain character types, themes, situations and conflicts, and resolutions.

It is also true that in the absence of detailed knowledge of early modern staging methods, or any assurance that they would please a later audience, all theatrical productions of Shakespeare texts are shaped by existing traditions. In our era, we have Shakespeare in modes Chekhovian, Pirandellian, Shavian, Odetsian, Brechtian, Beckettian and so forth. But while the shaping of Shakespeare texts by performance tradition is an old practice, the audience for films is larger and the commercial pressures on film-makers greater than those prevailing in theatre. Leo Braudy, an exponent of the importance of genre, observes that 'the text, the screenplay, is at best the skeleton from which the film grows, often unrecognizably'; the film as experienced by audiences is the product of a director's conception, a cinematographer's vision, and – my point here – genre conventions.[5] Star actors and recognised *auteurs* are, we know, bankable; so is genre, if well used.

Genres change over time, impelled by the imperatives of form, commercial pressures or historic events, but they compose coherent and recognisable types of literature with their own appropriate patterns (past ages might call them 'rules') and traditions. Genre – no less for us than for Shakespeare – shapes the form of the artwork and mediates its reception. It serves artists, audiences, marketers and critics.

Genre gives artists a shape and vocabulary for their work and constitutes a specific tradition to which they may contribute, by way of continuity or innovation (usually both). More significantly, genre dictates the psychology and philosophy of an artwork, and has a decisive influence upon its incidents and themes, moral values, characterisation, plot outcome, treatment of gender, use of language and degree of naturalism.

Genre films appeal by reminding us of other movies with which they share conventions. 'Genre' Shakespeare, too, reminds us of other kinds of movies. The relationship of Olivier's *Hamlet* to *film noir* has often been noted, at least by Shakespeareans. But it is a poor genre film that merely incorporates conventions. Genres evolve – Braudy speaks of their 'inner histories' – and may build on or play out variations on their basic conventions. The primitive form evolves into a classic one, which shifts on to various revisionist modes and finally becomes parody – self-conscious and self-referential – unless and until the form is reinvented and renewed. Western movies, over several generations, retained the tradition of the climactic gun duel, but their protagonists manifested themselves in many guises during that time – from the singing cowboy of the early 1930s on through the mythic figures of the 1930s and the post-war years, to the neurotics and anti-heroes of later decades, the bumptious parodies of Mel Brooks and, most recently, the frosty demigods favoured by Clint Eastwood.

I want to illustrate the relationship of Shakespeare movies to movie genre by comparing four film *Hamlet*s and their cinematic traditions: Olivier's *film noir*, Zeffirelli's action-adventure, Branagh's epic and Michael Almereyda's media-savvy, self-reflexive 'Indie' take on the material. The characters and plot situations of Shakespeare's large and open texts accommodate themselves to the template of the genre in which each production is conceived.

Film noir is most easily identified in terms of its visual style and camera strategies: low key lighting, shadows and fog; a *mise-en-scène* that makes settings as important as people; canted camera angles (expressing subjectivity), tight framing (showing entrapment) and slow tracking shots (suggesting the unravelling of mystery). Conditions of entrapment and moral ambiguity abound in *noir* films; taboos are tested and broken; a sense of destiny reigns. Typically, protagonists (the private detective was a favourite) face situations of existential solitude in isolation from the legal order. A typical foil for the crime film protagonist was the unreliable, often fatal, *femme noire*, a sultry figure representing a puzzle related but secondary to the main murder plot. And *noir* was drenched in a smouldering sexuality that energises such subsidiary passions as greed, revenge and jealousy.

If we write Olivier's *Hamlet* into the history of *film noir*, we are likely to begin with the obvious technical similarities – extensive tracking shots through

Elsinore, inventive dramatisations of subjectivity (including the voice-overs and the camera's memorable passage through Hamlet's skull during 'To be or not to be'), the wonderful use of shadows and deep focus to express the isolation that afflicts the protagonist.

But beyond these technical connections, we can see the familiar characters of the play fitting themselves into the genre's template. R. Barton Palmer's *Hollywood's Dark Cinema: The American Film Noir* breaks the genre down to subtypes and thereby offers several contexts for Olivier's *Hamlet* to occupy. One could, for example, write the film into Palmer's chapter on 'Noir Crime Melodrama', where he relates the cinematic type to pulp fiction of the 1930s and 1940s that promoted a wish fulfilment 'energised by the breaking of laws and taboos'. In the process, this fiction '[took] the side of those outside of or opposed to the established legal order'.[6] Such is Hamlet the snide riddler, mocking Polonius in the hallways of Elsinore; and Hamlet the criminal on the run, hiding a corpse and evading his pursuers down those same halls.

Discussing the 'Noir Thriller', Palmer cites the subgenre's use of 'a sensational crime [that] calls into question the effectivity of the law, making it necessary for an ordinary citizen to become a hero in order to save himself'. The protagonist must play a dual role: 'he must keep the authorities at bay while he identifies and and defeats the villains'. He must do this even when (indeed, especially when) the authorities *are* the villains. Olivier's Hamlet can be written into this chapter as a man 'selected by the randomness of the event' who 'becomes capable of feats of great strength and intellectual skill'; who is 'the only social force capable of preventing whatever disaster the villains have in mind'. He's no Hercules, but he walks those mean corridors by himself to make his world right again.

Hamlet (like other *noir* thriller heroes) acts out of a 'licit transgressiveness' in a situation in which 'the law [or justice] is represented as both initially wrong and ultimately inadequate; and the protagonist is deprived of his identity or social standing [that is, as an obedient subject of the law] and is able to regain it only with great difficulty and after severe trial'.[7]

Finally, Palmer offers the 'Noir Woman's Picture' – *Detour, The Stranger* and *Vertigo* are his prime examples – in which 'women often appear as victims of fate or circumstance who frustrate male desire'. He offers as an example *The Stranger*, in which – consider the parallel with *Hamlet* – the wife of a war criminal is the only one who can reveal his guilt. 'Faced with the impossible choice between identifying her husband as a genocidal maniac and living with a man she knows is a monster, Mary retreats into a suicidal self-abandonment, asking Kindler to kill her and even offering him a weapon.'[8] This *noir* motif is realised in Olivier's directorial decision to have Gertrude – whose allegiance Hamlet doubts – drink Claudius's poisoned wine fully aware of its contents. As Annette

Kuhn notes, in *noir* films structured around crimes and their investigation by detective figures, 'it is very common for a woman character to be set up as an additional mystery demanding solution, a mystery independent of the crime enigma'.[9]

Hamlet also contains material for a Hollywood action movie, a natural format for a star like Mel Gibson because it provides the occasion for enjoyable violence. In action movies, especially those centring on revenge, the social institutions charged with providing justice either don't exist, fail to function or have become corrupt. The victims themselves may retaliate, or their cause may be taken up by avengers who become champions of justice. Gibson's previous films tended to be revenge entertainments, melodramas in which the line between villains and heroes is clearly drawn. In *Mad Max*, the Gibson character tracks down the gang responsible for killing his best friend and his family. In the *Lethal Weapon* movies he plays an outrageous police detective whose sanity is in doubt.

Hamlet is entertaining, but it is not an entertainment: it is a revenge tragedy, in which the protagonist manifests flaws that lead to his death. One of the challenges that Zeffirelli faced in joining actor and role was to assimilate an icon of revenge entertainment into the format of a revenge tragedy, to combine optimal Gibson with optimal Hamlet.

Daniel Quigley has observed that the 'semiotic "noise"' created by the casting of Gibson makes the actor himself 'part of the performance text' and 'encourages the audience to see the Gibson that they have come to expect from his other films'. In evidence, he cites the way Hamlet confronts the Ghost. Olivier is 'turned inward, concerned about his soul and the internal damage a potentially evil spirit might inflict'; he adopts 'a protective, defensive posture, holding his sword in the form of the cross'. Gibson, on the other hand, 'pursues the Ghost with the point of the sword outward, ready to strike'; his Hamlet 'does not ponder the best way to act in a situation; he simply reacts, usually in a physical manner'.[10]

Other production choices also seem influenced by the presence of action-star Gibson. For example, the careful unfolding of the mystery of the Ghost that opens the playtext is replaced by a direct plunge into the Hamlet–Gertrude–Claudius relationship during the invented scene of King Hamlet's funeral service. To Claudius's 'Think of me as of a father', Hamlet responds with a non-committal nod, but he catches the exchange of glances between the sobbing Gertrude (whose face reads, 'I need to be comforted') and the opportunistic Claudius ('I'm here to comfort'), which causes him to stride from the tomb. We see at first hand what offends him and puts him on his guard.[11]

Nor does he suffer in silence: he is barely able to contain his feelings. Gertrude's energetic run down the castle steps to join Claudius for a ride elicits a truncated 'Oh that this too too solid flesh'; 'Things rank and gross in nature' visually include his mother, and he shouts after her through a window, though unheard, 'Frailty, thy name is woman.' This is accusation, not introspection. Olivier's direction emphasises Hamlet's entrapment; close-ups stress his inwardness and long shots make him seem diminished and isolated in the context of Elsinore. Left to his own devices, Olivier's Hamlet would decline and die of grief. Gibson's Hamlet snarls; low-angle shots and vibrant close-ups make him dominate each moment on screen.

Whatever else Zeffirelli's film did, it aimed to satisfy fans who went to the theatre to see a Gibson movie.[12] Gibson's fans seem to take special pleasure in the actor's explosive moments – his startling bursts of temper and flashes of violence. His Hamlet has an interesting way of reading a book, for example: as he finishes each page, he tears it out and throws it away – an existential gesture if there ever was one. Later ('words, words, words') he throws pages at Polonius and pushes away the ladder on which he is standing. Still later, Hamlet kicks a chair out from under an equivocating Rosencrantz and nearly strangles an unmusical Guildenstern in the recorder scene. Olivier omits the recorder scene (along with Rosencrantz and Guildenstern) and thereby robs himself of a very good theatrical moment.

In a cinematic strategy that sharpens the revenge theme by encouraging us to adopt the protagonist's frame of mind, Zeffirelli lets his audience share Hamlet's vivid impressions of the decadence of Claudius's court. Olivier's Hamlet got a glimpse of the king's raucous feast while on watch with Horatio and Marcellus, but Gibson's Hamlet gets a much better view, from a gallery above the dining hall ('The king doth wake tonight'), while on his way to the platform; and when he reaches the platform, he continues to see that irritating scene through a ceiling grate, so that it is before his eyes and ours when he remarks the harm done to national pride by the king's revels – 'They clep us drunkards' – and the fragility of fame – 'How oft it chances'.

Branagh's *Hamlet* (1996) seems, in terms of pacing, settings and scope, to follow the cinematic model of the epic – to court comparison to *Ben Hur*, *The Ten Commandments* and *Dr Zhivago*. Epic films tend to be paced majestically, prizing plenitude and variety over compactness and consistency of tone. Events tend to be broken up into episodes that are linked but self-contained, and enacted in a wide assortment of places. The movie epic, says Vivian Sobchack, 'defines history as occurring to music – persuasive symphonic music underscoring every moment by overscoring it'; it employs 'spectacular, fantastic costumes' and displays an 'extravagance of action and place'; its massive sets mythify the mundane into ' "imperialist" and "orientalist" fantasies of History'; the costs and difficulty of production, often stressed in promoting epic movies, elevate them 'into a *historical eventfulness* that exceeds its already excessive screen boundaries'.

The use of recognised stars 'doubles the film's temporal dimension'; they serve to '*generalize* historical specificity through their own *iconographic* presence. Stars are cast not *as* characters but *in* character – as "types" who, however physically particular and concrete, signify universal and general characteristics.' 'Stars literally lend *magnitude* to the representation.' She calls this 'conceptual mimesis', 'cinematic onomatopoeia'.[13]

Branagh's *Hamlet* participates in the epic tradition by several means. First, by producing a 'full text' *Hamlet* that runs over four hours, he required a commitment of audience time, and he required of himself a lavish production that would supply a variety of incidents, an epic arc and pace, and above all a sense of scope – enough, in Geoffrey O'Brien's words, 'to bring back memories of the early-Sixties heyday of blockbuster filmmaking, the days of *Spartacus* and *Lawrence of Arabia*'. He cautions us that 'streamline' Shakespeare, while achieving sharp narrative focus, also sacrifices the messy abundance that the playwright offers: '*Hamlet* is a much more interesting and surprising work – and, with its roundabout strategies and gradual buildups and contradictions of tone, a more realistic one – when all of it is allowed to be heard.'[14]

Branagh's use of flashbacks adds to the effect: they bring many elements of the Hamlet 'story' into the *Hamlet* plot; they undertake, through flashback, to explain what the play leaves unsettled (such as Hamlet's affair with Ophelia) and make elements of exposition explicit (the affection of Hamlet for Yorick).

The film is certainly visually opulent: Blenheim provides a lavish setting for the action. The 'Elsinores' of Olivier and Zeffirelli are not frugal, but the former is filmed in austere black and white and the latter is more functional than decorative. Branagh impresses by the inclusion of luxurious exteriors and props (like the miniature train that brings Rosencrantz and Guildenstern to Elsinore). Hamlet's sense of isolation is well dramatised by the very extravagance of the set for Act I scene 2, culminating in the great shower of confetti that accompanies the departure of Claudius and Gertrude. By showing soldiers training and providing other signs of a functioning bureacracy, Branagh suggests the practical needs of a nation threatened by invasion. Indeed, the cast seems large enough to be a small state.

Branagh's use of the statue of King Hamlet as an emblem of his reign – to be torn down to mark the advent of Fortinbras – gives the film a sense of expansiveness by alluding to the cycles of history, making the individual story of Prince Hamlet an episode in a larger process. (The motif also related clearly to the dissolution of the Soviet empire and the dismantling of its symbols.) As Sobchack says of the film epic in general, such a treatment gives a sense 'not of individually being toward Death, but of social being in History'.[15]

Branagh's casting of Hollywood 'stars' in minor roles has been criticised – justly, sometimes – from the point of view of performance quality. Such casting does, however, work as a strategy of amplification. Jack Lemmon is no Marcellus, but he is Jack Lemmon, and brings to the film the weight of rich career. His presence – and that of Charlton Heston, whose player-king needs no apology – sets the movie in film history, alluding to the larger story of the film medium itself. Billy Crystal and Robin Williams adapt aspects of their popular comic personae to the play's humour.

Though Shakespeare (or his early editors) had their doubts about the dramatic virtues of the 'How all occasions' soliloquy (present in the Second Quarto, absent in the First Folio), Branagh makes it essential to his epic scheme. Coming at the end of the cinematic 'second act'[16] and preceding intermission, it flamboyantly declares that the resolution of great issues is at hand for those in the audience who return to their seats. In terms of its tone, visualisation and emotional force, the soliloquy as located by Branagh has been appropriately compared to Scarlett O'Hara's cry, 'As God is my witness, I'll never go hungry again.' This treatment is not a necessary consequence of the playtext's dramatic rhythms; rather, it well fits and serves epic form.

Finally, the requirements of epic may explain Branagh's otherwise eccentric treatment of Fortinbras's invasion. Whereas the playtext rests the fate of the nation on the duel between Hamlet and Laertes, with the arrival of Fortinbras a formulaically necessary afterthought, Branagh diminishes the duel to an irrelevancy. Since Fortinbras was determined and bound to take over Denmark no matter who was on the throne, it mattered not at all (except to himself) whether Hamlet won or lost the duel, or whether he killed the king or not. So after a dramatic duel in the style of *Robin Hood* sword-and-buckler genres (pushed temporally up into the *Zorro* era, and not blushing to include a long swing *of* a chandelier that seems to suggest Hamlet has reached the side of the dying Claudius by means of a long swing *on* a chandelier), the film provides a wholesale, noisy castle-smashing as Fortinbras's troops launch themselves through the windows of the palace. Kenneth Branagh himself invokes genre in his directions to actors: in his script for *Hamlet*, he invokes the conventional Western gunfight to describe the duel scene: 'For several seconds it's *High Noon* as they stand facing each other.' Regarding Fortinbras's spectacular invasion of Elsinore, Branagh is quoted in the diary of the production published with the screenplay as commenting, 'I'm making six films at once. This is *Diehard*.'[17]

This *Hamlet* is, to be sure, not reflective of the early epic, which tends to celebrate national values and aspirations, but rather of a later, revisionist kind, full of subversive ironies and demythification. Still, it follows the dramatic rhythms of the genre; the logic of the invasion scene, while not the logic of the playtext, does reflect the conventions of the film epic, which often ends with some spectacular event prodigal in its effects. In this case, the imposition of a 'foreign' pattern may have diluted the tragedy of the Prince of Denmark, but it forwarded the epic's sense of a civilisation in turmoil through a historical era.

The films of Olivier, Zeffirelli and Branagh discussed so far have fit comfortably, I think, into familiar commercial genres. Michael Almereyda's 2000 *Hamlet* enters this mix with mischief on its mind, resisting easy categorisation. As an 'Independent Film', Michael Almereyda's work is the product of a movement that often disregards Hollywood's genre system, potentially freeing creators to fulfil their personal visions, adopt distinctive forms, and play imaginatively with and against the expectations of commercial cinema. Sometimes, of course, these efforts go on to great financial success, as happened to *The Blair Witch Project*, but 'indies' more generally create an alternative space for filmmakers to work outside 'the system'.

Almereyda's film sets *Hamlet* in contemporary New York City, transforming the 'state' of Denmark into the Denmark Corporation, which, following the death of its 'King and CEO', has passed into the hands of his younger brother. For this setting, Almereyda has acknowledged the inspiration of another quirky product, Finnish director Aki Kaurismäki's 1987 *Hamlet Goes Business*, a satirical work, set in Helsinki, in which Hamlet- and Claudius-equivalents struggle for control of a toy factory which the latter wants to turn into the world's leading manufacturer of rubber ducks. (Almereyda's homage to Kaurismäki comes when a little rubber duck appears among the 'remembrances' that Ophelia has 'longed long to redeliver' to Hamlet.) Almereyda's film differs, however, by restoring Shakespeare's language and by largely eliminating Kaurismäki's satire, opting instead to respect the play's tragic spine.

It could be argued, of course, that a Hamlet who is an experimental filmmaker with no interest whatsoever in controlling the corporation that is Denmark, with no concern for the state or his duties as 'prince', is no Hamlet at all. But 'reduced' Hamlets have been around for some time, at least since the sensibilities of the Romantics (Coleridge in particular) legitimated a purely private, inward formulation of the character and his dilemmas. Almereyda's self-absorbed prince has roots both in Hamlet-history and in film tradition, in which he shares iconic space with James Dean and the young Marlon Brando.

Kenneth Rothwell and Douglas Lanier, among others, have associated Almereyda's work with *film noir*.[18] Lanier sees Almereyda paying homage to the *noir* form through

> the film's brooding atmosphere; its use of the city as a character; its images of an oppressive, urban night-world of blue-lit neon, chrome, and asphalt; its emphasis on systematic corruption, surveillance, and violence behind a façade of benign normalcy; and its characterization of the protagonist as a fallen innocent who struggles against his own impotence, alienation, and complicity with the system he resists.[19]

Lacking the black-and-white aesthetic of 'classic' *noir*, the film is not fully comparable to Olivier's, but Lanier is correct to identify the urban settings of *noir* films as most characteristic of the form. (There's nothing urban about that remote, stony Elsinore of the earlier film.) And, perhaps as a homage nod to Olivier's earlier homage to *noir*, Almereyda too has his Gertrude (Diane Venora) drink that fatal glass of wine in full awareness of its contents.

Neither of the critics seems fully satisfied with the identification of Almereyda's work with *noir*, however – Rothwell settling for 'noirish' and Lanier wondering whether the elements he has identified might in the end be more 'a superficial stylistic homage' than a genuine parallel. More to the point, perhaps, are what Lanier and Samuel Crowl[20] term the work's 'metacinematic' aspects, its persistent referencing and incorporation of film technologies, its reminders that it is a movie about a person who makes movies, and about the tools he uses to do so. Perhaps we would do well to think of Almereyda's film as a 'metageneric' *Hamlet*, playfully aware of its place among cinematic forms. By turning Hamlet into a filmmaker and showing him as a creator and consumer of video images – e.g., by setting the 'To be or not be' soliloquy in the 'Action' aisle of a video store – Almereyda wittily references the alternative world of commercial cinema without participating in it.

Moreover, Almereyda's Prince is an experimental filmmaker, a category of artist that disdains even the limited commercial market cultivated by 'independents'. Hamlet's cluttered apartment contains various kinds of film and video technology, used not as means to make a living, but as instruments of self-reflection and self-understanding. The film opens with Hamlet's film of himself expressing his personal misery ('I have of late lost all my mirth') and his disillusionment with the world ('A sterile promontory'). In other clips, he rehearses suicide or compulsively replays images of his parents and Ophelia. Yet other images offer alternative Hamlets, Hamlets that have been, as in the clip of John Gielgud with Yorick's skull, and near-Hamlets, as in the segments from the *Hamlet* offshoot *Crow II: City of Angels*. Almereyda has himself noted the self-referential quality of his film in his use of surveillance cameras (to see the Ghost, to monitor Hamlet, etc.):

> A lot of the play is about people spying on each other and being watched and playing parts and being aware of themselves playing parts. And that corresponds to contemporary reality where cameras are on the present and images within images are on the present, at least in the city. So that seemed like a natural way of mirroring things that were going on in Shakespeare's text.[21]

Almereyda points out that in the screening of Hamlet's film *The Mousetrap: A Tragedy* – what Almereyda has called 'the film within the film' – 'the audience of the movie is watching an audience watch a movie. It's a hall of mirrors.'

Hamlet attempts to use cinema as a weapon: screening *The Mousetrap* is his effort to break out of that hall of mirrors and 'catch the conscience of the king'. A collage of home movies, symbolic stop-action cinema, and pornography, its shots linked by associative editing, *The Mousetrap* shakes Claudius's complacency and propels Hamlet to action. That his action leads inadvertently to disaster – Polonius is shot by Hamlet, yes, while he is hiding behind a mirror – fulfils the play's sense of the irony of fate, leaving us aware of both the power and the speciousness of the image. Lisa Starks and Courtney Lehmann see in Almereyda's work a critique of the effects of modern media culture, maintaining that the director 'appropriates Shakespeare to define the state of the art of film in the new millennium', in which the ability of technology to store images of reality defeats rather than forwards an ability 'to generate sincere connection and presence'.[22] Echoing this idea, Almereyda's film contains a film clip of Buddhist teacher Thich Nhat Hanh unpacking Hamlet's 'big question' ('To be or not to be') by posing the impossibility of anyone 'being' alone, and the need, rather, to 'inter Be'.[23] Using the freedom accorded him as an independent filmmaker, Almermeyda gives cinematic form to metadramatic elements present in Shakespeare's original playtext, thereby making his film a contribution to the genre of introspective, self-referential films that his own Hamlet might have been proud to make.

It is easy to predict, I think, that as more Shakespeare comes to the screen, it will not develop towards some standard, self-contained genre, but will instead be more fully dispersed among existing genres. (And not necessarily only the 'commercial' ones, as Almereyda's film shows.) Assimilating Shakespeare cannot help but challenge and enrich these genres for general film audiences; seeing the playtexts configured for mass-market consumption may do the same for Shakespeareans. Interesting times lie ahead.

NOTES

1 Geoffrey O'Brien, 'The Ghost at the Feast', *The New York Review of Books*, 44.2 (6 February 1997), 12.
2 Lynda E. Boose and Richard Burt, eds., *Shakespeare, The Movie. Popularising the Plays on Film, TV and Video* (London and New York, 1997), p. 13.
3 Jack J. Jorgens, *Shakespeare on Film* (Bloomington, IN, 1977). The quotations are taken from Jorgens's analyses of the films named at points throughout the work.
4 Kenneth S. Rothwell and Annabelle Henkin Melzer, eds., *Shakespeare on Screen: an International Filmography and Videography* (New York, 1990), p. 191.
5 Leo Braudy, *The World in a Frame: What We See in Films* (Garden City, NY, 1976), pp. 10–11.
6 R. Barton Palmer, *Hollywood's Dark Cinema: The American Film Noir* (New York, 1994), pp. 34, 35.
7 *Ibid.*, p. 107.

8 *Ibid.*, pp. 139, 140.

9 Annette Kuhn, *Women's Pictures: Feminism and Cinema* (London, 1982) p. 35.

10 Daniel Quigley, ' "Double Exposure": The Semiotic Ramifications of Mel Gibson in Zeffirelli's *Hamlet*', *Shakespeare Bulletin* (Winter 1993), 38–9.

11 For a close reading of opening scenes in several productions of *Hamlet*, see H. R. Coursen, *Shakespeare in Production: Whose History?* (Athens, OH, 1996), pp. 54–73.

12 A colleague who saw the film in a theatre full of teenagers reports that a loud whoop went up at the first appearance of the star, and a louder one at Gertrude's lingering kiss at 'Let not thy mother lose her prayers.'

13 Vivian Sobchack, ' "Surge and Splendor": A Phenomenology of the Hollywood Historical Epic', in Barry Keith Grant, *Film Genre Reader II* (Austin, TX, 1995), pp. 281, 290, 294.

14 O'Brien, 'The Ghost at the Feast', p. 15.

15 Sobchack, 'Surge and Splendor', pp. 296–7.

16 Screenwriters speak of the 'three-act' structure of movies: set-up, complications, resolution. In cinematic terms, Branagh's intermission sets up Act 3 of his *Hamlet*.

17 Kenneth Branagh, *Hamlet By William Shakespeare: Screenplay and Introduction by Kenneth Branagh* (London and New York, 1996), pp. 167, 205.

18 Kenneth S. Rothwell, *A History of Shakespeare on Screen and Film: A Century of Film and Television* (2nd edn, Cambridge, 2004); Douglas M. Lanier, 'Shakescorp Noir', *Shakespeare Quarterly*, 53/2 (Summer 2002), 157–80; 167.

19 *Ibid.*, p. 160

20 Samuel Crowl, *Shakespeare at the Cineplex: The Kenneth Branagh Era* (Athens, OH, 2003).

21 Cynthia Fuchs, 'Interview with Michael Almereyda' www.popmatters.com/film/interview/almereyda-michael.html.

22 Lisa S. Starks and Courtney Lehmann, *The Reel Shakespeare: Alternative Cinema and Theory* (Madison, NJ, 20–).

23 On this, and the film's use of technology, see Alessandro Abbate's ' "To Be or Inter-Be": Almereyda's End of the Millennium *Hamlet*', *Literature/Film Quarterly*, 32/2 (2004), 82–9.

PART II

Genres and plays

5

MICHAEL HATTAWAY

The comedies on film

Compared with screen versions of the tragedies and histories, there have been few distinguished films based on the comedies. Max Reinhardt's *A Midsummer Night's Dream* (1935) may be the only film in this genre to be acclaimed for its pioneering cinematography,[1] and Franco Zeffirelli's *The Taming of the Shrew* (1967), Kenneth Branagh's *Much Ado About Nothing* (1993),[2] and Michael Radford's *The Merchant of Venice* (2004) are the only three to have achieved popular (if not necessarily critical) success: the first for its use of actors (Richard Burton and Elizabeth Taylor) who were the co-supremes of their age, the second for cameo performances by photogenic stars, high spirits and picturesque settings,[3] and the third for fine cinematography and superb performances from Jeremy Irons and Al Pacino. Shakespeare's comedies create relationships with their theatre audiences for which very few directors have managed to find cinematic equivalents, and it is not surprising that some of the comedies (*The Comedy of Errors*, *The Merry Wives of Windsor* and *The Two Gentlemen of Verona*) have not been filmed in sound and in English for the cinema (although a couple have been the basis of adaptations).

The problem plays or 'dark comedies' have not been filmed for the cinema: presumably their sexual politics and toughness of analysis have never been thought likely to appeal to mass audiences, while *The Taming of the Shrew*, open as it is to both the idealisation and subjugation of women, has received a lot of attention, including versions from D. W. Griffith in 1908, Edward J. Collins in 1923, Sam Taylor in 1929, Paul Nickell in 1950 for American television, Franco Zeffirelli in 1966 – who placed it in the Hollywood genre of the battle-of-the-sexes movie – and, in a considered against-the-grain television version for the BBC/Time-Life Shakespeare Series, from Jonathan Miller in 1980.[4]

Directors of the other Shakespearean genres found conventions that, comparatively early in the history of filmed Shakespeare, made texts accessible to mass audiences. Spectacular screen adaptations of the history plays, shot on location, have held those vasty fields of France that cannot be represented in the theatre. Tragedy has been well served by virtue of the fact that film does not merely record spectacle but can document the gaze, project psychological occasions onto the screen. The eye of the camera may register objects as focuses of the attention of the characters rather than as components of nature, and may use, for example, familiar signifiers of the elemental or primitive to serve as landscapes of consciousness. Screen versions of the tragedies have exploited this interiority, have deployed special effects for the supernatural, and have used salient visual images (Iago's cage in Welles's *Othello*, the shadows in Olivier's *Richard III*) to conjure portentous themes appropriate to the genre or to create for their characters a distinctive consciousness.

Characters in the comedies, on the other hand, tend to the typical rather than the individuated and require settings that are neither wholly exterior nor wholly interiorised. The stories are enacted in distinctive fictional worlds that were designed for representation within the frames of specifically theatrical architecture. In the theatre, frames for the playing space are generally perpetually visible, essential signs of those conventions for game and revelry that govern the action. Indeed the best films of the comedies seem to be those that have avoided the use of location shooting throughout and thus evaded the untranslatable solidity of exterior nature.

For it is difficult to find cinematic equivalents for Elizabethan theatrical codes of place and space. Although they traded in spectacle, Shakespeare's playhouses had no mechanism for illusion. Such scenic devices as were used tended to establish genre rather than place – the mossy banks of the sort that may have been used in *As You Like It* presumably signalled not 'forest' but 'pastoral'.[5] And yet, for cinema, illusionism is the traditional – if not the essential – mode, and directors have found it hard to escape from its claims or the demands of their producers for immediacy or the picturesque. What could be worryingly improbable or outlandish can be naturalised or authenticated by a 'real' setting: a shot of a gondola legitimates the antique fable of a Venetian Jew. Reinhardt intended to authenticate his *Midsummer Night's Dream* with a shot near its opening of the ' "original Shakespearian folio" with the "authentic signature" of the author on its cover'.[6] (In implicit response, Baz Luhrmann's 1996 translation of a Shakespearean text into the present was wittily entitled *William Shakespeare's Romeo + Juliet*.) Period settings in reconstructed Renaissance cityscapes may also derive from Hollywood's veneration for European antiquity, indeed from a conservatising ideology: Shakespeare is commonly held to be the guardian of timeless moral and civil values. Indeed, as William Uricchio and Roberta E. Pearson showed, defusing 'perceived threats to the social order through the construction of consensual cultural values'[7] was one of the objects of some of the earliest Shakespearean film ventures, the Vitagraph Quality Films.

Film, in contrast to theatre, does not deploy frames but uses *masks*: the screen functions as a window onto a 'real' world that we deem to extend beyond its edges. What Fabian in *Twelfth Night* terms the 'improbable fictions' of comic texts are therefore difficult to render. Moreover, using a camera to shoot a theatrical set, in the manner of the earliest directors, just will not do: as Erwin Panofsky put it, 'To prestylize reality prior to tackling it amounts to dodging the problem. The problem is to manipulate and shoot unstylized reality in such a way that the result has style.'[8] Sometimes directors have chosen a very painterly mode of *mise-en-scène*: in 1955 Y. Fried's Russian version of *Twelfth Night* used shots that recalled the themes, patterns and lighting of Renaissance paintings, but offered a first view by Viola of 'the coast of Illyria' that looked like a symbolist painting. Jonathan Miller's television productions for the BBC/Time-Life series were often not only *painterly* – using settings that recalled the style of interiors used by European masters, often from periods other than the age of Shakespeare – but *architectural* in that the director often used rooms to 'make entrances' for his players to use. They could then appear, as onto a theatrical set, through the on-screen frame of an arch or doorway rather than just materialising in shot or emerging from the edge of the screen's mask.[9]

Trevor Nunn's *Twelfth Night* of 1996, some of which was shot at St Michael's Mount in Cornwall, created a successful 'prestylised reality' within a natural landscape that verged on the abstract or symbolic, and used a restrained and iconic autumnal palette. Similarly, in 2000, Kenneth Branagh offered a *Love's Labour's Lost* set in the 1930s in a stylised Oxford bathed in golden sepia, sprinkled with autumn leaves. (It has become a commonplace on stage and screen to underscore the melancholy in what were once called the 'happy comedies'.[10]) It picked up the on-Broadway exuberance as well as the jollity of the British stage musical *Salad Days* (1954) and, with the help of the composer Patrick Doyle, interspersed dance routines and songs by George Gershwin, Irving Berlin and Cole Porter into the play's verse – in the film's titles it was billed as a 'Romantic Musical Comedy'.

Other directors have introduced the comic worlds by using the equivalents of early modern theatrical inductions to institute a narrative frame as a surrogate for the theatre's visual frame. Some directors create establishing or 'translation' sequences to mark the journey into inset worlds, filming what is described as part of an exposition in Shakespeare's text. Sometimes, as in Lucentio's approach towards Padua in Zeffirelli's *The Taming of the Shrew* and in the shipboard and wreck sequence of Nunn's *Twelfth Night*, this 'induction' takes the form of a pre-title sequence. In the latter, in which the twins took the part of onboard entertainers, they came to Illyria immediately after a near-death experience (struggling for air under stormy waves) that endowed the action of the play with a visionary quality. After his inductive journey shots, Franco Zeffirelli's *Shrew* offered a long dialogue-free carnival sequence before the appearance of Katherine and Petruchio. Perhaps this sought to naturalise within the context of revelry what, in the case of Elizabeth Taylor's performance as Katherine, constituted pathological behaviour. (She was cured of her psychological problems by a little therapeutic house-work.)

Christine Edzard's *As You Like It* of 1992 opened with Jaques (James Fox) proclaiming the seven ages of man. Even Kenneth Branagh's location-based *Much Ado about Nothing* included in its opening sequence shots that were intended to make problematic the mode of what was to follow, a gesture towards intertextuality by means of joky visual quotations from John Sturges's western *The Magnificent Seven* (1960), then a dissolve from a painting to a cinema shot of the Tuscan villa where the action was set. The film ended with a bravura long take in which all of the characters were caught up in a farandole that wove in and through the villa and its garden. This de-individuated characters who had been presented as in a mode that was largely naturalistic.

Branagh's *Love's Labour's Lost* was also framed. It began with newspaper headlines detailing the King's plan to study and forsake women, shot in black and white in the style of upbeat 1940s 'Cinetone' newsreels. There followed an introduction to the characters, for the sake presumably of an implied 'popular' audience. The Pageant of the Nine Worthies that Merzade interrupts ended on the cutting-room floor – it can be seen on the out-takes section of the DVD. In place of the play's concluding songs Branagh added an epilogue, 'You that way, we this way', introduced by a medley of Berlin's 'The melody lingers on' and Gershwin's 'They can't take that away from me'. At its end the film modulated back into black and white and showed the young men translating the tasks imposed by the ladies into military heroics, an affectionate pastiche of sentimental movies of the Second World War. The lovers were reunited in shots of victory crowds that were again shot in colour.

Instead of introducing the plot in that way, the opening of Michael Radford's *Merchant* made explicit in the pre-title sequence the issues raised by the film: between establishing shots, brief statements scrolled up on the origins of racist discrimination, usury, and the Venetian Ghetto. As well as gondolas, we saw the burning of Jewish holy texts. This was a serious tale of two religions and two cultures: Venice's gilded youth, in carnival masks, and bare-breasted prostitutes were set against the asceticism of Shylock. Belmont, as its name suggests, was a villa on a high rocky island, the journeying to which marked its separation from the assiduous commercialism and religious fanaticism of Venice. In a nice piece of business, in one of the film's final shots, Jessica was shown wearing her mother's ring that, according to Tubal, she had swapped for a monkey (3.1.93–4).

The choice of *mise-en-scène* for the inset comic worlds had proved a formidable problem for some of the earliest screen versions of Shakespearean comedies. Max Reinhardt, as he winched himself into the fantastic world of the Athenian woods in his *Midsummer Night's Dream* (1935), offered a long prelude created out of music as well as a montage of very painterly shots, mixing real and imaginary animals, owls and unicorns – the latter surprisingly innocent for a post-Freudian age. He also used self-evident 'process' or trick shots that revelled in their own accomplishment. The fairies appeared on occasion in Busby Berkeley routines that seemed like animations and which were superimposed on 'real' backgrounds.[11] The protractedness of the sequence was an index of Reinhardt's struggle – and partial failure – to move away from the D. W. Griffith-like set of 'ancient Greece' on which he had opened the film. The next year Paul Czinner boldly but very unsuccessfully used a studio set but with real sheep for his *As You Like It*.

There are problems not only with place but also with space. Some Shakespearean comedies contain inset plays or prominent overhearing scenes: *Love's Labour's Lost*, *Much Ado* and *Twelfth Night* have set-pieces of this kind at their centre. On stage, actors playing characters who serve as spectators or overhearers have a special relationship with the audience, helping the other actors to manipulate audience response. This choric function means that they occupy a space that is both 'on-' and 'off-stage', a positioning that is difficult to re-create in the cinema since an actor cannot be both in and out of shot at the same time. Voice-overs would not be funny since the humour depends upon the audience enjoying the game of on-stage actors being invisible to those that are being watched. In his *Much Ado*, Branagh showed Benedick and Don Pedro with Leonato and Claudio only fleetingly in the same shots, whereas Nunn in the box-tree scene of *Twelfth Night* managed, on occasion, to include all members of the interlude by the cunning use of a hole in the hedge.

Equally problematic are the expectations of audiences. Theatrical versions of Shakespearean texts generally approach them as classics, a notion that defines them against one definition of the 'popular'. These tend to be produced for elite audiences that seek a distinctive 'directorial signature'[12] since they are likely to have some knowledge of, and therefore expectations concerning, the play. *Films* of classics, on the other hand, are often designed to tell the story for the first time to a mass audience, and therefore tend to avoid the allusiveness and delight in pastiche that distinguish some theatre productions – Branagh's inductive sequences in *Much Ado* are exceptional. Openness is the customary signature of this director, as well as of Zeffirelli and many of the TV versions. Perhaps, moreover, because movie producers assume that films of comedies should be funny – Ben Jonson actually argued that comedy was no laughing matter[13] – directors have generally eschewed anything that smacks of cinematic art, the interesting camera angles, deep focus, or lighting effects explored by directors of the tragedies. (Radford's *Merchant of Venice* is an exception: Venice was rain-drenched rather than sun-drenched and as little lighting as was practicable was used for interiors.) As soon as colour became available it was used: the desire seemed to be to make the medium as transparent as possible, to create the simplest and most direct relationship between star performers and movie audiences. It is notable that, in *Chimes at Midnight* (1966), Orson Welles eschewed colour for his cinematic meditation upon the greatest comic figure of them all, Falstaff.

Adrian Noble's *A Midsummer Night's Dream* made in association with British television's Channel 4 is an interesting exception. Like Ingmar Bergman's film of Mozart's *The Magic Flute*, it uses the equivalent of the *Sprecher* in a mannerist painting who gestures towards the principal subjects in the composition.[14] In both films there was a young child through whose vision the action is mediated, creating a double or 'natural' perspective that seems particularly appropriate for this anatomy of dreams.[15] The film opens in the boy's nursery; the camera pans over his toys, which include a toy theatre. The little boy awakens and walks along a corridor to see through a keyhole Theseus caressing Hippolyta. Thereafter the action is set in the house. The little boy hides under a table to watch the strange follies of the first scene. He then, in a moment that recalls *Alice in Wonderland*, seems to fall down a hole until his head emerges through the top of a stove in the hall where the mechanicals are about to rehearse. At the conclusion of this sequence an umbrella soars aloft and Puck and a fairy appear, holding umbrella handles. Later the child draws umbrellas up through the flies of his toy theatre. Much use is made of doors standing in frames independent of walls, a common motif in surrealist paintings. The film switches between special effects like those used in the films of Powell and Pressburger and a deliberate staginess translated from the Stratford production from which the film derived, and contains nicely placed quotations from *The Wizard of Oz*, *Father Christmas*, etc.

In contrast Trevor Nunn's *Twelfth Night* documented in realist mode the shipwreck that precipitated the action. The director also chose to foreground the conflict between Illyria and Messalina, and introduced an Illyrian army scouring the beaches for enemy survivors of the wreck, its mounted soldiers filmed from low angles to make them more threatening. Film's capacity for expanding the setting to show this conflict between the city-states darkens the action, giving a greater sense of political threat than the majority of stage productions.

As that brief analysis of Noble's *Dream* showed, the 'happy side' of Shakespearean comedies may depend more upon wonder, delight and wit than the stirring of laughter. These texts are based upon *play*, upon an implicit contract between players and spectators to enjoy not only, on occasion, physical knockabout, but sets of wit and virtuoso flourishes of *verbal* artistry – the display of recognised theatrical styles.[16] Shakespearean comedies are not as easily translated into film whose origins and essence have always been moving *pictures*. As Erwin Panofsky pointed out:

In a film, that which we hear remains, for good or worse, inextricably fused with that which we see; the sound, articulate or not, cannot express any more than is expressed, at the same time, by visible movement; and in a good film it does not even attempt to do so. To put it briefly, the . . . "script" of a moving picture may be subject to what might be termed the *principle of coexpressibilty*.[17]

If Panofsky is right – and he is not entirely right – Shakespeare's sets of wit and what Holofernes calls 'flowers of fancy, jerks of invention' cannot be 'coexpressed', are at least going to be difficult to film, and are likely to be pruned from the play-text to create a screenplay. Because of this, moreover, it is all too easy for the cinematic treatment of a character speaking verse in a comedy to appear as the record of an implied theatrical performance rather than as a performance for film, perhaps because the eye of the camera is likely to be unmoving and to occupy an 'objective' position, rather than figuring by its movement, as it often does in a tragedy, as the focus of the hero's consciousness. On other occasions poetical or lyric passages are deemed to need music to signal their 'abnormality'.[18]

Now the first Shakespearean films, of course, used fixed cameras to photograph or reproduce complete performances, generally including the whole of the actor's body in the shot. The innovation of the moving camera, however, created problems for comedy. In particular, the camera's ability to approach the subject for a revealing close-up may serve to psychologise characters whose being in the theatre may be primarily ontological.[19] Varying the point of gaze may tend to sexualise the bodies of actresses who may, in any case, have been chosen for their photogenic rather than acting abilities. The wit of Emma Thompson's Beatrice in Kenneth Branagh's *Much Ado* seemed something put on, affected, rather than an index of a fiercely ironic intelligence – a reading that was exacerbated in the opening sequence by glimpses of nudity that betokened a 'natural' world of premarital desire.

Another way of analysing the difficulties in this area is to point out that theatrical techniques for delivering such comic sequences imply some element of aesthetic estrangement or alienation between actor and role, whereas film generally creates an identification between actor and role[20] – an identification that is exploited by the star system where an actor donates his or her self-fashioned 'personality' to the performance. Stars may be particularly inappropriate in comedies that depend upon ensemble acting. Moreover, the acting of major roles in the theatre, particularly major comic roles, demands a degree of collusion with the audience that may even be modulated over different performances of the same production. This is particularly apparent in passages of bawdy, which are remarkably difficult to film since there is no live audience to signal the bounds of decorum – and which can hardly be 'coexpressed' with visual images.[21] Directors often tend to authorise the *double entendres* with chortles from on-screen spectators that can be as unconvincing as canned laughter in television shows. (This happens in the masked ball sequence in Branagh's *Much Ado*.) Certain roles contain asides or single lines that demand to be delivered directly to the audience: on film Groucho Marx was able to do this, but few Shakespearean film clowns or their directors seem to want to emulate him.[22] Theatre in fact, unlike many of the other arts, may not be a 'medium':[23] audiences relish the *presence* of actor/characters. Moreover, this reactive mode, characteristic of acting in a playhouse, can move towards – where appropriate and when the audience is ready for it – excess; excess on the screen can be embarrassing or simply 'theatrical', reminding spectators that what they are watching was originally a play. Energetic acting that can breed delight in the theatre can seem merely frenetic on screen: clowns turn into buffoons. The problem does not affect cameo roles, perhaps best defined as not only short parts but also those in which the character played and the persona of the actor are identical – roles that arguably constitute part of the *mise-en-scène*. An example would be Giancarlo Cobelli as the priest in Zeffirelli's *The Taming of the Shrew*. (Non-English-speaking directors, spared by the necessities of translation from the text's aura of respect, may have been more able to think cinematically.)

Theatre's dependence upon audiences can be seen in a very amusing tele-film of the American Conservatory Theater's production of *The Taming of the Shrew* in 1976 which used *lazzi*, the stock verbal and physical routines of Italian *commedia dell'arte* to disguise – and critique – the politically correct feminism that obtained at the time of its making. The film's record of audience response is crucial for its effect.

Normative film acting is familiar from those American movies that take their acting styles from Stanislavskian method. Actors in these films paradoxically reach the audience by pretending they are not there, whereas actors in Shakespearean comedy in the theatre depend upon audience response in order to conjure the folly of the play, to demonstrate and exploit the difference between themselves and their roles. The problem of the disassociated spectator is compounded when films are viewed on television by an individual or a very small group. (That identity between character and role, so salient a feature of many forms of popular drama, may be achieved on screen in genre movies and in those television sit-coms that enjoy long runs where actors exploit the predictability of the comic types they play.[24])

Comedy sequences often parade a variety of dramatic styles whose effect depends upon their being recognised – strings of Petrarchan conceits in *A Midsummer Night's Dream*, cross-talk routines in *As You Like It*, flyting-matches in *Much Ado*. There are often invisible inverted commas around each speech act in the theatre, and its style is as important as the sentiments it evokes. Speeches can veer towards pastiche, are sometimes so obviously 'theatrical' that they become metatheatrical. Yet what makes them delightful in a playhouse may make them ungainly or grotesque in another medium. The great topic of Shakespearean comedy is love, but, for Hollywood, 'falling in love', the necessary prelude to bourgeois marriage, is too serious to be treated as either a sport or a crucial negotiation.

There was also, at the time that early and silent films of Shakespearean comedies were being made, a repertory of stock sentiments with a matching theatricalised language of gesture that derived from Victorian melodrama: its persistence in the new medium of the talkies and its incongruity with both the verbal subtleties of Shakespearean texts and the more modulated gestures of modern film is displayed by Elizabeth Bergner's performance as Rosalind in Czinner's *As You Like It* which now looks not like cinematic acting but a record of an atrociously stagy and egoistic performance that made nothing of the subtle and complex communion between herself, Rosalind, and Rosalind's forest role as Ganymede. That kind of display acting is a habitual mode of melodrama; so of course is moralism. Kenneth Branagh moralised – and depoliticised – his *Much Ado* by casting against the grain: the sex-symbol Keanu Reeves was Don John, so demonising the role in inverse proportion to the star's supposed attractiveness. As Leo Braudy puts it, 'The film actor emphasizes display, while the stage actor explores disguise.'[25]

The example of Elizabeth Bergner also reminds us of how delivery has to be different. In the theatre actors generally have to find some way of facing the front or nearly so: they are required to speak both to the audience and for the play and not just to each other. This theatrical 'frontality' of itself creates a double perspective on actor and role. Film actors, on the other hand, can face each other, their expressions often recorded by cross-shooting and over-the-shoulder shots. There may be gains in visibility, but the temptation – especially on television – to film speeches rather than dialogues, means that pace, all important in comedy, is then established by the editor rather than by players reacting with audiences.[26] Moreover, directors often seem to have forgotten that the use of close-ups or reverse-angle shots deprives the audience of a necessity for comedy, the sight of *both* players in a comic match.[27] Moreover, when we reflect that the unit of theatrical construction is the scene whereas the unit of cinematographic construction is the shot or take, we realise how difficult it is for players to modulate those sequences, the effect of which is often verbal rather than situational. Of comic actors in such sequences in the theatre we would generally want to say that they are not just behaving – as film celebrities trained in the method school consider themselves to be doing – but behaving, reacting, demonstrating and interpreting. Indeed in certain films all the actors can do is behave, the other dimensions of the scene being established by director and editor.

The acting in early movie versions of the comedies reminds us how cinema readily appropriated not only the styles of theatre but also, specifically, the conventions of melodrama. Melodrama, of course, used music to work on the imaginary emotional forces of its audiences. Yet again there are problems for comedy: in Olivier's *Henry V*, Walton's score played by a full symphony orchestra was used to splendid effect for both exaltation and pathos, but the perfunctory and incongruent set-pieces he composed for Czinner's *As You Like It* reveal that tone in a comedy of wit is probably best modulated primarily through verbal delivery. Music can in fact be used to ironise a sequence, but Branagh's decision to use music almost throughout *Much Ado* seemed designed to smooth over the prickliness of the text. By inflating the play's brittle epitaph scene (5.3) with orchestra and full chorus accompanying a procession of penitents, Branagh made the sequence operatic and compounded the film's leaning towards melodrama. In a film notable for the excellence of its verse-speaking, Michael Radford boldly used no music in the trial scene of *The Merchant of Venice* until Shylock had rejected Portia's plea for mercy.

Directors have also used music as yet another means to authenticate décor: in Zeffirelli's *The Taming of The Shrew*, the opening romantic melody that accompanied Lucentio's approach to Padua was given an Elizabethan flavour once the action moved inside the city walls. Later the director used a similarly sentimental tune to romanticise one of the most theatrical moments in the text, Lucentio's recognition of his father Vincentio (5.1.87ff.).

Comedy is as much concerned with the life of groups as with central characters: many commercial directors, having found stars to play the leads, have not found satisfactory ways of creating those microcosmic communities in which their players might put their talents to work. Some early Hollywood movie versions of the comedies took the bait of inflation born of reverence – Reinhardt created that architecturally imposing 'Athens' for his *Midsummer Night's Dream* which, arguably, dwarfed the families whose tensions generate the action. Others played the role of iconoclasts: Sam Taylor's *The Taming of the Shrew* (1929) offered an equivalent to the play's induction in the form of a Punch and Judy show and then relegated the whole film to the proletarian art of Vaudeville wherein, despite a 'Renaissance' setting, Mary Pickford played Katherine as a truculent vamp, and Douglas Fairbanks buckled his swash as a pirate. Both were armed with whips for the wooing scene: Pickford gave up when she discovered that Fairbanks's was longer. (The intemperate acting may be accounted for by the fact that the film was released in both silent and sound versions.) Some created a picturesque merrie England inspired by nineteenth-century theatre design for the setting – Paul Czinner's *As You Like It* provides an example. (In this case it was Merrie France with a thatched mushroom-shaped cottage that anticipates the décor of *The Wizard of Oz* of 1939.) These seem both inappropriate and dated now – and yet, of course, if we could see *stage productions* of the same era as those recorded on film, we might find them as seemingly ill-fitted to what we now take to be conventions of Shakespearean comic playing as are the film sequences.

That brings us to another important difference between plays and films. A play has three ages: the age in which the story was set, the age when it was written, the age when it was performed. In the case of Shakespearean texts, the action is set in what we might call a mythical present, and they were performed almost immediately after they were written, using, we believe, contemporary costumes along with 'antic' suits for the mythic roles.[28] The production of text and performance were virtually simultaneous – and presumably influenced one another. One of the ways a community defines itself is by the identification of stock comic roles. For the community of London, Shakespeare almost certainly created some roles to fit the stage personalities of popular players. Today's comic personalities are unlikely to fit those created for either Elizabethan London or the period of the revival of a film. (Ben Elton's mutedly frenzied Verges in the Branagh *Much Ado* is an egregious example of this kind of misfit.) Shakespearean clowns define themselves by their direct rapport with their spectators: as this difference is difficult to recreate on screen, an alternative is to make them outsiders. Ben Kingsley's Feste in Nunn's *Twelfth Night* was neither Olivia's servant nor her friend, rather a neutral sexless confidant, clad in a sou'wester and dossing in a stable, possessed of a melancholy sardonicism.

Now 'classic' plays are today, by definition, performed after they were written: the gap between writing and performance is lengthened, and one of the first tasks for a theatrical director is to find an age in which to set the production. A film director has the same decision to make, but also has to bear in mind that the film is likely to be *shown* long after it was made, unlike a theatrical production which cannot be reproduced. Films have a kind of fourth age. For that reason a film is a record not only of what was filmed but also of the styles in décor and cinematography that went into its own making. Movies are by nature period pieces, and, given that social topics of comedy are not akin, for example, to the kind of 'prehistory of conscience'[29] that Orson Welles used for his *Macbeth*, both contemporary and 'Elizabethan' milieux for films of the comedies are quickly going to seem particularly quaint and period-specific. Peter Hall's 1968 film of *A Midsummer Night's Dream*, with a Royal Shakespeare Company cast, was shot on location in a country-house park, the house's interior being used for 'Athens'. The men wore Elizabethan costumes, the women were 1960s dolly-birds in mini-skirts. Censorship was being relaxed and we see a near-naked Oberon and Titania – perhaps as a consequence, and to avoid embarrassment, there were a large number of head-only shots. (A fading shot suggested that Bottom and Titania actually made love.) The fairies' roles were taken by children, cute little girl fairies and baleful boys. The fairies came and went by the use of jump-cuts, the director cheerfully removing them or adding them to shots where exits and entrances were required without the camera seeming to stop. The film stands as a *record* of a charade played as part of a country party to which London swingers had been invited rather than as an exploration of the text's transgressions of the boundaries between erotic fantasy and the nightmare of power misused.

Because of the dangers of dating or inappropriate contemporary resonance, some film directors have chosen to set their films in a kind of fifth age, a period neither Shakespearean nor modern. Miller's television *Merchant of Venice* (1973), deriving from an important National Theatre production starring Laurence Olivier and Joan Plowright, was set in a Venice of 1860. Nunn's film of *Twelfth Night* was set in high Victorian England and Michael Hoffman's *A Midsummer Night's Dream* (1999), starring Kevin Kline and Michelle Pfeiffer, was shot in a 'nineteenth-century' Tuscany using grotesque garden sculptures as markers of the fairy world. As Jonathan Miller notes, the revival of a dramatic work from the distant past is a conceptual problem and not simply a theatrical task. He figures the processes of dramatic reproduction in the patina that appears on a sculpture and which reminds us how even such 'autographed' works of art change, given that they carry with them a load of historically specific cultural connotations.[30]

Comedies in the English tradition are generally 'impure' and can contain embedded sub-genres such as pastoral or masquerade. Christine Edzard's *As You Like It* was a bold, but not wholly successful, attempt to locate 'pastoral' in a modern urban setting: an unemployed Orlando appeared in the vestibule of a contemporary commercial building surrounded by people with mobile phones. In the 'forest', odd sheep filmed amid the wastes of London docklands betokened the artificiality of all pastoral conventions. A 'natural perspective' became a double perspective. The film seemed to be saying, 'The text has a few things to say about social deprivation: let's see if we can bring this home to the audience by playing the game of pastoral in a modern city-scape.' Accordingly, and not surprisingly perhaps, the final wedding ceremony was cut. Part of the problem came from the strident over-determination of the setting: having established a strong sense of milieu, the urban wasteland that signified the dispossession of a modern underclass, it seems unlikely that an audience unfamiliar with the text could match its heightened speech to the naturalistic décor. References to killing venison sounded bizarre, and even Touchstone's prose encounter with Audrey (Grif Rhys Jones as a spiv and Miriam Margolies as the proprietor of a roadside caravan 'caf') could not work since the theatricality of lines like the former's semi-aside, 'sluttishness may come hereafter' (3.4.27–8), depends upon direct collusion with an audience comprised of spectators and not cinematic 'overhearers'. This is simply not the language to be heard in that milieu, particularly when filmed in the manner of television social documentaries of the 1960s. For an audience familiar with the play, the game of translation from the implied world of precocity in the theatre to in-your-face social relevance was labour lost.

Film directors have to find their own conventions. Theatre is an actor's medium, film a director's medium, and it is a director, with a totalising control of *mise-en-scène*, and, with his editor, master not only of pace but also of sequence, who inevitably displaces the author of the text and becomes the *auteur* of the film. Film may not be suited to Shakespearean acting, but what it can do wonderfully is offer readings of the text by specifically cinematographic methods. The expressiveness of language may have to give way to the suggestiveness of montage. Trevor Nunn's adaptation of *Twelfth Night* made, to a degree, a collage of the text, dissolved from Antonio's announcement of his intention to visit Orsino's court to a belated shot of Orsino speaking of his desires for Olivia. Later, while Feste was singing 'O mistress mine' to Sir Toby and company, the camera crosscut between Orsino and Olivia. Similarly, Radford moved the duet between Lorenzo and Jessica that opens the last act of *The Merchant* to before the trial of Shylock.

It may well be the case, even more than with histories and tragedies, that the value of a film version of a text will depend upon its formal *differences from* rather than its '*fidelity*' *to* the original, upon whether the director is able to make a 'filmic' film that, by delighting in its own conventions of narrative and diegesis, matches the metatheatricality that is so prominent in Shakespeare's comic texts. We will enjoy the director's signature; we must not expect Shakespeare's autograph on a representation that, by virtue of its medium, *cannot* be 'authentic'. A director derives his film from – does not merely 'adapt' – a Shakespearean text. Formal difference, moreover, will dictate changes in content – cuts from the text, and narrative rearrangement. A screenplay's fidelity to a play-text is likely to be a sign of failure rather than of success. The 'text' of the film is the film itself, not the text by Shakespeare that generated the treatment and screenplay that in turn generated the film. It must be judged alongside other films, other adaptations. Zeffirelli's *The Taming of the Shrew* and Branagh's *Much Ado* ran their texts through cinematic terrains that were also suited to television idylls: the latter recalled John Mortimer's series about beautiful expatriates in Tuscany, *Summer's Lease*, broadcast shortly before the film was made. These directorial decisions make any evaluating comparison with Shakespeare's text difficult to sustain. Noble's *A Midsummer Night's Dream* derived, through its ur-production in the theatre, from Brook's 1970 theatrical production that itself reconceptualised the text by virtue of its radical *mise-en-scène*. This both provided a laboratory for the exploration of Elizabethan playing conventions and an exhibition of the cultural paradigms that had informed later readings of the play. In the cinema, Noble could also draw upon non-theatrical renditions of interiority ranging from *Alice in Wonderland* to *The Wizard of Oz*, and upon films in the expressionist tradition: he was successful by virtue of this synopticism. This inventiveness is needed to match the modes of representation in the text. Perhaps a truly great film of a comedy has yet to be made: it may well be far more of a reflection upon a Shakespearean theme, rather than a film adaptation, akin to Welles's *Chimes at Midnight* or Greenaway's *Prospero's Books*. *Vive la différence.*

NOTES

1 Panofsky, however, called it 'probably the most unfortunate major film ever produced' (Erwin Panofsky, 'Style and Medium in the Motion Pictures' (1934), in Gerald Mast, Marshall Cohen and Leo Braudy, eds., *Film Theory and Criticism: Introductory Readings* (New York, 1992), pp. 233–48; p. 238).

2 For a critique, see Michael Hattaway, ' "I've Processed my Guilt": Shakespeare, Branagh, and the Movies', in Jonathan Bate, Jill L. Levenson and Dieter Mehl, eds., *Shakespeare and the Twentieth Century* (Newark, DE, 1998), pp. 194–214.

3 See Samuel Crowl, *Shakespeare at the Cineplex: The Kenneth Branagh Era* (Athens, OH, 2003).

4 Diana E. Henderson, 'A Shrew for the Times', in Lynda E. Boose and Richard Burt, eds., *Shakespeare, the Movie* (London and New York, 1997), pp. 148–68; Gil Junger's *10 Things I Hate about You* (1999) rewrites the play and sets it in a modern high-school.

5 R. A. Foakes and R. T. Rickert, eds., *Henslowe's Diary* (Cambridge, 1961), p. 320.

6 Russell Jackson, 'A Shooting Script for the Reinhardt–Dieterle *Dream*; The War with the Amazons, Bottom's Wife, and other "Missing" Scenes', *Shakespeare Bulletin*, 164 (1998), 39–41.

7 William Uricchio and Roberta E. Pearson, *Reframing Culture: The Case of the Vitagraph Quality Films* (Princeton, 1993), p. 7.

8 Panofsky, 'Style and Medium', p. 248; for a critique of this position, see Susan Sontag, 'Film and Theatre', in Mast, *Film Theory and Criticism*, pp. 362–74.

9 Jonathan Miller, *Subsequent Performances* (London, 1986), pp. 63–5.

10 See John Dover Wilson, *Shakespeare's Happy Comedies* (London, 1962).

11 For the fetishising of its supernatural elements by 'ultrareactionary critics', see Walter Benjamin, 'The Work of Art in the Age of Mechanical Reproduction', in Hannah Arendt, ed., *Illuminations*, trans. Harry Zohn (London, 1970), pp. 219–53; pp. 229–30; and for the contribution of Reinhardt's thirteen productions of *A Midsummer Night's Dream* to the German Shakespearean tradition, see Werner Habicht, 'Shakespeare and the German Imagination', in Heather Kerr, Robin Eaden and Madge Mitton, eds., *Shakespeare: World Views* (Newark, DE, 1996), pp. 87–101.

12 Barbara Hodgdon, 'Two *King Lears*: Uncovering the Filmtext', *Literature and Film Quarterly*, 11 (1983), 143–51, defines two *auteurs*, the 'so-called directorial signature' and 'another textual authority . . . – what I call the expectational text – [that] contains my private notions about the play and about performed Shakespeare, notions that I may not even recognize until I find them denied'.

13 'The moving of laughter is a fault in comedy' (Ben Jonson, *Timber or Discoveries*, in *Works*, ed. C. H. Herford and Percy Simpson, 11 vols. (Oxford, 1925–52), vol. VIII,

p. 643; Jonson was quoting from Heinsius, *Ad Horatii de Plauto et Terentio Judicium, Dissertatio*, 1618.

14 See Wylie Sypher, *Four Stages of Renaissance Style* (New York, 1955), pp. 143–4.

15 Compare Orsino in *Twelfth Night*, 'A natural perspective, that is and is not' (5.1.214).

16 Jonson made the contract explicit in the induction to his *Bartholomew Fair*.

17 Panofsky, 'Style and Medium', p. 237.

18 As in 'She never told her love' in Nunn's *Twelfth Night*, which was also intercut by images of crashing breakers.

19 I owe this distinction to André Bazin, 'Theater and Cinema', in Mast, *Film Theory and Criticism*, pp. 375–86; p. 378.

20 Walter Benjamin, however, argues that the piecemeal processes of shooting prevent 'identification' (Benjamin, 'Work of Art', p. 232).

21 In Zeffirelli's *Shrew* the lines bidding Hortensio to tune his 'instrument' (3.1.37ff.) were merely heard from an off-camera Lucentio.

22 Bottom did deliver his soliloquy to camera in Hall's *A Midsummer Night's Dream*, as, very effectively, did John Cleese playing Petruchio in Miller's *The Taming of the Shrew*.

23 See Sontag, 'Film and Theatre', p. 368.

24 I owe this insight to a conversation with Alberto Paolucci.

25 Leo Braudy, *The World in a Frame*, in Mast, *Film Theory and Criticism*, p. 391.

26 'The camera that presents the performance of the film actor to the public need not respect the performance as an integral whole' (Benjamin, 'Work of Art', p. 230).

27 Theatrical actors can be 'masked' by placing them in a solo spot-light, but the technique is not one that will be used much in comedy.

28 Foakes and Rickert, *Henslowe's Diary*, p. 318.

29 André Bazin, *Orson Welles: A Critical Review* (London, 1978), p. 101, cited Anthony Davies, 'Shakespeare on Film and Television: A Retrospect', in Anthony Davies and Stanley Wells, eds., *Shakespeare and the Moving Image* (Cambridge, 1994), pp. 1–17; p. 4.

30 Miller, *Subsequent Performances*, pp. 28, 68, 69.

6

H. R. COURSEN

Filming Shakespeare's history: three films of *Richard III*

Sir Laurence Olivier's 1955 film of *Richard III* centres on a single character and has, according to Anthony Davies in *Filming Shakespeare's Plays*, more links with his *Hamlet* than with his *Henry V*. It is, says Davies, a 'psychological study developed along the lines of attitudes to and conceptions of power'.[1] The film is unabashedly theatrical, with the kind of stylised sets that Peter Holland labels 'fake medievalism'.[2] As Davies shows, however, the play becomes cinema. 'The primary articulation of Olivier's *Richard III* is essentially filmic.' *Richard III*, writes Jack Jorgens, is 'not really a history play'. Olivier depicts a 'renaissance wolf among medieval sheep . . . Richard's opponents [in the film] are weak and stupid, but they do not seem as evil as they do in Shakespeare'.[3] Indeed, his victims tend to yield to him without resistance. Clarence does, of course, not reading his own vivid treachery as a family trait that inheres in his brother. Hastings does, ignoring Stanley's dream and his own stumbling horse. But Lady Anne, we notice, has taken off her wedding ring before her second meeting with Richard. It is as if she is waiting for him to ask 'Is not the causer of the timeless deaths . . . As blameful as the executioner?' in the second confrontation that Olivier crafts from the script.

Olivier notoriously includes some of Cibber's lines ('So much for Buckingham' and 'Richard is himself again'), some of Garrick's structural improvements and segments of Richard's speeches from 3 *Henry IV* ('Clarence beware. Thou keep'st me from the light; / But I will sort a pitchy day for thee': 5.7.85–6) and parts of the long speech beginning at 3.2.124. Olivier's choice is shrewd here, because that speech marks the 'invention of Richard of Gloucester' and his 'differentiation from the comparatively colorless orators and warriors who populate the *Henry VI* plays'.[4]

The film does not, as Constance Brown asserts, reflect a 'structure placed on the action of the play . . . the parabolic curve from legitimate king to tyrant to legitimate king'.[5] Olivier begins with Edward saying 'Once more we sit in England's royal seat.' Clearly, whether we know the previous plays or not, the seat has been subject to contestation. The Duchess of York is given part of her speech about the 'accursed and unquiet wrangling days', in whose aftermath, despite the apparent end of 'domestic broils',

> themselves the conquerors
> Make war upon themselves, brother to brother
> Blood to blood, self against self   (3.1.60–2)

This suggests that Richard's tyranny, however extreme, is part of a pattern, not an exception. It is Richmond, with his pious prayer before battle, who is the exception here.

Olivier does well to end the film shortly after Richard becomes king. He has been playing roles until then – suddenly he has the power those roles have acquired, but no role to play. He *is* king, and all excitement flees, replaced by fear. His becoming king has been like the wooing of Anne, a joy in process, but nothing once the goal is gained. He will have it but he will not keep it long. As Jorgens says, 'he becomes king and need pretend no longer'. Pretence has been his identity – as he tells us from the first. Jorgens links Richard with those 'other unfestive outsiders – Malvolio, Shylock, and Iago'.[6] But Richard, unlike Malvolio, makes it to the top, only to find no place to go from there. He is an outsider, as he himself sees it, but he is not outside of history. His character is the culmination of an alienated and alienating politics, which seeks power without purpose. This is revealed by his paranoid musings on the throne, even as Buckingham pesters Richard with conventional greed and ambition.

As Jorgens points out, the camera consistently takes his point of view. Indeed, Richard serves as a narrator and master of ceremonies during the early parts of the film, moving out from the dramatic space and telling us what he will do next. That continues up to the point of the sudden movement, along a dark chord, into the Tower, for Clarence's terror and death. Clarence has orchestrated some of that in previous history, of course. The denouement is Richard's drama, as he almost hands the murderers the warrant for Clarence's release. Richard holds life and death in his hands, and corrects himself to turn over the 'right' document. But once Richard is on the throne, Olivier cedes narrative command to Buckingham ('Made I him king for this?'), Tyrrel's description of the murder of the princes, and Stanley's conversation with Buckingham, in which Stanley tells Buckingham that Elizabeth will marry Richmond. Richard gets the story back as Tyrrel returns the ring whereby he has gained admittance to the Tower, but is immediately hit with many reports. He rushes off to Salisbury, leaving an empty throne behind.

Before the battle at Bosworth, Richard draws his plan on the plain with his sword. The diagram becomes real – and in a nice touch, the sky remains a painted sky for a moment behind the ranks of Richard's army. We then see Richard in front of the army. The drawing of the battle shows what he might have been, a creator of armies, of men, not a fomenter of desertion, finally dying in the midst of a savage pack. That is his allusion to Henry V, who creates a 'band of brothers' before Agincourt, promising long life and old age to an army that, until that moment, thought it was doomed. The play shows that Richard loses with a superior army. In the film, Richard's concern during the battle with the disposition of Stanley's troops permits an enemy soldier to slip in and stab his horse in the belly. Henry V, who had knocked off traitors before his expedition, would not have been similarly distracted.

Olivier omits Richard's soliloquy upon awakening after his nightmare. The enraged shade of Buckingham, seemingly about to throttle Richard, has startled him into fearful cries that rouse his camp. The Augustinian premises[7] that Richard so blithely ignored in his bustle are not stated, but at the end, in his death throes, he struggles to get the cross of the sword-hilt to his eyes. Those who have set upon him back away to watch this debate between body and soul. Body has failed soul so far, but Richard gets the sword up in front of his face before it falls. Are we to believe that he has become that Renaissance favourite, the Thief on the Cross, whose last-minute repentance saves him for paradise, or that Richard is as damned as the omitted soliloquy says he is? A horse does arrive and Richard is tossed over it. The camera shows his garter encircling a dead leg now bouncing from a living horse for which he would have traded his kingdom only a few minutes before.

Critics claim that Olivier 'sacrificed the larger significance of the work' and that his Richard verges 'on Victorian melodrama'.[8] Both objections have merit, but Olivier's is a brisk and vivid film that stands up well on reviewing. While it certainly concentrates on a single individual, it incorporates more of the ambiguous politics of the play than some believed it did at the time, and it even raises the issue of the destiny of Richard's soul by showing us that spasmodic final effort to look upon the cross. Clarence had done so earlier and had been subjected to a perverse Eucharist in which his own blood mingled with the wine. At the end, the various God-contacting rituals that Richard so distorted and perverted catch up with him, as his soul rebels against what his will has done. In holding the sword up at last to his eyes, Richard may be acknowledging this. Norman Wooland, who had been Olivier's Horatio, plays Catesby, but no one speaks of flights of angels here. Stanley finds the crown in a bush and takes it to Richmond. The film ends where it began, with a crown hanging in the air.

Having seen Richard Eyre's stage production of *Richard III* at the National Theatre in London in August of 1990, I went to see the film version when it finally arrived in my neighbourhood with considerable anticipation. The film, after all, arrived in North America with positive advance notices, including a promise from Richard Corliss in *Time* that it offered 'the fetid, enthralling goods, the *Nixon* that Oliver Stone didn't quite dare to make'.[9]

Peter Holland claimed in his *Times Literary Supplement* review that the film 'is far more successful than Kenneth Branagh's *Henry V* and *Much Ado About Nothing*', because it pursues 'an alternative history extrapolating from the perception that the English aristocracy's close alignment with fascism could make Richard into a potential Hitler'. 'By avoiding the fake medievalism of conventional representation', writes Holland, 'Loncraine and McKellen offer a precise cinematic analogy to the Shakespearean play . . . [The film] finds reasons within the conventions of filmic naturalism for its choices . . . The conjunctions of styles and voices that Branagh has been prepared to accept are here turned into a carefully controlled polyphony.'[10]

My own experience of the film was that it seemed a parody of Hollywood films, at times mildly amusing, most of the time simply grotesque, a shallow, meretricious shadow of the stage production. The film's explicitness robbed the play's metaphor of its suggestive bridge between unlike things. Pulled in the direction of its 1930-ish motif, the film loses contact with all but the words of the originating script. They are not enough. The film detaches from its archetype – whatever it is. I would suggest that the archetype might be the still 'religious' world that Richard thinks he can simultaneously manipulate for his own purposes and ignore as it might apply to his soul. The 1930s surface erases any medieval levels and convinces us that the surface is all there is. This is a film about the 1930s – Loncraine even finds an authentic De Havilland Dragon Rapide for Queen Elizabeth's escape to the 'sanctuary' of France – but it fails on these terms as well. The film does more than strain credulity. At the beginning, Prince Edward and King Henry, together at Tewkesbury, forget to post any guards. A tank rumbles up and crashes through their headquarters. Richard leaps out and kills them.

At the end, the abandoned Bankside Power Station, established as the Tower, becomes, it seems, Richard's redoubt for the final battle. Bosworth Field thus resembles the small unit struggles in the Krasny Oktyabr factory in Stalingrad during that pivotal battle. The analogy is that history itself can turn on the hinge of a tiny moment within a larger war. *If only* Richard had had a horse to pull his staff car out of the mud . . . ! But Richard, the Nazi here, has no air force. Until Dunkirk and the Battle of Britain, Hitler's Stukas and Messerschmidts had dominated the skies. But in the film Air Marshall Stanley has the only plane! If one imitates history, particularly on film, that history must be depicted with fidelity and not be 'transparently fake',[11] particularly when the rest of the late 1930s details, down to the smallest Tiffany pin, have been so meticulously recreated. But then it does not matter by the end of this travesty. We have to see horses, since they are mentioned in this botched-up filmscript, but they are as heavily anachronistic in an otherwise mechanised world as an army that has Tiger tanks but neither an air force nor some early warning system to show the approach of enemy planes.

If one is to avoid 'fake medievalism', one had better know the world into which one places the script. What we get in the film, as Samuel Crowl says, 'is visual overload . . . a ripe, garish cartoon . . . visual jokes, which, unfortunately, only work to fragment and dissipate the propelling energy of McKellen's performance'.[12] Richard delivers the first part of the opening speech into a microphone at the Tewkesbury Victory Party and then to himself in the palace men's room. He includes a slighter borrowing from 3 Henry VI than had Olivier. He notices us half-way through the speech, accusing us implicitly of being Toms peeping on his peeing. Unlike Olivier's charming Richard, McKellen's Richard never does ask 'us to join him', as Stephen Holden says he does. He sneers at us as he sneers at the feeble characters he manipulates in the film. The result is an alienation from him, as opposed to the fascinated emotional participation in his schemes and our sharing in his response to their success that Olivier's evil schemer invites.

Clarence delivers his 'dream' speech outside during a heavy and sudden downpour as he moves on to a grim circle of concrete surrounded by a foul moat, while the guard he is addressing stays in the shelter of the access doorway. (It seems to be the duke's exercise period.) The speech demands quiet and a re-engendered fear. Here it is not only pointless, but largely lost to the downpour. Clarence is not drowned in that droll butt of malmsey but has his throat cut in a bathtub, a borrowing from the enforced suicide of the old capo in The Godfather.

Robert Downey Jr. plays Rivers, apparently as an American seeking a title: the actor is presumably imported into the production to provide a dash of sexuality and to be dispatched suddenly. He reads his few lines as if reciting today's specials. While simultaneously smoking, drinking brandy and being massaged by his friendly air stewardess, he is startled to see a knife emerge from his stomach. Trick or treat! This also borrows from The Godfather, where a hood and his moll are tommy-gunned in bed while the christening is going on.

The final chase-scene up the steps and along the floor of a ruined building is on loan from a thousand old films – how many detectives and courageous cops have pursued their culprits upwards into the scaffolding? How many criminals have run out of ammunition and tossed their guns away in disgust? How many crooks or crookbacks have tumbled from their perches? Richard falls away into the flames, a Faustian end, as Al Jolson warbles the 1925 song, 'Sitting on Top of the World'. Yes, it may remind us of James Cagney's defiance on top of the exploding petroleum tank in White Heat ('Top of the world, ma!') but the sudden intrusion of Jolson is inconsistent with the tunes that have been a leitmotif here. Marlowe's lyric 'Come live with me, and be my love' is sung by a chanteuse at the outset, as a bandleader made up to look like Glenn Miller waves his stick. It might have been fun had we heard versions of 'It Was a Lover and His Lass' or

'O, Mistress Mine' with Bert Ambrose or Ray Noble settings in the background from time to time, but the promising beginning is not pursued. Richard does put on a gramophone record as he delectates over photos of Hastings's execution by hanging. (Hitler had watched the films of the slow strangulation of the Stauffenberg plotters in July 1944.) Later, Richard eavesdrops on the garrotting of Buckingham, who is cut off, it seems, with piano wire, as the Stauffenberg conspirators had been. (In the 1990 stage version, however, Hastings's head had been brought to Richard in a bucket. He reached delicately into the bucket, apparently to close Hastings's eyes. It was macabre, but funny.)

The film erases the play's rhythms – Richard's brilliant step-by-step progress to the throne and the nemesis that begins at the moment he is in the throne are gone here. Even the sequence of frantic reports in Act IV scene 4 is edited out, although we do get Richard's striking of the messenger who brings word of Buckingham's capture and Richard's subsequent 'I cry thee mercy' (4.4.444). In the inherited script, however, the striking is motivated by Richard's belief that here is *more* bad news. What we get, as Stephen Holden says, 'is little more than a collection of famous speeches connected by the Cliff notes'. It is as if some of the original words are obligatory amid the dreary drift of a 1930s world ignoring the Depression around it and colluding in a slide towards war. Holden calls the film 'a glib equation between the rise of Fascism and upper-class ennui. But it makes that equation with such a campy exaggeration that it finally seems tongue-in-cheek.'[13] If so, why? It is Richard himself who shows us how effete and/or naive his rivals are. All that reinforcement from the film diminishes Richard's brilliant skill in exploiting weaknesses that would probably be survivable if it were not for his malevolence. And, of course, the reality of Hitler's pre-war Germany needs no fictional embellishment. Many upper-middle-class German men were happy to accept honorary rank as officers in the SS to join the fashionable uniformed set of the late 1930s. We do see Buckingham precisely that here.

This production has almost no humour. Richard does turn to us to say 'I am not made of stone', but otherwise the film's literalisation of what even Richard recognises as improbable fiction flattens the story into sheer and unrelenting grimness, with no variation in tone.

Richard does not appear 'aloft, betweene two Bishops' (the First Folio stage direction), but is secreted in a room with two manicurists. That is a modern analogue to that old-time religion, one assumes, but it is not as funny as the scene can be as scripted. Buckingham does not get his amusing line 'This general applause and cheerful shout / Argues your wisdom . . .' Buckingham and Richard do not create for the Lord Mayor the farcical pretence that Lovel and Ratcliff are enemies approaching (3.5.18–19). And Richard does not say to Buckingham, after all the talk of bastardy, 'Yet touch this sparingly, as't were far off; / Because, my lord, you know my mother lives' (3.5.91–2).

The effort here goes into a simulation of Nazism. Like Hitler, Richard operates from a railway car. Buckingham, in uniform, looks just a bit like Hermann Goering, Ratcliff like Martin Bormann, Catesby like Rudolf Hess and Tyrrel like the model of a perfect Aryan. The hall in which cheering blackshirts greet Richard is a colourised replica of the one filmed by Leni Riefenstahl on the night of the 1934 Nuremberg Party Conference. Simply by its nature as a mechanically reproduced depiction of 'reality', the film insists on the Hitler–Richard comparison. The parallels melt away – so does the play.

The film's best moment, with Richard, his cronies and his queen viewing the newsreel of their own elevation to power, is isolated. It reminds us that the Nazis used film as part of their propaganda, and the film-makers might have shown Buckingham deploying an edited film of the population's less than enthusiastic response to his pitch for Richard (perhaps in the manner of the opening sequences of Leni Riefenstahl's *Triumph of the Will*), to convince others. Films about films can be exciting. But that does not happen here. In the isolation of the cinema, the excited involvement that the stage version demanded did not occur, and in the film the historical parallels that might generate excitement keep breaking down.

While Hitler demanded personal allegiance and insisted on the '*Führer Prinzip*', Nazi Germany was the epitome of *state* power, with a vast and complicated and conflicted apparatus. When Richard gets to the throne, there is no state, no structure and no programme for the *Volk*. He is only personally a Machiavel. Hitler outlined one of the sources for his own power in *Mein Kampf*: 'Inasmuch as one's own propaganda recognized a shadow of right upon the opponent's side, the ground is prepared for questioning one's own right . . . The people see in unfailing ruthless attack upon an opponent the proof of one's own right. Seen in this light hesitation leads to uncertainty, weakness, and ultimately failure.'[14] His party newspaper defined the goal of Hitler's propaganda: 'complete knowledge of and mastery over the soul and the mind, the bearing and the inner conviction of the people'[15]

By all accounts Hitler was dull in private, except when having a tantrum. In public, backed and surrounded by the pageantry of Nazism – torches, bands, concrete swastikas, flags and outstretched arms – he was hypnotic, magnetic. Richard, as depicted by Olivier, is scintillating in *private*. Olivier serves as narrator and master of ceremonies for his film until we move to the grey interior of the Tower and the murder of Clarence, which Richard orchestrates from a politic distance. McKellen in his film tends to be overshadowed by the trappings that, for Hitler, were background for one of his addresses. Shakespeare's Richard is a poor manipulator of the masses, which would make Buckingham a Goebbels without a Hitler. Richard, superb in his single-minded and solitary game of duplicity, is a wonderful actor. As Jorgens observes, 'He shifts effortlessly from "concerned brother," to "repentant murderer," and "flattering wooer," to "plain honest man overflowing with righteous indignation," to "friendly peacemaker," and "dutiful son," to "jolly playful uncle," to "pious unworldly man".'[16] And, of course, he *enjoys* playing these roles, stroking his skill against his inner cynicism. Hitler is here in the cynicism, but otherwise, Hitler was 'rigid and humorless', as Robert G. L. Waite says.[17] That Hitler was paranoid and that he indulged in scapegoating merely links him with most politicians. Those traits do not argue for a full-scale fascist architecture to accompany them.

Hitler's political ideas are summarised by Waite: 'exaltation of the *Führer* and the degradation of democracy; militarism and war; conquest of *Lebensraum* and the enslavement of other people; anti-Semitism and racism; propaganda and terror to force a nation to do the will of one man'. The film forces us to wander from the script in pursuing the parallel. Waite quotes a German doctor who, after witnessing a boy willing to die for Hitler (and doing so), asks 'What is this strange ideology that can even pervert instincts?'[18] The play makes clear, modern readings to the contrary, that Richard's world is Augustinian, and that the spiritual coding must then inhere in him, as his own basic instinct, and as part of the collective unconscious which, in this case, has a Christian configuration. He cannot pervert it in himself. He certainly does not pervert it in others into loyalty to him. They defect, even if he catches up with some of them.

Olivier performed the role on stage in 1944, and, according to Kenneth Tynan, he later said: 'There was Hitler across the way, one was playing it definitely as a paranoiac; so that there was a core of something to which the audience could immediately respond.'[19] Assuming that Richard's flexibility and sense of humour are not suppressed, Hitler can be used as characterisation, as subtext, but not as the centrepiece for a fully articulated fascist setting.

Richard Eyre's stage version pulled the audience into a nightmare world of black uniforms, kleig lights and summary executions. The grim rooms around the single lightbulbs under which prisoners were interrogated became visible to us and multiplied down a terrifying regress into other countries and other times. We could sense, just out of sight, the thousand outstretched arms of the Riefenstahl film and the clump of the goosestep down the Champs-Elysées (or Oxford Street) in 1940. The stage forced us to fill in its suggestions with our imagination, but by trying to make it 'real', the film did not permit us to believe any of it.

Stage, of course, places us in that remarkable zone in which we suspend our disbelief, or, to put it more positively, in which we awaken our imaginations. Paulina, staging a resurrection in *The Winter's Tale*, insists on a precondition: 'It is requir'd / You do awake your faith.' On film, the fascist analogy becomes glib. It is certainly true, as John Gray says, that 'we are curious whether fascist movements and regimes are so linked to the conditions of Europe between the world wars that nothing having their peculiar combination of features can be found in other historical contexts – such as our own'. Add to that curiosity the fascination of many of us who lived in that interwar interlude with fascism and particularly Nazi Germany, and the metaphor between late medieval times and modern becomes potentially potent. Superficially, Richard can be seen as fascistic: 'fascist movements', says Gray, 'distinguished themselves from even the authoritarian far right by their uncompromising modernism, their rejection of any kind of reactionary nostalgia for the past and, in many cases, by their pronounced hostility to Christianity'. At base, however, Richard's drive to the throne is not a 'movement'. It does not promise, as in the National Socialist oxymoron, to be 'at once the embodiment of a new world order and the savior of the social order in Germany and Europe'. Richard's career cannot be identified with even a contradictory social programme. Gray warns that 'we will not advance our understanding of fascism if we rest content with the cliché that fascism represented a regression into atavism, a step backward in historical development'.[20] Machiavelli may have been the first modern man, and Shakespeare seems to come to understand him as such in the construction of Henry V. But for Richard, before the publication in English of *The Prince*, Machiavelli is 'murderous', a version of devil. Hitler has come to represent that evil for this century, but he did so as the voice of a political movement which, however vicious and perverse, did have massive popular support as the documentaries demonstrate so chillingly.

Furthermore, Richard's is a perverse 'evolution'. He is as much a function of social Darwinism as of his self-invention. He comes from that brutal and often confusing sequence of battles that killed his father, York, and his brother, Rutland, and the Lancastrian prince, Edward, and that made his brother Edward king. The Yorkists win by having won the battles, not, like Hitler, as a reaction to having *lost* a war. Furthermore, as David Schoenbaum suggests,

> fascism has been among the most baffling of the great political movements. Liberalism and conservatism can still be recognized as fallout from the French Revolution. Western democracy and Marxist–Leninist Communism can still be traced to their common origins in the European Enlightenment. Only fascism seems to come from nowhere and lead to nowhere: a critical mass of negatives – anti-individual, anti-rational, anti-feminist, anti-Western – with little as a common core save a deep sense of collective grievance and, in the most notable cases, a charismatic leader. Before World War I . . . no one had ever heard of fascism.[21]

Fascism is a movement, based on collective grievances. It has no background save the trauma suddenly apparent at the end of a war, among both winners (Italy) *and* losers (Germany). Where is the link between Shakespeare's Richard and history's fascists? Richard emerges from a continuing power struggle of which many of his victims are unaware and in which the victims who know what he is doing are powerless to stop him.

We get a brief touch of Zeffirelli at the end. Richmond and Elizabeth have been married. Their wedding night is also the eve of battle. Dawn's rosy fingers trip across their rumpled sheets. Kate Steavenson-Payne, who has been pulled empty-faced from place to place throughout the film, finally gets a line. (One expected her to say, 'Wilt thou be gone? It is not yet near day.') Richmond blows her a kiss and strides cheerily off to war.

The film does have a few good moments, like a cut from King Edward pulling oxygen into his wasted lungs to one of Richard smoking and about to burn Clarence's pardon. We observe Edward's survivors from his deathbed, as if his shade has hung around for an instant before descending down through the royal wine cellar. At the railway station, when young York says his uncle Richard should bear him on his shoulders, he jumps on Richard's back and throws him to the platform, where Richard writhes in agony. This is a violent homage to Olivier, who had shown his naked hatred for a terrifying instant when York had taunted him about his lumpy back. We watch Richard's coronation and then, after a glimpse of Lady Anne's vacant face, see the same thing in black and white. It is as if Lady Anne were hallucinating until we realise that we are in the royal screening room as the royal party watches a newsreel. Later, we learn that Lady Anne is a heroin addict. We know that she is dead when a spider crawls over an unblinking eye.

The young princes play at war, one wielding a bi-plane above a toy locomotive, but the film provides no sense of Richard's 'playing', either as actor or as intellectual athlete. McKellen's Richard, as Terence Rafferty observed in the *New Yorker*, 'is a dull, efficient, affectless sort of monster'.[22] He was not much more than that in the stage version, but a fuller script permitted McKellen to suggest the concentric circles of institutionalised evil radiating outward from the still centre which his presence created. The effect was achieved because he stood alone on a vast stage, not surrounded by the busy 1930s *mise-en-scène* that Loncraine constructs.

As with other anachronistic productions of a Shakespeare script, we have in this film two plays competing against each other, with the Shakespeare script a distant runner-up. On stage (Rafferty noted) McKellen did not need Olivier's 'startling animal vitality'. On film, however, he needs Hitler's mesmerising presence. Another actor might bring that to Richard III; it is not inherent in the role. The Richard delivered from the womb of the *Henry VI* plays is no head of even a fascist party, but represents, as E. Pearlman says, a 'narrow and perverse individualism'.[23]

Richard Eyre's stage version was the imitation of an action. We watched the virtuoso performance of McKellen *and* Richard. On stage, McKellen, with one hand, extracted a cigarette from a silver case and lit it – a performance in itself. The closest he comes to this facility on film is to pull a ring from his hand with his teeth then place it on Anne's finger. On stage, McKellen accosted Lady Anne as she pursued the trolley on which Henry VI lay. His wooing was self-amused and convincing. On stage, McKellen could convince us of an ironic distance which the many close-ups in the film erase. In the film, the scene occurs in a white-tiled mortuary, as Anne mourns not Henry VI but Prince Edward, plugged through the head. Terrence Rafferty rightly complains that the sequence lacks an 'appalling magnetism . . . potent enough to win the grieving widow over. As the charmless McKellen and the wan Thomas play it, Anne's capitulation is wholly incomprehensible, not a breath of sexual passion is visible.'[24] Furthermore, McKellen seems to be playing the scene 'straight' in the film. Afterwards, as Ben Brantley observed in the New York Times, 'he waltzes through the casualty-cluttered corridors of a hospital to a jazzland beat, like the boy who has just won the girl in a 30s musical'.[25] On stage, as noted earlier, McKellen had a mourning band already in place as he entered the scene in which the others learn that Clarence is dead. That band predicted the fascist armbands to come. Buckingham threw his own armband on to the empty throne as he said, 'Made I him king for this?' In the film, Buckingham says the line just before his windpipe is slit. In Richard's stage dream, Lady Anne (Eve Matheson) danced briefly with Richmond (Colin Hurley) and Richard, suddenly desiring what he had cast away, felt a stab of sexual jealousy.[26] In the film, a sweating Richard hears angry voices from the past. The formal, stylised dream is discarded, one assumes, for something more psychologically plausible. (A surreal moment *does* come earlier when a boar-faced Richard embodies Stanley's dream, but that is an isolated effect that might better have tasted the cutting-room floor.) McKellen virtually throws the subsequent soliloquy away, sweating and mumbling. The style of this film can make nothing of an Augustinian anagnorisis, or moment of recognition. As Samuel Crowl suggests, when stage directors 'mount modern dress productions of Shakespeare . . . they do so by inviting our own imaginations to fill in the details their period suggests'. Loncraine's 'locations distract by rivaling, and often swallowing, the performances they contain'.[27] 'Modern' conceptions can also erase meanings still available to Shakespeare's early modern audiences, concepts like heaven and hell, that were still alive for many of them.

Al Pacino's Looking for Richard is a film about a film, a documentary which documents the issues and resistances involved in making a film of Richard III. The film of the play itself – the finished product that cuts in and out of the narrative of its making – would have made a solid entry among the many other Shakespeare films being produced in 1995–6. It is comparable in its setting and costuming with the Olivier version of 1955. It avoids the 'fake medievalism' of most productions of the play by going up to The Cloisters, the New York Metropolitan Museum's collection of medieval art, thereby gaining a kind of authenticity. The elegant artefacts of The Cloisters – golden chalices and reliquaries, and wafer boxes encrusted in jewels – are themselves metaphors for the play, in which religion serves as a cover for power politics. The particular 'fake medievalism' of the buildings and hallways of The Cloisters offers another metaphor. Within this fabricated world and in the chapels moved, stone by stone, from the old world, lies a long-dead reality, a 'sea of faith' like that imagined in Matthew Arnold's 'Dover Beach', that was once 'at the full' for much of the western world. Within Richard, under the bustling energy of his will to power, lies that ineradicable faith, waiting to slither past the lowered defences of a nightmare. It is *there*, a fragment of a human nature that belongs to the divine, and Richard cannot contradict it.

The McKellen–Loncraine modernised version of the script could not allow for that Augustinian moment when Richard awakens to the truth that is down there within him, a coding of the cosmic imperative at which he has sneered as he played with it and used it to doom others. An irony of Pacino's film is that he gives us so many worlds that we can believe in one that does not exist for most of us any more, that world in which speaks the voice of the archetype, of conscience, of a living God deep within and surrounding the secular mind. It is remarkable that a relentlessly modern and artfully 'random' film could remind us 'of a vast struggle of absolute good and absolute evil in the cosmos, one in which every event in human life has divine meaning and cause', as David Bevington says of the world of *Richard III*.[28]

We forget, but Pacino does not, that Shakespeare often frames his plays. Framing is central to Stoppard's wonderful *Rosencrantz and Guildenstern Are Dead*. Pacino's frame is contrived to seem more casual, but it is 'Shakespearean', showing us as do frames elsewhere in Shakespeare the inner art for what it is, and proving that it is capable of being invaded and of escaping its frame. Janet Maslin misses the point when she says in her *New York Times* review that Pacino 'manages to keep this *Richard III* furiously alive despite his film's frequent interruptions'.[29] The interruptions are what give life to the costumed segments, to the film being produced within the film. The interruptions are the search, implied in the film's title. Pacino frames the inner production with one of the oldest of the archetypes. It reaches back to the *Odyssey* and the Grail and *Don Quixote* and comes forward through Gatsby and the Joads and Jack Kerouac.

Loncraine's 1930s said nothing to the script, nor did the script inform that time of impending doom. And thus the film says nothing to us. It is a film about recreating a glittering art deco surface. Pacino does get back to the play's premises. He holds one culture up to another until gradually an infinite regress develops. We bounce down the hall of mirrors to that place where souls were

things immortal and destined to spend eternity in some place other than obliv-
ion. Watching an actor develop a character suddenly makes the character 'real',
partly because the struggle of the actor is real. The character sweats too, more
than vicariously. We observe the actor's craft *creating* character, as if a camera
dissolving from one plane of being to another – from human face to werewolf,
from Jekyll to Hyde, from Pacino to Richard.

If Richard is surprised by what finds him on that dark dawn before the Battle
of Bosworth Field, Pacino surprises himself in his own search for Richard. What
do we find when we look at the film? The play is about an 'actor-manager' whose
theatre turns out to be just a bit larger than he thought – it includes a cosmic
dimension that communicates with him, as the cosmic dimension is wont to do,
upon an emergent occasion. Pacino, the impresario of a project that may or may
not work out as he records the project, gets back there by reflecting the old script
against a gritty New York City – pigeon droppings in all the corners – showing
that any production must account for the dimensions around it, any actor must,
any director must. If all of that is taken into account – the old church with the
playground in front of it, the ignorance and the intelligence of the intended audience, the debates in which the actors engage as they read the script, the ways in
which the script has to be translated into a modern idiom before the reasons for
Shakespeare's words become apparent, the script itself may come in to view. If
so, it will emerge in a context that allows it to make sense – of itself, of the
context and of the relationships between script and context that are the meanings communicated by any production of Shakespeare, that is, unless the play is
hidden from its audience behind layers of velvet diction and reverence. Here, the
finished production – the goal – is a function of the process. The film, the story
surrounding the final *inner* film, becomes its own artefact. The effect is of a film
looking in upon a play and also a play looking out upon the ways in which it has
come into being.

There is nothing cosmic about New York – except in the ways that size itself
has become its own religious system – but it is there and Pacino accounts for it.
Richard fails to account for the outer circle of his own existence. *Richard III* is
the most medieval of Shakespeare's scripts, with the possible exception of
Macbeth, which, after the Gunpowder Plot, must be framed so that the murder
of a king becomes a crime against God and His scheme of things. For Richard
and Macbeth, as the latter is well aware, that outer circle is also the core of his
being. This is Augustine and Saint Bernard. The film, at times weirdly, almost
always wonderfully, reflects the methods of its creation against the script so as
to illuminate the heart of the script as well. The Loncraine film does not come
close. Pacino could have gone further, had he wished. We can imagine the voice
of a guide telling us that The Bonnefont Cloister was originally a Cistercian
abbey, built to house an ascetic monastic order that shunned any decoration that

might distract from the worship of God. The film makes Richard just another politician by showing Kevin Spacey (who plays Buckingham) campaigning for Shakespeare with a New York crowd in a city park, a modern analogue to Buckingham's plea to the London citizenry on behalf of Richard.

Pacino's technique is to keep building areas of activity that can then become points of reference. Few films are so self-allusive as this. Pacino establishes rehearsals for his production of *Richard III*. He cuts back and forth from Richard's opening soliloquy to a discussion of what it means. He establishes the performance itself, a costumed drama amid the arches and against the tapestries of The Cloisters. He and his director walk the streets around Times Square, interrogating the sidewalkers and panhandlers of New York. The effort to make the film also incorporates a seeking after an elusive 'Shakespeare'. Who is he, or it, to the people amid the horns and police whistles? Will the film be made? One Italian man, claiming ignorance of Shakespeare, leaves Pacino at a 'Walk' sign, saying 'To be or not to be, that is the question!' The line suddenly absorbs meaning from its context. When a panhandler talks about Shakespeare and *feeling*, we suddenly pick up on Pacino's leaving in so many lines from the play about 'a giving vein' and about begging: 'impotent and snail-pac'd beggary', 'the famish'd beggars, weary of their bones'.

Once Pacino's technique is established and once we have been educated to it, all the worlds of the film became available as points of reference. Two Richards – one an actor in rehearsal on the floor of The Cloisters and another sweating in the dawn before death of life and soul, in a close-up and in a side-shot as if lying in state – can alternate in reading the lines. This is a brilliant way of suggesting the split that the character perceives within himself, monarch versus truth-speaking jester, as well as the technique that goes into making a character who runs into the ranks of inalterable law deeper than his consummate skills. Richard's dream looks ahead to his battle, as the film incorporates brief glimpses of its own future in creating the shattered imagery of nightmare. The soliloquy is turned into a dramatic film. Clarence, about to be smothered in a belfry, flashes back *within* the crafted drama to the moment of Richard's pious hopes for his brother's freedom. Performance itself has convinced him, and performance, including his own – that of the actor playing Clarence – comes back to remind him of and mock him with his earlier credulity. Too late, he literally glimpses Richard's duplicity.

The production within the film does work. A wonderful moment comes when Richard says, 'What though I kill'd her husband and her father?' The line is accompanied by that most practised and instinctive of movements, the New York shrug. Anne, alone, bereft of her husband, and burying her father-in-law, buys into Richard's sexuality. The subtext is absolutely convincing. The camera catches the exchange between Richard and Anne in a series of dissolves. It then cuts from one to the other. Then they are in the same frame. The camera, then, simulates the process of initial emotional distance and of a gradual physical coming together. The film demonstrates that, although the camera moves very quickly, the words – which *must* move quickly on stage – do not have to pursue the rhythms of the camera. The film can circle the words with their emotional emphasis. It can watch faces and create weight within a demonstration of the rapidity of language and the slower development of insight. Here, as later with Kevin Spacey's hesitant Buckingham, the relative lack of rehearsal creates a tentativeness that is itself convincing. Alec Baldwin's Clarence is splendid as he pleads with the Murderers.

In Olivier's film the actor-director's glittering Richard generates a lot of sexuality, but Claire Bloom's wan Anne surrenders without a struggle. Most of her lines are cut. The scene in the Loncraine film, conducted in a white-tiled mortuary, 'works' because the scripted lines tell us it does. One area that does not work for Pacino is the substitution of 'C' for 'G' in the prophecy that gets George Clarence locked up. 'G' also stands for 'Gloucester', of course, among Edward's relatives. (Where were Pacino's college professors on *that* one?) A neat reference within the inner production links Elizabeth's silver hair, as her face grieves on top of the dead Edward, and the coins placed in his dead eyes. The scene in which Hastings is condemned is powerful, dominated by Kevin Conway's dignified Hastings. Pacino identifies the heart of the scene and generously cedes it from Richard to Hastings. The film cuts back and forth between Richard's speech to his troops, which sneers at the enemy they are about to face, and Richmond's prayer. This approach provides a vivid contrast between the two. As Richard says 'vomit forth', the camera cuts to a clean-cut Richmond and his 'watchful soul'. He is no 'milksop', though we see his face as Richard labels him and his army thus.

The film undercuts itself with its own ironies. The title, 'King Richard', becomes 'Looking for Richard', so that we are told immediately that the film incorporates at least two worlds, each one searching for the other. The goal, we are told is to establish a relationship between the old play and 'how we feel and how we think today'. The costumes for the inner film – the *Richard* being sought – were borrowed from New York's Public Theater, a fact that would have pleased Joseph Papp, himself so deeply engaged in bringing Shakespeare and city together. As Pacino sings 'he's got the whole world in his hands' the camera cuts to the Globe replica on Bankside. As Pacino glances at the script of *Richard the Third*, he says, 'It's good to open it up and know it's not *Hamlet.*' As he discusses his research into the play he holds up the *Cliff's Notes*. As Queen Elizabeth worries about her young prince – 'He is young!' – an unscripted siren sounds along the canyon floor below the rehearsal room. Later, as Pacino and Kimball look at the bed on which Shakespeare was born, a smoke detector goes off. It is a synecdoche for Kimball's disappointment at not having arrived with the Wise

Men at the manger. 'Shakespeare' appears early, sitting on a bench in what looks like the small theatre in the Bear Gardens Museum, which later holds a group of mocking students refusing to even begin to answer questions – every teacher's nightmare. Towards the end, 'Shakespeare' smiles scornfully at Pacino, as if to say, no, that's not what I meant at all. By this time, though, the film, like any script of Shakespeare's, has been out there finding its own meanings. At moments here we cannot be sure exactly which of his worlds Pacino is showing us. The princes, for example, wave from the Tower, which is also an upper porch of The Cloisters, little boys doomed by power politics and the children of tourists in a home video to be shown later in Scarsdale.

The final battle finds Pacino's Richard talking about his horse too much, as if the line were a mantra. I had hoped that the distant view of the horse on a hillside would stand as a metonym for the line. The earlier parts of the battle had been shot through a red filter, which created a powerful quasi-documentary effect. Queen Elizabeth and Richard's other victims, usefully saved from his nightmare, stand on a hillside. 'See – they're deserting him!' she cries. Richard is plugged by a couple of arrows, though avoiding the pincushion fate of Washizu in Kurosawa's *Throne of Blood*. The scene is redeemed when producer Michael Hadge says, 'If he knew we had another ten rolls of film, he'd want to use it.' The camera cuts to the open left eye of Pacino/Richard lying there in the grass. Suddenly it is Pacino at once indicting his film editor and pondering that unused footage. Just in case that final battle is too fakily medieval – as it is – it is under-cut at the last moment by a reminder of the process that had created it. Richard then 'dies' on a doorstep in the city in the arms of co-director Kimball, who says, 'We can rest.' The search is completed. The 'story', says Margo Jefferson, is 'of hardy, ambitious Americans who take on a powerful Old World and come out winners' – a revenge for Newman, Isabel Archer, Strether and other Americans of Henry James.[30] These Americans come out winners and still give us a hint of their insecurity at the end by providing us a laugh at the expense of the 'victory' within the frame.

The film, fortunately, does not bow down too reverently before the so-called Bard. We get lines from *Twelfth Night*, *Hamlet* and – at beginning and end – from Prospero ('leave not a *wisp* behind'). Perhaps there is too much deference to British actors and to academics both British and American, though the talking heads seem to be undercut by the irony of juxtaposed scenes and, at times, by their own self-mockery.

The film is about the tense business of making a film. How to make a film of a play becomes a deconstruction of the inherited script. The tension gets released into the inner production, which then dissolves back into the issues of making it, even the issue of whether it can or should be made. (To be or not to be?) Fortunately, good as the inner production is, the production surrounding it becomes much more than the sum of its parts. The parts comment on each other, directly and in our own imaginative fusing of the montage. Technique becomes meaning. We see that clearly when Pacino and his director discuss a site for Clarence's murder. The director verbalises it splendidly. But it is the wrong physical site, and words won't make up for that. The demonstration of a wrong choice here and there shows us how many right choices this wonderful film has made.

A Guide created to accompany Pacino's film suggests that 'You and your students may want to read *Richard III* by William Shakespeare in conjunction with viewing the film *Looking for Richard*.'[31] Once upon a time, such a statement would have enraged most teachers. Once upon a time, the film might have been used as a visual aid in conjunction with reading the play. In our post-modernist world, cultural artefacts have cut adrift from their sources. It is also true, though, that films are 'out there' fighting their own battles and achieving an identity of their own.

NOTES

On the Richard Eyre stage production, see my '*Richard III*: Large and Small', in *Reading Shakespeare on Stage* (Newark, DE, 1995), pp. 232–40. I am grateful to Marion O'Connor for an incisive critique of my response to the Loncraine/McKellen film.

1 Anthony Davies, *Filming Shakespeare's Plays* (Cambridge, 1988), p. 66.
2 Peter Holland, 'Hand in Hand to Hell', *Times Literary Supplement* (10 May 1996).
3 Jack J. Jorgens, *Shakespeare on Film* (Bloomington, IN, 1977), pp. 136; p. 144.
4 E. Pearlman, 'The Invention of Richard of Gloucester', *Shakespeare Quarterly*, 43/4 (Winter 1992), 410–29; p. 411.
5 Constance Brown, 'Olivier's *Richard III*: a Revaluation', in Charles W. Eckert, ed., *Focus on Shakespearean Film* (Englewood Cliffs, NJ, 1972), pp. 131–46; p. 136.
6 Jorgens, *Shakespeare on Film*, pp. 143; 142.
7 The Augustinian concept of the 'magister interior'. See Etienne Gibson, *The Spirit of Medieval Philosophy* (New York, 1936).
8 Alice Griffin, 'Shakespeare through the Camera's Eye', *Shakespeare Quarterly*, 7 (1956), 235–6; p. 236; Virginia Graham, review in the *Spectator* (16 December 1956).
9 Richard Corliss, *Time* (15 January 1996).
10 Holland, 'Hand in Hand to Hell'.
11 Stephen Holden, *New York Times* (29 December 1995).
12 Samuel Crowl, '*Richard III*', *Shakespeare Bulletin*, 14/2 (1996), 38.
13 Holden, *New York Times*.
14 Adolf Hitler, *Mein Kampf* (English translation) (Boston, MA, 1971), p. 313.
15 Aryeh L. Unger, *The Totalitarian Party: Party and People in Nazi Germany and Soviet Russia* (Cambridge, 1974), p. 34.
16 Jorgens, *Shakespeare on Film*, pp. 142–3.
17 Robert G. L. Waite, *The Psychopathic God: Adolf Hitler* (New York, 1977), pp. 13–15.
18 *Ibid.*, p. 89.
19 Kenneth Tynan, 'Sir Laurence's Richard', *New York Times* (21 August 1966).

20 John Gray, 'Defining Evil', *New York Times Book Review* (25 February 1996), p. 14.
21 David Schoenbaum, 'Out of Nowhere', *New York Times Book Review* (22 December 1996), p. 17.
22 Terence Rafferty, *New Yorker* (22 January 1996).
23 Pearlman, 'The Invention of Richard of Gloucester', p. 429.
24 Rafferty, *New Yorker*.
25 Ben Brantley, *New York Times* (21 January 1996).
26 See my '*Richard III*: Large and Small', pp. 232–40.
27 Crowl, '*Richard III*', p. 38.
28 David Bevington, ed., *The Complete Works of William Shakespeare* (Glenview, IL, 1980), p. 670.
29 Janet Maslin, *New York Times* (11 October 1996).
30 Margo Jefferson, 'Welcoming Shakespeare into the Caliban Family', *New York Times* (12 November 1996).
31 Roberta Nusim, *Study Guide to 'Looking for Richard'* (New York, 1996), p. 2.

7

J. LAWRENCE GUNTNER

Hamlet, *Macbeth* and *King Lear* on film

Ask the man on the street what comes to mind when you mention 'Shakespeare', and the chances are that he will reply, 'to be, or not to be'. We have come to associate Shakespeare with tragedy, especially with *Hamlet*, and in fact the first century of Shakespeare on film began with *Hamlet*, in the form of a five-minute film directed by Maurice Clément and shown at the Paris Exhibition in 1900. It starred Sarah Bernhardt as Hamlet and Pierre Magnier as Laertes. The predominance of the tragedies on screen until 1990 is confirmed by Kenneth Rothwell's and Annabelle Melzer's definitive filmography and videography that lists 184 entries for *Hamlet*, *Macbeth* and *King Lear*, i.e. 27 per cent of the total entries, even though they comprise only 8 per cent of Shakespeare's work.[1] Not surprisingly the film adaptations of the tragedies have received the most attention from (predominantly male) film critics as well. How and why Shakespearean tragedy on film has been able to transcend the temporal, national, ideological and cultural boundaries of Elizabethan England, even without Shakespeare's language, will be the question I am going to pursue.[2]

'Who's there?': the question of Fortinbras

Hamlet opens with a question, 'Who's there?' and by the the time the play has ended, more questions have been raised than answered. The opening question also points to the end of the play when Fortinbras enters to clear the stage of carnage and assume the throne as Hamlet's successor. It suggests that there is a circularity in the play and that Fortinbras may have been more important to Shakespeare than he has been to some directors.[3] Among Hamlet's final words are: 'Fortinbras; he has my dying voice' (5.2.308), and a central question to any production of the play, on the stage or on the screen, is whether to include Fortinbras and what he stands for. To cut Fortinbras, as Laurence Olivier (1948) and Franco Zeffirelli (1990) do in their film adaptations of *Hamlet*, shortens a lengthy play but amputates an important 'political' element. Svend Gade, Grigori Kozintsev and Kenneth Branagh leave him in as a central figure; in fact,

Branagh even foregrounds the presence of Fortinbras and the danger of war via cross-cutting and inserting extra visual material. It is on the character of Fortinbras that the 'politics' of *Hamlet* hinge.[4]

In *Hamlet, the Drama of Vengeance* (1920), directed in Germany by Svend Gade and Heinz Schall, with Asta Nielsen as the protagonist, Fortinbras appears three times: as Hamlet's student friend in Wittenberg, as the befriender of the exiled Hamlet who follows Hamlet to Elsinore to aid him in his revenge against Claudius, and as Hamlet's successor, who mourns and presides over the funeral procession. In 1920 the depiction of Fortinbras and Hamlet as reconciled sons of hostile fathers stems from the wish for reconciliation between the youth of Europe after the senseless slaughter of World War I. It is a decidedly political message speaking to the collective mentality of its German audience.[5] Nielsen's Hamlet is more than a cross-dressed Hamlet; it is the story of the daughter who is forced to conceal her female identity for reasons of *Realpolitik* – that is, for lack of a male heir. The scholarly justification for this reading of the play was found in Edward P. Vining's *The Mystery of Hamlet* (1881), translated into German in 1883. Vining suggested that the 'mystery' of Hamlet lay in the fact that 'he' was in reality a woman in disguise. This radical wrenching of Shakespeare's text to fit the circumstances of Germany's favourite starlet playing Germany's favourite male protagonist (and the audience came to see Nielsen as much as to see Shakespeare), this readiness of a relatively young medium of mass, or 'low' culture, to reshape an icon of 'high' culture to its own needs, is an example of the cinema's new self-confidence.

The Gade/Nielsen *Hamlet* established a number of conventions still alive in the genre of *Hamlet* on film: an androgynous, understated, sometimes comic Hamlet; a visual code that counterpoints indoor and outdoor scenes; a lengthy funeral procession at the close of the film; a radical reworking of Shakespeare's text; the use of conventions from contemporary film genres (in this case the scenography and lighting of Expressionism); and the casting of an established star as the prince to insure a financial return. It is the first truly successful adaptation of Shakespeare to the screen rather than a film of a theatre performance. Nielsen's recipe for success would be the key for later films: a box office star, the use of current and familiar film conventions and codes to visually frame Shakespeare's story.[6]

Laurence Olivier's 'essay' in *Hamlet*, as he himself calls it in the *The Film HAMLET* (edited by Brenda Cross and published in 1948), is probably the most influential Shakespeare film and Hamlet portrayal of the twentieth century. Together with Alan Dent, Olivier radically cut the text (by about one half), omitting whole scenes and even important characters (notably Rosencrantz, Guildenstern and Fortinbras). Although the omission of Fortinbras as well as Rosencrantz and Guildenstern excises a strong political element from the play,

Olivier's decision was in line with the dominant political opinion of the day, i.e. that the rise of fascism, World War II and the horrors of the Holocaust, were due to delayed political action on the part of France, Great Britain and the United States. By cutting Fortinbras and coding the visual strategy of the film as he does, Olivier suggests that this is a circular pattern of history doomed to be repeated if we do not act against injustice.

The film opens with a shot of waves pounding against a rocky shore, above which a castle stands, enclosed by swirling mists. From a bird's eye perspective the camera boom moves slowly in on the ramparts of High Tor encased in fog, while Olivier recites in voice-over: 'So, oft it chances in particular men, / That for some vicious mole of nature in them, / . . . Carrying, I say, the stamp of one defect . . . His virtues else, be they as pure as grace . . . Shall in the general censure take corruption, / From that particular fault' (Quarto lines preceding the ghost's appearance in Act I scene 4). Hamlet's reverie ends abruptly with Olivier's stern voice-over: 'This is the tragedy of a man who could not make up his mind.' With a long pan from above, the camera boom closes in on the ramparts until we discern a tableau of four solitary guardsmen keeping watch over a dead body. (In fact, Olivier claimed in *The Film* HAMLET, his vision of the entire film developed from his vision of this shot.) This establishes the atmosphere in Hamlet's private microcosm and stakes out the visual narrative strategy for the rest of the film. It is also the final shot of the film, suggesting that the cyclical nature of the story we have just seen, in which all actions are merely symbolic, is determined by menacing forces beyond Hamlet's (or our) control.

The debt to German Expressionist film techniques is obvious: the omnipresent stairs, empty hallways and corridors, the light and shadow dramaturgy of the lighting (emphasised by Olivier's choice of black and white film), the dazzling camera angles that often suggest everyone is being watched by someone or something else. Less obvious is Olivier's debt to *film noir*, the creation of emigrant German Expressionist directors in Hollywood: Hamlet the alienated sleuth in the tradition of Raymond Chandler's Philip Marlowe or Dashiell Hammet's Sam Spade.[7] This alienation is expressed visually through his use of deep-focus photography to emphasise Hamlet's feelings of powerlessness confronted with an overbearing environment. Roger Furse's cavernous sets correspond to the shadowy labyrinths of Hamlet's psyche and remind the viewer that Denmark is a prison, not only of the mind. The parameters of this prison are the High Tor where Hamlet must confront the Ghost of his father, and Great Hall, the arena into which he must descend to do battle with Claudius, his uncle, stepfather and father's murderer. In between are seemingly endless dark hallways and twisting stairways. The camera prowls with Hamlet, and the viewer with him, through seemingly endless corridors in search of 'who is there', ascending and descending steep and winding stairs, often preceded by a shadow that symbolises danger.

The stairs serve as bridges between appearance and reality, normalcy and the abyss of the human soul, the conscious and the subconscious, and they provide acting space for the agile Olivier. Hamlet climbs stairs to the ramparts to meet the Ghost, to his mother's closet to confront her conscience, and to the top of Great Hall from which he will spring, like an avenging angel, on to Claudius, thrusting his sword into him again and again.

It is above all the camera work that informs the inimitable style of this *Hamlet* film: deep-focus, the dazzling camera angles and the meandering camera that accompanies Hamlet on his search for his Self. The ever-changing camera perspective mirrors Hamlet's frame of mind and links it to his environment. The shifting point of view reminds the viewer that fixed points of view are impossible in a constantly changing world. On its wanderings through the castle, the camera takes us past the symbolic props: the oversized bed, the empty throne, the ever-changing columned hall, that remind Hamlet of his mother's incest and his repulsion at it, his delayed succession and his enforced separation from his beloved Ophelia.

From the opening credits over classical Greek masks for comedy and tragedy to Horatio's final command: 'Let four captains, / Bear Hamlet like a soldier to the stage', Olivier continually reminds us that we are watching a play and that the world is actually a stage. All entrances are carefully orchestrated: characters stand framed in a doorway (the opening of the 'nunnery scene') or descend a stairway to use a gallery as a platform (in the 'fishmonger scene'), or a sequence ends with a wipe or fade-out to suggest a curtain. Yet despite his insistence on its roots in the theatre, Olivier has succeeded not only in adapting Shakespeare to the screen but the screen to Shakespeare.

Olivier's film of *Hamlet* is psychoanalytic and personal.[8] That of Grigori Kozintsev (1964) is political and public. The critique of this Soviet film is directed at both Stalinism and 'Hamletism', the pose of alienated intellectuals under totalitarian regimes: both the translator of the text, Boris Pasternak, and the actor playing Hamlet, Innokenti Smoktunovski, had bitter experience of Stalin's regime. The central theme, 'Denmark is a prison', is embodied by the huge and threatening castle with its brooding rooms and gloomy corridors. However, the furnishings are luxurious and life there is comfortable, even though oppressive for a sensitive man of ideas.[9] Again and again the camera peers through screens, bars and grates. Ophelia, unable to dance because an iron farthingale is encasing her body, becomes an emblem for the fate of the sensitive and intelligent in this environment. Except for his journey to England, Hamlet will leave the castle only as a corpse. As with Olivier, the end recalls the beginning. In the opening sequence the hooves of Hamlet's horse thunder across the wooden drawbridge, and the massive portcullis is slowly lowered and locked behind him. In the final sequence Fortinbras stomps across the same bridge to succeed Claudius in the exercise of power. Like Olivier's Elsinore, Kozintsev's Elsinore is full of stairways and halls, but whereas Olivier's stairways are narrow, private spaces for personal encounter, Kozintsev's are broad public avenues populated by courtiers and ambassadors. Kozintsev and Pasternak virtually rewrite the text, cutting even more than Olivier, and Kozintsev's camera is more mobile, panning and zooming, yet the average length of the shots (twenty-four seconds) allows the viewers to note the careful *mise-en-scène* of each frame. Olivier's shifting camera perspectives and his penchant for the high-angle shot reflect Hamlet's frame of mind, while Kozintsev's shifting compositions reflect the complexity of historical reality. Olivier's film mirrors Hamlet's psychological and emotional isolation, but Kozintsev shows us his political alienation. Olivier places Hamlet in an abstract, symbolic environment, but Kozintsev situates him in a realistic environment, authentic down to minute details. Examples of this are his alternating long and medium tracking shots of Fortinbras's army on its way to Poland or the scenes with the common people, replete with rubbish and cackling chickens. It is from the people that Hamlet has come and to them he will return, but the people are oblivious to him; what counts in the end are the unrelenting forces of nature: earth, stone, water, fire. Walton's musical score is subordinated to Olivier's visual imagery, but Dimitri Shostakovich's score counterpoints, highlights and comments on the action itself, transforming each shot into a microcosmic *Gesamtkunsterk*, a unified work of art in image and sound. Hamlet's final words are 'the rest is silence', as he points along the granite wall of the castle with his arm outstreched towards the approaching Fortinbras. There is nothing more to say, the action has now come full circle and can begin again.

Franco Zeffirelli's *Hamlet* (1990) is a *Hamlet* of and for the 1980s. It pairs Mel Gibson, the suicidally inclined action hero from Richard Donner's *Lethal Weapon* (1987), as Hamlet, and Glenn Close, the threatening 'other woman' from Adrian Lyne's *Fatal Attraction* (1987) as Gertrude, with such first-rate stage actors as Alan Bates (Claudius), Paul Scofield (Ghost), Ian Holm (Polonius) and Helena Bonham-Carter (Ophelia). It is indebted to Olivier in, for example, its strong emphasis on the incestuous attraction of Gertrude to Hamlet, its omission of Fortinbras and the final high-level shot of the dead Hamlet, as well as to the narrative conventions and shooting style of 1980s Hollywood action films which made Gibson an international star. Like Olivier, Zeffirelli simplifies Shakespeare's script, but unlike Olivier, he breaks down longer speeches and scenes into bits and pieces. He interrupts longer dialogues and soliloquies with reaction shots between the actors or between actor and audience, which detracts from Shakespeare's spoken language and highlights the sense of directorial control. Unlike Olivier and Kozintsev, Zeffirelli's camera remains relatively stable but his shots are shorter than any other director's (an average of less than six seconds). The first court scene (1.2.1–126) is divided between four locations. It begins in the state hall where Claudius announces that he has 'taken [Gertrude] to wife', cuts first to the library where Claudius enquires about the plans of Laertes, then to Gertrude and Claudius frolicking on the steps of the castle and finally to a darkened room where Gertrude and Claudius try to console the bereaved Hamlet.

Gibson as Hamlet is less frequently seen than any other screen Hamlets. Instead, Zeffirelli focuses his camera often on Glenn Close as a sexually attractive and active Gertrude involved with three different men. Her proximity in age to her son foregrounds the incest theme, especially in the closet scene where the explicit motions of Hamlet with his mother on her bed and Gertrude's passionate kiss of her son leave little to our post-Freudian imagination. Zeffirelli's *Hamlet* tries to match Hollywood and Stratford, and the outcome is a film that has received uneven criticism, yet remains popular with young viewers.[10]

Kenneth Branagh's lavish colour production (1996), filmed in the 'epic' 70mm format, is a *Hamlet* for the approaching millennium. It pays homage to those living actors and actresses who have shaped our perception of Shakespeare on the stage and screen in the twentieth century, and exorcises the spectre of Laurence Olivier, mentor, actor, film-maker, for the twenty-first century. The film begins with a close-up of the name 'HAMLET' chiselled in a stone block. Later we discover it is the pedestal of a huge monument to Old Hamlet in front of Elsinore (Blenheim Palace) that will be systematically demolished as the film ends. Branagh pays his dues to Olivier, plays with him, quotes him and finally deconstructs him while having a good time in the process.

In the tradition of Olivier and Smoktunovski, Hamlet is blond-haired, and like Olivier and Kozintsev, Branagh keeps his camera in perpetual motion, tracking, panning, craning, zooming in and out, and circling only to rest in close-up on such details as the liquid blue eyes of the Ghost (Brian Blessed). Having learned from Olivier, he does not interrupt long soliloquies but begins with a close-up and moves up and away with the crane to emphasise Hamlet's isolation. In Act 4 scene 4, he begins 'How all occasions do inform against me / And spur my dull revenge' by addressing the camera, and the viewer, directly. The camera slowly pulls up and back to reveal Hamlet as a tiny, isolated figure on an icy plain across which Fortinbras's men march off to Poland. But here the similarities end.

Unlike Olivier, Branagh gives us a 'full-text' version of the play from the Folio and supplements it when necessary with passages from the Second Quarto.[11] The result is a film that takes four hours to watch, a film for Shakespeare devotees and English teachers as much as – or more than – the man on the street. Branagh leaves in every character, even foregrounding Fortinbras through cross-cutting. Throughout the film he seems to be marching relentlessly across the frozen Danish plain towards Elsinore, like the Bolsheviks storming the Winter Palace (there is an air of David Lean's *Doctor Zhivago* about the film, intensified by the casting of Julie Christie, Zhivago's Lara, as Gertrude). This is a decidedly 'polit-ical' *Hamlet* located in the Europe of the nineteenth century: inside it is warm, colourful, classical Denmark, but outside it is cold, grey England. Branagh sup-presses any psychologising, Freudian overtones, or suggestions of an incestuous attraction to Gertrude. Julie Christie is an attractive, middle-aged queen, yet Hamlet's passion is clearly for Ophelia (Kate Winslet), whose nights of love with a California-tanned Hamlet are explicitly visualised for the audience via two flashbacks. Whereas Olivier chose his cast from non-celebrities who would not detract from his own performance, Branagh picked an ensemble of heavyweights from screen and the Shakespearean stage and from both sides of the Atlantic (Derek Jacobi, Julie Christie, Charlton Heston, Kate Winslet, Billy Crystal, Jack Lemmon, Robin Williams, Judi Dench, Rosemary Harris, and even Richard Attenborough as the English Ambassador and John Gielgud as Priam). He seems to direct his camera at least as frequently at Derek Jacobi as Claudius as at himself as Hamlet. When Hamlet delivers his 'To be, or not to be' soliloquy to a mirror, we later discover that it is the two-way mirror behind which Claudius and Polonius (Richard Briers) have been standing. Thus, Hamlet (Branagh) is holding a mirror up, not only to himself but also to Claudius (Jacobi) whom he resembles closely down to his blond-dyed hair. It is an uneven film but never dull and would profit from abbreviation. It brings to a close nearly a century of Hamlet on film that began with Sarah Bernhardt, and had she still been alive, Branagh certainly would have found a role for her in his film as well.[12]

Michael Almereyda's *Hamlet* is an American *Hamlet* for the twenty-first century. It features a complete cast of actors better known for their performances on American movie and television screens than on the stage: Ethan Hawke (Hamlet), Bill Murray (Polonius), Kyle McLachlan (Claudius), Diane Venora (Gertrude), Sam Shepard (Ghost), and they recite Shakespeare's blank verse as flatly and unpretentiously as if *Hamlet* were a television sitcom or *Saturday Night Live*. This Hamlet is young (Hawke was twenty-seven when production began), 'a bright young man struggling with his identity, his moral code, his rela-tionship to his parents and to his entire surrounding community'.[13] His roots are not in a British Hamlet tradition stretching from Olivier and Gielgud to Jacobi and Branagh, a tradition of actors in their prime, but in 'Generation X' and the alienated icons of American popular culture: Kurt Cobain, James Dean and Holden Caulfield.

Almereyda sets the film in downtown Manhattan, symbol of globalised cor-porate capitalism. The centre of power resides no longer in the British Empire, nor in the Danish royal court. Claudius is not King but CEO of the Denmark Corporation; he occupies not a throne but a chair as head of the board, and Elsinore is not a castle but a glossy high-rise hotel. Hamlet is faced by a world of corporate anonymity in which brand names, logos and surfaces prevail. Human communication, experience and interaction – the human voice itself – have been replaced by video technology, monitors, pixelvision cameras, walkmen, floppy disks and telephone answering machines. Where Branagh puts all the words on the screen, Almereyda leaves them out (this *Hamlet* is 112 minutes long, over two hours shorter than Branagh's).[14] Yet, despite post-modernised setting and costumes and all of the attention paid to contemporary media virtuosity, Almereyda retains Shakespeare's Elizabethan English and its anachronistic frame of reference: Claudius is referred to as 'the King', Hamlet studies in 'Wittenberg' and is told 'the bark is ready and the wind at help' before boarding an airliner to England, while Ophelia passes out 'rosemary', 'pansies', 'fennel' and 'columbines' in the form of Polaroid snapshots. Where Branagh strives for completeness, Almereyda, like Welles, prefers 'a rough charcoal sketch' (albeit in Technicolor).[15] And like Welles, Almereyda uses media techniques self-consciously to dislocate the film's historical reference.[16] He directs the focus of the film away from the character of the protagonist and his historical mission and onto Hamlet's feelings of entrapment in a featureless, post-modern land-scape of 'hard surfaces, mirrors, screens and signs'[17] straight out of *film noir* : dark, towering buildings, sinister black limousines, glassed-in penthouse rooms and hotel elevators.[18]

In this world, human communication is constantly mediated and monitored via technology. Hamlet interrupts his admonition to Ophelia to 'get thee to a nunnery' and finishes it via an answering machine. He berates his mother from a pay phone in the basement of the hotel where he has 'lugged the guts' of the dead Polonius, and even the Ghost of his father appears for the first time on the monitor of the CCTV–video surveillance system. His complaint that he is 'for the day confined to fast in fires', is accompanied by footage from the Gulf War on a television monitor in Hamlet's bedroom. As Almereyda himself remarks: 'images currently keep pace with words, or outstrip them, creating a kind of overwhelming alternate reality. So nearly every scene features a photograph, a TV monitor, an electronic recording device of some kind.'[19] While Hamlet stalks the aisles of a Blockbuster video shop, stocked significantly with action films, reciting lines from the 'To be, or not to be' soliloquy, the fiery climax from Tim Pope's *The Crow II: City of Angels* (1996) is playing in the background on the overhead monitor.

Shortly before that Almereyda interpolates a video clip in which the Vietnamese Buddhist monk Thich Nhat Hanh, a preacher of non-violence, pro-poses that the verb 'to be' should be replaced by 'inter-be'. The text is vital to Hamlet's dilemma: 'it is not possible to be alone. To be yourself. You need other people in order to be . . . father, mother . . . uncle, brother, sister, society . . . therefore to be means to interbe.'[20] Yet, the very same media technology that mis-represents both past and present simultaneously empowers Hamlet to break out of the confinement of the present and, with his pixelvision camera, retrieve and make sense out of the past, be it in his film *The Mousetrap* or in his personal videos of Ophelia.[21] As Katherine Rowe remarks: 'For Almereyda's Hamlet, the personal video is *the* technology of interiority . . . . What Hamlet seeks in his videos is not history but a connection between collective experience and his own loss.'[22]

In the end even death is mediated by electronic technology, e.g. Hamlet re-types Claudius's command that he be put to death upon arrival in England in a Word document in Rosencrantz and Guildenstern's Notebook, and electronic devices keep track of the hits in the final deadly duel. In the end, neither Hamlet nor Fortinbras has the final word – instead Robin MacNeil, a retired newscaster. Fortinbras's face can be seen on the background monitor, but MacNeil speaks Fortinbras's words: 'This quarry cries on havoc, O proud death, / What feast is toward in thine eternal cell, / That thou so many princes at a shot / So bloodily hast struck?' Then he adds the first line of the First Ambassador's comment: 'The sight is dismal.' MacNeil's final words are from the Player King in Shakespeare's *The Mousetrap*: 'Our wills and fates do so contrary run / That our devices still are overthrown; / Our thoughts are ours, their ends none of our own.' Even these words are mediated by a teleprompter, a fitting final image for a film that fore-grounds how the media is a questionable means of representing history or con-structing subjectivity.

Macbeth: of kings, castles and witches

Macbeth is Shakespeare's most straightforwardly political play. It celebrates Stuart absolutism in the person of Duncan, warns against its deposition in the person of Macbeth and confirms its cyclical renewal in Malcolm.[23] Shakespeare's *Macbeth* was a timely play. James was troubled about his succession, so Shakespeare staged his direct descent from Banquo. Witches troubled James as well, so much so that he even wrote a book about them, so Shakespeare created the 'Weird Sisters'. At the end of the twentieth century, the royal family has been reduced to a media event, but witches continue to exercise a strong fascination on contemporary audiences and film-makers. Like James I we are fascinated by the politics of the supernatural.

In 1948 the memories of self-proclaimed *Übermenschen* of the Nazi regime and the destruction they had wrought were still vivid in the minds of Europeans, and Orson Welles's *Macbeth* can be read as the actor-director's answer to the question of how this could have happened. Egomania was a topic that he had explored brilliantly in *Citizen Kane* (1941), and for Welles, Macbeth, like Kane, was an example of uncontrolled ambition, a 'brave' soldier who falls prey to the temptations of the witches (voice-over in the prologue). Welles uses his familiar, idiosyncratic repertoire of Expressionistic camera techniques, décor, lighting and editing to transform Shakespeare's political parable into a 'violently sketched charcoal drawing of a great play', a cinematic expedition into the dark reaches of Macbeth's heart and mind.[24] However, his plans to film the play pre-dated *Citizen Kane*. In 1936 Welles had directed an all-African American *Macbeth* in Harlem for the Federal Theatre. In 1947 he had staged the play again at the Utah Centennial Festival, and he used the Surreal-Expressionist sets from this production in the movie to cut expenses. The origin of this film in the 1930s explains why the faceless masses who march with Celtic crosses resemble the pre-World War II mass parades at Nazi *Reichsparteitage* in Nuremberg, and its pre-history on the stage explains why the blocking of Welles's deliveries is so obviously theatrical despite the Expressionistic camera work.

Shakespeare's *Macbeth* may celebrate James I: this film certainly celebrates Orson Welles, who is at once the producer, director, adaptor and star actor, omnipresent before and behind the camera. The kings – Duncan (Erskine Sandford) and Malcolm (Roddy McDowell) – are reduced to ciphers, while the overreaching Macbeth is thrust into the foreground. The remaining characters, including Lady Macbeth (Jeanette Nolan) and Macduff (Dan O'Herlihy), pale in the overbearing presence of the protagonist. Ross has been cut, Seyton made into a feeble servant, and the 'Holy Father' (Alan Napier), a creation of Welles, can do little to hinder the forces of evil. The film contains some five hundred shots, and the majority focus directly on Welles as Macbeth or include him in the *mise-en-scène*. Frequently low-angle or high-angle shots or deep focus close-ups distort his size in comparison to the other figures. It is Welles's face and voice, directly and in voice-over, that dominate the film. The rest belong to the faceless masses.

A massive bulwark in the midst of a bleak and savage landscape (blasted heath, gnarled trees, fog), Macbeth's castle becomes a metaphor for his ambitions as well as his psyche. As the film progresses the protagonist, and the viewer with him, descend into the subterranean interior of the castle which resembles more a stone quarry than a domicile. Down damp and leaking tunnels we descend into the dark caverns of Macbeth's nightmare fantasies. In the banquet hall, the huge flat stone over the massive table accentuates the claustrophobic confinement of Macbeth's mind and situation. On entering for the banquet scene, he is dwarfed by two enormous wine butts, and he has discarded his garish, outsized crown, the sign of monarchal authority. When he upsets the massive banquet table, he also upsets the last vestiges of decorum and the fellowship of the court. Hereafter he becomes the isolated murderous despot.

The downfall of the *Übermensch* Macbeth is wrought not by Macduff, Malcolm, or their troops, but by the witches, those 'plotters against law and order . . . the agents of chaos, priests of hell and magic' (Welles's voice-over in the prologue). The precise motivation for murdering Duncan, Banquo, or Lady

Macduff remains nebulous, like the witches themselves: we hear their voices but never see their faces, and Hecate has been cut altogether. They have been replaced by a Lady Macbeth in a light-coloured, tight-fitting gown, writhing on her skin-covered bed like an itchy lioness in a cage. The witches with their forked staffs serve as a metaphor for evil and a druidic antipode to the Celtic cross. The film opens with the witches shaping a voodoo doll out of clay. Macbeth is their creation and their toy, and when he has served their purposes, they lop off the doll's head. Macduff announces that 'the time is free', throws Macbeth's severed head down to the masses, and they roar back their approval. In a brief inter-spliced shot, Macbeth's crown is picked up by young Fleance, and we cut to a long shot of the craggy outlines of Macbeth's castle, a rough-hewn Stonehenge-like crown in swirling mists. In the foreground the three witches with their forked staffs wait on the heath for the next victim on which to work their powers.

Kumonosu-Djo (1957), Akira Kurosawa's universally acclaimed transmutation of *Macbeth* into another medium and culture, locates the story during the *Sengoku Jidai*, 'The Age of the Country at War' (corresponding to 1392–1568 in Western chronology), a period of civil wars roughly equivalent to the English Wars of the Roses. This is a period picture with masterful attention to authentic detail, and it combines elements from traditional Noh drama, the American Western film and classical Japanese scroll painting. The film is known in English-speaking countries as *Throne of Blood*, but the title, as explained by Kurosawa himself, actually means 'the Castle of the Spider's Web': 'castles were constructed . . . of the wood which was grown as if it had been a maze. Therefore, the wood was named "the wood of spiders' hair", meaning the wood that catches up the invaders as if in a spider's web. The title . . . came to me this way.'[25]

The film opens not with the Weird Sisters but with an extreme long shot of a barren, misty, mountain landscape. In this film, long shots will predominate: foggy mountain vistas, horse and rider processions, feudal decorum and ceremony on display. As the camera pans to a lonely monolith, we hear voices chanting 'within this place / Stood once a mighty fortress'. Here there 'Lived a proud warrior / Murdered by ambition / . . . For what once was is now yet true / Murderous ambition will pursue.'[26] Kurosawa – like Welles at once producer, director, scriptwriter and editor – warns us against uncontrolled ambition while the Castle of the Spider's Web slowly emerges from the swirling mists. In the course of the film it will become an icon of a rigid social order as impenetrable and inescapable as the labyrinthine forest from the wood of whose trees it is made, and from which it takes its name.

The castle is characterised by low ceilings, squat pillars, wide empty rooms dominated by horizontals: beams, floors and sliding doors 'to create the effect of oppression'. The Spider's Web Forest, its metaphorical counterpart, stands for an inscrutable natural order. It is a latticework maze of tangled branches and vines dominated by the vertical lines of great tree trunks, yet there are paths that lead through it if you do not deviate. When Noriyasu leads Kunimaru's (Malcolm) troops against Washizu (Macbeth), he does not sidestep but marches directly through the Forest to the Castle. The Forest is the home of the Spirit, an old hag at her spinning wheel, a Noh equivalent to the Weird Sisters, who spins the threads of ambition in Washizu's mind that will eventually entrap him as a spider traps a fly. In pursuit of the Forest Spirit Washizu and Miki (Banquo) gallop wildly though the rain, and with Kurosawa's tracking camera we accompany them, catching only an occasional glimpse of the riders through a screen of branches and vines. From the beginning Kurosawa shows Washizu as entangled in a tight web from which there is no escape, even though it is Washizu's personal decision to pursue the Spirit.

Interior scenes show us Washizu locked in by a rigid geometry of rectilinear interior design and low ceilings that leave him no alternative but to cower in the corner. Confined by his environment, under pressure from his wife, Asaji, Washizu's only recourse is to enter the Forbidden Chamber, to descend into the dark and uncharted recesses of his mind, and murder his master Tsuzuki (Duncan). There is no other way out, nor can there be an escape when Washizu is besieged by Kunimaru's troops. They conjoin forest and castle by bringing trees and branches for camouflage. In the spectacular final sequence, Washizu is cornered and then pumped full of arrows shot by his own troops. Like a giant porcupine he staggers on the stairways, along the galleries and into the corners of the castle before an arrow out of nowhere pierces his throat, stopping his voice and ending his life. For Kurosawa, Washizu is as much a victim of a constraining feudal order and social decorum as of his personal transgression.

Whereas Welles transforms Shakespeare's *Macbeth* into an Expressionistic morality play and Kurosawa transmutes it into a Japanese parable, Roman Polanski's *Macbeth* (1971) takes Macbeth at his word: 'Life . . . is a tale . . . signifying nothing.' The Polish director transforms the tragedy into a cruel and absurd nightmare that perpetually repeats itself. Like his countryman Jan Kott, Polanski presents us the world as a never-ending cycle of gratuitous violence and murder determined by an inscrutable 'Grand Mechanism' whose central metaphor is blood and whose agents are demons in human form.[27] To underpin this message, Polanski adds an epilogue to the play. We see an abandoned stone ruin in the pouring rain and hear the sound of sour bagpipes and discordant strings which we recognise as the signature tune for the Weird Sisters. A rider approaches and lifts his hood; it is Donalbain, Malcolm's disenfranchised and crippled brother. Curious about the sounds he hears, he dismounts and limps around the ruin in the direction of smoke and keening emanating from the witches' cave. Cut to the riderless horse: dissonant chimes and a heavy drum grow louder as the credits appear on the screen. The murderous cycle can begin again. The witches have virtually the final word. Like everything else in this film, they are concretely real. Despots may come and go, but the witches will remain, and they live in a nearby cave.

Macbeth (Jon Finch) and Lady Macbeth (Francesca Annis) are a young, attractive and sympathetic couple, securely in royal favour. Their physical attractiveness visually reinforces the 'fair is foul, and foul is fair' motif with which the witches open the film. There is no pressing reason for them to murder Duncan. However, the Macbeths are childless and will remain so, as opposed to Banquo, Macduff, Duncan, Seyward or even the father and son Murderers. This childlessness becomes their driving fear, and Macbeth attempts to wipe out all sons, visualised by Polanski in chilling detail: young Macduff, wrapped in a towel, is stabbed in the back after bathing, young Seyward humiliated before Macbeth slits his throat, and even the Murderers are dumped down a chute. Polanski motivates Macbeth's ambition by emphasising the scene in which Duncan introduces primogeniture by naming his son Malcolm as his successor, a reading of the play closer to Holinshed than to Shakespeare.

Polanski makes extensive use of close-ups and voice-overs (more than in any other Shakespeare film) to allow the audience to be privy to the secret thoughts and desires of the young couple. From the outset we are included in their conspiracy, wayfarers on their self-imposed psychological journey into emotional isolation and self-imprisonment. By the end Lady Macbeth has cast off crown and robes, the last semblances of social station and mental decorum, to become a restless sleepwalker, vulnerable in her nakedness (compare young Macduff), and her fragile corpse barely warrants a comment in passing from Macbeth. Macbeth, clean-shaven as the film opens, increasingly develops a full beard. He has aged as well as hardened in his sensibilities, as if the foul wilderness of his mind has been turned inside out.[28]

The opening shot presents us with a Technicolor picture-postcard vista: a broad, sandy beach at dawn bathed in rich reds, oranges and purples that change to the pale light of day. All is still. Suddenly in the foreground a crooked stick held by a grimy hand bisects the vista diagonally. Three Weird Sisters, two crones old and withered, one of whom is blind, the third young, pocked-marked and mute, scrape out a grave on the beach in which they bury a dirty noose, a severed lower arm and a dagger, which they lay in the hand. They strew the objects with grasses and herbs, cover them with sand and sprinkle them with blood. Mumbling 'Fair is foul, and foul is fair / Hover through the fog and filthy air', they agree to meet again before trudging off in different directions.[29] Credits and the same beach becomes the scene of a battle, now over, as if the witches have pre-ordained the severance, death and mutilation that has come to pass. The film will end in silence from the vantage-point of Macbeth's severed head as it is carried on a pike and raised above the castle gates.

Macbeth's castle 'hath a pleasant seat', to quote Duncan. Like its owners, it is attractive. It bustles with domestic life as the preparations are made for Duncan's visit: servants sweep the banquet hall and catch pigs, Lady Macbeth prepares Duncan's bed with rose petals, and the lord is welcomed home from the wars.[30] However, as the film progresses, the castle is no longer a hostel of hospitality, and the cheerful domestic population is replaced by surly cut-throats and rogues. When they abandon Macbeth in the end, the empty castle becomes a metaphor for his own isolation.

A major change is the 'privileging' of Ross (John Stride) whom Polanski advances to one of the prime agents for defining the politics of the film. At a second glance he seems omnipresent on screen, even when in the background. He is at once the 'maker' and 'unmaker' of kings, a likeable but facile fellow-traveller, opportunistic and unscrupulous, who always goes unpunished. He serves Duncan, Macbeth and finally Malcolm. He is ever hovering in the background: when Banquo is assassinated and when Lady Macduff is raped and her children slaughtered. Not rewarded, Ross abandons Macbeth, journeys to Malcolm, informs Macduff of the extermination of his family and then hands him the sword that will be the undoing of Macbeth. He literally 'makes' Malcolm King of Scotland when he hands the crown just off of Macbeth's head and with a smirk cries out, 'Hail, King of Scotland.' Like the Macbeths, he is proof of the witches' dictum that 'fair is foul'. The film closes with Ross. For Polanski, kings are not determined by divine right but 'made' by the likes of Ross.[31]

King Lear: a play for our times

King Lear is a play about a world grown old and cold, brutal and uncaring, a world at the mercy of egoistic old men, deaf to those who love them, and their vicious children who lust for power and possession. It is a world in which the gods, if any, no longer care, in which humanity no longer matters. Shakespeare presents the world as 'this great stage of fools' (4.5.179) on which the blind are the true seers, the madmen the true philosophers and from which the only exit is death. *King Lear* is also a play about landscapes, exterior and interior, human and natural, mental and material. Storm-swept heaths and steep cliffs are hard to realise on stage but lend themselves admirably to the wide screen.

In fact, the 1970s and 1980s, the period between Polanski's *Macbeth* and Kenneth Branagh's *Henry V* (1989), saw a veritable boom in *King Lear*s: cinema films by Grigori Kozintsev (1970) and Peter Brook (1971); Michael Elliot's production for Granada Television (1983), a moving farewell performance for Laurence Olivier; and most memorably, Akira Kurosawa's *Ran* (1985).[32]

The stark landscape of Kozintsev's *King Lear* is cold and grey, a primeval stone garden through which the poor, the crippled, the hungry and the mute stumble on their way to a massive and formidable fortress to which they have no access. There their rulers, closeted in warmth and comfort before a huge, roaring hearth, have gathered for Lear's announcement. Lear's approach is heralded by the bells and laughter of the Fool (Oleg Dal). The door opens and Lear (Yuri Yarvet), his face hidden by a mask, enters. He is fragile, senile and unpredictable in his moods and whimsy, and too small for his throne. His division of the kingdom is read aloud to the court while he plays with the Fool and peers into the flames. A counter shot of Lear and the court from the back of the flaming hearth fore-shadows the conflagration that will ensue from his misjudgement. Later, on the battlements of his fortress, he appears tiny, insignificant and absurd against the epic proportions of this backdrop. The 'division of the kingdom' sequence takes nearly twenty-five minutes, twice as long as it will for Brook. It ends with the exit procession of Lear and his train of knights in authentic detail, complete with wolfhounds, falcons and the Fool bound and collared.

The interior/exterior dichotomy between the bright, stony wasteland, and the dark, gloomy castle, between the neglected and suffering people and the greedy and malicious court, established in the first sequence, visualises the parameters of Lear's own *via dolorosa* from stubborn egocentrism to pitiable humanity. His testament will be burning houses and countless corpses, a landscape more rem-iniscent of his own scorched homeland in World War II than the devastated Hiroshima that Kozintsev himself cites.[33] In the final sequence the Fool, artist and comedian, weeps amid the charred remnants of what was once Lear's kingdom and is then coldly kicked aside by the soldiers bearing Lear and Cordelia to their graves. There is no safe place for the artist in this world. The mournful melody of his flute will accompany the end of the film – an image that foreshadows the meditative closing scene of Kurosawa's *Ran*.

If Shakespeare's tragedy is the story of a man who estranges himself from his own humanity, Kozintsev's *King Lear* is a film in which humanity continually suffers death and destruction, yet keeps moving forward in a never-ending pro-cession whatever its leaders subject it to. From the grotesque procession with which the film opens to the closing shots of the charred remains of Lear's kingdom, Kozintsev's camera is always trained on masses of human beings on the move and positions Lear in relationship to them. The camera follows Lear down into Poor Tom's damp and fetid hovel that is populated by a whole cell-block of other half-crazed outcasts, and it tracks Lear and Cordelia as they trudge through the mud and the cold with hundreds of other refugees.

Kozintsev also uses the camera to frame the increasing isolation of Lear's cold-blooded daughters and the rise and the fall of Edmund. As the film progresses, Goneril (Elza Radzin), Regan (Galina Volchek) and Edmund (Regimentas Adomajtis) are shown ever more frequently by themselves, progressively isolated from the rest of humanity until in the final battle Goneril and Regan stagger with heads uncovered, their hair undone, separated from everyone else. Low-angle medium shots and low-angle close-ups emphasise Edmund's threat until the trial by combat with Edgar. Now the camera shifts its angle to above to emphasise Edmund's increasing diminution, until it hovers directly over him cringing on the ground ('the wheel has come full circle'). In these sequences Lear and Cordelia are shot consistently straight on, slightly from above in long and medium shots, and the *mise-en-scène* locates them among other people. Kozintsev's camera technique stems from the Soviet tradition of Eisenstein and Pudovkin: that is, a camera that employs pans, zooms, angles, tracking shots and montage for cinematic effect. And yet his study of Lear remains contemplative and introspective, 'a serene dignity' as Kenneth Rothwell calls it.[34] Kozintsev is the only director to show the corpse of Cordelia dangling at the end of a rope (five seconds), yet the image that transcends the film is that of the fragile, broken Lear and the serenely beautiful Cordelia (Valentina Shendrikova) standing triumphant in the muck, surrounded by grey, helmeted soldiers. It is a *mise-en-scène* that recalls a carved crucifixion tableau from a medieval altar. The final shot is of Edgar's (Leonard Merzin) face against the background of ruined houses, the embodiment of hope for a humanitarian future.

Peter Brook's *King Lear* (1971) is also about faces, and about heads, in close-up, in and out of focus, in full-view, in eyes-only close-ups and often askew. It is a film about heads that have lost touch with hearts and reason, and heads bear the brunt of the punishment: Gloucester's eyes are gouged out with a spoon, Edmund is slain with a battle axe to the neck, Goneril bashes Regan's brains out and then like a whirling dervish works herself into a frenzy before banging her own head against the rocks. From the opening pan of a hall full of strangely motionless faces, the camera focuses on heads and faces as if probing their surface representation for a clue to their inner character, and characters talk straight into the camera as if directly to the spectator. The second shot of the opening 'division of the kingdom' sequence is an oversized low-angle close-up of the hard and massive face of white-haired Paul Scofield as Lear, who says, 'Know . . .' followed by a seemingly endless pause. This film is about learning to 'know' and the consequences of not 'knowing'.

Brook confronts us with the grim winter landscape of the Anglo-Saxon 'King Leir' of Geoffrey of Monmouth's *Historia Regum Britanniae* (it was filmed on location in northern Jutland), the frozen outdoor world of the Old English poems *The Wanderer* and *The Seafarer*. The 'castles' resemble dug-outs from World War I trench warfare, and this will be a film about trench warfare slugged out without quarter in a barren no-man's-land. The combatants are clothed in furs, hides, rough-woven shirts and heavy leather dresses, their faces darkened by the weather and grime. They travel in primitive wagons covered with hides and resting on huge, solid wooden wheels.

In *King Lear* humanity has alienated itself from its humanness, and Brook reinforces this alienation with his camera. His Lear owes as much to Godard and the camera shenanigans of the French 'New Wave' as it does to the oft-cited influence of Brecht and Kott (in particular, the chapter '*King Lear*, or Endgame' in Kott's *Shakespeare our Contemporary*, 1965). Brook consistently and insistently interrupts the narrative flow with the hand-held camera, rapid acceleration, out-of-focus shots, printed subtitles, zooms, fades, jump-cutting and cross-cutting to suggest the rupture and discontinuity in Lear's mind. Here Brook transfers the lessons of Brecht's *Verfremdungseffekt* from the stage to the screen to create a cinematically noisy and theatrical *King Lear* that is in direct contrast to the vast stretches of 'silence' in the film. Accordingly, the *mise-en-scène*, like Lear's own grasp of reality, is constantly off-balance, and out of focus, especially during the storm on the heath that switches back and forth from the rain-drenched heath to the smoke-filled dug-out. The sequence ends with a shot of drowned rats about which Lear has never cared and which now become a metaphor for his own situation. For Brook, King Lear is Shakespeare's *Endgame*, a suggestion mirrored in the shot of Lear carrying Cordelia's lifeless body up the beach into a blank sky, and it is with a shot that pans from a part of Lear's face to his shoulder to the empty, grey sky that the film ends.

Akira Kurosawa's *Ran* is an epic colour version of the *King Lear* story adapted to Japanese culture: Hidetora (Lear) abdicates his throne and divides his kingdom between his three sons, Taro (Goneril), Jiro (Regan) and Saburo (Cordelia), rather than any daughters. Whereas the worlds of Kozintsev's and Brook's films are drab, cold and grey, that of Kurosawa's *Ran* is full of vast vistas of bright sunshine, brilliant colours and an eerie stillness. In the outdoor scenes yellows, blues and green dominate (also the colours of Hidetora and Saburo), whereas in the indoor scenes the predominant colours are browns and ambers. In the outdoor scenes we often hear the sound of crickets chirping in the background, a sound effect more effective than a musical score. On display is the love of ceremony, procession and hierarchy. Everything has its place, and all in life has been preordained. This sense of continuity will be transformed into chaos (the meaning of the film's title) by Hidetora's ill-guided decision.

Kursosawa's camerawork is reminiscent of that in his *Kumonosu-Djo*: extreme long shots of mountain vistas, lines of horsemen against the horizon, faceless armies, riders shown from the rear, mysterious castles in the distance, interiors defined by stark horizontal and vertical lines suggesting strict hierarchy, order, confinement and massive wooden gates that open and close on Hidetora, reminding us of the trap he has set for himself. The natural outdoors, bright and vast, is the world of men, loyalty and familial solidarity, while the forts, symbols of power, are breeding grounds for treason, betrayal and fratricide. Here, in the inner chambers, Lady Kaede (Mieko Harada), Taro's widow and later Jiro's wife, a mixture of Goneril and Lady Macbeth, can manipulate the downfall of the Ichimonji dynasty who have destroyed her own family and taken possession of this fort that once belonged to them.

The film opens with an old boar being hunted down by mounted samurai using bows and arrows, but when they finally slay him, the meat turns out to be inedible, old, stinky and foul. The boar will become a metaphor for Hidetora, who himself will later be banished by his own son Jiro and hunted by his former subjects. The division of the kingdom sequence ends with a back shot of Hidetora and his sons striding up the hill towards the approaching storm. The apocalypse of Hidetora's world is the ambush in the Third Fort by the forces of his own sons Taro and Jiro. Kurosawa films this epic battle sequence mainly without sound. Hidetora sits stoically, like a Buddha, at the top of his burning tower while his loyal samurai are massacred by the fusillades of faceless riflemen, and his concubines kill each other in a mutal act of *harakiri*. After all are dead and the tower is in flames, Hidetora slowly descends the stairway like an apparition already embarked on a voyage into madness which is his only rescue.

Ran is a *King Lear* for and of the eighties, when the world seemed poised on the brink of nuclear destruction. Although (like the same director's *Macbeth* film) it is set in the 'Age of the Country at War', the film is a commentary on the twentieth century: the decay of culture, the loss of humanity and the disproportionate destruction that can be loosed if we were to make a mistake and a nuclear holocaust ensued. Accordingly, major segments of the film are devoted to battle sequences. A mixture of motifs, shots and codes borrowed from Western and knights-in-armour films, these sequences fascinate through the orchestration of wave-like movement and surging colour. Yet, the spectator is granted no chance to lapse into nostalgia or reverie but is confronted with the chilling brutality of war in which it is faceless material, not palpable human beings, that make the difference. The personalised art of swordplay of Hidetora's samurai has no chance against the muskets. Likewise, Hidetora's sons, Taro and Saburo, are ambushed by faceless, nameless gunmen who remain unrevealed and go unapprehended. When Hidetora laments how unjust and unfair the world is, that there are no more gods, no Buddha who cares, Fujikada (who corresponds to the play's King of France) admonishes him not to slander the gods because they are unhappy when they see how we humans slaughter each other. Fujikada's final verdict is that human beings would rather suffer than live in peace. In the final shot the camera pulls back to show us Tsumuramu, the blind boy from the hut, now tapping alone towards the edge of an abyss. Jan Kott, reviewing the film in the *New York Review of Books* ('The Edo Lear', 24 April 1986), found in this a metaphor for our predicament at the end of the twentieth century.

NOTES

1 Percentages are based on Kenneth S. Rothwell and Annabelle Henkin Melzer, eds., *Shakespeare on Screen: an International Filmography and Videography* (London, 1990). For the critical reception by academic critics, see in particular the works by Collick, Davies, Jorgens, Kliman and Rothwell listed in the further reading section at the end of this volume.

2 See also Dennis Kennedy, 'Shakespeare Without his Language', in James Bulman, ed., *Shakespeare, Theory and Performance* (London, 1996), pp. 133–48.

3 On the circularity of the play, see Terence Hawkes, 'Telmah', in *That Shakespehearean Rag* (London, 1986), pp. 96f. I have written on the cyclical nature of Olivier's film in 'A Microcosm of Art: Olivier's Expressionist *Hamlet*', in Holger Klein and Dimiter Daphinoff, eds., *'Hamlet' on Screen. Shakespeare Yearbook*, 8 (Lampeter, 1997), p. 135.

4 See Jan Kott, 'Hamlet of the Mid-Century', in *Shakespeare Our Contemporary*, trans. Boris Taborski (London, 1964), pp. 57–60, and David Walton, 'The Fortunes of Fortinbras in Three Film Versions of *Hamlet*', *Shakespeare Bulletin* 16/3 (Summer 1998), 36–7.

5 Siegfried Kracauer, *From Caligari to Hitler. A Psychological History of the German Film* (Princeton, 1957), pp. 3–11. On the Gade/Nielsen *Hamlet* see Lawrence Danson, 'Gazing at Hamlet, or the Danish Cabaret', *Shakespeare Survey 45: Hamlet and its Afterlife* (1993), 37–52; Robert A. Duffy, 'Gade, Olivier, Richardson: Visual Strategy in *Hamlet* Adaptations', *Literature/Film Quarterly*, 4 (1976), 141–52; Ann Thompson's essay in Linda E. Boose and Richard Burt, eds., *Shakespeare, the Movie. Popularising the Plays on Film, TV and Video* (London and New York, 1997); and J. Lawrence Guntner, 'Expressionist Shakespeare: the Gade/Nielsen *Hamlet* (1920) and the History of Shakespeare on Film', *Post Script*, 17/2 (1998), 88–100.

6 See J. Lawrence Guntner and Peter Drexler, 'Recycled Film Codes and the Study of Shakespeare on Film', *Shakespeare Jahrbuch* (1993), 31–41.

7 See Harry Keyishian's chapter above in the present volume, and my own essay in Klein and Daphinoff, *Hamlet on Screen*, pp. 133–52.

8 See also Peter S. Donaldson, *Shakespearean Films/Shakespearean Directors* (Boston, MA, 1990).

9 See Grigori Kozintsev, '*Hamlet* and *King Lear*: Stage and Film', in Clifford Leech and J. M. R. Margeson, eds., *Shakespeare 1971* (Toronto, 1972), p. 192.

10 On Zeffirelli's film see Deborah Cartmell's chapter below in the present volume, the essays by Ace G. Pilkington (on the director) and Neil Taylor (on *Hamlet* films) in Anthony Davies and Stanley Wells, eds., *Shakespeare and the Moving Image* (Cambridge, 1994) and Edward Quinn, 'Zeffirelli's Hamlet', *Shakespeare on Film Newsletter*, 15 (1991), 1–2, 12.

11 Some details are given by Russell Jackson, 'Kenneth Branagh's Film of *Hamlet*: the Textual Choices', *Shakespeare Bulletin*, 15/2 (Spring 1997), 37–8.

12 For more on this *Hamlet*, see Robert F. Willson, Jr., 'Kenneth Branagh's Hamlet, or the Revenge of Fortinbras', *Shakespeare Newsletter*, 47 (Spring 1997), 7, 9; reviews by Thomas Pendleton, *Shakespeare Newsletter*, 46 (Fall 1996), 60 and Samuel Crowl, *Shakespeare Bulletin*, 15/1 (Winter 1997), 43–5.

13 Ethan Hawke, 'Introduction', in Michael Almereyda, *William Shakespeare's 'Hamlet' adapted by Michael Almereyda* (London: 2000), p. xiii.

14 See Almereyda for the original film script, which does not necessarily coincide with the edited version of the film.

15 *Ibid.*, p. vii.

16 For an argument that the new technology of film reception, e.g. VCR and DVD, have made the act of film reception post-historical, see Richard Burt, 'Introduction: Editors cut', in Richard Burt and Lynda E. Boose, eds., *Shakespeare, The Movie, II* (London, 2003), pp. 2–5.

17 Almereyda, p. xi.

18 According to Almereyda himself, 'in movies . . . the locations are manifestations of the way your characters are feeling' (in Cynthia Fuchs, 'Looking Around Corners. Interview with Michael Almereyda', www.popmatters.com/film/interviews/almereyda-michael.html) see also Alexander Leggat, 'Urban Poetry in the Almereyda *Hamlet*', *Shakespeare Studies Today*, 4 (2004), 169–81.

19 Almereyda, p. x.

20 *Ibid.*, p. 37; see also Richard Burt, 'Shakespeare and Asia in Postdiasporic Cinemas: Spin-offs and Citations of the Plays from Bollywood to Hollywood', in Burt and Boose, pp. 292–7.

21 See Mark Thornton Burnett, ' "To Hear and See the Matter": Communicating Technology in Michael Almereyda's *Hamlet* (2000)', *Cinema Journal*, 42/3 (2003), 57–60, and Leggat, 'Urban Poetry in the Almereyda *Hamlet*'.

22 ' "Remember Me": Technologies of Memory in Michael Almereyda's *Hamlet*', in Burt and Boose, pp. 46–7.

23 See E. Pearlman, '*Macbeth* on Film', in Davies and Wells, *Shakespeare and the Moving Image*, pp. 250–60.

24 Welles quoted in Roger Manvell, *Shakespeare and the Film* (New York, 1971), p. 59. See also James Naremore, 'The Walking Shadow: Welles's Expressionist *Macbeth*', *Literature/Film Quarterly*, 1 (1973), 360–6.

25 Kurosawa quoted in Manvell, *Shakespeare and the Film*, p. 104. The major source of information on the director's work remains Donald Ritchie's *The Films of Akira Kurosawa* (3rd edn, Berkeley, CA, 1996). See also Robert Hapgood, 'Kurosawa's Shakespeare Films', in Davies and Wells, *Shakespeare and the Moving Image*; Anna Zambrano, '*Throne of Blood*: Kurosawa's *Macbeth*', *Literature/Film Quarterly*, 2 (1974), 262–74; J. Blumenthal, '*Macbeth* into *Throne of Blood*', *Sight and Sound*, 34 (1965), 190–5; and John Gerlach, 'Shakespeare, Kurosawa and *Macbeth*: A Response to J. Blumenthal', *Literature/Film Quarterly*, 1 (1973), 352–9.

26 Translation in Ritchie, *The Films of Akira Kurosawa*, p. 117.

27 Jan Kott, *Shakespeare our Contemporary* (London, 1965), pp. 68–78.

28 See Lorne M. Buchman, *Still in Movement: Shakespeare on Screen* (New York, 1991), p. 77.

29 Discussions of the sequence include Kenneth Rothwell, 'Roman Polanski's *Macbeth*: Golgotha Triumphant', *Literature/Film Quarterly*, 1 (1973), 71–4; Norman Silverstein, 'The Opening Shot of Polanski's *Macbeth*', *Literature/Film Quarterly*, 2 (1974), 88–90; and Jack Jorgens, 'The Opening Scene of Polanski's *Macbeth*', *Literature/Film Quarterly*, 3 (1975), 271–8; and Buchman, *Still in Movement*, pp. 70–2.

30 See Nigel Andrews, '*Macbeth*', *Sight and Sound*, 41 (Spring, 1972), 108.

31 See Kenneth Rothwell, 'Roman Polanski's *Macbeth*: the "Privileging" of Ross', *The CEA Critic*, 46 (1983), 50–5.

32 Rothwell and Meltzer (*Shakespeare on Screen*) list twenty-three films and/or video versions of the play or 'offshoots' from it between 1970 and 1985, but only fifteen between 1899 and 1970.

33 Grigori Kozintsev, *King Lear, The Space of Tragedy* (London, 1977), p. 108.

34 Kenneth Rothwell, 'Representing *King Lear* on Screen: from Metatheatre to "Metacinema"', in Davies and Wells, *Shakespeare and the Moving Image*, pp. 216–24.

8

PATRICIA TATSPAUGH

The tragedies of love on film

The celluloid fortunes of Shakespeare's tragedies of love mirror their stage history. Most popular of the three tragedies, *Romeo and Juliet* has the richest stage history.[1] Shakespeare's earliest tragedy of love invites an exploration of social issues, survives transpositions of time and place, accommodates multi-cultural casting and, of course, dramatises the timeless conflict between generations. Although there are numerous important productions of *Othello* – and memorable portrayals of Othello and his adversary, the script presents greater challenges than does *Romeo and Juliet*. Contemporary audiences expect, for example, a black actor in the title role and find the racist and sexist language offensive. In the late twentieth century Shakespeare's study of jealousy in *The Winter's Tale* was staged more often than *Othello*. Least popular of the three tragedies of love, *Antony and Cleopatra* is also the most demanding to stage or film.

Film directors, like their theatrical counterparts, face the challenge of trans-lating English Renaissance play-scripts to a new medium and for a contempo-rary audience. A particular challenge of the tragedies of love is the limited number of crowd-pulling scenes of bliss and fulfilment, or as in the case of Shakespeare's mature Othello and Desdemona and to a lesser extent with the adulterous Antony and Cleopatra, face-to-face confrontation and conflict. One focus of this study will be an examination of ways in which film directors open out the plays to provide scenes for the tragic lovers, who would otherwise spend little time with each other. Directors must also place Romeo and Juliet, Othello and Desdemona, Antony and Cleopatra in a social context that illu-minates their characters and mediates between the Renaissance play and the target audience – and between the Renaissance play and the extended audience watching in film archives and on video or DVD. Another focus of this chapter will be on the way directors present and define the communities in Verona, Venice and Cyprus, Egypt and Rome and the effects of those communities on the tragic figures.

Romeo and Juliet

In 1970 George Cukor suggested several reasons why his *Romeo and Juliet* (1936), which had been nominated for four Academy Awards,[2] had 'fallen into great disrepute'. Perhaps it was 'too stately', its lovers 'too stodgy', it should have looked 'more Italian, Mediterranean', Shakespeare's play was 'unfamiliar territory'. Given the chance to film it again, 'I'd know how. I'd get the garlic and the Mediterranean into it'[3] In the late twentieth century, Cukor's film may be viewed as a flawed product of 1930s Hollywood. Romeo (Leslie Howard, b. 1893) is too old – and he wears gloves during the balcony scene; Juliet's 'youthful' gestures and her pet fawn are unconvincing attempts to make Norma Shearer (b. 1902) seem younger. The inserted scenes on the road to Mantua, where the hapless Friar John is quarantined with a plague victim, induce tedium, not dramatic tension.

But Cukor's film offers an excellent starting point for an introduction to filmed adaptations of Shakespeare's earliest tragedy of love. Although the four films themselves are wildly different, the adaptations of *Romeo and Juliet* share two common goals: to make Shakespeare's famous young lovers attractive to the cinema audience and to portray realistically the society in which Romeo and Juliet live. Cukor worked within the Hollywood system, and the influence of his translation of the play from stage to screen may be seen in the filmed versions of *Romeo and Juliet* of Renato Castellani (1954), Franco Zeffirelli (1968) and Baz Luhrmann (1996).

Cukor's opening sequence highlights the care taken to ensure authenticity.[4] His technique may be dated, but each of his successors borrowed something from the three movements of Cukor's opening sequence. First, Cukor seeks approval from authorities: he displays a bust of Shakespeare and his impressive list of credits includes a literary adviser. Next, he appeals to his audience by linking the film with familiar theatrical customs, such as illustrated programmes, publicity shots and formal scenes: he introduces actors in character and in a shot of a scene staged before a drop curtain on a proscenium platform. Finally, he sets the scene of the play: an overview of Verona narrows the focus to the cathedral square, then to the cathedral. Castellani's Chorus was John Gielgud, a famous Romeo in the 1930s (New Theatre, London, 1935). Gielgud wears Elizabethan doublet and hose and reads the Chorus from what appears to be the First Folio. Zeffirelli also set the scene with an overview of Verona, and Laurence Olivier, who had alternated the roles of Romeo and Mercutio with Gielgud, read the Chorus in voice-over.[5] In 1996 Luhrmann appealed to a much younger audience by introducing the framework of television and print journalism.

Cukor treats the script seriously, but not as seriously as his appeal to the authority of the First Folio and a literary adviser would suggest. His scenarist,

Talbot Jennings, abridged Shakespeare's script. He plays approximately 45 per cent,[6] excising passages that are traditionally cut (such as Chorus 2, the musicians), substituting action for dialogue (Capulet's servants, taking their cue from Capulet's instructions in Act 4 scene 4, convey the grief of the household and bridegroom), reassigning dialogue from several servants to enlarge the comic role of Peter, a faint-hearted bully. Jennings rearranges scenes to introduce characters in longer narrative sequences: for example, he focuses first on the Capulets, then on Romeo and his friends. Jennings retains several crucial scenes and passages cut by some or all of his successors, including most of Juliet's soliloquy 'I have a faint cold fear thrills through my veins' (4.3.14–59), which Zeffirelli and Lurhmann cut and from which Castellani cuts nearly one third; he entrusts to Romeo and Juliet more of Shakespeare's poetry than do his successors. Most of Jennings's interpolations, such as the three sequences portraying Friar John's travails in Mantua (as related in Act 5 scene 2), have some basis in the text. Songs are taken from two of Shakespeare's other plays: the shepherd sings 'Come away death' (from *Twelfth Night*) and a boys' choir sings Juno's hymn, 'Honour, riches, marriage blessing' (from *The Tempest*) at Capulet's feast.[7]

Most of the spectacle Cukor introduces has a basis in the text: three events – Capulet's feast and the two fights – encourage spectacle; four other events embedded in the lines – the wedding, Act 3 scene 5 ('Wilt thou be gone?'), Juliet's funeral and the play's final twenty lines – also invite translation to film.[8] Cukor sets the opening feud within the realistic context of a religious procession. The Capulets and Montagues, displaying their wealth, glide imperiously through Verona's streets, across its square and up the steps into the cathedral. During the procession Peter, the Nurse's dim-witted servant, provokes a quarrel with Montague's servants. The brawling draws the worshippers from their prayers to the cathedral steps. Capulet's feast takes an Italian Renaissance theme, with jousting knights on hobby-horses and an elaborate dance (choreographer: Agnes de Mille) in which Juliet is presented. In a game of blind man's bluff, Rosaline huffily rebuffs a crestfallen Romeo. The long sequence, with its entertainments and party games, contrasts with folk entertainment on a Veronese piazza (in Act 2 scene 4 when the Nurse is giving her message to Romeo) and within the village where Friar John is quarantined. Both the marriage and its consummation are handled with brief shots of the couple, a fade-out and a sequence of evocative shots of birds, sky, stars, gardens, rippling water, tolling bells.[9] Cukor stages an elaborate funeral procession for Juliet, which draws upon the Friar's and Capulet's instructions in Act 4 scene 5 and which resembles a Renaissance painting. Mourners wend their way along a cypress-lined path in perspective from unseen Verona to a secluded churchyard. Privacy characterises Cukor's understated final segment: the Prince, Capulet and Montague speak the last twenty lines at the entrance to Capulet's monument, attended by the Ladies Capulet and

Montague, Friar Laurence and other mourners. The film closes with two images from the opening sequence: actors on the forestage and an overview of Verona.

Clusters of images help present Romeo, Juliet and Mercutio. Enlarging upon Benvolio's and Montague's description of Romeo in the play's first scene, Cukor introduces Romeo in an Arcadian scene: a pipe-playing shepherd and his sheep-dog tend the flock; nearby, day-dreaming Romeo reclines against a classical ruin. Howard plays Romeo as a lovesick young man, who quickly shifts his devotion from Rosaline to Juliet and as quickly assumes the toughness necessary to avenge Mercutio's murder. Juliet is associated with a cultivated garden which features a decorative fish pond. She is livelier and more energetic than Romeo. Three images of her linger in the memory: Juliet and the Nurse walking together down a long corridor after the feast, a servant behind them extinguishing candles in the wall sconces; Juliet practising with the rope Romeo has provided; Juliet considering the terrorising effects of the 'distilling liquor'. The camera lingers on their hands during the dance and the balcony scenes.

John Barrymore, by then in his late fifties, plays Mercutio as a flirtatious tease, a foil to Howard's serious Romeo. *En route* to the feast, Mercutio kisses women through a grille and gives them flowers. In two scenes that playfully mock the balcony scene, he passes a carafe of wine to women on a balcony (Act 2 scene 4) and begs a fan from them (Act 3 scene 1).

To modern viewers, Cukor's middle-aged cast looks and sounds distinctly middle-aged.[10] Especially in the early scenes the attempt to portray the youthfulness of Romeo and Juliet calls attention to the ages of Shearer and Howard. The 1930s technique also dates the actors and the film: reverential speaking of the verse and romantic shots, such as the montage sequences that follow the wedding and wedding night and further heighten the poetry. The other three directors sacrifice the verse in favour of younger, less experienced but more photogenic actors.

In its attention to the recreation of a realistic Verona, Castellani's colour film, which won the Grand Prix at the Venice Film Festival,[11] is a bridge between Cukor's black and white Hollywood sets and Zeffirelli's lavish photography. Castellani, who shot some scenes on location,[12] interpolated sequences to portray Renaissance Verona, its rigid class system, Roman Catholicism and feuding families. Guards at the gate to Verona welcome farmers who carry their produce to a market held in the piazza dominated by the cathedral; the Capulets and Montagues pursue each other through narrow streets lined with mellow stone buildings; Capulet's mansion, with its large courtyard and grand rooms, his comfortable study,[13] his numerous servants, and his elaborate feast, testify to his wealth and status; monks announce Friar Laurence's visitors and sing a steady round of devotional services in their Romanesque chapel. Throughout the film, costumes and sets and groupings resemble Italian Renaissance paintings; the music (composer: Roman Vlad) contributes to the effect of *Quattrocento* Italy.[14] The wealth and feuding of Veronese families contrast with an inserted scene which depicts poverty and plague in a household just inside the gates of Mantua.

Castellani's screenplay, which retains approximately 36 per cent (approx 1,081 lines) of Shakespeare's script, significantly alters the original.[15] Castellani sets the Prince apart from his subjects. Instead of having the Prince interrupt the two brawls, Castellani stages two formal hearings, an alteration that in the second case destroys the spontaneity of Benvolio's defence of his friend. For interpolated scenes with minor characters, he scripts dialogue, much of it banal. Friar John's chastisement of the plague-ridden man blames the sickness of the poor man's soul for his terminal disease. Another set of changes complicates the action without gaining any apparent benefit: the first fight, Friar Laurence's plan for reuniting the banished Romeo and the revived Juliet and Romeo's return to Verona. Realistic presentation of place, so carefully handled with Capulet's mansion and the monastery, goes seriously off the rails when it comes to the Capulets' vault.[16]

But Castellani's most important alterations are those that redefine Romeo's character. A series of excisions and insertions intensify the loneliness of Romeo. He enjoys very little companionship with his friends (cuts include Act 1 scene 4 and Act 2 scene 4) and goes to the feast alone, where the haughty Rosaline orders her lovelorn suitor to leave immediately. Castellani cuts the Montagues' concern for their absent son (1.1.113 etc.) and inserts a leaving scene (before Act 3 scene 5) in which Montague coldly pulls Romeo from his mother's farewell embrace.[17] The alterations increase the importance of Mervyn Johns's affectionate but dotty Friar Laurence. In two sets of parallel scenes rearranged so that they follow each other, Castellani draws further attention to Romeo's solitude by contrasting his situation with Juliet's. Romeo, heartsick in a meadow outside the walls of Verona (1.1.57 etc.), contrasts with Juliet, surrounded by servants who bathe her (Act 1 scene 3). The second pair contrasts Romeo's dependence on Friar Laurence (Act 2 scene 3) with Juliet, who awaits the Nurse's return in a room full of seamstresses, who may be preparing a trousseau for her intended wedding with Paris (Act 2 scene 5). To mark the shift in Juliet's fortunes, Castellani reorders lines and draws on imagery from the domestic scenes and, especially, the seamstresses in Act 2 scene 5. In lines transferred from 4.1. 24–34, Paris woos Juliet immediately after she has obtained the potion; her wedding gown, displayed on a tailor's dummy, stands nearby. After she drinks the draught, Juliet crawls over to the wedding gown (it has been moved to her room), which she is wearing when the Nurse discovers her. Another set of sequences intensifies Juliet's situation. The film cuts from the gloomy, plague-infested room in Mantua to the darkness in which Juliet contemplates awakening in the vault (Act 4 scene 3).

Castellani's textual alterations and embellishments lessen the effectiveness of the big scenes. The fights spill into the streets off the piazza and conclude in confusion in the courtyards of mansions, where women keen the death of their kin and where Juliet, in the balcony overlooking the Capulets' courtyard, learns Romeo has killed Tybalt. (The body of the much-lamented Tybalt seems to have been abandoned unceremoniously on a stone bench in the vault.) Castellani films a brief wedding in the friars' chapel, treats the consummation in a chaste manner (shots of skies, sunrise over Verona and birdsong). He cross-cuts Juliet's funeral with sequences of Romeo's return to Verona.[18] He closes with a double funeral, with the Prince and other mourners processing into a church; Benvolio comforts the Montagues; Capulet begs forgiveness of Montague.

Romeo and Juliet are associated with two sets of visual images. Grilles and shadows cast by grilles heighten the darkness introduced by Castellani's revision of Romeo's character and foreshadow Friar John's quarantine and its disastrous effect. In the balcony scene, a grille bars Romeo from Juliet and casts a shadow behind him; at Friar Laurence's, a grille over the window separates the couple during the brief wedding ceremony. Castellani also associates them with a more optimistic set of visual images: bells, a nest of young birds, numerous shots of blue sky.

Nearly thirty years separate the two most popular films of *Romeo and Juliet*. Both directors – Franco Zeffirelli (1968) and Baz Luhrmann (1996) – appealed to a youthful audience by casting young actors as Romeo and Juliet and by presenting the conflict between generations within a contemporary context. Zeffirelli's film spoke to the generation that rebelled against the Vietnamese war and demanded 'relevance' in secondary and higher education. The film was, as Sarah Munson Deats points out, 'particularly intended to attract the counter-culture youth, a generation of young people, like Romeo and Juliet, estranged from their parents, torn by the conflict between their youthful cult of passion and the military traditions of their elders'.[19] Luhrmann's film and the soundtrack released with it very successfully targeted a younger audience, the MTV generation of teenagers roughly the age of Romeo and Juliet.[20] 'It's a grave understatement,' intones Peter Matthews, 'to say that this *Romeo and Juliet* is youth-oriented.'[21] The radically different films are themselves an ironic comment on the generation gap: the Zeffirelli generation parented Lurhmann's audience.

Zeffirelli's debt to Castellani, the influence of his 1960 production for the Old Vic and productions in Italy and New York and his appeal to youth culture have been well documented.[22] This discussion will centre on aspects of Zeffirelli's presentation of Romeo and Juliet: his adaptation of the script; his attention to various representations of love; his use of spectacle and interpolated scenes to attribute meaning to geographical locations.

Retaining 35 per cent (approximately 1,044.5 lines) of Shakespeare's script,[23] Zeffirelli concentrated on the central characters. He shaped the roles to minimise the disadvantages of casting inexperienced actors, to make the characters less complex, and to make them more attractive to his target audience. He excised, for example, Juliet's soliloquy before drinking the potion and Romeo's attempted suicide, his visit to the apothecary and his murder of Paris.

Zeffirelli imbues his film with a zest for life and love, best illustrated by looking at his handling of Capulets' splendid feast. He juxtaposes the betrothal of Juliet to Paris with the Capulets' crumbling marriage, introduced by Capulet's telling delivery of 'too soon marred' (1.2.13) and here demonstrated by Lady Capulet's disdain for Capulet and her flirting with Tybalt. He focuses on an array of listeners' responses – romantic, transported, bemused, questioning – to the vocalist, whose theme is *carpe diem*:

> What is a youth? Impetuous fire.
> What is a maid? Ice and desire.
> The world wags on,
> A rose will bloom . . .
> It then will fade,
> So does a youth,
> So does the fairest maid.

And he juxtaposes the interpolated song and the listeners' expressions with Romeo, who pursues Juliet around the circle of listeners and grabs her hand on 'so does the fairest maid'. Other views of love include Rosaline's rejection of Romeo with a cruel glance and the Nurse's fondness for Juliet. The sequence introduces an important visual image – Romeo's and Juliet's hands – and their theme music.[24] It introduces also, through Lady Capulet's treatment of Capulet, behaviour traits that will mark Juliet's transition to maturity: the ability to dissemble and to command.

Other sequences further explore the theme of love, some more fully than had earlier films: the Friar's concern for Romeo, Balthazar's loyalty to Romeo, the inclusion of Romeo's farewell to Balthazar. The zest for life, explored most fully by John McEnery's excellent Mercutio, and zest for love, represented by Leonard Whiting's young Romeo, make their scenes poignant. Presciently masked as death, Mercutio attends the feast. Exhausted after his energetic delivery of Queen Mab, Mercutio collapses against Romeo; mortally wounded, he again collapses on Romeo. Zeffirelli has been credited with introducing homosexual undertones to this relationship.[25]

A distinguishing feature of Zeffirelli's realism is its disassociation from the kinds of sources Cukor and Castellani had relied on. The advantage of drawing on paintings of Renaissance Italy for things such as costumes, scenery and pictorial composition becomes a liability when the audience slips into student mode, identifying painter and painting as though sitting for a slide examination in art history. Zeffirelli's treatment of the market square illustrates his quite different method. His opening shot, which pans over Verona, introduces the centrality of Verona and its market square.[26] Zeffirelli imbues the square with more significance than had Cukor, whose film had an opening sequence with a religious procession, and Castellani, whose film had an opening sequence of the market traders arriving. All three directors set many of the public sequences in the square. But only Zeffirelli capitalises on the church which forms one side of the square. He associates the church, with its Romanesque arches, fading frescoes and mosaic pavement, exclusively with Romeo and Juliet. The Nurse delivers Juliet's message to Romeo there and Friar Laurence marries the couple there. Mercutio dies on its steps. The film closes not with feuding factions in opposing lines but with the bodies of Romeo and Juliet, dressed in their wedding finery and carried in a single cortège past lines of black-clad mourners, through the square and up the steps to the entrance of the cathedral. As the cortège passes through the square, one does not remember Renaissance paintings such as those evoked by Cukor's and Castellani's interpolations of Juliet's funeral. Instead one revisits events that had taken place in the square and the church. Zeffirelli's visual strategy is similar to Olivier's in the closing sequence of his *Hamlet* (1948), in which Hamlet's bier is carried past significant places in the castle at Elsinore. The final visual image is pairs of familiar faces, as the grief-stricken families, their households and friends pause at the threshold to exchange condolences and forgiveness.

By far the darker of the two films, Luhrmann's modern-dress adaptation isolates Romeo (Leonardo DiCaprio) and Juliet (Claire Danes) within the crass, violent and superficial society of Verona Beach and Sycamore Grove, its shabby seaside amusement park. The Capulets' ostentatious and tasteless display of wealth, Capulet's physical violence with his disobedient daughter, the city-paralysing violence of the feuding families, the omnipresent guns and readily accessible drugs, Christian symbols stripped of meaning and translated into designer ornaments or rococo artefacts – all serve to heighten the vulnerability and attractiveness of Romeo and Juliet.

Luhrmann is preoccupied with creating a distinctive aura for Romeo and Juliet. Costuming Romeo as a medieval knight and Juliet as an angel for Capulet's fancy-dress extravaganza, Luhrmann offers a bold visual statement. Romeo and Juliet alone possess a stillness and serenity, which Luhrmann conveys through symbols associated with them (the tiny cross Juliet wears on a chain about her neck and an engraved ring), by filming their scenes in softer focus and longer sequences, by making their theme a lyrical torch song and by contrasting their love with the absence of love in Verona Beach and Sycamore Grove. During the feast 'Capulet ogles some passing young ladies';[27] the self-obsessed Paris,

costumed in a NASA space suit, does not notice that the angelic Juliet's attention has strayed to a gate-crashing medieval knight; at Sycamore Grove punters
proposition prostitutes. Juliet, on the other hand, is surprised by Romeo's
sudden 'wilt thou leave me so unsatisfied' and the parting scene – 'Wilt thou be
gone?' (Act 3 scene 5) – is, by contemporary standards, chaste and witty.

The richness of Luhrmann's visual images and his soundtrack offer several
fruitful veins of enquiry; they are, for example, witty, allusive, provocative.[28]
Darkly parodic visual images and scenes link love with the violence that will
destroy it, foreshadow tragedy and characterise the tragedy of love. Surprised by
Juliet in the balcony scene, Romeo falls backwards into the Capulets' swimming
pool; mortally wounded by Romeo, Tybalt falls backwards into water.
Dominated by Gloria Capulet in Act 1 scene 3, Juliet takes a teenager's revenge:
she speaks 'Farewell! God knows when we shall meet again' directly to her
mother, not to herself. The boys' choir, which sings evocative music, and the
Nurse, who watches from the back of the church, would seem welcome guests at
the 'secret' wedding; but who is the unidentifiable man just behind the Nurse and
why is he there? Romeo and Juliet carry pistols; Juliet's designer pistol rests
beside her on the bier. Used as a visual for the television news reports, the ring
loses its privacy as a symbol.

Luhrmann's framing device, which transforms the narrative into a series of
front page stories and television news items,[29] can also be read on several levels.
It cleverly provides convenient and slick exposition and transition between
scenes. Reporting the feud on the evening news, a television commentator identifies the characters for her viewers; later she announces the party as an important social event. Banner headlines and news flashes move the plot along. But the
device, far from immortalising the young lovers, gives them nothing more than
their fifteen minutes of fame, teenaged suicides in a sensational crime story. At
the close of the long sequence in the church, its aisles marked by garish neon
crosses, the camera lingers over the candle- and angel-banked bier of Juliet and
Romeo, draws away once more to place Romeo and Juliet in the context of empty
symbols and then cuts to a sequence composed of brief, rapid shots of the emer-
gency services arriving and the media coverage. Luhrmann excises the exchange
of forgiveness and closes with the bleak image of a flickering, unwatched television set. Did the watcher fall asleep or walk away during the news? Was the news
bulletin too painful? Or was s/he untouched by the latest round of violence in
the community?

Othello

In three of the four films of *Othello* – Orson Welles (1952), Sergei Yutkevich
(1956) and Oliver Parker (1995) – the opening sequences introduce a point of

view and visual images that will contribute significantly to the way the director presents Othello and Desdemona and Iago's destruction of their marriage. Each director establishes a dominant tone for his film, reveals an aspect of the Venetians' respect for Othello, presents Othello and Desdemona in a religious or social ceremony and anticipates the closing sequences. The films may share traits, but most of the apparent similarities stem from the common source and especially Shakespeare's imagery and the locations of Venice and Cyprus. Resonating with other images in the film, the apparent borrowings assume a singularity.

In the pre-credit sequence, Welles establishes the formal tone, stately pace and visual images that will dominate his filmic adaptation of Shakespeare's tragedy. Cowled, chanting monks process behind the biers of Othello and Desdemona; mourning soldiers and villagers crowd against the castle wall; chained Iago is dragged through the crowd and imprisoned in an iron cage, which is raised high over a fortress wall; Emilia's casket joins the procession. The sequence anticipates the Venetians' affording Othello a Christian funeral and, presumably, the forgiveness implicit in the act. It also introduces a number of visual motifs: silhouettes and shadows; sequences shot from a number of angles; imagery of containment; contrasts between horizontal and vertical; significant architectural details.[30] Welles relies on visual effects to amplify the heavily cut text and to contribute significantly to the presentation of Othello (Welles), Desdemona (Suzanne Cloutier) and Iago (Micheál MacLiammóir).

Welles's Othello is statuesque and controlled. His first words are the formal, measured speech to the senators, 'Most potent, grave, and reverend signors' (1.3.76 etc.); his reunion with Desdemona is coldly formal; he sends an emissary to summon the brawlers before him; and his face conveys little of the turmoil evoked by Iago. Welles's dignified Othello, whose long robes accentuate his noble stature, contrasts sharply with MacLiammóir's scrappy loner, his unbecoming costume inspired by Carpaccio. In his diary of the filming, *Put Money in Thy Purse*, MacLiammóir describes Iago's appearance: 'hair falling wispishly to shoulders, small round hats of plummy red felt . . . very short belted jackets, undershirt pulled in puffs through apertures in sleeves laced with ribbons and leather thongs, long hose, and laced boots'.[31] MacLiammóir spits out Iago's words in a matter-of-fact manner. Whereas Othello fills a frame, Iago typically enters the frame from behind his target and adjusts his pace to accommodate that of the character he is manipulating. Two other visual images characterise Iago: he is seldom still, and he almost always gets the dominant physical position from which he literally looks down on Othello, as well as on Roderigo (Robert Coote) and Cassio (Michael Lawrence). Iago is diminished by Roderigo's cuddly white lapdog, who seems to comment ironically on Iago's disloyalty and to call attention to the ensign's mongrel appearance.[32]

Like Yutkevich and Parker, Welles interpolates scenes to introduce and define the marriage. He films Othello and Desdemona in a gondola *en route* to the wedding, a brief glimpse of the secret ceremony and Desdemona, her loose blond hair arranged decoratively on the pillow, awaiting Othello for the consummation of their marriage. Their Cypriot bed figures in three other brief interpolated scenes: before the brawl, the couple, with lines transferred from Act 2 scene 2. ('If it were now to die / 'Twere now to die most happy'); Othello, his rest disturbed by rioting. In Act 3 scene 3, seeking evidence for Desdemona's alleged adultery, Othello draws the curtains and looks at their bed.

Welles's script helps establish Desdemona's loyalty: on her own initiative she attends the Senate and she arrives at the brawl immediately after Othello. Despite the interpolated sequences, the bedroom shots and Desdemona's loyalty, Welles's film falls short of conveying the marriage as a love-match and the tragedy of love. The formality of concept and Welles's stately Othello raise the film to a lofty plain, but the sharp and moving visual images, which appeal primarily to the eye, undermine the tragic intent.

Throughout the film, shots of the empty cage foreshadow Iago's punishment and fit into a pattern of images that confine Desdemona and Othello. Desdemona's braided hair and, later, her snood, both decorated with pearls, signal her innocence. But they also anticipate the imagery of imprisonment in three key scenes. Desdemona's second plea for Cassio takes place in the armoury where Iago had, literally, disarmed Othello. Shot through a rack of spears, Desdemona seems to be behind bars. Separated from Emilia (Fay Compton) by a window grille with spikes on one side, Desdemona hums the willow song and discusses adultery with her companion (Act 4 scene 3). Immediately after, Othello, whose approach is filmed as shadows on stone walls, peers at Desdemona through another barred window. Nets and cages also help portray Iago's entrapment of Othello. But another set of images works in much the same way as do those which resonate with Desdemona's pearls, braids and snood. Othello's triumphant arrival at the fortress in Cyprus contrasts with his loss of command and Iago's confinement of his general to stony rooms and narrow stairwells. Welles encouraged MacLiammóir to play Iago as impotent and explained 'that's why he hates life so much'.[33] MacLiammóir summarises Welles's view:

> No single trace of the Mephistophelean Iago is to be used: no conscious villainy; a common man, clever as a waggonload of monkeys, his thought never on the present moment but always on the move after the move after next: a business man dealing in destruction with neatness, method, and a proper pleasure in his work: the honest Iago reputation is accepted because it has become almost the truth.[34]

MacLiammóir's Iago is passionless, even somewhat mechanical, and he makes no concessions to companionability. Emilia makes clear her bitter disgust with him, especially in her delivery of "'Tis not a year or two shows us a man. / They are all but stomachs, and we all but food; / They eat us hungerly, and when they are full, / They belch us' (3.4.99–102) and in her angry glance and quick departure when Iago dismisses her.

The films of Welles and Sergei Yutkevich, both of which won first prizes at Cannes, open with interpolated sequences in two quite different moods. Yutkevich records the closing moments of Othello's (Sergei Bondarchuk) visit to Brabantio (E. Teterin) and Desdemona's (I. Skobtseva) romantic fantasy of a heroic Othello's exploits at sea. Gazing at the celestial globe Othello had rested his hand on, Desdemona imagines 'the dangers' Othello 'had passed', endows Othello's countenance with power to stay the hand that would whip him, and pictures him in triumphant command of a Venetian ship.[35] Yutkevich's interpolation invites three interrelated lines of enquiry: the juxtaposition of Othello's unintentional seduction of Desdemona with Iago's intentional destruction of Othello; the pattern of visual images introduced in the sequence; its relationship with the portrayal of the marriage and with the closing sequences.

Yutkevich's presentation of Desdemona and Othello focuses on the romantic aspect of their courtship and marriage. Before the Venetian Senate, Othello is polite, modest but not deferential; his bearing, statuesque but not overpowering; his reception, cordial. Desdemona clutches the handkerchief[36] and gazes fondly on her husband. Yutkevich stages a dramatic reunion in Cyprus for which Desdemona dresses in tights and jacket with military trim. He films their Cypriot scenes in picture-postcard settings and enhances the image by costuming Desdemona with attractive dresses and changes in hairstyle. By not showing their bedroom until Shakespeare's script calls for it, he gives power to the scene and the symbol. Yutkevich, who has introduced Brabantio's discovery of his daughter's empty bed, also links Desdemona's elopement in Venice with her murder in Cyprus. In Act 5 scene 2 Yutkevich films Othello's entrance from Desdemona's perspective, his face in red light, his outstretched hands directed towards her. An organ plays, as it had at their wedding. After he murders Desdemona, Othello disappears behind drapery; when he reappears his hair is silver.

Iago (A. Popov) employs one strategy for Roderigo (E. Vesnik) and Cassio (V. Soshalsky) and another for Othello. Typically, Iago works on Roderigo and Cassio in cramped spaces in obscuring night-time. With them he affects a familiar comradeship, putting his arm around their shoulders in gestures of comfort and understanding and touching Roderigo's face and Cassio's head in disarmingly fond gestures. His strategy with Othello is more complex: he relies on and, sometimes, redefines images from Desdemona's evocation of Othello's bravery at sea and from the General's appearance before the Senate. Iago and Othello walk along the ramparts and along the strand; they ride horses through scrubby, barren countryside; they talk by an anchor and in the empty cabin of a moored ship. An increasingly complex series of fishing nets, an image Welles had used, signifies the stages of Othello's entanglement. With Othello, Iago affects respect and does not initiate any touching. As he had with Emilia (A. Maximova), Iago looks away when Othello rests his head on the ensign's shoulder: 'Now art thou my lieutentant' – 'I am your own for ever' (3.3.481–2). The two men are held in focus, but Iago's expression does not seem to signify an unstated love for Othello. Rather, with Emilia and with Othello, Iago pulls away from those he deceives. The gesture anticipates the final sequence, in which Iago, bound to the mast of the ship that carries the bodies of Othello and Desdemona, is unable to raise his head and to avert looking at the bodies of the couple he has destroyed. Yutkevich reads *Othello* as 'the tragedy of faith, the tragedy of trust and treachery'.[37]

Much of Yutkevich's film is set out of doors and in bright sunlight.[38] The treachery is played out against a backdrop of blue sky and seas, rocky cliffs and hills; Desdemona receives Cassio beneath an arbour ripe with grapes. The film takes 'every advantage of the spectacular coastal scenery of the Crimea', and Anthony Davies has examined 'the extent to which [Yutkevich] achieves an integrated dramatization of nature, and the extent to which there is an ironic relationship between exterior and interior (psychological) action'.[39] By evoking the supernatural, another cluster of visual images underscores the mythic, universal aspects of the tragedy. When Othello recalls Desdemona as 'an admirable musician! O, she will sing the savageness out of a bear!' Yutkevich presents her as a siren leading Othello to destruction on the rocks.[40] The zodiacal signs on the celestial globe in Brabantio's sitting-room, the winged lion of St Mark, the mythical sea beasts on the mosaic, the grizzled face of an ancient god carved on rock against which Othello delivers the speech beginning 'This fellow's of exceeding honesty' (3.3.262 etc.),[41] the classical ruins, the portrayal of Desdemona as a siren – all tend to relocate the action from a spot on the globe to a storied universe, where one might meet 'the Anthropophagi, and men whose heads / Do grow beneath their shoulders' (1.3.143–4).

The closing sequences of Yutkevich's film are evocative of the opening sequences and resonate also with the celebration in Cyprus. Othello, as he had in Desdemona's fantasy, gradually regains command: he closes the bed curtain so that the assembly cannot stare at Desdemona; he dismisses them and carries Desdemona's body to the tower from which he and Desdemona had watched the celebratory fireworks. Lodovico (P. Brilling), the prisoner Iago and attendants discover him obeisant at Desdemona's feet. After he stabs himself, he kisses her and shrouds their bodies with his white cape. Iago pounds his fist in fury and defeat.[42] The scene dissolves to the ship, which carries their bodies and which resembles the one Othello had commanded.[43]

Although the influence of Welles and Yutkevich can be seen in Oliver Parker's adaptation, his film is closer to the Zeffirelli tradition of realism and follows the recent stage practice of casting younger actors as Othello and Desdemona. Parker films Venice, warts and all, and the fortress that is its military outpost in Cyprus, providing realistic detail for both locations. Parker's presentation of place, his playing a higher percentage of the text than Zeffirelli – or Welles and Yutkevich – and his staging of unscripted scenes help Laurence Fishburne and Irène Jacob portray a convincing attraction between Othello and Desdemona.

Parker's interpolations portray several stages of the romance and help to give the marriage a solid and believable basis. He films Desdemona's journey to the church, which takes her through deserted, rubbish-strewn arcades, and the final moments of the wedding ceremony. During Othello's appearance before the senators he uses flashback to film two of Othello's visits to Brabantio's (Pierre Vaneck) residence. In the first sequence, Brabantio and his guest walk and talk in a garden; Desdemona and Othello exchange glances, but she and her attendants seem to be too far away to hear Othello's stories. In the second sequence, in which the romance has blossomed, Othello uses the handkerchief to wipe a tear from Desdemona's eyes. Parker further visualises their attraction to and fondness for each other in the long sequence of the feast in Cyprus, which includes a formal banquet and dancing. And, of course, Parker films the couple disrobing for the consummation of their marriage. Their intertwined hands and rose petals on the bridal linens, symbolic of their love, will recur in the second series of interpolated scenes, which charts Iago's (Kenneth Branagh) destruction of the marriage. Othello twists these scenes into haunting evidence of Desdemona's alleged affair with Cassio (Nathaniel Parker). As Iago poisons Othello's mind, Othello sees Desdemona's adultery in increasingly detailed and tormenting visions: in Act 3 scene 3, Desdemona and Cassio dancing flirtatiously, Desdemona's mocking smile, Cassio and Desdemona's hands and bodies interwined and the rose petals, and in flashback Brabantio's warning. In Act 4 scene 1 he sees an extended sexual encounter.

It has been argued that the interpolations take away from Fishburne's performance the misery Othello imagines.[44] They contribute though to the integrity of the overall design of the film and point to other aspects of Fishburne's strong performance. First, his relationship with Desdemona. The romantic tone in which he describes their courtship and his delivery of lines such as 'Excellent wretch! Perdition catch my soul / But I do love thee!' (3.3.91–2) convey his fondness for Desdemona. Othello sheds tears in his Act 4 scene 2 confrontation of Desdemona and at the beginning of Act 5 scene 2. Parker juxtaposes Desdemona singing the willow song with a shot of a pensive Othello standing under the branches of a weeping willow on a moonlit shore. Next, in his commanding and assured presence before the Senate, his eye contact with the senators conveys his confidence. He represses his anger towards the changed Brabantio; he steps in front of him to speak 'Her father loved me' directly to Brabantio, who is then portrayed in flashback as a welcoming host. On Cyprus Fishburne expresses Othello's anger: he pulls Montano (Nicholas Farrell) by the hair (2.3.158), he strips Cassio of his lieutenant's sash and slaps him with it (2.3.245), he threatens Emilia (Anna Patrick) with a sword against her neck (5.2.157). More crucially, Othello's anger sharpens the scenes with Iago: he holds a pistol to Iago's chest ('By heaven, I'll know thy thoughts' – 3.3.167); subsequently he hounds Iago along the strand, plunges him into the water, and holds his head under for a frighteningly long time, and he grabs him by the collar to demand 'Give me a living reason she's disloyal' (3.3.414).

Instead of casting Desdemona in the tradition of beautiful blond cipher, photographing her in static or romantic situations, and redefining her character with a heavily cut text, Parker presents a Desdemona whose firmness with the Senate, fondness for Othello and feistiness when accused make her a suitable match for Fishburne's Othello. She struggles to save her life.

Parker introduces Iago's destruction of Othello as moves in a chess match.[45] Iago places the black king and white queen on a board and puts the white knight between them as he deliberates on his course of action (1.3.386); in Act 4 scene 2, as he says 'This is the night / That either makes me, or fordoes me quite'; in Act 5 scene 1, he pushes the chess king and queen off the castle wall and into the sea, a move presaging the burial at sea of Othello and Desdemona. The image is appropriate to the calculating aspect of Branagh's Iago, who is quietly efficient in his dealings with Othello. But the pre-eminence given the fortress and the military make the image of a naval engagement, illustrated with a map and model ship at the very beginning of the film, more fitting. Parker reorders the script to make the first words Venice's need to defend Cyprus. Parker places most of the Cypriot scenes in the fortress; Act 3 scene 3 moves from a bright, sunlit exercise field, where Othello gets the better of Iago, to an armory well stocked with swords and guns, where Iago and Othello clean and load guns and Iago gets the better of Othello; Act 4 scene 1 takes place in the dungeon. Parker's use of the fortress does more than pay homage to Welles: it establishes the centrality of a military ethos. Iago adopts a jocular, barrack-room camaraderie with Cassio, who responds in kind to Iago's smutty innuendoes about Desdemona in Act 2 scene 3. Parker's interpolations, such as the lusty and drunken soldiers who celebrate the victory, add another dimension to the military setting. Iago plays the quietly efficient ensign to Othello's general. The key scene between them is the close of Act 3 scene 3, which Parker repositions just before the arrival of the Venetians in Act 4 scene 1. As is now fairly regular practice on the stage, Parker introduces Iago's love for Othello as a motivating factor. Othello and Iago seal a blood bond with a handshake; Iago addresses the first part of his speech to the heavens:

> Witness you ever-burning lights above,
> You elements, that clip us round about,
> Witness that here Iago doth give up
> The execution of his wit, hands, –

but from 'heart', the next word, to the end of the speech he directs his words to Othello

>   – heart,
> To wronged Othello's service. Let him commmand,
> And to obey shall be in me remorse,
> What bloody business ever.   (3.3.466–72)

They embrace; the camera focuses on Iago's face, etched in pain of his unexpressed love for Othello. In his next scene Iago wears the sash of office, now symbolic of his being bound to Othello. He forces himself into the tableau which forms the final image: Iago drags himself on to the bed and rests his head on Othello's leg.

Unlike the versions conceived as film scripts, which open with interpolated sequences of a cortège, the courtship, or the marriage ceremony, Stuart Burge's film (1965) of the National Theatre production (1964, directed by John Dexter) opens with Roderigo (Robert Lang) speaking the first line of Shakespeare's script. Roger Manvell and others recount the background of filming and evaluate the film's place in the history of filmed accounts of theatrical performances.[46] In the context of this tragedy of love on film, three interrelated points are important: key scenes and speeches cry out for a stage and a live audience; Laurence Olivier's Othello is the central performance; the consistently strong acting explores the differences in military and social rank of Othello, Cassio (Derek Jacobi) and Iago (Frank Finlay) and the relationships between men and women. In other words, the gains may be balanced against the losses.

Not surprisingly, most of the scenes that would work better on stage centre on Olivier's Othello. The film exaggerates the intensity of his performance, especially in Act 3 scene 3 and Act 4 scene 1. The commanding physicality of Olivier's gestures and movement, which on stage would seem to reach out in pain and disbelief and appeal, are filmed in medium shots and close-ups and, as a consequence, his head and torso fill the frame and his gestures and movement are too broad or awkward. Similarly, in Act 3 scene 3 the crescendo of speeches such as 'Ha, ha, false to me, to me', 'Farewell the tranquil mind!', 'Now do I see 'tis true', and 'Damn her, lewd minx!' projects Othello's words to the gods, far beyond the last row of a typical cinema – or, still worse – a video audience.[47] In these and other scenes one wishes for a fuller picture not only of Othello but also of responses to him. In transferring Iago to the screen, Finlay misjudges a number of scenes shared with one other character. With Roderigo (1.3.301 etc.) and with Cassio (2.3.253 etc.), for example, he directs some speeches to a larger audience.

On the other hand, Finlay uses the camera well for Iago's soliloquies, and, as Alice Griffin points out, reinstates Iago, who in the stage production had been 'demoted . . . to a definitely secondary role, a hating and hateful non-com'.[48] The opening scene and the revelry and quarrelling on Cyprus also make an unsatisfactory transfer to film. In Act 2 scene 3, for example, the director introduces details that contribute to the larger motif of relationships between men and women. The film teases with unanswered questions (who is the boyish woman resting against Iago's chest?) and hints at unexplored conflicts between the garrison and the Cypriot community when a Cypriot spits in Bianca's (Sheila Reid) face. The half light and the movement of characters off-camera deny us answers. However – and more crucially – the concept of the production is very firmly based on the eponymous character and does not seek, as the other films do, to portray realistically Venice and Cyprus.

The most controversial aspect of Olivier's portrayal is his blacking-up. The effect today is troubling, not only because seldom is a white actor now cast as Othello but also because of the glistening black make-up, some aspects of Olivier's carefully detailed portrait and the film's highlighting of the virtuosity of his performance and revealing the inadequacies of make-up. (On the other hand, the softer tones of Sergei Bondarchuk's make-up, together with his performance and the concept of Yutkevitch's film, are less offensive.) Some 1960s reviewers found Olivier's portrayal unacceptable: 'his primitivism is an embarrassment';[49] he gives 'the by-now outrageous impression of a theatrical Negro stereotype';[50] 'he is . . . an effeminate and querulous West Indian beach boy'.[51] More recently, Barbara Hodgdon: 'Olivier's Othello confirms an absolute fidelity to white stereotypes of blackness and to the fantasies, cultural as well as theatrical, that such stereotypes engender . . . The "real" black body, and the histories it carries, can be elided, displaced into and contained by theatricality, which embraces a long tradition of whites blacking up, primarily, as in minstrelsy, for comic effect.'[52]

Other critics sought the concept behind the portrayal: 'Olivier, both in characterization and makeup, stressed the blackness of Othello, the exotic alien surrounded by respectful but potentially hostile whites';[53] 'but what could slip easily into racial parody becomes instead a sympathetic portrait of a man who has made himself indispensable to a society which denies him full membership'.[54] James E. Fisher and Jorgens, especially, consider how Olivier and Dexter adapted F. R. Leavis's thesis that Othello's downfall is greatly contributed to by his 'habit of self-approving self-dramatization'.[55] Fisher identifies Othello's 'pride in his stature, his prowess, his power to captivate admiration [as] the chief determinant of [his] character and fate' and asserts that Olivier's appearance and bearing are central to Othello's personality and character: 'What Olivier's Othello himself commands with is a triumphant sense of his own blackness, which not simply sets him apart from others but, in his own view, sets him above them as well.'[56]

The most striking attribute of Othello's 'command' is his self-assured stillness, his confidence that 'my services, which I have done the signory' (1.2.18) will out-weigh Brabantio's (Anthony Nicholls) complaint and that he will quell the disturbance in Cyprus and his playing the trump card with Brabantio:

> How may the Duke be therewith satisfied,
> Whose messengers are here about my side,
> Upon some present business of the state
> To bring me to him?   (1.2.89–92)

Olivier's proud carriage is well supported by his voice, trained an octave lower for the part and deeper, richer than the Venetian voices. When Othello speaks or thinks of Desdemona (Maggie Smith), Olivier interpolates self-satisfied grunts and hums. In Act 1 scene 2 his appearance is simple and striking: a white caftan, a bulky chain and cross around his neck, thick bracelets on his wrists, and a long-stemmed red rose, which he sniffs and toys with. In these early scenes Olivier reveals fissures in Othello's proud facade. Encouraged by the senators' response to the Anthropophagi, the general misjudges his audience with 'men whose heads / Do grow beneath their shoulders' and lapses, very briefly, into a com-radeship or equality with the Duke (Harry Lomax) and senators. Stung, he takes refuge in 'his power to captivate admiration'. More seriously, in Act 1 scene 3 his pride blinds him to Iago's grinning response to 'My life upon her faith!'

In sun-drenched Cyprus and with Iago as agent, Othello's command disinte-grates and his distinguishing traits are parodied: manic gestures and a voice enraged replace his stillness; with Desdemona at the beginning of Act 3 scene 4, tension now marks the interpolated noises. The bracelet conceals a knife, which Othello pulls on Iago at 'If thou dost slander her and torture me' (3.3.373). Othello's silence and rigid inertness during the fit juxtapose ironically with the commanding composure in Act 1; Iago restrains Othello's tongue with the general's dagger. Before Lodovico's (Kenneth Mackintosh) arrival, Iago's checking Othello's tongue for foam visualises the distance he has fallen since his confident perfor-mance before the Senate. In Welles and Parker, Iago helps Othello out of a military costume in a military setting. In Burge/Dexter, on a bare stage backed by golden stone walls, Iago removes Othello's splendid caftan, a full-length garment of bold stripes in tones of black and yellow, designed to give Othello height, to broaden his shoulders, to obscure the middle-aged paunch he had displayed proudly in Act 1 scene 2. The disrobing reveals a close-fitting black cassock which ages Othello by calling attention to his narrow shoulders and paunch – 'I am declined / Into the vale of years' (3.3.269–70) – and makes him more vulnerable to Iago.

A lethal mixture of sexual, social and professional jealousy propels Finlay's Iago. Convinced of Emilia's (Joyce Redmond) infidelity with Othello, he misreads her pleasant, trusting manner; he does not return Emilia's kiss and pushes her from him (3.3.324). His gulling of Othello has an air of sexual seduction.[57] Class difference intensifies his professional jealousy of Jacobi's sophisticated Cassio, every detail of whose appearance and performance sets him above the plain ensign.[58] Iago, not Othello, strips Cassio of his sword; Cassio takes off the lieutenant's sash, folds it carefully and gazes at it. Against Iago's brown tunic, decorated only with rows of medal studs, the richly embroidered sash sits uneasily.

Dignity, intelligence and maturity (marred occasionally by a girlish gesture) are the defining characteristics of Smith's Desdemona. The film script retains a higher percentage of her lines than are retained in the other versions. The cuts, which affect Emilia as well as Desdemona, delete much of the cynicism about relationships between men and women. Desdemona loses her exchange with Iago (2.1.106–64), in which she accuses him of telling the 'old fond paradoxes [that] make fools laugh i'th' alehouse'; Emilia's sharp retort is cut (3.4.101–4) as is the women's discussion of adultery in Act 4 scene 3. Redmond's soliloquy in Act 3 scene 3 after she picks up the handkerchief and especially her delivery of 'I'll have the work ta'en out' make clear her loyalty to Desdemona. Only Iago's arrival interrupts her determination to have a copy made for Iago. Desdemona's relationship with Emilia is, as a consequence, companionable rather than complex. With Othello, Desdemona is flirtatious without demeaning herself and compassionate, seeking in illness an explanation for his unexpected behaviour. Desdemona is, as Cassio says, 'exquisite'. Although Smith's Desdemona is a suitable wife for Olivier's Othello, the power of Olivier's performance and the film's concentration on him privilege, as does the text itself, the tragedy of Othello rather than the tragedy of Desdemona and Othello.

Antony and Cleopatra

With its promise of legendary characters in a splendid Mediterranean world, *Antony and Cleopatra* seems ideally suited for the large screen. But, as others have pointed out, Shakespeare's often intimate script is more suitable for television or small theatres.[59] Shakespeare presents the eponymous characters through image-rich language that defies translation to visual effects and through the observations of almost all of the other characters, a number of them little more than cameo roles. Charlton Heston's flawed film (1972), which was not released theatrically in the USA, grapples with the dichotomy between promise and reality and with the major conflicts between Egypt and Rome, between love and war. The actor-director attempts to bring order to Shakespeare's sprawling script: he cuts numerous lines and speeches, reorders scenes, substitutes large-scale battles at sea and on land for Shakespeare's two groups of short scenes, and reduces the number of minor characters.[60] Although the film script is promising and actors such as Eric Porter (Enobarbus), John Castle (Octavius Caesar),

Freddie Jones (Pompey), Joe Melia (Messenger), Jane Lapotaire (Charmian) and Julian Glover (Proculeius) are strong, the film fails, as so many stage productions have failed, because the central characters are not convincing and do not convey the range Shakespeare invests them with. Hildegarde Neil falls far short of Cleopatra's 'infinite variety' and Heston's Antony is not, even allowing for Cleopatra's elegiac hyperbole, the 'noblest of men'.

The film opens with shots of a Roman ship arriving in Egypt. Proculeius mounts the waiting horse and races through the streets, upsetting citizens and smashing their property, to Cleopatra's palace, where he learns that Antony is 'in the garden'. Although the inserted dialogue is banal, the scene itself is a more dramatic opening than Philo's description of Cleopatra, establishes the urgency of the message from Rome, introduces the enhanced character of Proculeius and provides a dramatic unity with the final scene, in which Proculeius returns to Egypt.

Proculeius, to whom Heston reassigns lines, gains several scenes and is Caesar's follower with the most intimate knowledge of Antony's Egyptian life. As Caesar's messenger in Act 1 scene 1 and Act 1 scene 2, he is the first and most important of Caesar's followers to travel to Cleopatra's court. In the early scenes, Proculeius hears Enobarbus describe Antony's flaws. Enobarbus is assigned, significantly, Philo's speech beginning 'nay, but this dotage'; asking the question Shakespeare assigns to Demetrius – 'Is Caesar with Antonius prized so slight?' – Proculeius hears Philo's brief assessment of Antony's opinion of Caesar, lines also reassigned to Enobarbus (1.1.59–61). In the final scene Proculeius serves as the guard who discovers Cleopatra's suicide and the dying Charmian. Proculeius also gains lines from Dolabella and carries the drunken Lepidus (Fernando Rey) (2.7). In addition to creating a recognisable character, there are two important effects of Heston's redefinition of the part: Caesar sends one of his followers, not an anonymous emissary to Antony; the more generous Proculeius is a foil to Agrippa (Doug Wilmer) in scenes such as the party on Pompey's barge, where the sour Agrippa takes his cue from stony-faced Caesar.

Heston also increases the importance of the Soothsayer (Roger Delgardo). Reassigning lines from three characters, Heston links the Soothsayer with events he has foreseen: he announces to the dying Antony that Cleopatra is alive (Diomedes, Act 4 scene 14), reports Antony's death to Caesar (Decretas, Act 5 scene 1), and speaks with Cleopatra (Clown, Act 5 scene 2) before she applies the asp, supplied by Mardian (Emiliano Redondo). The Soothsayer's totem, a white Roman helmet with a red plume, is introduced in Act 1 scene 2; it recurs in Act 2 scene 3, when Antony decides to return to Cleopatra, and in Act 4 scene 14, where the Soothsayer drops it on the ground next to Antony's bloody sword.

In Rome, an interpolated show of strength by two gladiators comments on the power struggle between Antony and Caesar. As Octavius Caesar and Lepidus wait for Antony's arrival, two gladiators, one of whom is armed with a symbolic triton, entertain the tribunes (Act 2 scene 2). Heston cross-cuts between fighters and rulers to shed light on Caesar, who insults Antony by calling for the battle to resume immediately after he enters. Caesar agrees simultaneously to the marriage between Octavia (Carmen Sevilla) and Antony and to the release of one gladiator, whose arm had been pinned by the triton.

Reordered scenes alter the presentation of Antony and Cleopatra, Antony and Octavia. Heston makes bitter-sweet the presentation of Antony's gift to Cleopatra (Act 1 scene 5) by placing it immediately after Antony has agreed to marry Octavia (Act 2 scene 2). Heston creates curiosity about Caesar's sister by withholding the introduction of Octavia, placing it in Act 3 scene 2, not Act 2 scene 3 and repositioning the scene after the Pompey scenes (Act 2 scenes 6, 7) and after the messenger to Cleopatra announces Antony's marriage (Act 2 scene 5). He postpones Antony's first conversation with Octavia (Act 2 scene 3) until immediately after the Messenger's canny description of Octavia (Act 3 scene 3). His revisions culminate in Antony's decision to return to Cleopatra. Antony explains that his 'great office' will sometimes take him from Octavia, who brushes her hair in preparation for bed. Turning his advance aside, Octavia dismisses him. Leaving, Antony hears Cleopatra say 'Eternity was in our lips and eyes / Bliss in our brows' bent' (1.3.35–6); after his exchanges with the Soothsayer and Ventidius (Aldo Sambrel), Antony overhears Enobarbus describing Antony's first view of and meeting with Cleopatra (Act 2 scene 2). Cleopatra's charms, so effectively evoked in Enobarbus' description, again draw Antony to her. The episode closes with shots of the ship at sea, waves crashing on rocks. Unfortunately the voyage is more compelling than the reunion. Heston's Antony is respectable, but Hildegarde Neil's disappointing Cleopatra, who seems to have wandered in from a 1970s domestic drama, bears little resemblance to the queen Enobarbus so famously describes.

NOTES

1 On the film adaptations of *Romeo and Juliet* in the context of earlier stage versions, see Kenneth Rothwell, 'Hollywood and Some Versions of *Romeo and Juliet*: Toward a "Substantial Pageant"', *Literature/Film Quarterly*, 1 (Fall, 1973), 343–51, and Paul A. Jorgenson, 'Castellani's *Romeo and Juliet*: Intention and Response', *Quarterly of Film, Radio and Television*, 10 (1955), 1–10.

2 Derek Elley, ed., *Variety Movie Guide 1994* (New York, 1993), p. 654, lists nominations for best picture, best actress (Norma Shearer), best supporting actor (Basil Rathbone), best art direction.

3 Gavin Lambert, *On Cukor* (London, 1973).

4 Two years before the film was shot, the production crew undertook research in Italy; inspiration for the sets and costumes include 'Botticelli, Bellini, Signorelli and such narrative artists as Benozzo Gozzoli and Carpaccio' (Meredith Lillich, 'Shakespeare on the Screen', *Films in Review*, 7 (1956), 250–1).

5 Franco Zeffirelli, *Zeffirelli: The Autobiography of Franco Zeffirelli* (London, 1986), p. 229, records that Olivier dubbed Lord Montague and 'insisted on dubbing all sorts of small parts and crowd noises in a hilarious variety of assumed voices'.

6 This estimate and all others, unless noted otherwise, are based on the New Penguin edition ed. T. J. B. Spencer (Harmondsworth, 1967). All citations, however, are to the Oxford one-volume edition of the *Complete Works* (1988). Jennings's film script gave the impression of including more of Shakespeare's play. Albert R. Cirillo, 'The Art of Franco Zeffirelli and Shakespeare's *Romeo and Juliet*', *Triquarterly*, 16 (1969–70), 69–92; p. 70: 'Unless my memory . . . fails me, the text was presented virtually uncut.'

7 Typically, the completed film does not always correspond to the shooting script. On the music see Charles Hurtgen, 'The Operatic Character of Background Music in Film Adaptations of Shakespeare', *Shakespeare Quarterly*, 20 (1969), 53–64.

8 David Garrick had staged a funeral procession for Juliet and the tradition continued throughout the nineteenth century.

9 Neil McDonald, 'The Relationship between Shakespeare's Stagecraft and Modern Film Technique', *Australian Journal of Film Theory*, 7 (1980), 18–33; p. 24, points out that Shakespeare's imagery inspires the montage.

10 Frank S. Nugent announced that 'the performances *en masse* . . . are splendid', and did not refer to the ages of Shearer, Howard or Barrymore (*New York Times*, 21 August 1936). Shearer was married to the film's producer, Irving Thalberg.

11 Francis Koval, 'Report from Venice', *Films in Review* (October 1954), 5:394, records the excitement generated by Castellani's film.

12 Lillich, 'Shakespeare on the Screen', 258–9.

13 *Ibid.*, p. 258: 'Capulet in his study was straight from Raphael's portrait of the Pope.'

14 *Ibid.*, p. 259, identifies paintings. On the music see Roman Vlad, 'Notes on the Music for *Romeo and Juliet*', *Film Music*, 14 (1955), 3–5.

15 Lauro Venturi praises the unity of the film and argues that Castellani 'emphasize[s] the humanistic, and Latin, aspects of the story . . . and . . . minimize[s] the Anglo-Saxon and the Elizabethan' ('*Romeo and Juliet*', *Films in Review*, 5 (1954), 538–40; p. 538).

16 Juliet's burial seems to take place within the cathedral; but Romeo enters the cloister, with great difficulty pries the stone lid from a vault, and makes an awkward descent to an underground chamber.

17 Castellani cast Guilo Garbinetti, a Venetian gondolier, not an actor, as Montague for his face.

18 Jorgenson ('Castellani's Romeo and Juliet', 3) admires the chase (Act 1 scene 1) and the long sequence of Romeo's return from Mantua and identfies these sequences as rooted in the play's text.

19 Sarah Munson Deats, 'Zeffirelli's *Romeo and Juliet*; Shakespeare for the Sixties', *Studies in Popular Culture*, 6 (1983), 62. See also Jack J. Jorgens, *Shakespeare on Film* (Bloomington, IN, 1977), pp. 86–7. On the popularity of the film, see also Jay L. Halio, 'Zeffirelli's *Romeo and Juliet*: The Camera *versus* the Text', *Literature/Film Quarterly*, 5 (1977), 324 and Zeffirelli's *Autobiography*, where he observes, wryly, 'I don't believe that millions of young people throughout the world wept . . . just because the costumes were splendid' (p. 341).

20 Peter Newman, 'Luhrmann's Young Lovers As Seen By Their Peers', *Shakespeare Bulletin*, 15/3 (Summer 1997), 36–7. See also Jim Welsh, 'Postmodern Shakespeare: Strictly *Romeo*', *Literature/Film Quarterly*, 25 (1997), 152–3.

21 Peter Matthews, 'William Shakespeare's *Romeo+Juliet*', *Sight and Sound*, 7 (April 1997), 55.

22 See especially Jill L. Levenson *Shakespeare in Performance: Romeo and Juliet* (Manchester, 1987), pp. 82–123. See also Zeffirelli, *Autobiography*, pp. 161–5, on the Old Vic production.

23 Ace G. Pilkington, 'Zeffirelli's Shakespeare', in Anthony Davies and Stanley Wells, eds., *Shakespeare and the Moving Image* (Cambridge, 1994), p. 165. Halio, 'Zeffirelli's *Romeo and Juliet*', 324, estimates that Zeffirelli cut 60 per cent of Shakespeare's script.

24 Zeffirelli explores more fully an image introduced by Cukor. On music, see Page Cook, 'The Sound Track', *Films in Review*, 19 (October 1968), 571–2, and Rothwell, 'Hollywood', pp. 326–31, especially pp. 327–8.

25 Renata Adler (*New York Times*, 9 October 1968): 'There is a softly homosexual cast over the film – not just with Romeo and Mercutio, but with Juliet's bodice being much too tight, or a kind of Greek attention lavished on Romeo in the bedroom scene.' See also Peter S. Donaldson, *Shakespearean Films/Shakespearean Directors* (Boston, MA, 1990), ch. 6, and William Van Watson, 'Shakespeare, Zeffirelli, and the Homosexual Gaze', *Literature/Film Quarterly*, 20 (1992), 308–25.

26 See also Jorgens's reading of the opening sequence, (*Shakespeare on Film*, pp. 81–2), and Anthony Davies, *Filming Shakespeare's Plays* (Cambridge, 1988), p. 16. Zeffirelli's opening shot is in homage to Olivier's *Henry V* (Pilkington, 'Zeffirelli's Shakespeare', p. 166).

27 Craig Pearce and Baz Luhrmann, *William Shakespeare's 'Romeo and Juliet'* (London, 1996), p. 46.

28 José Arroyo, 'Kiss Kiss Bang Bang', *Sight and Sound*, n.s. 7/3 (March 1997), 6–9, identifies several influences on Lurhmann's 'very hybrid film'. Luhrmann includes one seam of allusions to Shakespeare and (unintentionally?) to other films of *Romeo and Juliet*.

29 Theatre directors have also used this framing device. See, for example, Michael Bogdanov's history cycle and, more recently, his *Antony and Cleopatra* (UK tour, 1998), which opened with a series of on-the-scene reports from various Mediterranean locations.

30 See Jorgens, *Shakespeare on Film*, pp. 175–90 and Davies, *Filming Shakespeare's Plays*, pp. 100–18.

31 Micheál MacLiammóir, *Put Money in Thy Purse. The Making of Orson Welles's Othello* (1952; rpt. London, 1994) p. 13.

32 Welles identifies the dog as a 'tenerife', and indicates the inspiration: 'Carpaccio's full of them . . . all the dandies in Carpaccio fondle exactly that dog' (Jonathan Rosenbaum, ed., *This is Orson Welles: Orson Welles and Peter Bogdanovitch* (New York, 1992), p. 235). MacLiammóir did not like the dog.

33 MacLiammóir, *Put Money in Thy Purse*, p. 26. See also Rosenbaum, *This is Orson Welles*, p. 234.

34 MacLiammóir, *Put Money in Thy Purse*, p. 27.

35 Sergei Yutkevich, 'My Way with Shakespeare', *Films and Filming*, 4 (1957), 32, discusses his use of hands as a symbol.

36 Leaving the council chamber with Othello, Desdemona drops the handkerchief, which Iago retrieves and returns to her. Yutkevich, *ibid.*, discusses his use of the handkerchief as a symbol.

37 *Ibid.*, 8.

38 Derek Prouse, '*Othello*', *Sight and Sound*, 26 (1956), 30.

39 Roger Manvell, *Shakespeare and the Film* (1971; revised edn, London, 1979), p. 73; Davies, 'Filming *Othello*', in Davies and Wells, *Shakespeare and the Moving Image*, pp. 196–210; p. 202.

40 Manvell (*Shakespeare and the Film*, p. 76) suggests the 'solitary man' accompanying her 'by implication . . . might well be Cassio'. He could as easily be a mariner.

41 Welles films 3.3.450–64 before a Madonna, but neither Othello nor Iago kneels.

42 Yutkevich, cited in Prouse, 'Othello', 30: 'When Othello raises his dagger, it is Iago who leaps forward to stop him, having understood his intention. Othello's death negates the victory of Iago. The Moor pays for his crime with blood. His courage and his honesty elevate him above Iago.'

43 Laurie É. Osborne, 'Filming Shakespeare in a Cultural Thaw: Soviet Appropriations of Shakespearean Treacheries in 1955–6', *Textual Practice*, 9 (1995), 325, argues that 'Othello becomes a sacrifice which frees the state from the lies and double-dealing of Iago, while the filming works to defuse Othello's own misguided violence against the innocent.'

44 Samuel Crowl, '*Othello*', *Shakespeare Bulletin*, 14 (1996), 41–2.

45 Crowl, *ibid.*, 41, notes that 'chess is too rational and pure for Iago's mind (particularly as reflected in Branagh's performance)'.

46 Manvell, *Shakespeare and the Film*, pp. 117–19; Harland S. Nelson, '*Othello*', *Film Heritage*, 2 (1966), 18–22.

47 Constance Brown, '*Othello*', *Film Quarterly* (1965–6), 49, finds evidence that television was the intended market.

48 Alice Griffin, 'Shakespeare through the Camera's Eye: IV', *Shakespeare Quarterly*, 17 (1966), 384.

49 Nelson, '*Othello*', 1966, p. 18.

50 Bosley Crowther, *New York Times* (2 February 1966), rpt. in *NYT Film Reviews*, 5 (1959–68), 3594.

51 Brendan Gill, 'The Current Cinema', *New Yorker* (19 February 1966), 145.

52 Barbara Hodgdon, 'Race-ing *Othello*, Re-engendering White-Out', in Lynda E. Boose and Richard Burt, eds, *Shakespeare, the Movie. Popularising the Plays on Film, TV and Video* (London and New York, 1997), p. 26.

53 Griffin, 'Shakespeare Through the Camera's Eye', 384.

54 Brown, '*Othello*', 50

55 James E. Fisher, 'Olivier and the Realistic *Othello*', *Literature/Film Quarterly*, 2 (1973), 321–31; Jorgens, *Shakespeare on Film*; F. R. Leavis, 'Diabolic Intellect and the Noble Hero: or the Sentimentalist's Othello', in *The Common Pursuit* (London, 1952), pp. 136–59; p. 142. The essay first appeared in *Scrutiny* in 1937.

56 Fisher, 'Olivier and the Realistic *Othello*', pp. 322, 325.

57 See Brown, '*Othello*', 50; Jorgens, *Shakespeare on Film*, p. 200. Fisher, 'Olivier', 330–1.

58 For a description of Cassio and class distinction, see Fisher, 'Olivier', 329–30.

59 Samuel Crowl, 'A world Elsewhere: The Roman Plays on Film and Television', in Davies and Wells, *Shakespeare and the Moving Image*, p. 153. See also Keith Miles, *English Review*, 4 (1994), 1.

60 On the battles on sea and on land see Charlton Heston, *The Actor's Life: Journals 1956–1976*, ed. Hollis Alpert (London, 1978), pp. 357, 359.

PART III

Directors

9

ANTHONY DAVIES

The Shakespeare films of Laurence Olivier

Olivier made his three Shakespeare films as the result of multiple promptings. Despite uneasiness about his own Orlando in the *As You Like It* film directed by Paul Czinner in 1936, he became interested in exploring the potential of the cinema for the presentation of Shakespeare's plays and he managed never to abandon the theatricality implicit in the plays in the films he directed. He was conscious, too, of the different and wider cinema audience to which he would be bringing Shakespeare, and which in the 1940s still retained 'its slight preponderance of women, its heavy working class bias and its very strong "youth" bias'.[1] In the case of his first film, *Henry V*, there was, of course, also the persuasive power of the wartime Ministry of Information, anxious to promote a film which would boost national morale. This chapter will approach the films in the first instance through the diverse opinions of critics, in particular those of their first reviewers.

All Olivier's films are remarkable for their constant oscillation between the cinematic and the theatrical, and their fusion of the two distinctly different dramatic languages. Not only does this arise from the unconscious instincts of Olivier the film maker, an indication of his claim to be an *auteur*, but there is, too, a conscious shifting between the elements of the two media. Some argue that this oscillation is less a distinguishing feature than a flaw. 'Try as he would to be cinematic in his directing and acting', Robert Hapgood has written, 'Olivier often fell between the two stools of theatre and film . . . One must acknowledge that as a film director his blocking now seems static and stage-bound.'[2] Yet when one considers the deliberateness and the subtlety with which Olivier incorporates theatrical elements it is difficult to agree with Hapgood. Nearer the mark is James Agee's recognition in a *Time Magazine* review that 'Olivier's films set up an equilateral triangle between the screen, the stage and literature', and his suggestion that 'between the screen, the stage and literature they establish an interplay, a shimmering splendour of the disciplined vitality which is an art'.[3]

One other point needs to be made: Olivier's ability to devise a cinematic strategy which arises from the particular opportunities presented intrinsically by individual plays. So in *Henry V* the film draws upon the Chorus's prologue to make the move out from and back to the confines of the Globe integral in fusing cinema and theatre; in *Hamlet* the camera becomes an elegiac narrator completing a cyclic journey; in *Richard III* the camera becomes Richard's confidant, ensuring that we become intimate accomplices in watching the fall and rise of the crown of England.

Henry V (1944)

A reviewer of his 1937 stage performance noted, 'Laurence Olivier's Henry is not the hearty young Rugby forward with a leaning for poetry that we usually get. He is a man conscious of his destiny, sober under the weight of responsibility.'[4] Reviewers of the 1944 film of *Henry V* did not consider the extent to which Olivier's characterisation had drawn on his earlier stage performance and it is clear that reviewers and critics found themselves in a new field when called upon to judge the effectiveness of filmed Shakespeare. On one thing they concurred: they were no longer judging an actor's performance. It was now a matter of judging the appropriateness of a relatively unexplored medium for the presentation of Shakespeare's dramatic material. Understandably there was some hedging of bets. The reviewer for the *Monthly Film Bulletin* of the British Film Institute saw fit to nail his colours to the mast before setting off. 'The present reviewer', he wrote,

> believes that a very high proportion of the beauty of Shakespeare's plays resides in the superb language properly spoken and that stage action is secondary in importance. *Henry V* is no exception to the other plays. The audience is expected to concentrate on hearing the great speeches, but the film medium demands a movement which has to be artificially introduced. In the reviewer's opinion, this detracts not a little from the force of all these scenes. The need to keep the screen alive has caused the producers to make the first act of the play – as the reviewer thinks unwisely as later it becomes realist – a picture of the first performance as given at the Globe Theatre . . .

He then goes on to rate the colour 'as excellent', the sets as 'gems of exquisite design' and the charge of the French cavalry as 'unforgettable cinema'.[5] This tentativeness and ambivalence is found in other early reviews. Richard Winnington in the *News Chronicle* considered the film to be 'in over-bright Technicolor, half an hour too long, at its worst . . . vulgar and obscure, but at its best . . . an indication of what could be done with Shakespeare on the screen'.[6] 'What could be done' suggesting, perhaps, that it hadn't been done yet!

The ambivalence of response is perhaps most powerfully felt in Ernest Betts's *Sunday Express* review. While complaining that 'so much artistry has so little consequence on the screen', he considered *Henry V* 'the most ambitious film of our time', but qualified the assertion by observing that it was 'also the most difficult, annoying, beautiful, exciting, wordy, baffling picture yet made'. The film had 'a sort of damnable excellence'.[7]

The temperature of the water having been taken, the general tenor of the reviews became more boldly favourable. Under an eye-catching headline 'HENRY V A FEAST OF COLOUR', in the *Evening News*, Jympson Harman allowed himself a more adventurous response. ' "Old men forget; yet all shall be forgot / But he'll remember with advantages . . ." today's date for it marks a great step forward in the art of film . . . Here is the film not tied down to mundane realism, but free to roam through pictorial fantasy in the creation of a mood.'[8] Dilys Powell in the *Sunday Times* acknowledged that 'the first problem awaiting the film producer who attempts Shakespeare [is] the avoidance of pictorial redundancy; the cinema must of its nature proceed by pictorial narrative, yet here the pictures, the background and detail are already painted in words. The cinema is also of its nature movement; take movement away and the film dies . . .' Olivier's *Henry V*, however, had convinced her 'that it is possible to keep the words and have the pictures'.[9] Helen Fletcher in *Sunday Graphic* and *Sunday News* concentrated on the importance of the film in making Shakespeare accessible. She lauded the film for '[giving] Shakespeare back to the groundlings. To you and me, to the people to whom he wanted to belong.' She 'pictured audiences in little market towns, wartime ports and garrisons and destroyers who will see *Henry V*'.[10]

Outside London, the response to the film encompassed a wider range of expression. By one British audience in the North the film was 'booed off the screen', an eruption of mindlessness which prompted Rank – who had had to be offered considerable inducements to back the film's production – to defend the film's potential appeal, to champion 'the intelligence of the British people', and to prophesy that the film 'will bring thousands of new patrons to the cinema'. On the other hand, the United States premiere in Boston in April 1946 drew the ringing and memorable acclaim from James Agee who found in the film 'the perfect marriage of great dramatic poetry with the greatest contemporary medium for expressing it'.[11] Interestingly, the responses of the American distributing companies were more guarded than those of the American public. It would never be understood in the United States, one executive told the producer, Filippo del Giudice. Another warned that the king's proposal to the French princess running to two thousand words would seem too long for the steel workers of Pittsburgh who 'were accustomed to make their proposals in two words or none at all'. Within a year of its United States release the film – with one or two minor verbal excisions – had been shown in twenty cities and had netted a profit of £275,000.[12]

J. Arthur Rank's prophecy so far as the British viewing public was concerned would seem to have been sound, for the film not only bridged the assumed gulf between the heightened expression of classical theatre on the one hand and cinema entertainment on the other, but it pointed the way to the cinema's becoming an educational medium. Reviewing the film for *Sight and Sound*, the Headmaster of the Latymer School, F. W.Wilkinson, wrote of the 'new Education Bill [whose] main aim will be to provide an adequate education for that sixty-odd per cent of the adolescent population which hitherto has been largely neglected after the age of fourteen . . . Mr Olivier's film opens a new prospect, rich in promise for the new schools and colleges as they begin to provide new audiences for the cinema.'[13] This perceptive comment was prophetic not only in foreseeing the later development of teaching Shakespeare through cinematic adaptation. It suggested too, that the 'new audiences' would be educated and so become increasingly active in their responses to film.

One direction this new critical energy took in its reception of Olivier's *Henry V* is recognisable in the strength of the anti-imperialistic currents which have gathered momentum since the late 1940s. Joan Lord Hall blames 'the iconoclastic Kenneth Branagh' for arousing in students of the 1990s a tendency to dismiss Olivier's version as 'pageant-like and overstylized, a glorified version of King Henry that beefs up the chauvinism at the expense of the play's ambiguities'.[14] But film is a document of its time and given the historical moment of the birth of Olivier's film one might expect critical response to have shifted its stance more severely than it has. It is not surprising that there have been some attempts to belittle the film for its clearly patriotic line and for some of the excisions from Shakespeare's text which result in a film which tends to glamorise war and romanticise the English victory. The criticisms along this line are not unreasonable. Apprehended on one level the film does give to the play a strongly pro-English overlay, '[carrying] on a performance tradition that is both conservative and patriotic' and 'unquestionably [having] an ideological component'.[15]

There are three main reasons for this. Firstly, it was inevitable that a film made at the time amid the tide of wartime national sentiment would reflect those currents of feeling. Secondly, the circumstances surrounding the film's genesis were bound to carry their echoes into the film. Anthony Holden records that Olivier was 'summoned by Jack Beddington, the Information Ministry official in charge of showbiz propaganda work and enlisted for two projects [one of which] was to make a film of Shakespeare's *Henry V*'. Finally, the association of Olivier with both the rousing speeches from the play and with public morale-building rallies during the early 1940s was well established. Olivier's appearances as a patriotic speech-maker were numerous. 'A stirringly sub-Shakespearean address would invariably be followed, in grandiloquently Churchillian vein by "Once more unto the breach. . ."'[16]

Thomas Kiernan and Felix Barker both draw attention to the prominent part played by Filippo del Giudice, the Italian immigrant interned at the start of the war, but later released 'on the condition that he devote his energies, talents and financial resources to making wartime propaganda and morale-boosting films'. Olivier played the title role in a radio broadcast of *Henry V* in 1942, and on hearing this Del Giudice settled on the play as the basis of his next propaganda film.[17] Another name which deserves mention here is that of Dallas Bower, the first Producer-Director of BBC Television in the late 1930s, and later associated with the wartime Ministry of Information. Bower had written a TV script for *Henry V* which he later modified for film and submitted as the basis for Olivier's film, and it was 'at [his] instigation' that Del Guidice was persuaded to set up *Henry V* under the banner of his Two Cities production company. It was also through Bower that Olivier was induced, 'with some difficulty' to accept William Walton as composer. Bower points, too, to the important liaison role of John Betjeman in securing the agreement of the Irish government for shooting the Agincourt sequences at Powerscourt near Dublin.[18]

Dale Silviria explores the extent to which Olivier's *Henry V* is limited to a jingoistic patriotism, and provides interesting arguments to suggest that the film celebrates many things beyond the bounds of England and the English. 'The Globe and with it the entire tradition of the English stage and theatrical profession find honour.'[19] The inclusion of Falstaff's ghost accords to 'the fat knight' a place of affection and, as James Agee maintains, Olivier teaches us how to film Shakespeare's poetic language: 'I am not a Tory, a monarchist, a Catholic, a medievalist, an Englishman, or, despite all the good it engenders, a lover of war: but the beauty and power of this traditional exercise was such that, watching it, I wished I was, thought I was, and was proud of it.'[20] Even more interesting because of its placing in the political developments in Europe in the 1940s is Franco Zeffirelli's comment remembering his first viewing of the film in Florence at the end of the war: '[Olivier] was the flag bearer of so many things we did not have. I'd been educated and brought up in a fascist country. He was the emblematic personality of a great free democracy. The whole world was opening up for us and this *Henry V* was the beginning of a new era for us.'[21]

Much recent criticism has swung away from allowing the ideological component in the film its former prominence, partly because the argument has been very thoroughly pursued in discussions of Branagh's 1989 film as a more or less conscious critique of Olivier's film and partly because the wave of reaction against Olivier's film arose largely from critics who came from another and more aggressive political direction. The question of Olivier's patriotism as a possible intervention would seem now to be most profitably explored along the lines of cinematic codes. Comparing the overt propaganda strategies of Veit Harlan's *Der Grosse König* (Germany, 1942) with those in Olivier's *Henry V*, Peter Drexler concludes that while there are remarkable similarities in the way the two national heroes are treated by the camera at crucial moments, there is a playfulness in Olivier's film which is not to be found in Harlan's depiction of Frederick the Great. 'In the case of Olivier's film', he has written, 'the hypothesis would be that he used popular Hollywood film codes as well as the theatrical frame of the Globe theatre production to save the film from becoming as flat a piece of propaganda as its German counterpart(s) . . .'[22]

It is saved by other, more organic and less easily identified elements as well. Peter Donaldson and James Loehlin investigate detail in the film and reveal complexities, both in the transitions of time and space and in the character of Henry, which refuse inclusion under an arbitrary dismissive label. Donaldson deftly parallels the shift from Elizabethan stage convention where female parts were played by boys, to the film convention where realism demands real women as female characters with the problematic question which opens the play, the Salic Law of succession. 'Like the king, who must pursue a matrilineal claim and secure his conquest through a dynastic marriage, the boy player can succeed only by 'claiming from the female' (1.2.92), appropriating women's dress and manner, assimilating feminine traits to male performance. Film makes this possible in a unique way.' He argues further that as the action in the film moves from its presentation within the Globe Playhouse to the spaces outside and beyond it, the boy actors are replaced by women and that the ingenious return to the confines of the Globe '[unsettles] audience perceptions of gender and [imparts] to the final image of the "boy actress" an effect of the real beyond the range of the transvestite theatre'. Far from merely trying to make Henry into a heroic focus for jingoistic nostalgia and a rhetorical reincarnation of spirit, Olivier's reduction of the more violent dimensions of Henry's character allows for the acceptance of 'the feminine within the king's personality . . . For this Henry V outward success is matched by inward integration of a "feminine" capacity for tenderness, nurturance and intimacy.'[23]

After a thorough discussion of the critical approach that sees the film as debasing the play through a reduction of its complexity, James Loehlin acknowledges both 'the inevitable historical oscillation of interpretation' and the multiple layers of the film's potential reception. 'Various critics understand the film differently according to which elements of it they choose to weigh most heavily.'[24] Yes, England and things English are celebrated in Olivier's film. But rather than an England of military heroics, it is an 'England of the mind' and a 'homage to Shakespeare' as part of it that registers most forcefully for Ace Pilkington.[25] His response is accurately tuned. The Globe sequence covers a broad range of society as audience, from aristocrats to rowdy groundlings, a spectrum of bustling people about their work – orange-sellers, and stage hands who probably double as actors. There is a vigorous if rough-hewn camaraderie about the totality of the theatrical experience which mirrors that required of troops and generals in a war. There is, too, a precarious crudity, an irremediable unpredictability about it. Unlike the technical finish which is possible in cinema, this theatre is dependent upon humanity, its recurrent frailties and its momentary redeeming glories. So Richard Burbage clears his throat before going on; the fourth chime on the clock does not immediately ring; the Bishop of Ely abandons his character and becomes a costumed actor who gives way to personal petulance at his earlier humiliation backstage; the groundlings can noisily protest at the comments made about Falstaff and obviously disconcert the actors; the entire theatrical enterprise can be threatened with thunder and torrential rain. And yet, against all these odds and with no defence against them except spontaneous initiative, the play goes on and takes the audience into its illusory world of time and space. As Loehlin rightly maintains, much of the sustained opening Globe sequence makes theatre the essential subject matter, the primary action being 'between the players and the groundlings rather than between the characters on the stage'.[26]

Despite the substantial excisions from the play's text, Olivier's Henry is not projected as one-sidedly heroic. The groundlings' protests at the banishing of Falstaff suggest certain predilections about theatre, but also hint at their uncertainties as they gauge the priorities of the new king. The sequence filmed through an upstairs window, of Falstaff on his deathbed recalling his echoing cry to Hal and the young king's cold rejection of him, is presented not for the Globe audience, but for the cinema viewers. It is there to distance us from Henry, to remind us that with his inheritance has come also something of the steely, cold ruthlessness of Bolingbroke.

The extent to which the French can in fact be identified as the enemy is also a complicated question. Raymond Durgnat suggests that the placing of France shifts through the film, and that this frustrates any simplistic propagandist reading of the film. 'The English are the English, but Agincourt is D-Day where the French are the Germans until Henry courts Katherine, whereupon the French are probably the French.'[27] Even this, it seems to me, is to oversimplify the issue. The mutual respect which Henry and Mountjoy hold for one another, the French Constable's deeply held but icily masked contempt for the Dauphin, the poised elegance of the frankly one-dimensional and stylised castles and the landscape of France accompanied on the sound track by Walton's wistful music, Henry's prolonged contemplation of the distant French palace and finally Burgundy's portrait of 'this best garden of the world' spoken again over Walton's evocative music, all suggest qualities of civilised life which the English need and for which they unconsciously yearn, while the princess's watching absorbedly the departure of the English ambassadors in the distance coming just after her lesson in English invests her with an innate awareness of what France – presented in the film as essentially aristocratic and ornamental – needs from the English. It is the union of England and France rather than the annexation of one by the other that Olivier aims to reveal as desirable, and as finally achieved. Furthermore, Dallas

Bower has stressed the extent to which not the French, but the Vichy French, a puppet government installed by the Nazis in the south of the partitioned country, were the primary target of those scenes featuring the dithering of the French aristocracy.[28]

Ultimately the substance of the film centres on Henry himself and on that degree of complexity which makes up the heart of his mystery. As Loehlin and others have argued, the stripping of many of the episodes which come between Henry and our admiration of him leaves Olivier little material with which to give range and depth to Henry's character. Certainly some intricacy of mind and feeling is given to him by the camera's intimacy in his solitary night patrol, by the isolation of his self-exploration before the battle, his argument with Williams and his contemplation of a king's predicament with the boy, Court, sleeping beside him, momentarily under his wakeful guardianship. There is also the considerable weight given to the power of this sequence by the combination of elements at work in the film. Fluellen's insistence at full volume on the danger of speaking loudly, the king's contained valuing of the Welshman's unfashionable expressions of valour, his face surrounded by darkness, the small smoky fire, the contrast of voices as the two men and the boy give words, some simple and resigned, some sombre and some cynical, to their situation as soldiers of the king and the growing light in the east, all suggest the ordeal and the duration of the king's vigil. The brief remaining lines of the prayer, too, gain force from what has gone immediately before and from Olivier's quiet intensity as he speaks them, with smoke shadows in the dawn light still flickering faintly on his face and on the tent wall at his left to suggest that his private unhappiness aroused around the fire still smoulders in his mind and underlies his prayer.

Olivier's *Henry V* is a complex and intricately wrought film. The journey we travel over its 137 minutes ends not with the triumph of the English, but with the marriage of France and England; a marriage in the realm of the civilised mind, if not in the possibilities of the slippery world of international politics.

Hamlet (1948)

Ivor Brown, reviewing Olivier's performance in Tyrone Guthrie's 1937 Old Vic production of *Hamlet*, wrote that 'the dominating impression is of "the flash and outbreak of a fiery mind" and of a steely body too. The weakness here is that you begin to suspect that such a Hamlet would have put through his murderous work without so much . . . hesitation.'[29] He was not the only critic not to notice the influence of a Freudian exploration of Hamlet's apparent lack of resolution. Dr Ernest Jones's writings on Hamlet's character, first published in 1910 and later included in his 1923 publication, *Essays in Applied Psycho-Analysis*, profoundly fascinated both Guthrie and Olivier, and while not flaunted, this was a provocative feature of the thinking that underlay the production. Certainly both the Freudian implications and the athleticism which sprang from the stage production were powerfully woven into the film. Jack Jorgens has observed the camera's obsession with 'Gertrude's large, suggestively shaped bed':

> Hamlet's impotence is indicated by symbolic castration as he drops his dagger into the sea . . . his inability to strike home with his sword until the end, and his simultaneous fear of and longing for death . . . From the beginning when Claudius must break up a passionate kiss between mother and son . . . Hamlet's scenes with the Queen in her low-cut gowns are virtually love scenes. A setting dominated by archways, corridors, phallic pillars, cannon, and towers echoes the theme further, so the film becomes in a sense, an Oedipal cinepoem.[30]

More recently, Peter Donaldson has read the film as 'a psychoanalytic, Oedipal text' with the 'phallic symbolism of rapier and dagger, the repeated dolly-in down the long corridor to the queen's immense, enigmatic and vaginally hooded bed, the erotic treatment of the scenes between Olivier and Eileen Herlie as Gertrude all bespeak a robust and readily identifiable, if naive, Freudianism'.[31]

Olivier's film must be central among those which Lawrence Guntner has identified as having become a kind of 'Great Tradition of Shakespeare on Film', privileging the films directed by Olivier, Welles, Kurosawa, Kozintsev, Brook, Polanski and Zeffirelli. One reason for the status accorded these films is that their source plays are mostly the well-known tragedies with their strong story-lines, large-scale characters and symbolic dimensions which generate a powerful cinematic imagery on the big screen. Guntner persuasively argues that the success of these 'Great Tradition' films arises from their 'recycling' of film codes already current. In *Hamlet,* Olivier not only appropriated the codes of German Expressionism, to make Elsinore with its narrow tortuous passages, its winding stairs, the massive pillars and shadowy interiors an architecture of Hamlet's mind, but also those of the American *film noir* of the 1940s. His redeployment of these cinematic resources enabled him to 'locate Shakespeare's play in viewing traditions of the late 1940s and thus more readily evoke an imaginative response from eyes more accustomed to accompanying Humphrey Bogart as Sam Spade than Laurence Olivier as Hamlet'.[32]

Initial press reviews of Olivier's *Hamlet* suggest that the earlier success of *Henry V* had not made Shakespeare on film any easier to write about. One senses that reviewers were aware of handling something sacred in a new medium. There was the weight of theatrical tradition which it was hard to betray, and there was the material. This was no colourful celebration of a young king's glory on the battlefields of France, but a dark, shadowy exploration of what was in many minds the most deeply treasured play in the English language. The *Monthly Film Bulletin*, treading cautiously, spent most of its space in describing rather than evaluating the film's treatment of the play. Its reviewer went no further than to list 'a number of artistically questionable effects', these being 'the visualising of old King Hamlet's murder, the encounter of the ships at sea and . . . a recon-struction in movement of Millais' picture of Ophelia's drowning', and concluded with overall praise for the film as showing 'the range of imagination and artistic integrity which belong to all Sir Laurence Olivier's work'.[33]

Writing for *Sight and Sound*, Arthur Vesselo saw Olivier's *Hamlet* as 'rais[ing] the whole question of how best Shakespeare can be translated into film terms'. He referred to Olivier's attempt 'by some ingenious tricks of technique' to fuse the cinematic and theatrical, and later in his review he saw as 'dangerously mis-leading' both the claims of *Hamlet*'s evolving new screen techniques and 'the emergence of a Shakespeare film as the big prestige-picture of the year'.[34] The 'danger', it seems, was powerfully sensed also by the reviewer for the *Birmingham Mail*, who was unequivocally hostile: 'Cinema should work out its own salvation through its own stories, leaving severely alone Shakespeare who wrote for the stage and nothing but the stage . . .'[35]

Those who found faults in the film, it now seems, were attempting to justify a deeper, less tangible unease. While Eric Bentley protested that 'the film had no style' and that 'visually, it was simply grandiose in the academic manner', Jean Renoir considered that 'the style confuses the issue'. Olivier's restless camera moved John Mason Brown to complain that 'at least forty minutes are squan-dered in travelogues up and down Mr Furse's palace', and Alan Wood found in his use of deep focus a failure to select and make meaningful detail.[36] Despite continuing reservations from some quarters – a Yorkshire police chief is reported to have declared the film 'noisy, vulgar and even macabre . . . a poor film' and unsuitable for children – the tide of favourable reaction to the film was clearly beginning to make its way.[37] *The Times* praised the film's successful balance of action and reflection, seeing Olivier's Hamlet as 'a virile man, a prince, athletic in body and in temper masculine' but finding time to 'turn away from his dra-matic leaps and runs through the somewhat undistinguished architecture of this cinematic Elsinore, to commune with his own conscience and his secret self'. Conscious of the particular audience which a filmed *Hamlet* would reach, this reviewer saw the film as proving that 'the greatest of Shakespeare's plays can be translated to the screen without loss of dignity to the author and to the immense enjoyment of a public suspicious of his name'.[38] The *Manchester Guardian*'s film critic was especially impressed by the thrust of the film. 'This was a film of action; this Hamlet, too, could be swift and violent. This was, somehow, a unified and purposeful film; this Hamlet was more than usually like a brilliant leader of men.'[39]

The *Observer*'s C.A. Lejeune, one of the few early reviewers to sense the Freudian climate of the film, claimed to find it 'a study in simplification, a handsomely illustrated, handily abridged text-book for the general'. She, too, discerned a contradiction in Olivier's characterisation: 'He nullifies his own thesis in never for a moment leaving the impression of a man who cannot make up his mind; here, you feel rather, is an actor-producer-director who in every circumstance, knows exactly what he wants, and gets it'.[40]

There is some evidence that Olivier's *Hamlet* – or the publicity that surrounded it – did arouse an interest in 'the general public'. Under the headline, 'FACTORIES BLOCK-BOOK FOR HAMLET' the *Evening Dispatch* reported that for the gala opening at the West End Cinema in Birmingham a special box-office was opened three weeks in advance. Queues had started forming at 8.00 a.m., two hours before opening, and there was block-booking for factory workers.[41]

American response to the film, while generally enthusiastic, was not without some strong adverse reactions. Robert Duffy faults Olivier on '[having] chosen to cast his film in the form of a play, rather than to explore the true possibilities of cinema', and finds the camera '[reeling] around, rather drunkenly' or 'swivelling with . . . banality'.[42] The Massachusetts State Censors looked more askance at what Hamlet said to his mother than at his suggestions to Ophelia, and insisted on the deletion of 'The rank sweat of an adulterous bed' and 'To post with such dexterity to incestuous sheets' from the soundtrack.[43]

There is much to suggest that in the years between the colourful, at times flamboyant, celebrative mood of *Henry V* and *Hamlet* there developed a more sombre national climate of post-war austerity. Together with this there was the clear change in Britain's place as a nation in the post-war and post-imperial world. The introspection and searching for a national identity in an uncertain world of confusing and changed political priorities, a confusion and a cynicism made manifest in Carol Reed's *The Third Man* – with the growing threat of the Soviet Union, former ally, now rumbling enemy – is certainly not out of keeping with the dark, depressive and brooding Hamlet that Olivier gives us in the film: a Hamlet caught between the inevitability of a new order and the haunting of a ghost-father from the past requiring retribution for a past betrayal and implying that failure to vindicate values of the old order constitute a betrayal of self in the son. Anthony Dawson comments valuably on this relationship of Olivier's *Hamlet* to post-war Britain: 'After the election of the Labour government in 1945, social policy became increasingly collectivist and the transformation to the modern welfare state was quickly set into motion. Olivier's film turns away from both national and international politics towards an inner province of sovereign subjectivity.'[44]

Hamlet took the 1948 Academy Award for 'best picture' (the first non-American entry to be so honoured) and its success in the United States can be seen against the background of a more disturbing aspect of the Cold War politics there. In November 1947, The House Un-American Activities Committee convicted ten Hollywood writers and directors of contempt of Congress for refusing to co-operate with the Committee. This was followed by a decision reached by the major studio executives to dismiss the convicted ten and to block possible employment of anyone suspected of communist sympathies. And not unlike the situation which Hamlet has to confront, the moral lines were not clear. Arthur Miller has written of the 'moral confusion that no one seemed able to penetrate and clarify':

> The problem was that in New York the Committee members had all been elected democratically and were not plotting to take over the republic by violent terror. At least some of them, moreover, were genuinely alarmed by the recent Red victory in China, the Russian demonstration of the atomic bomb, and the expansion of Soviet territory into Eastern Europe. The mixture, in other words, of authentic naivete, soundly observed dangers, and unprincipled rabble-rousing was impossible to disentangle . . .[45]

Considered culturally respectable by the American Establishment and eschewing political and social dimensions, the film 'represents a move inward at a time when the social responsibilities of the artist were in retreat'.[46]

The spate of biographies of Olivier in recent years and the autobiographical writings of Olivier himself have prompted some critical approaches to Olivier's *Hamlet* to turn on the extent to which the Freudian interpretation of Hamlet's irresolution might be rooted within Olivier's own personal development. Foremost of those exploring this psychoanalytical angle on Olivier himself is Peter Donaldson. Taking an episode recounted by Olivier, of himself as victim in a homosexual rape attempt on a staircase at school, Donaldson argues that Olivier's description of the incident 'echoes powerfully in the visual design of Hamlet' and notes that 'Staircases are often the setting for violence, the locus of a repeated pattern in which someone is thrown down on the steps and the attacker flees upward.'[47] The pattern is interestingly observed, pointing as it does, to an overlap of Freudian with personal autobiographical impulses behind the imagery of the film. Hamlet's treatment of Ophelia echoes what the Ghost has done to him, and that, suggests Donaldson, 'is, in part a reenactment of a key incident of abuse the director suffered as a child'. While the erotic desires of Gertrude and the fusion of violence with Hamlet's desire for her are identifiable as influences from Ernest Jones, 'also central to Olivier's conception of the scene are elements that derive not from Jones but from his own engagement with the issue of passivity and the compulsively cyclical character of abuse'.[48]

Donaldson illuminates Olivier's *Hamlet* most usefully when he takes the imagery of the film as essential evidence and analyses his responses to that. The emptiness of Elsinore has been seen as integral to Olivier's interpretation – 'related to Olivier's interest in Hamlet's self-absorption and in the special way in which, for him, Oedipal confusion manifests itself in an irresolution of roles and meanings . . . pregnant with significances we cannot fully grasp', and allowing the camera to explore symbols that are essentially Hamlet's and allowing us to share a penetration of the 'world of Elsinore that is privileged and private'. In this world places, objects and spaces are given gravity and consequence, and in their silence they represent a past and more heroic matrix of values, now mute accomplices in a subsequent collapse into modern expediency, betrayal and desecration.[49]

Olivier went far beyond the limits he would seem to have imposed upon the play when he prefaced his film as 'the tragedy of a man who could not make up his mind'. His is a Hamlet of exceptional dignity and nobility who gives to everything he touches a significance and a meaning. In retrospect, Olivier's verdict on his own film of *Hamlet* was 'a rattling good story, inside and outside Hamlet's mind, told cinematically'.[50] 'Told cinematically' it certainly is, but the film gathers and sustains the force of its impact from its refusal to abandon the theatrical resonance so intricately woven into the play. It is certainly more than Olivier acknowledged. Mary McCarthy identified with incisive insight another of the qualities that give to the film its enduring relevance. It is, she maintains, 'the only *Hamlet* that seizes [the] inconsecutiveness' implicit in the play and in the character of its protagonist, and 'makes of it an image of suffering, of the failure to feel steadily, to be able to compose a continuous pattern, which is the most harassing experience of man'.[51]

Richard III (1955)

Writing of Olivier's 1949 stage performance, the reviewer for *New Statesman and Nation* took issue with the kind of humour that Olivier brought out in the role.

> Exactly what kind of laughter is he to evoke in us? Very early on Sir Laurence seemed to me to be getting the wrong kind. The first time it happened I felt a pang of sympathy for him as an actor – he was being misunderstood by the more obvious-minded of his audience, who seemed to think Richard Crookback 'funny'. Not, that is to say, funny in some mordant, macabre way, but just ordinarily funny. I expected to hear him being more careful next time to point the edge more sharply. But no, it comes again, and again, until one realises that he is deliberately playing for that kind of ordinary laugh.[52]

The *Daily Telegraph* found the 'chief surprise' of the film to be the amount of comedy Olivier 'extracts from [the title role] . . . He gives us a fellow of infinite grim jest, brisk and jaunty in his villainy, able to evoke almost uproarious laughter with lines most actors would play straight.'[53] *The Times* questioned the integrity of the film. Recognising that Shakespeare's Richard is 'the kind of full-blooded villain revelling in his own villainy who was much to Elizabethan

ANTHONY DAVIES

taste', its reviewer observed that 'before the film even begins the credit titles
throw doubt as to whether this *Richard III* will take the play as it is. The suspect
name of Colley Cibber is joined with that of David Garrick to suggest that adaptors other than Sir Laurence himself have been at work', and went on to accuse
Olivier of having chosen to play Richard 'like some demon king in pantomime'.
While this film, like *Henry V*, was 'lovely to look on' and carried 'a [pervading]
suggestion of illuminated medieval manuscripts' it never, 'with pennants flying
and trumpets sounding, storms to decisive victory'.[54]

The general tone of the reviews, however, was much more favourable than
those for *Hamlet*, as the *Manchester Guardian* reviewer foresaw they would be,
Richard being 'a much less holy subject' and the 'entanglement of cousinly
murders [making] cuts and [interpolated] explanations . . . not only pardonable
but essential'. He found the stylisations 'functional and unobtrusive but . . . a
little undistinguished' and the Battle of Bosworth, 'fought on an arid plateau
near Madrid', cinematically ineffective, there being too few soldiers for the 'wide
Spanish expanses'. Richard's death spasms were robbed of their drama by being
exactly synchronised with the music and Walton's score was 'masterly', but
lacking in subtlety.[55] C. A. Lejeune in the *Observer* praised Olivier's courage in
refusing to be drawn into yielding to modern sentiment which considered
Richard 'a man maligned by history'.[56]

Interestingly, the film was seen as celebrating something uniquely British. The
banner headlines which drew the eye to reviews and reports are dominated by
the word, 'triumph'. Olivier had returned to colour after the dark, brooding
journeys through the great Elsinore set. Here was the history of England presented with a splashy swagger and with a cinematic panache, but infused with
an odd element of solemnity by the music of Walton. The *Tottenham Herald*,
reviewing the film on its general release, hailed it as 'a memorable picture which
could have come from no country in the world but Britain'.[57]

The mid-1950s brought with them an awareness of a range of concerns that
had not electrified British journalistic writing in the 1940s. This film was not
judged only against any orthodox view of Shakespeare's play, nor simply in
terms of effectiveness as cinematic drama. The *Lancashire Daily Post* took up the
realism of the murders and the implicit permissiveness of the film and claimed
that the film's tone gave and encouraged a tacit approval of what was morally
reprehensible. The actions and attitudes of Richard, claimed the reviewer, were
given a licence because they emerged under the protective banner of art:

Today, amidst an outcry against violence, crime and evil, when any film that shows
the sinful and sordid side of life is given an 'X' certificate, up pops one that combines murder, evil, violent death and veiled hints at sex . . . and is passed with a 'U'
certificate for universal showing . . . One can only conclude that crime referred to

in cultural terms loses all its wickedness and emerges, in this case, as merely a play in which the central character, a deformed cripple and outcast of nature has a passionate scorn of men because they are weaker and more obtuse than he.[58]

American reaction, like that in England, was predominantly favourable. Bosley Crowther in the *New York Times* found Richard 'tremendous – a weird, poisonous portrait of a super-rogue whose dark designs are candidly acknowledged with lick-lip relish and sardonic wit'.[59] Much of the critical response, however, was deflected from probing in depth by an attempt to discuss the audience responses to two media presentations as though they were one. For simultaneous with the opening of the film at cinemas was the sponsored television broadcast to a national audience estimated by the NBC network at between 40 and 50 million.

The television showing was acknowledged as drawing 'the largest audience ever to watch a day-time entertainment programme (other than sports and political material)', and, said an NBC spokesman, 'it proves you can put on classical productions and still get a big audience'.[60] (Barbara Freedman dicusses this broadcast earlier in this *Companion*: pp. 47–71). Olivier's own response to it was unmitigatedly negative. Describing the experiment as 'deplorable', he maintained that 'the film was not made for television, which calls for the creation of its own productions. The varying long shot and close-up [effects] were almost lost on television screens. The impact of colour was lost because only a few thousand sets in the U.S. could receive colour.' He further found the cutting, in the interests of family viewing, of the smothering of the little princes in the Tower, the drowning of Clarence and the graphic detail in the killing of Richard, a distortion. Finally he weighed in against the 'overwhelming' power of the advertising breaks which intruded on the flow and cumulative thrust of the film. There were apparently three commercial interruptions to the film, and the identity of General Motors as the chief sponsor was stamped indelibly on the mind of one reviewer who complained that 'it was . . . a little disconcerting to be informed during a break three quarters through the play, that a certain motorcar has more power than all the horses in Richard III'.[61]

British reviewers were for the most part quite tolerant of the cuts which Olivier made in the text, no doubt because neither the play nor its historical context was likely to be well known to the cinema audience. More than one reviewer pointed out that Olivier's Richard woos Lady Anne over the coffin of her dead husband, Edward, Prince of Wales, not of her father-in-law, Henry VI – a change which implicates Anne more deeply in submitting to Richard's sexual appeal than in Shakespeare's original. Few, however, questioned the dramatic credibility of Richard's prompt success. Olivier himself recognised the difficulty. 'If it's too sudden on the screen the unaccustomed audience would cry, "Hold! We don't believe this!" So I cut the scene in two, let time pass and gave Richard two glorious climaxes.'[62] For James Phillips Olivier's cleverness here was '[a sacrifice] of subtle dramatic values in order to obtain simplified theatrical effects'. He argued that Shakespeare's scene involves Anne in a finely graded psychological process during which her resistance to Richard is broken down in stages – from hatred through confusion, submission and finally surprise – which are both subtle and convincing. While acknowledging that Richard's sexual appeal was the key to his successful wooing of Anne, Phillips maintained that Shakespeare sustained the complexities in the relationship, 'showing that only when sexual desire can be made acceptable to the participant in terms of a moral or religious rationalization does it become convincing in terms of recognizable patterns of human behaviour'.[63]

Two further omissions which Phillips saw as distorting the original balance of the play are the character of Margaret, and Clarence's subtle and skilful pleading with those who come, on Richard's instruction, to kill him. Margaret's function is to remind the audience of the complicity of Edward IV, Clarence, Elizabeth, Dorset, Rivers, Buckingham and Hastings in an endemic dynamic of self-serving corruption. Her absence from the film makes Richard emerge as a predatory aberration preying on the naive and the bewildered, 'a renaissance wolf among medieval sheep',[64] whereas her weight in the play is to reveal Richard as 'simply a smarter villain amongst a pack who morally and ethically are no better than he'.[65] Richard may indeed be 'hell's black intelligencer', but the power of Margaret's curses is directed against an organism of perfidy.

One can appreciate that Clarence's plea to his murderers in Act 1 scene 4 'that you depart and lay no hands on me' and its ensuing development might sensibly be seen as slowing the necessary narrative pace of the film, but one cannot help regretting that Gielgud was denied the dramatic opportunities in the elaboration of this eloquent entreaty, especially when one sets it against such preparatory lines from his killers as 'S'wounds, he dies. I had forgot the reward' and 'O excellent device! – and make a sop of him'.

The balance which Shakespeare has built into the play's structure is further distorted in Olivier's film by the omission of Richard's soliloquy on waking from his ghost-infested dream and of Richmond's oration to his soldiers before the battle. In contemplating the nature and the totality of his isolation Richard's 'There is no creature loves me, / And if I die no soul will pity me' not only reveals a more complex dimension within Richard himself, but the close compression of love, death and pity in the lines offer a reminiscent flash of his abrupt halting of the coffin-bearers and his short-lived satisfaction in the wooing of Anne. Richmond, addressing his soldiers not in 'dead midnight' but in the light of morning brings a refreshing, and essentially responsible perspective on Richard and his contorted ambitions.

> For what is he they follow? Truly, friends,
> A bloody tyrant and a homicide;
> One raised in blood, and one in blood established;
> One that made means to come by what he hath,
> And slaughtered those that were the means to help him;
> A base, foul stone, made precious by the foil
> Of England's chair, where he is falsely set;
> One that hath ever been God's enemy.   (5.5.199–206)

There emerges more promise of a desirable and genuine restoration of good government in these lines than in Lord Stanley's smile of happy relief as he picks up the crown and holds it aloft after Richard's death on the field of Bosworth.

This Richard has been criticised as lacking in psychological complexity. Harry Schein maintains that Olivier presents the usurper 'just as univocally as he depicted Henry – he replaces the uprightness with a completely self-integrated wickedness'. The notable exception emerges not from the lines of the text, but from an unspoken moment (at 3.1.131) that follows the young Duke of York's

> Uncle, my brother mocks both you and me.
> Because that I am little, like an ape,
> He thinks that you should bear me on your shoulders.

The sudden close-up on Richard's expression of frightening malice and the abruptness with which his avuncular charm collapses give intensity and depth to the response brought forth by the child's innocent arousal of Richard's deep sense of his own deformity. The flash of the hunchback's envious hate for the delicate vitality and radiance of the child-prince 'fills a psychological need, the dramatic vacuum which Olivier has left through his one-sided interpretation of the role', a vacuum which, being momentarily filled, in Schein's words 'all at once lifts the film from historical thriller to the realm of the essential'.[66]

If Olivier has arguably stripped the play of its broader range of complexities and concentrated on the character of Richard as the source of dramatic energy in the film, he sustains a magnetic hold on the viewer until the very end. Like the final encirclement of Claudius in *Hamlet*, there is a throng that closes upon Richard at the close of the battle. And just as the focus is upon Claudius, the victim in the centre, so we are forced, with Richard's slayers as they move back, to watch with a mixture of fascinated curiosity and horror, the convulsive violent throes of his body. Even the process of death has about it a hideous and contorted energy. We who have been borne along as Richard's accomplices through so much of the film are finally presented with a spectacle which suggests an intense, horrific entanglement of soul and body. At the edge of our apprehension of this grotesque struggle there begins to take shape the question of whether Richard's deformity reaches beyond the world of the physical. Rather than suggesting a finality and a cleansing of the realm of England, it is as though we remain infected with something of him that has refused to die. Why otherwise do we watch his body taken from the field, stretched across the back of a mule, with so dark a sense of uncertainty, almost of awe, as though we are witnessing a desecration?

Of Olivier's three Shakespeare films, *Richard III* invites less penetrating analysis as a film than either *Henry V* with its ingenious transitions through time and space or *Hamlet* with its brooding and elegiac camera movement through Elsinore. This is partly because Richard is so clearly the axis of Shakespeare's play, but mainly because we are captivated by Olivier's performance, and (as Jorgens writes) by 'watching Olivier the consummate actor play Richard the consummate actor'.[67] In 1971 Roger Manvell maintained that Olivier's Shakespeare films 'belonged to an era of film-making which seems long superseded by very different techniques of presentation', and that they represent 'that great period of Shakespearean star-acting initiated largely by Laurence Olivier himself'.[68] This no longer stands as an adequate assessment. Olivier's Shakespeare films liberated Shakespeare's language and his dramatic energy from the confines of the theatre, the lecture hall and the classroom and cultivated them in the public mind with an immediacy and to an extent that no other film-maker has equalled. Paradoxically they have also become, as visual texts, the subjects of scrutiny, analysis and discussion in the seminar rooms of universities and on the shelves of research libraries. It has become something of a commonplace to draw attention to the evidence of dated cinematography in the Olivier films. Yet they glow with an instinctive theatrical rightness in important sequences, the energy, involvement and dramatic concentration on detail in the *Hamlet* duel scene being a classic instance. Olivier does not emerge as one who sought essentially to popularise Shakespeare. Yet the global reach of his Shakespeare films during the thirty years that followed the Second World War has been immensely significant.

NOTES

1 Mark Abrams, 'The British Cinema Audience 1949', *Hollywood Quarterly*, 4 (1949–50), 251–5. See also Felix Barker, *The Oliviers* (London, 1953), p. 262: 'Gertie was an imaginary young woman in the one-and-ninepennies who, [Thorold] Dickinson told Olivier early during the making of the film, would not understand a particular sequence. Throughout the film Gertie was constantly at Olivier's elbow, and he was careful never to forget her.'

2 Robert Hapgood, in Lynda E. Boose and Richard Burt, eds., *Shakespeare, the Movie. Popularising the Plays on Film, TV and Video* (London and New York, 1997), p. 85.

3 James Agee, *Time Magazine* (28 June 1948).

4 *Daily Telegraph* (7 April 1937).

5 *Monthly Film Bulletin*, 11, 132 (December 1944), 139–40.

6 Quoted by Anthony Holden, *Olivier* (London, 1988), p. 179.
7 Ernest Betts, *Sunday Express* (28 Novemer 1944).
8 Jympson Harman, *Evening News* (22 November 1944).
9 Dylis Powell, *Sunday Times* (26 November 1944).
10 Helen Fletcher, *Sunday Graphic* and *Sunday News* (26 November 1944).
11 *Ibid.*, pp. 179–80.
12 Barker, *The Oliviers*, p. 215.
13 F. W. Wilkinson, *Sight and Sound*, 13, 52 (1944), 85–6.
14 Joan Lord Hall, *'Henry V': a Guide to the Play* (London, 1997), p. 129.
15 James N. Loehlin, *Shakespeare in Performance: Henry V* (Manchester, 1996), p. 25.
16 Holden, *Olivier*, pp. 172–3.
17 Thomas Kiernan, *Olivier: the Life of Laurence Olivier* (London, 1981), pp. 204–5; Barker, *The Oliviers*, pp. 198–9.
18 Dallas Bower, interview in Brian MacFarlane, ed., *An Autobiography of British Cinema* (London, 1997), pp. 81–2.
19 Dale Silviria, *Laurence Olivier and the Art of Film Making* (Cranbury, NJ, 1985), p. 79.
20 James Agee, review, *The Nation* (New York), 163, 5 (3 August 1946).
21 Franco Zeffirelli in *Olivier at Work: the National Years* (London, 1989), p. 66.
22 Peter Drexler and Lawrence Guntner, eds., *Negotiations with Hal* (Braunschweig, 1995), p. 132.
23 Peter S. Donaldson, *Shakespearean Films/Shakespearean Directors* (Boston, MA, 1990), pp. 4, 6, 15–16.
24 Loehlin, *Henry V*, pp. 27–8.
25 Ace G. Pilkington, *Screening Shakespeare. From Richard II to Henry V* (Newark, DE and London, 1991), p. 114.
26 Loehlin, *Henry V*, p. 35.
27 Raymond Durgnat, *Films and Feelings* (London, 1967), p. 262.
28 Dallas Bower, interview, p. 83.
29 Review by Ivor Brown, quoted by Barker, *The Oliviers*, p. 121.
30 Jack J. Jorgens, *Shakespeare on Film* (Bloomington, IN, 1977), p. 217.
31 Donaldson, *Shakespearean Films*, p. 31.
32 Drexler and Guntner, *Negotiations with Hal*, p. 56.
33 *Monthly Film Bulletin*, 15, 173 (May 1948), 60.
34 Arthur Vesselo, *Sight and Sound*, 17, 66 (Summer 1948), 99–100.
35 *Birmingham Mail* (17 September 1948).
36 John Mason Brown and others quoted in Holden, *Olivier*, pp. 220–1.
37 *Yorkshire Post* (29 September 1948).
38 *The Times* (5 May 1948).
39 *Manchester Guardian* (6 May 1948).
40 C. A. Lejeune, *Observer* (9 May 1948).
41 *Evening Dispatch* (6 September 1948).
42 Robert A. Duffy, 'Gade, Olivier, Richardson: Visual Strategy in *Hamlet* Adaptations', *Literature/Film Quarterly*, 4/2 (1976), 141–52; p. 141.
43 Reports in the *Daily Worker* and the *Birmingham Gazette*, both 26 July 1948.
44 Anthony B. Dawson, 'Hamlet at the Movies: Olivier and Kozintsev', in *Shakespeare in Performance: Hamlet* (Manchester, 1995), pp. 170–84; p. 175.
45 Arthur Miller, *Timebends* (New York, 1987), p. 329.

46 Dawson, *Hamlet*, p. 176.
47 Donaldson, *Shakespearean Films*, pp. 35; 39.
48 *Ibid.*, pp. 47, 49.
49 *Ibid.*, p. 51.
50 Laurence Olivier, *On Acting* (London, 1986), p. 204.
51 Mary McCarthy, 'A Prince of Shreds and Patches', repr. in Charles W. Eckert, ed., *Focus on Shakespearean Film* (Englewood Cliffs, NJ, 1972), p. 66.
52 *New Statesman and Nation* (16 February 1949).
53 *Daily Telegraph* (14 December 1955).
54 *The Times* (14 December 1955).
55 *Manchester Guardian* (14 December 1955).
56 Lejeune, *Observer* (18 December 1955).
57 *Tottenham Herald* (13 April 1956).
58 *Lancashire Daily Post* (7 March 1956).
59 Bosley Crowther, *New York Times* (12 March 1956).
60 Report in *The Times* (14 March 1956).
61 Report in *The Times* (16 March 1956).
62 Olivier, *On Acting*, p. 206.
63 James E. Phillips, 'Some Glories and Some Discontents', *Quarterly of Film, Radio and Television*, 10 (1955–6), 399–407; p. 405.
64 Jorgens, *Shakespeare on Film*, p. 136.
65 Phillips, 'Some Glories', p. 402.
66 Harry Schein, 'A Magnificent Fiasco', *Quarterly of Film, Radio and Television*, 10 (1955–6), 407–15; p. 410.
67 Jorgens, *Shakespeare on Film*, p. 142.
68 Roger Manvell, *Shakespeare and the Film* (London, 1971), p. 52.

IO

PAMELA MASON

Orson Welles and filmed Shakespeare

Like Coleridge's Ancient Mariner, Orson Welles is an isolated figure, driven by his unrelenting passion: 'this heart within me burns'. After the precocious brilliance of *Citizen Kane* at the age of twenty-five, some critics have regarded his journey through the world as one of decline punctuated by failure. The compulsive nature of his vision has proved disconcerting and he has gathered an unseemly gaggle of detractors. The cinema industry with its priorities so firmly asserted by Hollywood's premium upon financial success has tended to regard him as something of a wild and unpredictable grey-beard loon. Whilst there have been some critics who have sensitively praised Welles as the supreme *auteur*[1] for his success in combining the roles of screenwriter, actor and director, they are possibly outnumbered by those who have an insatiable enthusiasm for fusing life and art. All too frequently the characters of Welles and Falstaff are yoked: 'In dramatising the simultaneous betrayal and self destruction of Falstaff, one can see Welles exploring a career of squandered talent and rejection.'[2] Similarly, a jeering obsession with his weight was accompanied by accusations of sloth and contempt for his appearance in commercials. His self-exile from America may have been driven as much by pragmatism as pique, but the evidence that he was appreciated so much more in Europe, as 'a wise madman, a solitude surrounded by humanity',[3] than at home, does contribute to the sense of his being a prophet without honour in his own land.

When Orson Welles amended Falstaff's words 'This that you heard was but a colour'[4] to 'This that you have seen is but a colour' he might seem simply to have been endorsing conventional assumptions about the superiority of the visual dimension in film. However, Welles's vision was more complex and more ambitious. In discussing *Chimes at Midnight* Welles acknowledged that in the film he aspired to discover 'not technical surprises or shocks, but a more complete unity of forms, of shapes. The true form, the interior, the musical form of a picture. I believe you should be able to enjoy a picture with your eyes closed, that a blind man should be able to enjoy a movie.'[5]

Welles was well aware of the power of the spoken word and early in his career he had challenged what he saw as complacency about what radio could offer. On 30 October 1938 his radio adaptation of *The War of the Worlds* succeeded in making many Americans believe that the Martians had landed in New Jersey. A similar commitment to challenge and extend the medium in which he was working informed his approach to filming Shakespeare. Although his film of *The Merchant of Venice* (1969) was made in colour, the theft of two reels prevented its release. When he died in 1988 Welles had been working on an adaptation of *King Lear*.[6] However, evaluation of his achievement can only be based upon the three films he made in black-and-white: *Macbeth* (1948), *Othello* (1952) and *Chimes at Midnight* (1966). Each of these completed films has its 'unity of form'. *Macbeth* has an etched sharpness in its settings and in its careful groupings of taut figures. In *Othello* there is a pervasive wind which gusts and swirls, embodying an energy and elemental responsiveness as well as summoning up an emotional turbulence. In *Chimes at Midnight* it is so often the clash of stone against wood which forces choice and denies compromise. At the heart of each film is Welles's commitment to accommodating the scale and grandeur of each protagonist whilst engaging with the details of their personal histories.

In acknowledging that Welles made a major contribution to the genre of Shakespeare on film David Cook describes Welles's films as 'extravagant and eccentric'.[7] Both adjectives are ambivalent in the balance of commendation and reservation that they contain but they offer a familiar judgement of Welles's work. When criticism does not focus upon the character of Welles himself, it too often gives undue attention to the circumstances in which the films were made. That *Macbeth* was made in twenty-one days whereas it took four years to complete *Othello*,[8] are factors which seem to condition the responses they provoke. Assessment of the films has also been hampered by their technical imperfections, particularly in the quality of the soundtracks. However, with the restoration of first *Macbeth* in 1980, then *Othello* in 1992 and now the promise of the same for *Chimes at Midnight*, it is perhaps timely to consider the films 'as they are, nothing extenuate'.

Macbeth (1948)

The swirling mists and vague outlines of three crouching figures lure an audience into a disturbing world where supernatural powers seem to be controlling events. Faceless witches defy our attempts at definition and the sight of them plunging their hands into the bubbling cauldron confirms our fear. They shape our thoughts as they shape the clay doll which will bring forth Macbeth.[9] The bleak, frightening world they conjure is expressed in a wild, barren landscape and a dark inhospitable castle. Cold stonework, cavernous cellars, exposed platforms and craggy promontories dominate and intimidate figures clothed in armour or thick rough fabrics. It is a primitive world and its society seems to be at the edge of civilisation. The execution of the Thane of Cawdor is witnessed by an undemonstrative crowd. The gaunt lines of the gallows against the skyline confirm an habitual brutality.

However, any assumption that this is to be a story of demonic possession is challenged by Orson Welles's interpretation of the protagonist's role. His Macbeth is consistently humanised. The film chooses to stress that he shares with Banquo the encounter with the Witches. The meeting is discussed within their group and Macbeth dictates his letter to his wife with no sense of secrecy or conspiracy. The early emphasis upon Macbeth's openness, sociability and camaraderie establishes what will be a rich interplay in the film between its iconography of Expressionist symbolism and its careful attention to human relationships.

The Witches have entered Macbeth's consciousness in an insidious way which he and the cinema audience only slowly recognise. His vision is at times distorted, such as when his wife's face is dissolved by the return of the swirling mists. The clay doll will be crowned to confirm his success but it will also break out in rivulets of blood to confront him with the reality of the means of his achievement. These are horrible imaginings that isolate him from those with whom he was once at ease. He is unable to maintain the equilibrium displayed by Banquo, whose own moral ambivalence the film also addresses. Developing the shared experience of their meeting with the Witches, it is Banquo rather than Lennox who protects Macbeth by confirming the guilt of the grooms before he confronts him directly with his suspicions:

> Thou hast it now, King, Cawdor, Glamis, all,
> As the weird women promised, and I fear
> Thou played'st most foully for it.   (3.1.1–3)

In Shakespeare's text the soliloquy provides a moment of reflection for a Banquo who generally avoids condemnation for his inaction. However, Welles creates anxieties about Banquo's integrity as he offers Macbeth the possibility of support yet prompts 'Our fears in Banquo'.

The sequence from the murder of Banquo to the banquet demonstrates how the film intertwines its various stylistic strands. Macbeth's lines:

> Come, seeling Night
> Scarf up the tender eye of pitiful day,
> And, with thy bloody and invisible hand
> Cancel and tear to pieces, that great bond
> Which keeps me pale. Light thickens, and the crow
> Makes wing to th' rooky wood
> Good things of day begin to droop and drowse,
> Whiles night's black agents to their preys do rouse . . .   (3.2.46–53)

inspire a visualisation which transmutes the Murderers into crouching, crow-like figures as night's black agents in the finger-like branches of the tree, poised until 'Let it come down' cues them to pounce.

From the bleakness of the woods we move to the claustrophobia of the tunnelled recesses of the castle to share Macbeth's sense of being 'cabin'd, cribb'd, confin'd' with the emphasis upon his obsession with Banquo. Although Macbeth has retreated into the bowels of the castle, he cannot escape hearing the repetition of Banquo's suspicions that Macbeth 'played falsely for it'. Macbeth hears himself tell Banquo 'Fail not our feast' which prompts an echoing response 'I will not, I will not, I will not fail your feast.' The echoic use of words here serves as memory and prophecy. Banquo seems to be mocking Macbeth's earlier anxiety lest 'we fail'. At the banquet which follows Macbeth's fear is understood and shared. We know the demons that are haunting him and how difficult he finds it to say 'I drink to our good friend Banquo – whom we miss – would he were here.' His careful invitation to his chief guest now seems to be serving as his own invocation for Banquo to haunt him.

The attention given to the bond between Macbeth and Banquo also serves to highlight what is the most important dimension in the film's humanising of Macbeth – his childlessness. He is haunted by his awareness of his 'fruitless crown' and 'barren sceptre'. He knows 'no son of mine succeeding'. The film makes us aware that Macbeth is continually striving to define himself within the context provided by Banquo and Fleance, by Duncan and his sons and by the Macduff family. It is not surprising that Macbeth sees them as antagonists. He is a man driven both by a hunger for power and by a fear of impotence.

His relationship with Lady Macbeth is overshadowed by the sterility of their marriage. When we first see her she is lying on a bed, but any easy assumptions about sexuality are challenged by the visual tension between the barbarism of the fur bed-covering and the forties' style, front-laced, high-necked dress with its zip-fastener and shoulder pads. Macbeth's letter makes her fearful. Her voice has a persuasive strength belied by her physical uncertainty. She seems aware of her own inadequacy and moves to the window to seek to invoke the 'spirits that tend on mortal thoughts', but the swirling mists which had revealed the Witches to Macbeth do not respond to her. She does offer an embrace of welcome on her husband's return and gives efficient assistance by drugging the wine and putting the daggers ready, but she lacks confidence. The film makes it clear that Macbeth's experience on the heath has entered his consciousness in a way that Lady Macbeth will never be able either to share or to understand. It is Macbeth and not his wife who says 'Leave all the rest to me.'

Their lack of a family serves as a nagging ache to both of them. When Lady Macbeth speaks about having given suck and utters her challenge 'if you were a man' she seems to be responding to familiar cues for support. Their relationship is always under pressure. Macbeth's plea to her 'Bring forth men children only' is immediately followed by Banquo's question to his son 'How goes the night, boy?' When Lady Macbeth urges Macbeth 'to bed, to bed' she cannot counter his vivid thoughts about 'the seed of Banquo' becoming kings. Her physical stiffness is an emblem of her awareness of inadequacy. Whilst Macbeth surveys his hangman's hands, she stands alone in the middle distance, a thin, frail, gaunt figure.

The Macduffs' marriage provides a touchstone of normality which accentuates the dysfunction of the Macbeths' relationship. In the uproar following the discovery of Duncan's murder we have a glimpse of the potential for sympathy and support in marriage as Macduff addresses 'horror, horror, horror' to his wife. By reshaping the text Welles also gives us a brief scene of leave-taking between them which not only reinforces the domestic truthfulness underpinning their partnership but also provides the motive for Lady Macduff's later frustration and her anxiety about her husband's absence.

Distanced from her husband, Lady Macbeth continually finds herself next to Lady Macduff. As Macbeth makes his crazed, uncertain amble towards the throne she is seen with Lady Macduff and her child. They share a snatch of dialogue transposed from the scene in which Lady Macduff's children will be murdered. At the banquet Macbeth is framed by the two women and they exchange words of challenge and rebuttal. Lady Macbeth seems drawn to her counterpart. Their earlier exchanges all took place within the Macbeths' castle but Lady Macbeth will visit Lady Macduff at home. It is Lady Macbeth who debates with Macduff's child, but positioned far from the camera she functions as both a naturalistic presence and in terms of an imaginative projection into a domestic world essentially prompted by her own feelings of frustration and inadequacy.

That the film is concerned with the psychology of both Macbeth and Lady Macbeth is expressed vividly when we see Macbeth questioning the Doctor, 'How does your patient?' whilst looking down at Lady Macbeth in bed. Macbeth speaks for both of them when he asks:

> Canst thou not minister to a mind diseased,
> Pluck from the memory a rooted sorrow,
> Raze out the written troubles of the brain,
> And with some sweet oblivious antidote
> Cleanse the stuff'd [sic] bosom of that perilous stuff
> Which weighs upon the heart?   (5.3.39–44)

The Doctor's diagnosis that 'therein the patient / Must minister to himself' makes it clear that neither partner can offer the other any support. So Macbeth's instruction 'Put mine armour on' is no expression of wild angry defiance but a moving realisation of the impossibility of physical or emotional defence. He moves to the window, and in that moment past and present are recalled. We are with him but then the perspective shifts and we move outside and view the moment more objectively. Macbeth's hand is stretched over his heart, but he feels only the unresponsive metal of his breast plate, which is itself scarred by the jagged metal of the bars of the window. On the other side of the central dividing rod, framed between two horizontal bars, is the small, prostrate figure of Lady Macbeth. Under all the barbarism of the stone and metal and the sculpted Expressionism of the composition is a tender tableau of marital breakdown, mental illness and intimations of mortality.

Macbeth makes a desperate attempt to help Lady Macbeth through a passionate embrace which wakes her from her sleepwalking. Terrified, she flees to the raised platform. The setting of sharp thorns and stylised trees that remind us of the projections of the castle windows provides a nightmare correlative for her inner anguish as she topples over the edge of the precipice. Her body bounces from the rocks in an anticipation of the way Macduff will later treat Macbeth's severed head. Standing on the platform from which she fell, Macbeth reflects on 'Tomorrow, and tomorrow and tomorrow' and as the screen swirls with cloud and mist we are prompted to remember the supernatural soliciting, but also, more importantly, we are forced to engage with the resonance of the words.

As originally released, the film began with a spoken prologue describing the action as an allegorised conflict: 'Plotting against Christian law and order are the agents of chaos, priests of hell and magic; sorcerers and witches.' Welles wrote the lines in response to the studio's decision to cut two reels of the film: 'People were getting a brisk version of the tragedy and we had to set things up for them', but he felt that it 'read like a trailer'.[10] When the film was restored to its full length and rereleased in 1980, the prologue was cut.[11] Freed from the dogmatism of the inserted text it is more clearly evident that the film's exploration of the struggle between good and evil is ambivalent. Of central importance is Welles's created figure of the 'Holy Father' whose lines come variously from Ross, Angus and the Old Man. Initially an agent of spiritual goodness, he has some power and the Witches leave at his gesture of dismissal. He functions as companion, attendant, even secretary to Macbeth, taking down the dictated letter to his wife. He leads prayers on the return from battle, offering an effective but unforceful spiritual leadership towards which Macbeth and his wife have shown a tolerance rather than an allegiance. After Macduff tells him of the 'sacrilegious murder' he runs into Duncan's chamber and witnesses Macbeth's killing of the grooms. An exchange of looks seals an uncomfortable compact and it is the 'Holy Father' who tells Malcolm of his father's death and confirms to him that 'those of his chamber, as it seemed, had done it'. Consequently, although he offers some of the Old Man's choric reflections upon the 'sore night' and judges events to be 'unnatural', his involvement in events complicates both his role and our evaluation of it. His function as Macbeth's attendant passes to Seyton, whose name undergoes a seamless transition to Satan during the course of the film.

The passivity of the 'Holy Father' eventually gives way to action as he warns Lady Macduff and flees Scotland. His fearful anxiety makes clear the fragility and inadequacy of his spiritual influence. In the England scene Macduff directs his fierce accusation 'Did heaven look on / And would not take their part?' directly at him. In this context Macduff's words offer a powerful challenge to spiritual leadership and his anger is the frequently voiced despair at the impossibility of sustaining faith in a seemingly godless world. By welding the spiritual, the domestic and the political in the role of the 'Holy Father', the film ensures that the complex layering of Shakespeare's play is not reduced to the simple dimensions of the morality tradition.

As Malcolm's forces gather outside Macbeth's fortified castle there is a moment of balance. The crowds of soldiers have battering rams but their staves seem woefully spindly. Macbeth is an isolated figure but the castle walls seem strong and impregnable. But it is the hurled spear that fells the 'Holy Father' which prompts the invasion. Macbeth's face is wracked with fear as he defiantly challenges Macduff, but the vision of the decapitated doll confirms the imminence of his death. Despite linking Macduff with the iconography of the cross, a moral and spiritual uncertainty remains. As the camera tracks back and the castle slips into the past, the Witches can be seen watching. Their forked staves offer an ironic mockery of the tall, spindly crosses carried by the triumphant troops. As the Witches announce 'Peace, the charm's wound up', Welles gives us both an ending and a beginning.

Othello (1952)

Welles's *Othello* gives a similar priority to intelligent interpretation of Shakespeare's text. The opening shots of the funeral procession express the inevitability of the tragedy, but the projected title page, also read to us, acknowledges the narrative dimension and gives the story the perspective of time. The film, true to the play, allows Othello to be introduced through Iago's perspective. At first we are given only glimpses of Othello as a man in a gondola, a glimpse of the back of a turbaned head, a figure descending a staircase. We are more than eight minutes into the film, hearing Brabantio's impassioned disbelief that his daughter would 'run from her father to the sooty-bosom of such a thing as that', before we are presented with our first view of Othello. There is an impressive stillness in his delivery of 'Most, potent, grave and reverend masters', and when he talks of his invitation to Brabantio's house there is a flurry of movement to enable us (but not Othello) to see Desdemona arrive. She stands, a still, rapt figure, illustrating the truth of Othello's claim that 'this to hear would

Desdemona seriously incline / And with a greedy ear devour up my discourse'. The sequence provides effective evidence of his conclusion that 'This only is the witchcraft I have used.' Although an audience can sympathise with Desdemona's choice, the film shows her disappointed and lonely father depart. Desdemona runs to him but the long shot allows Brabantio's words of warning, 'Look to her, Moor' to come from a figure receding into the past. With no face to focus upon, the words seem to be a continuation of the spoken narrative.

It is difficult for Othello to reconcile his public and private roles. His relationship with Desdemona is always subject to the pressure of time. A mechanical figure striking a bell had prefaced his words that he has but 'an hour of love to spend with thee' and his awareness that 'we must obey the time' will prove tragically prophetic. In Cyprus he speaks 'If I were now to die, 'twere now to be most happy' as he closes the bedroom door, but, as Cassio's drunkenness prompts anarchic chaos, a crane shot invades their private space.

As counterpart to the sexual intimacy of Othello and Desdemona, Iago will lead Othello into a pillared interior to remove his armour. In this enclosed space it is not so much that Othello cannot escape Iago's suggestions and insinuations but that he is trapped by his own self-awareness. Moving away from one mirror he finds himself regarding himself in another, as he seeks to contradict that he is 'not much moved'. A few moments later he breaks from Desdemona's attempts to 'bind' him with her 'napkin' and he returns to the mirror on the wall searching for a truth, whilst trying to loosen the armoured breast plate round his neck. We do not see him remove it but when he turns from the mirror to her he wears only a protective layer of soft suede. Both figures are crowded together in the glass as he frames her face with his hands, desperately seeking to know what is reality. This sequence defines the polarisation of choice for Othello as being one between Iago and Desdemona. This aspect is reinforced by the significant diminution of the Iago–Emilia relationship. We are nearly half-way through the film before Emilia appears. At this point she seems merely a plot device to deliver Desdemona's discarded handkerchief to her husband, announcing, 'I have a thing for you.'

However, although the film also reduces the sense of any real relationship between Othello and Cassio, it carefully acknowledges the structural means by which the three women, initially distinct and with no pre-existing relationships to bind them, become yoked by events to offer female perspectives upon the male attitudes which prevail in this world. In an invented sequence we see Iago pushing his way through a crowded street to call upon Cassio. There is no reply, but we hear a girl giggling. Iago drapes the handkerchief over the end of his swagger stick and drops it through the window, and we cut to hear Othello command Desdemona to 'Lend me thy handkerchief.' The narrative set up by Iago's visit shows how the piece of cloth binds the women together. We see Bianca looking suspiciously at the handkerchief she has been asked to copy before moving to Desdemona, telling Emilia, 'Surely there's some wonder in this handkerchief.' Iago's entrance prompts Emilia's lines about men treating women as food, but following a look from him she leaves. As in the play, it seems, at this point, that in this patriarchal world, all three women defer to their men in terms of 'whate'er you be I am obedient'.

The film also highlights the structural patterning of movement between Venice and Cyprus. While Iago prods and fans Othello's uncertainty and jealousy there are shots of an approaching ship. The crowds gathering at the shore sustain the sense of another arrival from Venice, signalling the replacement of Othello. The man who was earlier the heralded saviour of Cyprus crouches in an oppressively barred and latticed chamber, then stands cramped in a twisting stairwell as he tries to hear what Cassio is saying. He catches only snatches of an inconclusive narrative. He does not see the handkerchief, which Bianca returns, and pathetically asks Iago whether it was his. Indeed, the fact that the handkerchief is one 'spotted with strawberries' is not something that the camera registers. The piece of white silk or muslin is a more significant motif. It is what Othello uses to smother Desdemona and was the veil that covered Desdemona's face in the opening funeral procession. The device makes clear that, although Othello demands 'ocular proof' he neither is given it nor needs it. As F. R. Leavis phrased it, 'the mind that undoes Othello is not Iago's but his own'.[12]

Othello's collapse can be shared by members of the cinema audience who experience with him his vertigo and the disorientating sight of circling birds and peering faces. Moments later it is a quiet, reflective and controlled Othello who states quite calmly and factually that 'Othello's occupation's gone', with his use of the third person conveying the sense of a narrative slipping into history. The sounds made by the 'rude throats' of the 'mortal engines' are of cannon announcing the ship we had seen approaching earlier. There is no rhetoric, no wild passion, but merely the realisation of the inescapable imperative to 'obey the time'. The ship's sail is lowered and when Othello enters his exclusion is emphasised by the sight of Desdemona at ease and comfortable. She moves quickly to reassure him and her open, trusting face fills the screen. Othello's slap is truly shocking. As Othello alternates his comments to her and to Lodovico, the sight of her hair enclosed within a jewelled net symbolises Othello's sense of being enmeshed and trapped. The camera pans over the shocked faces of the many witnesses and Othello eyes them with contempt, defining them with his muttered 'Goats and monkeys'. After his departure Welles isolates a key exchange. Lodovico asks 'Is he not light of brain?' and Iago replies 'He is what he is.' It provides a telling echo of the latter's enigmatic 'I am not what I am.'

The play's insistent linear narrative is reordered to reinforce the sense of a continuous life for all these characters that the camera can allow us to visit. But

Welles is not blindly committed to the drama of minimal utterance, and the film gives space and authority to an Emilia who has seemed for much of the film to be only an instrument of the plot. In her brief appearances she has been inhibited, silenced or dismissed by Iago's presence. Their marriage lacks physical closeness, but the bond of allegiance she owes him is what he insists upon in his ever-careful watchfulness of her. Welles selects just the final section from Shakespeare's scene of Desdemona preparing for bed, where she asks whether there are women who 'do abuse their husbands'. Emilia's speech is a remarkable one. She not only explores and challenges the social *mores* which endorse a double standard in the matter of sexual infidelity, but more poignantly she makes both a claim for equality and a plea for kindness. In Welles's film she loses only three of her twenty lines. She finds a voice that is all the more effective because of her earlier constraint and repression.

The film emphasises how her new-found confidence informs her confrontation with Iago in the final scene. There is also an effective use of space. There is no need to crowd the action around the bed. Othello imprisons himself behind bars and Iago keeps a real and metaphoric distance from his wife until she whispers to herself her realisation: 'villainy, villainy, villainy'. Her face is shadowed by the metal bars as she tells Othello: 'that handkerchief / I found by fortune and did give my husband'. As she indicts him, Iago strikes from behind. The screen clears as all pursue the fleeing Iago and once again Emilia is empowered. Lying face down on the bare stones, her simple statement articulates the terrible tragedy implicit in 'she loved thee'. In awful silence Othello presses his face to the bars to register what she is saying. Quietly and simply she repeats 'she loved thee'.

The confirmation of his private loss is followed by Lodovico announcing: 'Your power and command is taken off / And Cassio rules in Cyprus' (5.2.340–1). Othello sharply unclasps his cloak and in the same movement stabs himself and discards the dagger. The importance of the sea and journeying has been emphasised throughout the film. The shift from Venice to Cyprus has proved significant, but the sea has also been the realm in which Othello has functioned as a military leader: 'Here is my journey's end, here is my butt / And very sea-mark of my utmost sail' (274–5). As a wounded animal he struggles to make his way back to the bedroom, and the dizzying shots of the arched ceiling invokes memories of earlier dislocations. As Othello holds Desdemona in his arms, the opening of a round porthole above locates them now in their own tomb-like space. With just his face in half-light, Othello speaks of 'these unlucky deeds', urges those watching to 'speak of me as I am', concluding with 'Set you down this.' These are the last words in the film and they emphasise once more the need to ensure that the events are a matter of record. Welles had responded to the ways in which the opening Venetian scenes of Shakespeare's text offer layers of recounted narratives which relate Othello's wooing but also underpin what we witness. So many events have preceded the action of a play which itself ultimately and self-consciously invites us to 'relate' its 'unlucky deeds'. The film's final sequence shows the funeral procession still weaving its way as both a conclusion to the film's narrative and a recollection of its opening. Although Roderigo's words, 'never tell me', are not spoken in the film, Welles carefully engages with Shakespeare's emphasis in *Othello* upon the need to tell and retell the story. His film acknowledges that the narrative imperative is both the play's method and its message.

Chimes at Midnight (1966)

The opening moments of *Chimes at Midnight* give priority to Falstaff as he and Shallow offer us a prologue of reflection and retrospection. The two old men on the snow-covered landscape encourage a feeling that this will be a story infused with nostalgia. However, personal memory and the perspective of time provide a correlative for the awareness of a historical frame that Shakespeare could have relied upon his own audience bringing to the play. The film moves from the old men's reminiscences to a narration which draws upon the combined authority of Holinshed's words and Ralph Richardson's voice. Welles's decisions about the way to begin the film offer the audience a personal point of contact in the wider perspective of history, whilst at the same time establishing a method of juxtaposition that will be central to the film's method.[13] For rather than rely upon extensive use of narration the film exploits Shakespeare's use of resembling contrast, exploiting paired characters and linked scenes to explore issues of kingship, public and private morality as well as the interplay of relationships.[14] *Chimes at Midnight* keeps faith with the dramatist's method and prompts an audience, in the manner of Brechtian epic theatre, to think, judge and assess.

The film acknowledges the importance of Hotspur as Hal's antagonist, giving early prominence to his wish that Hal might be 'poisoned with a pot of ale'. Hotspur is attractive as the energetic and forceful counterpart to a dissolute and idle Hal. We have the humour of Hotspur reading his letter in the bath, and there is an engaging lack of self-consciousness as he steps out of the bath, without worrying about his nakedness. His attentive servants with towels at the ready and his gently concerned wife depict a comfortable, domestic world, but the dark, sharp-edged armour reminds us of Hotspur's purpose and the political imperative that Hal is neglecting. The scene between Hotspur and his wife is played with love, tolerance and good humour, as Kate helps him dress. In contrast, Hal is seen helping Falstaff into his robes of disguise for the Gadshill robbery. The parallels work to define character but they also force us, in a Brechtian manner, into making connections which prompt judgement.

The early contrasts and comparisons all work against a Hal whom Welles depicts as self-seeking and manipulative. Hal has no compunction about picking Falstaff's pocket and will readily tip a tankard over him. What is ostensibly his soliloquy of self-justification is influenced by his growing awareness that he is being overheard by Falstaff. Hal's expressed awareness of the usefulness of a 'foil' can describe his own preparedness to play different roles, but in the film it becomes an acknowledgement of the way in which he is prepared to use his companions. It is an uncomfortable sequence and Hal's final wink at Falstaff increases the sense of unease.

The use of long shot in the presentation of the robbery at Gadshill enables us to see Hal's abuse of friendship. As Falstaff and his group pose as hooded, chanting Friars in white robes, Hal and Poins put on black cloaks before swooping to chase their friends. In juxtaposing Hal's careless treatment of his surrogate father with Henry's appeal 'Can no man tell me of my unthrifty son?' Welles allows Gielgud's austere father to claim our respect. The reordering of the sequence encourages us to sympathise with the king's evaluation of the relative merits of Hal and Hotspur, and in this Welles is once again exploiting the strength of film in juxtaposition. There is a satisfying shape in the screenplay which frames Henry's lines (from *Richard II*) about Hal 'robbing our passengers' by the scenes of the Gadshill robbery and its aftermath.

The contrasting settings of court and tavern offer another dimension of opposition. The unremitting perpendiculars of the cold stonework express a rigid commitment to order and restraint, whereas the timbered tavern with its low ceilings invites participation and embraces its inhabitants. It provides a natural theatre in which Falstaff and Hal can play out their play. When impersonating the king, Hal sounds uncannily like Gielgud, and the saucepan crown which had looked comic on Falstaff seems tight upon Hal's brow. He does not soften his list of insults to Falstaff and the resolution he expresses in 'I will' is intensely serious. Welles's support for the values of Eastcheap seems to be signalled as the Sheriff invades the room, accompanied by men and dogs. However, the Sheriff's courtesy dissolves the threat of subjugation and Hal's dismissal of him seems uncomfortably flippant. When Hal hits his head on the ceiling, it might indicate that he is at odds with his environment, but it could also suggest that a measure of knocking into shape is necessary.

In Shakespeare's text Henry summons the court only to dismiss them two lines later, having effectively wrong-footed a son expecting a private exchange with his father. Welles shows us Henry intimidating and humiliating Hal by leading him through the echoing stone hall, watched by the disciplined ranks of stave-bearing troops as well as the ordered court. Once on the throne the king orders 'Lords, give us leave. The Prince of Wales and I must have some needful conference alone.' Hal has been forced to recognise that the meeting is on the king's terms and the vast cold setting makes clear the calculation that is at work in Henry's expressions of regret and disappointment.

The montage that shows us paired characters as warring antagonists sets up powerfully the importance of the meeting at Shrewsbury in both political and personal terms. The vivid realism in the battle sequence is Welles's conscious rejoinder to what he described as Olivier's 'people riding out of the castle and suddenly they are on a golf course somewhere charging each other'.[15] The extended sequence shows the human cost of a war in which it is rapidly impossible to identify the mud-covered soldiers as either loyalist or rebel. Our judgement is continually challenged. With his feet planted firmly on the ground, Hotspur courageously embraces his fate, while Falstaff is seen scuttling across the screen, peering round a tree or comically caught stranded and incongruous amidst the horses, soldiers and brutal combat. He functions as a Brechtian device of ironic alienation, prompting evaluation. Hotspur's integrity is preserved and the tragic consequences of his 'ill-weaved ambition' are acknowledged. After his death the camera tracks back, allowing the battlefield to be replaced by a scene of natural growth and fertility. Hal and Hotspur are held in a moment of stillness that forces reflection upon the waste of war.

Falstaff's claim to have killed Hotspur is a challenge to the very notion of honour. Welles responds imaginatively to the potential of the sequence and reshapes the text to include the king in the tableau grouped over the body of Hotspur. A silent Henry looks steadily at Hal, and the camera shows Hal returning the look with equal steadiness while Falstaff shamelessly pursues his claim with 'I look to be either earl or duke, I assure you.' By implying that Henry believes Falstaff, the moment scars the recently healed bond with his son. As the king mounts to depart, our sympathy remains for a moment with Hal. But this shifts as Henry suffers a moment of physical frailty, falling forward before bracing himself to announce, 'Rebellion in this land shall lose its sway.' The yoking of his public responsibility and private disappointment ensure that we register his failure as king and father. Civil strife and familial friction are set to continue, and Welles's decisions effectively deal with the transition to the events of *Part Two*. When Michael Bogdanov and Michael Pennington staged their cycle of history plays, *The Wars of the Roses*, for the English Shakespeare Company, they took similar decisions to forge a link between *Part One* and *Part Two*, and acknowledged their debt to *Chimes at Midnight* with 'Thank you, Orson.'[16]

Although John Dover Wilson argues in *The Fortunes of Falstaff* that Hal's tolerance of Falstaff's claim is 'an instance of selflessness and generosity',[17] Welles indicates that any sense of triumph for Falstaff will be short-lived. The moment is transitional for Hal. Having been left behind with a surly-looking Prince John, Hal listens to Falstaff holding court about the benefits of 'sherris sack'. But as

Falstaff warms to his theme, Hal draws away to watch the king and the nobility leave. He is caught in the middle ground. Falstaff is then silent for what is one of the most powerful moments of departure in the film.[18]

In the absence of Hotspur, Poins functions as Hal's foil as well as his preferred companion, who takes precedence over Falstaff. Poins had been established early in the film as someone on whom Hal had relied for the business of stage management. Their bond is strengthened by the attention that is paid to Poins's plans for Hal and his sister to marry. Hal responds to Poins's definition of his role as 'Hal's shadow' by wrapping his arm round his shoulder. Rather than as tempter, it is more as his conscience that Poins responds to Hal's question 'What wouldst thou think of me if I should weep?', by telling him 'I would think thee a most princely hypocrite.' This prompts Hal's rapid departure, which is patterned by Falstaff's journey to Gloucestershire.

While Falstaff reminisces with Shallow and Silence, Hal is positioning himself closer to the crown. The alternation of sequences at court and in the country promotes objective assessment. In a strikingly choric moment, the three men on the bench play 'we have heard the chimes at midnight' straight to camera. Welles intensifies the characteristic shared by the plays and his film in that the central motifs of departure, rejection and betrayal exist in inset cameos throughout. There is a powerful sense of an ending as Falstaff, increasingly conscious both of his own death and the passing of an era, is on the point of fading into the past as he recedes into long shot. Pistol's arrival, though, has him thrusting back to fill the frame and a low camera angle makes him a towering figure to ask: 'Is the old King dead?' There is a burst of energy over snow-covered landscape which recalls events at Gadshill. In recalling an episode in which an energetic Falstaff was 'put down' by a 'plain tale' spoken by a deceitful and manipulative Hal, we are encouraged to consider how history is about to repeat itself.

Falstaff may be embarrassing as he salutes his 'sweet boy', but having to address Hal's back ensures that he keeps our sympathy. Falstaff's flicker of a smile may suggest paternal pride, but that does little to erase the pain and public humiliation explicit in Hal's rejection and in Falstaff's acknowledgement of his debt to Shallow. The film's use of montage once again ensures that our emotional involvement is tempered with a reasoned objectivity. The new regime is harsh. As the 'fair proceeding' of the king is commended, Doll is arrested, crying in vain for help from Falstaff, who is suffering the same fate at the hands of the Sheriff. Immediately the Boy announces that Falstaff is 'very sick' and an audience is prompted to consider and assess Bardolph's view that 'The King is a good King, but it must be as it may.'

In drawing upon *Henry V* for his screenplay, Welles illustrates how Falstaff continues to challenge Henry in both his public and private roles. Welles emends the text to identify the 'man committed yesterday' as Falstaff. The decision tidies the narrative by getting Falstaff freed and prompts a memory of the sermon on sack, for 'It was excess of wine that set him on.' Yet the film suggests that it is too little, too late. The closing sequence juxtaposes two narratives. The Hostess's account of Falstaff's death is given almost uncut. Then, as she watches the funeral procession bearing the coffin through the countryside, we hear the voice of history declaring how the new king will be regarded as 'a pattern of prince-hood, a lodestar in honour'.

Characteristically, the film once more urges reflection and prompts judgement. Just as he does at the end of *Macbeth* and *Othello*, Welles pays tribute to events that transcend time and proclaim universal truths. Each film is structured upon a cyclic pattern. Like Coleridge's Ancient Mariner, Welles recognises the necessity of going beyond reflection, which can be relatively passive, to embrace the imperative of the affirmation that is implicit in a more active commitment to recounting the story.

NOTES

1 See Ace G. Pilkington, *Screening Shakespeare. From Richard III to Henry V* (Newark, DE, and London, 1991) pp. 130–4. The relationship between Welles and his public(s), and the complex textual and contextual histories of his films, are examined in detail by Michael Anderegg, *Orson Welles, Shakespeare and Popular Culture* (New York, 1999).

2 Jack J. Jorgens, *Shakespeare on Film* (Bloomington, IN, 1977) p. 112.

3 Jean Cocteau, quoted by Peter Bogdanovich in Jonathan Rosenbaum, ed., *This is Orson Welles: Orson Welles and Peter Bogdanovich* (London, 1993), p. xxxiv.

4 *2 Henry IV*, 5.5.83–4.

5 Juan Cobos and Miguel Rubio, 'Welles and Falstaff', *Sight and Sound*, 35 (Autumn 1966), 158–61; reprinted in Bridget Gellert Lyons, ed., *Chimes at Midnight* (New Brunswick, NJ and London, 1988), pp. 259–66; p. 263.

6 Welles's shaping of *The Merchant of Venice* cut Portia. He was planning to emphasise Shakespeare's exploration of old age in *King Lear*; see Jonathan Rosenbaum, *Sight and Sound*, 55 (Summer 1986), 164–71; 168, 170.

7 David A. Cook, *A History of Narrative Film*, third edn (New York, 1996), p. 419.

8 A fascinating account of the process is provided in Mícheál MacLiammóir, *Put Money in Thy Purse. The Making of Orson Welles's Othello* (London, 1952).

9 This aspect had been central to Welles's 1936 production of *Macbeth* (known as the 'Voodoo' *Macbeth*) for the Federal Theatre Project in Harlem. See Simon Callow, *Orson Welles: the Road to Xanadu* (London, 1995), pp. 222–65.

10 Rosenbaum, *This is Orson Welles*, p. 214.

11 Jonathan Rosenbaum records that 'the release version, which contains the narrated prologue, is still available on film but not on tape', in *ibid.*, p. 510. See also Anderegg, *Orson Welles*, ch.5, and Simon Callow, *Orson Welles: Hello Americans* (London, 2006), ch. 22.

12 F. R. Leavis, 'Diabolic Intellect and the Noble Hero', *Scrutiny*, 6 (1937), 259–83; p. 267.

13 Welles had filmed two scenes, showing the murder of Richard II, and his coffin being presented to Henry, which were to follow the old men walking through the snow.

However, he judged that they would 'have hurt the real, internal rhythm of the picture' and rejected them. See Cobos and Rubio, 'Welles and Falstaff', reprinted in Lyons, *Chimes at Midnight*, pp. 259–66; p. 264.

14 Welles's fascination with the narrative sweep of Shakespeare's history plays had produced his *Five Kings* (Colonial Theatre, Boston 1939) (see Callow, *Orson Welles: the Road to Xanadu*, pp. 423–46) and the earlier version of *Chimes at Midnight* staged in Belfast in 1960. See 'Interview with Keith Baxter', in Lyons, *Chimes at Midnight*, pp. 267–83; p. 268.

15 Cobos and Rubio, 'Welles and Falstaff', reprinted in Lyons, *Chimes at Midnight*, pp. 259–66; p. 266.

16 Michael Bogdanov and Michael Pennington, *The Wars of the Roses* (London, 1990), p. 55.

17 John Dover Wilson, *The Fortunes of Falstaff* (Cambridge, 1943), p. 68.

18 See Samuel Crowl, 'The Long Goodbye: Welles and Falstaff', *Shakespeare Quarterly*, 31 (1980), 369–80.

11

MARK SOKOLYANSKY

Grigori Kozintsev's *Hamlet* and *King Lear*

More than two centuries ago Voltaire made a telling remark: 'All the arts are brothers, each one is a light to the other.' The career of Grigori Kozintsev (1905–73) as an interpreter of Shakespeare in Russian theatre, cinema and literary criticism is a striking illustration of this maxim.

Kozintsev's road to his two Shakespeare films was long and not very easy. It passed through three channels, the first of which was the theatre – the director's earliest passion. As early as 1923 the young Kozintsev was planning to perform *Hamlet* as a pantomime in the 'Factory of the Eccentric Actor' (FEKS), the experimental group he created with Leonid Trauberg and Sergei Yutkevich, but this plan was not realised.[1] Seventeen years later, already a well-known film director, he returned to Shakespeare on stage. In 1940 he wanted to perform *Henry IV* at one of the Leningrad theatres, but this, too, did not take place. It was a year later, in 1941, that Kozintsev achieved his first Shakespearean production, *King Lear*, at the Bolshoi Dramaticheski Teatr in Leningrad.

His next step was a production of *Othello* at the Pushkin Theatre: the play was performed during 1943–4 in Novosibirsk, where the Leningrad company had been evacuated during the war. In 1949 Kozintsev was offered the chance to stage *King Lear* at the famous Kamerny Teatr in Moscow, run by Alexandr Tairov, but this proposal coincided with the gloomy period of recurrent witch-hunts in the USSR, and the Kamerny, with its innovative aesthetics, was *de jure* renamed but *de facto* closed down by the authorities. The most important event in the history of Kozintsev's interpretations of Shakespeare was his *Hamlet* at the Pushkin Theatre in 1954. The performance was one of the two first productions of the play on the Soviet stage in the post-Stalin years.

The second channel of Kozintsev's approach to Shakespeare was literary criticism. He published several critical essays on Shakespeare and a seminal book, whose Russian title is *Nash Sovremennik Viliam Shekspir* – 'Our contemporary William Shakespeare'. The title of the 1966 English translation, *Shakespeare, Time and Conscience*, was presumably chosen to avoid confusion with Jan Kott's recently-published *Shakespeare Our Contemporary* (1964), a landmark in the modern understanding of Shakespeare's works.[2]

Most important, though not as remarkable in terms of quantity, was the third channel of Kozintsev's Shakespearean interpretation, the cinema. In 1945 he and Trauberg created a film about the Second World War under the title *Burya* – 'The Tempest'. Some elements of the plot paralleled Shakespeare's play, but the film was not shown until eleven years later, with its title changed by the censors to *Prostyie Lyudi* – 'The Common People'. Kozintsev's film of *Don Quixote* (1957) also has a bearing on his Shakespeare work: it was shot just after his theatrical production of *Hamlet*, and was closely connected with it in both feeling and style.

The film of *Hamlet* was in production in 1963, and was shown in the spring of 1964, when the quatercentenary of Shakespeare's birth was being celebrated. Ten years had passed since the Leningrad stage production of the tragedy. Within that decade was encompassed a whole era of post-war Soviet history, the so-called 'Thaw'. The term has commonly been used to define the post-Stalin decade (some Western authors call it the 'Khruschev era', with reference to Nikita Khruschev's ruling position). It was marked by a certain animation in social and cultural life, following the denunciation of Stalin's 'personality cult', the mass rehabilitation of innocent people and their homecoming from the prisons and concentration camps, and an obvious intensification of intellectual and spiritual life. The changes in cultural life in general were reflected in the treatment of Shakespeare's plays in particular.

The new possibilities for a deeper and closer reading of the Danish tragedy corresponded to the evident need for a topical interpretation. Collecting his reflections on *Hamlet* over many years, Kozintsev felt the play's topicality keenly and defined the dominant theme of his film very clearly. 'Conscience is the main theme of our age', he wrote in his notebook, and identified the theme in his favourite tragedy.[3] As for the central character, the director apprehended him as a man who can 'say *No* to all kinds of lie. But the revealing of falsehood in social order and human relations appeared also to be a kind of struggle.'[4] In other words, Hamlet's frank non-conformism was interpreted by Kozintsev as resistance by the person 'who gave too much vent to his mind'. Approaching his new work, the director told a reporter from the magazine *Films and Filming*:

> It is quite possible and permissible, to make an academic production of the play, but I think at the same time Shakespeare needs a kind of new, individual interpretation. Every new effort of every generation creates a new aspect of this character. A new aspect of history, the spirit of poetry, the sense of humanity, should be modern and absolutely lifelike for audiences today . . . I shall try to show the general feelings, the general philosophy of the poetry, but I shall not use the medium of traditional theatre staging. I want to go the way of the cinema . . .[5]

Kozintsev used a wide-screen format with black and white photography, and the choice was a matter of principle. There was no challenge to the tastes of contemporary Soviet audiences, with whom black and white films were then no less popular than colour. Nor was the decision dictated by the Lenfilm studios' financial problems: *Don Quixote* had been in colour. He wrote later that for *Don Quixote* he had wanted to capture the quality of the warm south but for *Hamlet* he needed the cool greys of the north. The black and white of *Hamlet* was also to some extent determined by a desire to avoid bright colouration as a way of glossing over the truth – the tendency encouraged by official Soviet ideology and despised by Kozintsev.

In the 1920s, before the appearance of colour films in Russia, one of the leaders of Russian theoretical formalism, Yuri Tynianov, observed that 'the black-and-white variant gives to cinematography an opportunity to present not the material, but the semantic comparison of sizes, the monstrous lack of coincidence of perspectives'.[6] Kozintsev was attracted by that opportunity. It was also very important for him to concentrate the audience's attention upon the main elements – the contrasts in the represented reality, the evolution of the characters, Shakespeare's poetry. Accordingly, he chose Boris Pasternak's translation, which is far from being literal but is in tune with Shakespeare's poetry, dramatic spirit and topicality.

Kozintsev's theatrical experience was especially apparent in the episodes and sequences limited by the space of Elsinore. In the course of the first discussions of the film some critics identified the influence of Alexander Tyshler's settings for the famous 1935 production of *King Lear* at the Moscow Jewish Theatre. This was not altogether correct. The set designer, Evgenii Enei, who had begun his collaboration with Kozintsev in the 1920s, had successfully learned lessons from various predecessors in theatre and cinema: he was trying to overcome theatricality in the setting by broadening the represented space and through the specific language of black and white cinematography. The costume designer, Soliko Virsaladze, supported this by representing only the outlines of Renaissance costumes, but omitting detail and ornament. The theatrical influence was also overcome by the skill of the cameraman, Ionas Gritsius, an apprentice and follower of the great Russian cameraman Andrei Moskvin, a longstanding collaborator of Kozintsev, Leonid Trauberg and Enei. Gritsius and Enei were the backbone of the team for *Hamlet*.

Music had an exceptionally important role in the film. It was created by one of the greatest composers of the century, Dmitri Shostakovich, who had written music for several films by Kozintsev and Trauberg as well as for Kozintsev's theatre productions of *Hamlet* and *King Lear*. For the film *Hamlet* he created what was essentially a new score, catching exactly the musical quality of Shakespeare's poetry, which (according to Pasternak) 'lies in the rhythmic interchange of solemnity and anxiety'.[7] Musicologists have noted that the main musical theme in the film score bears some resemblance to portions of the composer's eighth and eleventh symphonies, while the music for the ball in Elsinore and for the play-within-the-play recalls his famous scherzos.[8]

The approach to *Hamlet* in 1963–4 was basically new in comparison with that of 1954, and this required a new cast. Only a few actors from the Leningrad stage performance came with Kozintsev to the film. But this raised other, more complicated problems of adjustment. For instance, according to Kozintsev himself, Yuri Tolubeev, who had played the part in Leningrad, completely revised his interpretation of Polonius for the film, avoiding anything exaggerated and drawing a detailed portrait of a courtier who can be every monarch's ears, mouth and counsellor.[9]

In selecting the actors, Kozintsev resolutely expanded the scope of his team. Side by side with those he brought from the Pushkin Theatre (Tolubeev, Vladimir Erenberg as Horatio, Vadim Medvedev as Guildenstern and Igor Dmitriev as Rosencrantz) was a Moscow actor of the 'psychological' school, Mikhail Nazvanov, as Claudius. The delicate, child-like Moscow actress Anastasia Vertinskaia played Ophelia. With some misgivings, but nevertheless consistently, Kozintsev cast actors whose first language was not Russian: Latvian Elza Radzin as Gertrude, Ukrainian Stepan Oleksenko as Laertes and Estonian Ants Laurer as the priest. They brought some shades of other national traditions into the film. But the main problem was to find an actor for the prince himself.

Almost all the reviewers agreed that the Leningrad stage production of 1954 had not been a really great success for the principal reason that there was no adequate performer for the title role. As the most authoritative critic of the day expressed it – an opinion shared by many educated and experienced spectators – the '*Hamlet* of our time' could not be adequately presented without a really great actor.[10] Even the ingenuity of the director and the enthusiasm of the audience could not make up for this lack in such a complex tragedy.

Innokenti Smoktunovski appeared to have the required resources, and Kozintsev chose him for the film. Like the director, Smoktunovski began his path towards Hamlet in the theatre. He had been a theatrical actor *par excellence*, and his greatest success before Hamlet had been the role of Prince Myshkin in Georgi Tovstonogov's Leningrad production of *The Idiot*. It was the prologue in his career to the great tragic role. (It should be added that the history of Smoktunovski's Hamlet had a *comic* epilogue in the cinema: a year after the appearance of Kozintsev's film he played a comic version of the role in El'dar Riazonov's comedy *Beregis' Avtomobilia!* – 'Beware of the Car!' – where the hero, an insurance agent, plays the prince in an amateur production.)

The outward appearance of Smoktunovski's Hamlet was rather traditional. The director did not wish to declare his innovations by means of purely external details. In his book on Shakespeare he has clearly explained his intentions: 'Hamlet is often staged in modern dress, but the performance tells a tale of ancient life. The tragedy must be played in sixteenth-century costumes but must be comprehended as a modern story.'[11] Playing this 'modern story' the actor was quite reserved, in accordance with the character's instructions to the Players. However, this reserved manner of acting also helped to indicate the depth of the protagonist's personal tragedy, which was also that of the world represented in the film.

Above all, it was Smoktunovski's individual manner of acting that distinguished the film from all previous cinema versions of the play. The manner became a tuning fork that gave the pitch for all the actors. As he saw him, Prince Hamlet was not only the centre of the whole action, but also its leader. The hero's nervousness was played without any affectation, shown in nuances, but it made clear the intensity and scale of his inner shock. This is evident in his dialogue with Ophelia, his conversation with the Players, and especially his tirade about the recorder in the dialogue with Rosencrantz and Guildenstern after *The Murder of Gonzago*. Hamlet/Smoktunovski exposes falsehood at several stages of the plot's development, but most of all in this episode, which many critics thought the climax of the film.

An outstanding Russian psychologist, Lev Vygotskii, has observed acutely in an essay on the play that Hamlet often speaks in monologues because he is absolutely alone.[12] In the limits of the conventions chosen for the film, the performance of the monologues was especially difficult. Kozintsev preferred the off-screen reading of the soliloquies accompanying silent behaviour. This device was contemplated in Russian film-making as far back as the 1930s by Sergei Yutkevich, who had planned several Shakespeare films many years before his 1956 *Othello*. The device was used by Olivier in his 1948 film of *Hamlet*.

In Kozintsev's film the world of Elsinore is concentrated in a reserved, very compact space: there is practically no empty space in it. Perhaps the single exception is the walls of the castle, where the Ghost appears. Many spectators were impressed by the sequences with Hamlet walking nervously through the crowded court: he can be alone nowhere, and everywhere there are people who make up the prison that is Denmark. In the palace all the walls have ears, and the ears are embodied not only by Polonius hiding behind the arras but by the numerous courtiers. The second distinctive quality of this universe is that we encounter armed men at every step: a symbol of the 'new order' and the people's devotion to the new monarch. Even Ophelia's insanity is shown against the background of the crowd of soldiers, who are an emblem of the all-pervading coarseness and servility. Among these loyal subjects of Claudius only Marcellus and Barnardo are picked out as friends of Hamlet and Horatio. The total effect of this world is to determine Hamlet's tragedy as that of an unsleeping conscience. As a British critic observed, 'Kozintsev portrayed the tragedy of a whole society where real justice was impossible.'[13]

But what is juxtaposed with this monotonous world of Elsinore? The occasional alternatives appear to be fictions, which are being destroyed like a house of cards. The assumed Renaissance worldiness and *bonhomie* of Rosencrantz and Guildenstern during their first meeting with Hamlet transforms into betrayal; Ophelia's love for him coexists with espionage and the combination of the two leads to her insanity; the queen's feeling for her son is outweighed by her lust for Claudius; Laertes's 'giant-like rebellion' is concluded by his collaboration with the king. There are few exceptions to this rule. The principal one is of course Horatio, with the face and garb of a Renaissance humanist rather than a man of action. The other exceptions are the players and the grave-diggers, but they are marginal figures, literally outside the world of the court. The single conscious fighter against this 'sea of troubles' is Hamlet. In the episode of the duel with Laertes, Smoktunovski's Hamlet is no longer a hesitating philosopher, but a rebel, sure of his own righteousness.

As has been mentioned already, Kozintsev's *Hamlet* appeared in Russia in the year of Shakespeare's quatercentenary, and it was an undoubted success at home and abroad from its first showing. It remained a 'Russian *Hamlet*', embodying in the first instance an acute reaction to Soviet reality, but at the same time it aroused enormous interest among Western audiences and critics.

It is noteworthy that the success of the film also coincided with the end of the 'Thaw' in the Soviet Union. In the autumn of 1964 a *coup d'état* took place in Moscow, and Leonid Brezhnev's 'much more Claudian' era began.[14] Even moderate attempts at overcoming totalitarian dictatorship were blocked. The role of the party's dictatorship increased considerably in cultural and spiritual life. It is enough here to mention the several notorious trials sentencing writers to imprisonment, the dismissal of the editorial boards of progressive periodicals, the banning of many books, theatrical performances, films and so on.

Kozintsev began work on his film version of *King Lear* in this new historical and political situation. Among the events which occurred between his two Shakespeare films were the 'Prague Spring' of 1968 and the Soviet invasion of Czechoslovakia in August of the same year, and the principal phases of the Vietnam War. The toughening of Soviet foreign and internal policy as well as an aggravation of East–West antagonism made the traditional, somewhat romantic approach to Shakespeare impossible. The new artistic trends in theatre and cinema also impacted on Kozintsev. In an interview given while shooting the new film, he tried to define the main themes of *King Lear*: 'Personality and history are the tragedy's theme. And further, I could go on all night listing various themes: personality and power, society and personality, old age and youth, the fate of a clan and of one person, the fate of a group of people, and the fate of human thought, too . . .'[15] In this knot of themes, the eternal and universal coexist with topical motifs. Kozintsev was seeking for new approaches, though the work's continuity with his *Hamlet* was quite noticeable. The film was completed in 1970.

King Lear was produced by the same studios – Lenfilm – and the director enlisted the services of the principal members of the team with which he had worked on *Hamlet*: the cameraman Ionas Gritsius, and designers Evgenii Enei and Soliko Virsaladze, with Dmitri Shostakovich as composer. (The film turned out to be his last work for the cinema.)

Kozintsev again chose to film in black and white, carefully avoiding any hint of chocolate-box prettiness. One difference from *Hamlet* was immediately obvious: the whole atmosphere was much more ascetic – or restrained. To some extent this was connected with an orientation towards the Dark Ages as the historical time of the 'medieval' Lear, the prototype of Shakespeare's hero. Thirty years earlier, in 1941, in his theatrical production of the play, Kozintsev had presented a widened, 'universal' Middle Ages. In the film the accent moved to a 'dark' age, its ascetic character more concentrated. In his diary Kozintsev wrote about the simple stage properties for the play: 'the crown, the map of the kingdom, a rope for hanging'.[16] He enlarged the list for the film, but remained true to his first idea of the tragedy's ascetic spirit.

King Lear was shot in various locations in the Soviet Union – in the mountains of Crimea, in the old small north-western town of Ivangorod on the river Narva and on a plain near the Caspian Sea. Very different as they are from each other, those places had something in common – desolate nature. In fact 'stone is a key image' throughout the film.[17] The costumes were designed for corresponding effect. One cannot say that Virsaladze recreated the dress of sixth-century Britain, rather he was aiming for the same timeless, 'universal' and dark sense of period. In every respect the material environment of the characters is primitive, from an open fire in Lear's castle to the stocks in which Kent suffers. The actors' manner of playing is also simpler in comparison with the technique adopted in *Hamlet*.

The new purposes of the director determined his choice of actors. Elsa Radzin (Goneril) apart, none of the *Hamlet* cast were invited to work in the new film. This time almost all the leading roles were played by actors from the Baltic theatres, despite the need to dub most of them with the voices of Russian actors. Besides the Latvian Radzin, the team included an Estonian as Lear (Yuri Yarvet), the prominent Lithuanian actors Regimantas Adomajtis (Edmund), Donatas Banionis (Albany) and Iozas Budrajtis (France), and the Latvians Leonard Merzin (Edgar) and Karl Sebris (Gloucester).

As Lear, Yarvet is a short and frail old man. Such a Lear seems quite as appropriate to the scene of the storm as one of the 'poor naked wretches' he encounters, or to the circumstances of his death, but has nothing of the majestic monarch. However, Yarvet demonstrates brilliantly in physical bearing and the expressiveness of his eyes how this Lear has a different bearing as king from the one he adopts as one of the 'wretches'. The arrogant bearing and sparkling eyes of Lear show that without a doubt this personage was born to be a king, that he is used to his vassals' implicit obedience and cannot accept the changes that have taken place in his life. Such, for instance, is Yarvet's appearance in the coach that takes him from one castle to another – a vehicle absolutely unlike a royal carriage, with the Fool perched outside it – that the situation almost seems parodic. Besides majestic manners and senile weakness, there is one more quality which Yarvet plays perfectly: the gentle humaneness of Lear before his death. This Lear has passed through madness to the higher wisdom.

The motif of madness is important in both Kozintsev's films of Shakespearean tragedies. As Hamlet, Smoktunovski only seems mad in the presence of Elsinore's inhabitants: he plays an insane person. The madness of Vertinskaia's Ophelia stands out against the brutal armed guards (as has been noted) and is completely determined by Elsinore's moral climate. In *King Lear*, Edgar, like Hamlet, represents insanity and the Fool (Oleg Dal) plays a real fool to avoid the penalty for his wit. Lear really goes mad not because his inner world is 'out of joint' but because all surrounding life is out of its senses. The change from majesty to madness is skilfully played by Yarvet, and the dubbing of his Russian dialogue is done wonderfully by the unique Moscow actor Zinovi Gerdt, who is completely in tune with the Estonian's performance.

While Hamlet is himself a keen philosopher and needs no Fool to unmask the hypocrisy of Elsinore, as F. W. Sternfeld notes, 'there are two clowns in *King Lear*, the professional fool and Edgar, disguised as Mad Tom'.[18] In the film the fool's role played by Edgar is not accentuated, which makes the figure of the professional Fool even more significant. In the performance of Oleg Dal the restrained manner of playing reaches its peak. He is quite unlike most Fools in stage and film versions of the play: a skinny boy with a shaved head and large sad eyes – 'a boy from Auschwitz' as Kozintsev himself called him. This Fool's jokes are not designed to make people laugh; more often they are bitter truth covered by irony. Life is too tragic for insouciant laughter, and in this world 'the Fool in accordance with his philosophy of life is a bitter realist and a moral realist by his behaviour'.[19] In some sequences the king and the Fool are shown as a syncretic pair. The Fool often produces ironic comments on the king's actions. In Kozintsev's opinion irony gives to the character of Lear the 'range of negation' and 'convincingness' in critical analysis of social links. That is why the Fool, with his sarcastic intonation, is so important. He cannot be separated from Lear and when he disappears his functions are taken over by the king himself.

The moral idealism in *King Lear* is expressed by different means than those employed in *Hamlet*. In several sequences of the earlier film romantic feeling was quite appropriate. First of all it can be located in what Hamlet himself says. For instance, as some critics have noted, Hamlet's exclamation 'We'll have a play tomorrow!' sounds like the announcement 'We'll have a battle tomorrow!' In *King Lear* such expression of feeling in intonation was impossible. The world represented in the film is full of the cruellest prose. Kozintsev's approach to it was quite in tune with the opinion of Boris Pasternak, whose translation was used. 'In *King Lear* only the criminals – hypocritically – use notions of duty and honour. The positive heroes of the tragedy are fools and madmen, perishing and vanquished ones.'[20] The tragic outlook of the prominent Russian poet and translator was very close to the director's own at the end of the 1960s. The theme of moral idealism is also accentuated by Shostakovich's sad melody, played by the Fool, which seems to frame the whole film.

Whereas in his *Hamlet* the director actively used Shakespearean metaphors and translated them into the language of cinema (a classical example being Hamlet's outburst about the recorder), in *King Lear* he created new metaphors, which help to represent the tragedy's message more precisely. These are linked above all with the tragic nature of the play. 'The metaphors of tortures and torments pass through all the tragedy', wrote Kozintsev in his book on Shakespeare.[21] One can identify a number of them in the film, including the Fool's appearance (wisdom assuming the aspect of a martyr) and Kent in the stocks (generosity and loyalty with chained legs). The cinematic metaphors do not break the stylistic unity of the tragedy, and at the same time they strengthen the effect of artistic generalisation. These metaphors can be associated with the famous laconic formulas from Sonnet 66: 'right perfection wrongfully disgrac'd', 'art made tongue-tied by authority' and 'captive good attending captain ill'.

In search of a balance between conventional and natural, Kozintsev took issue not only with his own earlier works, but also with his contemporaries among theatre and film directors. He enjoyed Peter Brook's 1962 production of *King Lear* in Stratford-upon-Avon, with Paul Scofield, but in his own work he did not accept any of the Brechtian mannerisms. 'Brechtian aesthetics have won in Stratford', he wrote. 'In Peter Brook's *King Lear* the realistic entourage is absent.'[22] To the Russian director's way of thinking that was an 'algebraic formula', but he needed the 'realistic entourage', material as well as human. We can see it in his representation of the places of the action (the designer's and cinematographer's work), in the costumes and in the acting. Such actors of the traditional, realistic school as those playing Kent, Regan, Cornwall, Cordelia and Oswald might seem alien to the prevailing stylisation of the film, but at the same time their manner of acting corresponded altogether to Kozintsev's intention.

Brook's stage production was not the only object for artistic discussion. As has already been mentioned, Kozintsev's book shares the same title as the second edition of Jan Kott's *Essays on Shakespeare* published in Poland a year earlier. For all the coincidence of their claim to consider Shakespeare a 'contemporary', the approach of the two authors could hardly be more different. In particular, their interpretations of *King Lear* were contradictory. Kott analysed the British tragedy as a kind of absurd drama, an *Endgame* for the Shakespearean epoch. As a director and literary critic, Kozintsev saw the deep meaning of *King Lear* in its presentation of the greatest human and social collisions – in themselves altogether topical for modern audiences. To screen this tragedy he needed more concrete reality, more closeness to the audience's social and historical experience.

Maybe that is why there are so many crowd scenes in the film, and why the common people occupy such an important place in the world Kozintsev creates for the tragedy. In his *Hamlet* film, besides the soldiers, the common people are evident at the beginning of the film (townspeople listening to the herald), in the episode in the churchyard and in the finale. Nevertheless, these appearances are episodic. Although in *King Lear* the common people are represented as a formless, silent mob, we cannot imagine the film's world without them. The mob makes the space of tragedy live – it is not an 'empty space'. In spite of its ascetic appearance, it is a full, dynamic space.

In some moments the characters in the foreground appear to be part of this mob, to be amongst the common people. It is clear that the tragedy seen by the audience is also that of the people. These scenes represent a great disorder as a symbol of a national tragedy. 'This, not the storm, is the chaos that really matters', writes Alexander Leggatt. 'As the procession of beggars, with Lear, Gloucester and Edgar in their company, trudges along the road, they encounter a stream of refugees fleeing in the opposite direction.'[23]

In *Hamlet*, Elsinore's inhabitants are not themselves responsible for the 'sea of troubles', with the exceptions of Claudius, who is responsible for the murder of his brother, and Gertrude, who has turned traitor. 'Polonius, Guildenstern, Rosencrantz are by no means villains . . . It is awful that they are quite typical people – moderately clever, moderately honest, moderately kind. But Hamlet is not satisfied with this moderation . . .'[24] So the director and Shakespeare scholar drew a boundary between the protagonist of the Danish tragedy and the people who embodied to a great extent this *world-prison*. These people have become capable of evil because of the circumstances of life in Elsinore.

In Shakespeare's *King Lear* this verdict, with its debt to Hegel, is not to be found. The circumstances are not less terrible there, but every character is responsible for his personal actions. In the film those personally responsible are the personages whose guilt is evident. Lear is guilty of despotic actions, when he could not distinguish truth from lies. 'Lear is not insane. What is insane is the social system, at the central point of which he stands. But the king has created this system himself.' [25] He is especially guilty because his actions lead to war in his country.[26] Having betrayed their father for the sake of the crown, Goneril and Regan can kill each other out of jealousy and lust: they also are guilty, as is Gloucester who acts like his king.

But a logical question occurs: who is qualified to be a judge in Kozintsev's version? The answer is the same Lear, as played by Yarvet and spoken by Gerdt – but Lear in his new image. The judge Lear is not the arrogant tyrant but a common old man, who has lost everything in his life and through his sufferings has attained the higher justice.

The film's main moral message is connected with that simple but eternal wisdom. For Kozintsev the crucial point is not that several men (Albany, Kent, Edgar) have survived and could consolidate the kingdom. Who can foresee the results of what they might do? Political forecasts were of no interest for Kozintsev. His deep historical optimism had an ethical basis. In the film the director and his team made a protest against the cynical, Edmundian view of life and stated that there are real moral values in this world – and that every epoch begets defenders of those values.

Having put *King Lear* on the screen, Kozintsev did not intend to stop his work on Shakespeare in the cinema. Time was passing, and he felt keenly many changes in both private and public spheres. On the threshold of the 1970s he noticed some anachronistic details in his previous works. Even in the 1960s, considering the opinions of critics and audiences on his *Hamlet*, he had remarked that 'the critics could be divided into two camps: some of them did not like symbolic sequences, others did not like hens'.[27] He felt the necessity to seek for a new reading of the tragedy. He was thinking about the imagery, though if he had made a new version of *Hamlet*, there would probably have been more hens and fewer symbols in it. Kozintsev himself wrote that he would willingly omit the seagull that figures as a symbol of freedom in his film.[28]

In 1973, almost ten years after his *Hamlet* appeared, he invented quite another finale for the tragedy:

> Now I know how to present the coming of Fortinbras. Machinegunners hold the posts. The telephone wires (let them be tongues of a bell) are being cut. Fortinbras occupies the office of Claudius. The frightened ministers appear . . . in underpants. Fortinbras breaks the safe's lock with his dagger and asks 'Where did the crime take place?' Horatio is in floods of tears. Fortinbras goes on giving orders, looks out of the window and by the way gives instructions concerning the ceremony of Hamlet's funeral.[29]

If Kozintsev had shot *Hamlet* in the 1970s, after his *King Lear*, it would certainly have been quite another film, especially in terms of cinematic style.

Tempora mutantur et nos mutamur in illis – the times change and we change in them. As thinker and director, Kozintsev did not stand still. Influenced by political events as well as by new aesthetic trends (sometimes in dispute with them) he was not afraid to revise his views of Shakespearean works and of the art of the cinema.[30]

In the 1970s, Kozintsev was maturing new plans for Shakespearean films, including *Measure for Measure*, *As You Like It* and *The Tempest*. His death in 1973 put an end to those plans, but Kozintsev remains as a creator of two films that have a place of honour in the history of cinematographic Shakespeare.

NOTES

1 Kozintsev's intentions are described in Sergei Gerasimov, *Zhizn', Fil'my, Spory* (Moscow, 1971), p. 6.
2 The English translation by Joyce Vining, *Shakespeare, Time and Conscience*, was published in London in 1966. The other work translated into English is *King Lear: the Space of Tragedy* (London, 1974), which includes notes, excerpts from production diaries and reflections, mainly on the *King Lear* film, but with some additional material on *Hamlet*. In the present chapter translations from these works and other Russian texts are by the author.
3 G. Kozintsev, 'Iz rabochikh tetradiej', *Iskusstvo kino*, 7 (1976), 112.
4 G. Kozintsev, *Sobranie socinenii v 5 tomakh* (Leningrad, 1982), vol. I, pp. 489–90 (referred to hereafter as *Sobranie*).
5 Quoted by Roger Manvell, *Shakespeare and the Film* (London, 1971), p. 78.
6 Yuri N. Tynianov, *Poetika. Istoria literatury. Kino* (Moscow, 1977), p. 239.
7 Boris Pasternak, *Izbrannoe v dvukh tomakh* (Moscow, 1985) vol. I, p. 308. For a discussion of the poet's views in English, see Anna Kay France, 'Boris Pasternak's Interpretation of Hamlet', *Russian Literature Triquarterly*, 7 (1974), 201–26.
8 G. Troitskaia, 'Muzyka Shostakovicha v kino', *Iskusstvo kino*, 12 (1981), 54–67.
9 Between his two Poloniuses the actor had also played Sancho Panza in the *Don Quixote* film.
10 Alexandr Anikst, 'Byt' ili nie byt' u nas Gamletu?', *Teatr*, 3 (1955), 72–81.
11 G. Kozintsev, *Nash sovremennik Viliam Shekspir* (2nd edn, Moscow and Leningrad, 1966), p. 291 (referred to hereafter as *NSVS*).
12 L. S. Vygotskii, *Psikhologia Iskusstva*, (2nd edn, Moscow, 1968), p. 391.
13 Manvell, *Shakespeare on Film*, p. 15.
14 Michael Hattaway, Boika Sokolova, Derek Roper, eds., *Shakespeare in the New Europe* (Sheffield, 1994), p. 43.
15 Kozintsev, *Iskusstvo kino*, 3 (1970), 116.
16 *Sobranie*, vol. IV, p. 431.
17 Alexander Leggatt, *King Lear* (Manchester, 1991), p. 84.
18 F. W. Sternfeld, *Music in Shakespearean Tragedy* (London, 1963), pp. 126–7.
19 N. Ia. Berkovski, *Literatura i teatr* (Moscow, 1969), p. 451.
20 Pastnerak, *Izbrannoe*, vol. II, p. 321.
21 *NSVS*, p. 42.
22 *Ibid.*
23 Leggatt, *King Lear*, p. 87.

24 *NSVS*, p. 268.

25 *Sobranie*, vol. I, p. 498.

26 Alexander Leggatt writes: 'In a manner that probably speaks with special urgency to a Russian audience, war is waged not just by sword play but by wholesale burning' (*King Lear*, p. 87). The depiction of the civil war might be said to 'speak with special urgency' not only to inhabitants of Russia, but of Poland, Vietnam, Yugoslavia and many other countries turned into battlefields during the wars of the last century.

27 *Sobranie*, vol. IV, p. 455.

28 *Shekspirovskie Chteniia, 1977* (Moscow, 1980), p. 295. Kozintsev's lines are an interesting anticipation of the conclusion to Kenneth Branagh's film of *Hamlet* (1996), with a cold-eyed Fortinbras trying on the Danish crown as his soldiers overthrow the statue of old Hamlet.

29 *Sobranie*, vol. IV, p. 544.

30 For a discussion, see A. Lipkov, 'Uroki Kozintseva', *Shekspirovskie Chteniia, 1993* (Moscow, 1993), pp. 103–16.

12

DEBORAH CARTMELL

Franco Zeffirelli and Shakespeare

Franco Zeffirelli's contribution to the Shakespeare on screen canon continues to receive considerable commentary even though his last film of Shakespeare, *Hamlet*, was made as long ago as 1990. Zeffirelli has made three films of Shakespeare's plays: *The Taming of the Shrew* (1966), *Romeo and Juliet* (1968), and *Hamlet* (1990). While each film clearly appropriates a particular cultural moment, they are stylistically similar in so far as they share an unmistakable operatic conception; it has been repeatedly observed that they make as much use of colour, movement and music as they do of Shakespeare's lines. Opera, for Zeffirelli, is the complete form: it combines dance, drama, poetry, music and the visual arts.[1] His films of Shakespeare, similarly, unashamedly aim to appeal to all the senses. Their appeal is largely sensual rather than cerebral and in this the director achieves his ambition, in defiance of his critics, to make Shakespeare, as he says, even more popular.[2]

In many respects, Zeffirelli's screen interpretations of Shakespeare owe as much to travelogues as they do to the playtexts. Zeffirelli has no qualms about imposing his own tastes on to Shakespeare's texts. Shakespeare is, for Zeffirelli, 'a frustrated traveller' with a desire to take his audience on a sight-seeing tour of Italy;[3] and his union of Shakespeare with Italian Renaissance culture earned him the nickname, 'Shakespirelli'. This 'Italianisation' of Shakespeare is precisely what happens in the films of *The Taming of the Shrew* and *Romeo and Juliet*, where the attention to visual detail often detracts from the spoken word. Critics of the former film repeatedly mention that 'Zeffirelli's approach to the problem . . . of understanding Shakespeare's language has seemed to be . . . to distract the audience from the words as much as possible.'[4] It was felt that 'Zeffirelli's aim seems to be to elicit from his audience an active contempt for the words. Visual extravagance is the keynote.'[5] Visual spectacle unashamedly takes precedence over the playtexts, which have been drastically reduced, sometimes rewritten and often bewilderingly cut: it has been estimated that roughly 30 per cent of *Shrew*, 35 per cent of *Romeo* and 37 per cent of *Hamlet* are retained.[6] On the set of *The Taming of the Shrew* John Francis Lane found cameraman Ossie Morris studying a book of Correggio reproductions in preparation for the lighting of a shot[7] and the vivid primary colours with the golden lighting of Italian Renaissance painting are unmistakably recreated in the two 1960s films of Shakespeare; certainly the look of the production takes precedence over the words of the plays.

Zeffirelli produced two films of Shakespeare in the sixties and one at the beginning of the nineties. In between, he directed opera and Shakespeare for the theatre in addition to a number of less popular films, including a version of Verdi's *Otello* for the screen (1986). His subjects have ranged from Jesus Christ (*Jesus of Nazareth*, 1977) to himself (*Tea with Mussolini*, 1998). He began his career by studying architecture in Florence and was interrupted by the war when he joined the Italian Resistance. Immediately after the war, he became an actor, a costume and set designer and a film technician (working and living with Luchino Visconti). He then moved into directing theatre, opera and film; his early career was dominated by his dealings with the actress Anna Magnani and the opera star Maria Callas, both renowned for their temperamental behaviour. Undoubtedly he is best known for his films of Shakespeare, both because of their longer shelf-life (their continual use in classrooms, for example) and their box-office returns. His *Romeo and Juliet* (1968) made him internationally famous, and, as he claims himself, at the time its fifty-million dollar gross virtually saved Paramount Studios, who were initially cautious and far from generous to the project.[8] Clearly, the popularity of Zeffirelli's films of Shakespeare is, in part, due to their appropriation of particular cultural/historical moments.

The trailer to *The Taming of the Shrew* is a case in point. The voice-over narrator introduces the film with 'if you haven't tamed any good shrews lately, she's just what you've been waiting for';[9] and we are tempted by a feast of images of Kate and Petruchio, played by the then Hollywood version of royalty, Richard Burton and Elizabeth Taylor, physically abusing each other, an obvious send-up of the stormy relationship they were known to have. The film, clearly, sought commercial success through its jokey objectification of women; the trailer voice-over explains that this is 'a motion picture for every man who ever gave the back of his hand to his beloved and for every woman who deserved it'. It's not only Taylor's sixties hairstyle and make-up that dates the film; Zeffirelli includes shots of her throughout lovingly gazing at Petruchio unobserved; the shot of her famous eyes gazing through a keyhole is used in the trailer and epitomises the message of the film: here is a woman who secretly wants to be abused (or tamed). Burton's comically imperious Petruchio (almost always seen clutching a wine goblet) bears an unnerving resemblance to Henry VIII (or Charles Laughton's Henry VIII in Alexander Korda's 1933 film), whose notorious treatment of wives augurs badly for Taylor's Kate. Her transformation of Petruchio's home tells it all: she becomes the ideal 1960s besotted housewife, complete with headscarf, having the time of her life tidying up and feminising a long neglected male domain. She belongs to the era which produced *The Honeymooners* (which spawned *The Flintstones*) in which a wife's virtue is in the way she perseveres with her boorish and self-centred husband.[10] Surely it is not the case, as Graham Holderness has claimed, that 'Zeffirelli's film is not so much anti-feminist as a-feminist'[11] or as Jack Jorgens notes that 'the "taming" is not the heart of the film'[12] while the play, he claims, is 'to a feminist . . . a piece of male chauvinist wishful thinking'.[13] The final speech, one of the few in the film which is kept virtually intact, is spoken without irony, reputedly Taylor's own decision.[14] However, she does play a final joke on her husband by getting up from her father's feast and farcically leaving her husband behind her. Yet, even here, the implication is that she loves the chase, and is begging for even more abuse.

The fact that Gil Junger's 1999 teen-pic *Ten Things I Hate About You*, based on *The Taming of the Shrew*, makes no attempt to recreate Kate's final speech, suggests that the play's sexual politics are far too complex and problematic for a cinema audience at the end of the twentieth century. The play Zeffirelli chose for his second Shakespeare film, *Romeo and Juliet*, remains less problematic, as the success of Baz Luhrmann's version suggests. Certainly *Romeo and Juliet* has received more positive criticism than any of the director's other works, yet like *The Taming of the Shrew* it is unmistakably of its time. The film (which originated in Zeffirelli's production for the Old Vic in 1960) has been read as much as a reworking of Mike Nichols's *The Graduate* (1967) as of Shakespeare's play, in so far as it appeals to its period's obsessive interest in the generation gap: Zeffirelli expands the divide between the generations. The extremely young Romeo and Juliet (Leonard Whiting and Olivia Hussey were sixteen and fifteen, respectively) can do no wrong (for example, Romeo's exploitation of the apothecary and his killing of Paris are eliminated in order to ensure his character remains pure); the older Capulets and Montagues are severely flawed. Lady Capulet is a Shakespearean Mrs Robinson (from *The Graduate*); her gaze at Tybalt (played by Michael York) during Capulet's feast implies that they are having an affair, a relationship which is made more explicit upon Tybalt's death when she displays an unnatural excess of grief. Lady Montague is alive for the final 'reconciliation' and the film suggests the unfairness of a society where the old live while the young (who have the potential to redeem their society) die. For instance, Juliet's final lines – 'Then I'll be brief. / O happy dagger, This is thy sheath! / There rust, and let me die' (5.8.168–9) – are almost the final lines of the film. The next hundred plus lines are eliminated, which include the arrival of the watchmen, the reaction of the families and Friar Laurence's explanation. Only nine lines remain, as Juliet's voice gives way to that of the Prince – 'Where be these enemies?' – which is quickly replaced by the voice-over epilogue, spoken by Laurence Olivier. The older generation are reduced and condemned in this production in order to give full expression to the young.

Twenty-three years later Zeffirelli returned to Shakespeare, releasing *Hamlet* with Mel Gibson and Glenn Close as co-stars. Gibson, best known for his portrayal of an action hero living on the edge (starring in George Miller's *Mad Max* (1979), *Mad Max 2* (1981), and *Mad Max Beyond Thunderdome* (1985)) and Close, fresh from Adrian Lyne's *Fatal Attraction* (1987) and Stephen Frears's *Dangerous Liaisons* (1988), are unusual choices for Hamlet and Gertrude. Ideologically, the film is the complete opposite of *The Taming of the Shrew*, although it markets itself in the same way by using extremely famous faces. The first impression we have of the film is that there are two stars: Mel Gibson as Hamlet and Glenn Close as Gertrude. In this drastically cut version of Shakespeare's play, Zeffirelli enlarges the roles of the women. Ophelia, played by Helena Bonham-Carter, defies her father through her rebellious looks and, unlike her predecessor, Jean Simmons (from Laurence Olivier's 1948 film), survives the nunnery scene; although hurt she is not destroyed by Hamlet's violent rejection. Jean Simmons, after Hamlet reluctantly abandons her, collapses on the staircase in the position of a rape victim while the camera moves up the stairs in the direction of Hamlet, her figure becoming smaller and increasingly insignificant. More strikingly, Glenn Close's Gertrude is a woman torn between two lovers. Gibson's Hamlet makes no secret of his sexual jealousy of Claudius and in the closet scene all but rapes his mother, simulating sex with her on the bed; accordingly, Zeffirelli ingeniously manages to insert the obligatory sex scene into this movie, satisfying the expectations of his audience. Her death is equally sexually climactic; she realises her mistake in her allegiance to Claudius after she has drunk the poison and she dies, after sexually suggestive jerking movements, with Hamlet positioned on top of her, his face covered with sweat. What is unusual about this *Hamlet* is the prominence of the women; and it is almost as if Zeffirelli has produced a feminist version of the play (or at least one in which the women are allowed an equal part) in order to appeal to a more 'politically correct' audience.

While each of the films is undeniably 'of an age' and not 'for all time', they share certain striking similarities. *Romeo and Juliet* opens with a panoramic shot recalling the opening of Olivier's *Henry V* (1944) and this, with Olivier's voice-over epilogue and prologue, firmly places the film within a tradition of Shakespeare on film, with Zeffirelli following in Olivier's footsteps. In fact, Zeffirelli arranged for Olivier to dub Lord Montague, smaller parts and crowd noises. As Zeffirelli recalls, 'audiences never knew just how much of Laurence Olivier they were getting on the sound-track of that film'.[15] Indeed Zeffirelli credits Olivier with his early decision to abandon a career in architecture, for one in opera, theatre and film. He remembers his first exposure to Olivier's *Henry V* in the mid forties:

> Then the lights went down and that glorious film began. There was Olivier at the height of his powers and there were the English defending their honour . . . and I knew then what I was going to do. Architecture was not for me; it had to be the stage. I wanted to do something like the production I was witnessing. When the lights went up my head was clearer than it had been for months.[16]

Zeffirelli's admiration of Olivier is well known and is most prominent in *Hamlet*, which, in many ways, is a homage to Olivier's 1948 film. Certainly the *mise-en-scène* inside the castle, with its seemingly never-ending staircase, is a replica of Olivier's claustrophobic interiors. Even Olivier's shirt, worn in his film, was relic-like, delivered to Mel Gibson while he prepared for the role.

Zeffirelli credits his success in adapting Shakespeare and opera to what he describes as a 'radical return' to the original.[17] For Zeffirelli, the 'only revolutionary claim any director can make is to have seen what no one has bothered to see since the author compiled the work'.[18] And while he comes to Shakespeare with a conservative reverence for 'tradition' (reflected in his homages to Olivier), his idea of the original involves recreating not the period in which the dramas were produced, but the earlier time and place in which they are set (which inevitably, dates the films in the periods in which they were produced). However, it is not only his additions to the text, including spectacular sets reconstructing the period and place, which distinguishes his work. His manipulation of the camera, especially the gaze, adds another layer to Shakespeare's narrative, a layer which can subvert or distort the actual words of the text. Zeffirelli's films invariably juxtapose the public with the private, or the spectacular with the intimate. Numerous examples could be cited. In *Otello*, private moments are juxtaposed with sensational ensemble sequences, involving an enormous cast.[19] Most notably, in *Romeo and Juliet*, Zeffirelli's meticulously orchestrated feast scene and street sequences are counterpointed with scenes of Romeo and Juliet alone. In all of the films discussed here, Zeffirelli establishes strikingly intimate contact between individuals amidst the big ensemble scenes through his manipulation of the gaze.

This dimension of his films goes against his declared reverence for Shakespeare and is a contradiction akin to his explanation of how he manages to reconcile his Catholic faith with his lifestyle: 'I believe totally in the teaching of the Church and this means admitting my way of life is sinful.'[20] What is sinful for Zeffirelli, it must be deduced, as it is never explicitly mentioned in his autobiography, is his homosexuality. Although self-consciously placing themselves within a tradition of Shakespeare on screen (or a 'belief' in Shakespeare), Zeffirelli's Shakespeare films are, at the same time, almost 'sinful' in so far as they manipulate the playtext through their use of the gaze. William Van Watson has argued that Zeffirelli's homosexuality – or more precisely, his homophobic homosexuality – informs his films through what he calls the director's 'homo-erotic' or 'sodomizing camera', which continually challenges Laura Mulvey's influential claim that cinema is characterised by an active male subject gazing at a passive female object.[21] Yet according to Watson, in *Hamlet*, an older Zeffirelli represses the homoerotic gaze in favour of 'an obsessive nostalgia for patriarchy which has led him into an increasingly reactionary position'.[22] Watson is quick to point out that the director, like Hamlet, is obsessed by his desire for the restoration of patriarchy as the result of having been stigmatised throughout his childhood by his father's refusal to officially recognise his bastard son. (Zeffirelli's well-documented, unusual and eventful life offers much scope to psychoanalytic critics, such as Peter S. Donaldson.)[23] Despite the problems in reading Zeffirelli's films as concealed confessions, Watson is convincing in identifying Zeffirelli's camerawork – the vehicle of the gaze – as the distinctive feature of his films. At its most effective, it interprets, subverts or transforms the words of the playtext. In fact, his knack for beguiling the eye, which he was initially attacked for in the sixties,[24] can be seen as his most significant achievement in his interpretations of Shakespeare. An analysis of the openings of the three films will demonstrate the ways in which Zeffirelli visually 'reads' the plays.

The Taming of the Shrew opens with Michael York's Lucentio speaking approximately half of his first speech in the play (1.1.1–24). He explains to Tranio (in the interpolated words of Zeffirelli and his scriptwriters, Suso Cecchi D'Amico and Paul Dehn) that it is the first day of the scholar's year. They arrive in a crowded Padua and find their way to a church where they listen to choral music which is broken by a cannon firing. The solemn hymn gives way to the exuberant theme music (composed by Nino Rota) and the title appears triumphantly on the screen. Graham Holderness (following Jack Jorgens) has described how Zeffirelli translates the Christopher Sly Induction (which Zeffirelli, like his many predecessors has chosen to leave out) in carnivalesque terms:

> Zeffirelli simply tapped the resources of his own national history to produce a detailed evocation of saturnalian ritual. In the course of the opening sequence (framed as an 'induction' by the superimposition of film titles), we observe the barbaric anti-ceremony of clerics wearing grotesque animal masks, sacred music giving way to obscene and cacophonous chants, a blasphemously parodic image of the Virgin.[25]

The carnival atmosphere of the film's opening functions like the Induction, to announce that this is a world of trickery, mockery and artificiality. The camera focuses on Michael York looking first at the elaborate church service and then at Bianca, who is surrounded by adoring men, a parodic object of the male gaze.

The focus moves to York's intent gaze as he speaks the words: 'I burn, I pine, I perish' (1.1.153).[26] Zeffirelli delays the first appearance of Kate by reversing the sequence of events of the first scene. While the camera looks down at Bianca, it looks up at the women in the windows, both on the streets of Padua, and at Hortensio's house where Kate initially appears from a window. We first see Kate's eye looking down at the street scene below her. She is next seen framed in the window, like a portrait, but a portrait which echoes the sight of the enormous blond and busty prostitute – who figures as the Madonna of the procession – in the window from the street scene moments before. Visually, this Madonna/whore is a parody of the 'good' Bianca (blonde) and the 'bad' Kate (busty); Tranio's look at Kate in the window clearly echoes his earlier goggle at the whore. This implied association (through Zeffirelli's relational editing) of Kate with the whore is reinforced by her first words: 'I pray you, father, is it your will / To make a whore of me amongst these mates?' (55–6: the screenplay replaces 'sir' with 'father' and 'stale' with the still current word 'whore'). Zeffirelli positions Kate with Lucentio, both deceived by what they see; and there is no doubt that Kate is in genuine need of taming. The film is, on one level, a public relations exercise which gradually transforms Taylor, notorious for having married so frequently, from female dissident to respectable wife.[27]

Filmed at Dino de Laurentis's studios in Rome, the set has a stagey quality; although painterly in its design, it in no way resembles a 'real' Padua and it is understandable why this aspect of Zeffirelli's sets was so disliked by the influential film critic Pauline Kael:

> Theatricality can be effective in a movie when it is consciously used, but it's very awkward when the director is trying for realism – which Zeffirelli apparently takes horse-play and opulent clutter, and dust, to be. He brings to the screen the filler of opera – all that coarse earthy stuff that comes on when the main singers are off. And Zeffirelli's 'robust' realistic detail is ludicrous; when he throws a close-up of the marketplace onto the screen and we see peppers and onions, it's like the obligatory setting of the scene in the first act of an opera when the peasant girl walks on with the basket on her arm.[28]

In his next film, *Romeo and Juliet*, Zeffirelli shot on location and, as a result, it is not as operatic as *The Shrew* in its design. The extremely gentle voice of Olivier opening the film is heard over a distant view of the city, replaced with a crowded market square where the liveried Capulet men enter. As critics like Watson are quick to point out, the camera focuses on the men's crotches, especially their elaborate codpieces. Again, the opening is drastically pruned (less than 30 per cent of the first scene is retained with some additions). Instead of the long exchange between Sampson and Gregory – 'A dog of that house shall move me to stand' (1.1.10–17) – Zeffirelli has Gregory kick a dog (presumably belonging to a Montague) in passing. The violent opening of the first half of Scene 1 is dramatically contrasted with the quietness of the second half, reflected in the vibrant colours turning to faded blues and greys. In the first half, it is Michael York's Tybalt who dominates; the camera tilts up from his feet to his crotch and finally lingers on a close-up of his face. Romeo's arrival, like Tybalt's, calls for similar close-up treatment. He arrives in soft focus, carrying a flower, in direct contrast to the sword-carrying Tybalt. For a 1960s audience, Tybalt, representative of his repressive and violent patriarchal Verona society, is visually defeated by Romeo, the flower-power pacifist.

As in *The Taming of the Shrew*, the women, Juliet and Lady Capulet, are first seen framed, like pictures, in a window. When Paris says of Juliet, 'Younger than she are happy mothers made' (1.2.12), a youthful, scornful Lady Capulet appears across the courtyard in a window. The music sours while Capulet, looking at her, retorts, 'And too soon marred are those so early made', unequivocally commenting on the failure of his own marriage.

At first glance, *Hamlet* appears completely different from Zeffirelli's earlier Shakespeare films. Its setting is grey and cold, beginning with a shot of the battlements and then a group of armed men outside the castle. This is followed by a scene in the tomb of Hamlet senior. Glenn Close's Gertrude is shown in close-up. Her excessive grief is contrasted with the face of Claudius (Alan Bates), who betrays no sign of emotion. A detail shot follows of a hand (seemingly belonging to Claudius), clutching dirt which is distributed slowly over the corpse. (The opening of the hand recalls visually the final scene in *Romeo and Juliet*, where the camera focuses on the opening of Juliet's hand when she awakes in the tomb of her forefathers. *Hamlet* thus begins where *Romeo and Juliet* ends.) The camera tilts slowly up the arm and finally, into the face of Mel Gibson's Hamlet.[29] He is given the fetishistic treatment we associate with leading women in the *film noir* tradition, where we are often teased with seeing parts of their bodies before their face is revealed for the first time on screen. Once again, Zeffirelli uses omitted lines from the text in the action of the film. The appearance of Hamlet's face is accompanied by Claudius's voice-over announcing, 'let the world take note / You are the most immediate to our throne' (1.2.108–9). The eliminated preceding line, 'we pray you throw to earth / This unprevailing woe', is preserved in the act of Hamlet throwing earth over his father's corpse.

The film begins in Act 1 scene 2 and is drastically cut and rearranged. The scenes change with uncanny speed. After the tomb sequence, the camera cuts to Claudius announcing his marriage to Gertrude, then cuts to Claudius visiting Laertes, jovially granting him his suit, then to Claudius and Gertrude searching out Hamlet, who is found in a secluded and barren study. Claudius speaks first, and then Gertrude is left alone to deliver her earlier lines, 'Good Hamlet, cast thy nightly colour off' (1.2. 68) together with those of Claudius, 'This gentle and unforced accord of Hamlet / Sits smiling to my heart' (1.2.123–4). More notice-able than the rapidity of the set changes (Close, looking like the Snow Queen, wears three different dresses in the space of Act 1 scene 2), are the looks between the central figures. In the first moments of the film, the weeping Gertrude looks up at Claudius and her face is transformed from one of mourning to one of hopefulness. Zeffirelli cuts immediately to Hamlet who, unobserved, looks at his mother, registering his awareness of her fickleness. Without doubt, Gertrude's first scene alone with Hamlet resembles a seduction (Close brings to her Gertrude shades of the seductress and homewrecker of *Dangerous Liaisons* and *Fatal Attraction)*. Gertrude pulls Hamlet to her, passionately kissing his lips, and then quickly leaves in order to cavort with Claudius (shot from Hamlet's point of view). While looking down at their antics from his window, Hamlet speaks his first soliloquy which, revealingly, stops with 'Frailty thy name is woman'(1.2.146).

Rather than taking Zeffirelli at his own word in his perception of his role as a populariser of Shakespeare, this chapter has argued that Zeffirelli's mission is a far more subtle one. He has persistently reduced the playtexts in his screenplays of Shakespeare through his creation of visual correlatives to the words. The use of and allusions to Olivier in his films serve not only to pay tribute to his declared hero, but to juxtapose a notion of Italianness (and European film traditions) with a notion of Englishness (and the tradition of Shakespearean theatre). Zeffirelli's *Autobiography* expresses a faint disgust for Olivier in its tactfully cen-sorious accounts of the actor's off-screen behaviour. In spite of his many pro-nouncements of his admiration of the English cultural icon, it seems as though Zeffirelli 'protests too much'. Undoubtedly, in his many allusions to Olivier, Zeffirelli sets himself next to the embodiment of English theatre and film, both in comparison and contrast. Above all, his films implicitly and daringly argue that pictures can speak as loudly and as eloquently as Shakespeare's words.

NOTES

1 Interview on *South Bank Show*, ITV, December 1997.
2 *Ibid.* This is Zeffirelli's response to criticism that his Shakespeare films are too popular.
3 Toby Cole and Helen Krich Chinoy, eds., *Directors on Directing: The Emergence of the Modern Theatre* (1973; rpt. London, 1964), p. 439.
4 *Financial Times* (3 March 1967).
5 *Monthly Film Bulletin*, 34, 399 (April 1967), 58.
6 These figures are based on those of Ace G. Pilkington, 'Zeffirelli's Shakespeare', in Anthony Davies and Stanley Wells, eds., *Shakespeare and the Moving Image. The Plays on Film and Television* (Cambridge, 1994), pp. 163–79; p. 165.
7 John Francis Lane, *Films and Filming* (October 1966), 50–3; p. 51.
8 Franco Zeffirelli, *Zeffirelli: The Autobiography of Franco Zeffirelli* (New York, 1986), pp. 229–30.

9 My source for the trailer is Columbia Pictures International video of Peter Brook's *King Lear*.

10 *The Honeymooners* ran from 1955–67, while *The Flintstones* first appeared in 1960. The tradition which features the comical pairing of a stupid but endearing husband with a 'sensible' wife has been resurrected and parodied in the cartoon series, *The Simpsons*, which first appeared in 1989.

11 Graham Holderness, *The Taming of the Shrew* (Manchester, 1989), p. 71.

12 Jack J. Jorgens, *Shakespeare on Film* (Bloomington, IN, 1977), p. 72.

13 *Ibid.*, p. 67.

14 Zeffirelli, *Autobiography*, p. 216.

15 *Ibid.*, p. 229.

16 *Ibid.*, p. 61.

17 *Ibid.*, p. 330.

18 *Ibid.*

19 See William Van Watson, 'Shakespeare, Zeffirelli, and the Homosexual Gaze', in Deborah E. Barker and Ivo Kamps, eds., *Shakespeare and Gender: A History* (London and New York, 1995) pp. 235–62; p. 236.

20 Zeffirelli, *Autobiography*, p. 240.

21 Watson, 'Shakespeare, Zeffirelli, and the Homosexual Gaze'. Mulvey identifies three types of gaze which involve men looking at women: the look of the camera in which the male director voyeuristically gazes at women, the gaze of the men within the film and the gaze of the male spectator of the film. ('Visual Pleasure and Narrative Cinema', *Screen*, 16, 3 (Autumn, 1975), 6–19.) Here the gaze is interpreted to include women looking at men, men looking at men and women looking at women.

22 Watson, 'Shakespeare, Zeffirelli, and the Homosexual Gaze', p. 259.

23 See Peter S. Donaldson, ' "Let Lips Do What Hands Do": Male Bonding, Eros and Loss in Zeffirelli's *Romeo and Juliet*', *Shakespearean Films/Shakespearean Directors* (Boston, MA, 1990), pp. 145–88.

24 See notes 3 and 4 above.

25 Holderness, *The Taming of the Shrew*, p. 57.

26 The prolonged gaze at Michael York becomes a regular feature in Zeffirelli's films.

27 See Barbara Hodgdon, 'Katherina Bound; or, Play(K)ating the Strictures of Everyday Life', in *The Shakespeare Trade. Performances and Appropriations* (Philadelphia, 1998).

28 Pauline Kael, *Going Steady* (1968; rpt. London, 1970), p. 156.

29 See Donaldson, 'Let Lips Do What Hands Do', for his analysis of the hand motif in Zeffirelli's *Romeo and Juliet*.

13

SAMUEL CROWL

Flamboyant realist: Kenneth Branagh

The release of Kenneth Branagh's film of *Henry V* in 1989 sparked a revival of creative and commercial interest in Shakespeare as a source for films, which had been dormant since the box-office failure of Roman Polanski's *Macbeth* in 1971. The surprising critical and financial success of Branagh's *Henry V* has proved to be as influential in the history of Shakespeare on film as was the equally unanticipated success almost fifty years earlier of Laurence Olivier's film of the play released in 1944. Olivier's *Henry V* led to a steady stream of international Shakespeare films over the next two decades by such directors as Orson Welles, Akira Kurosawa, Grigori Kozintsev, Franco Zeffirelli and Peter Brook.

Branagh's 1989 film helped to create the most intense explosion of English-language Shakespeare films in the century. The 1990s saw the release of ten major Shakespeare films as well as several interesting Shakespearean offshoots, including Branagh's own *In the Bleak Midwinter*. Branagh has now surpassed Olivier, Welles and Zeffirelli, to become the only director to have produced five Shakespeare films, though an examination of his films will reveal that Branagh has moulded his own cinematic style from elements present in the work of his distinguished predecessors.

Popular film culture, represented at one extreme by James Cagney and at the other by Orson Welles, lies deep in the soul of Branagh's creative sensibility. Branagh watchers have long recognised that he generates much of his artistic power – as an actor and director – from his unique stance as an outsider to mainstream English theatrical culture. His family roots are in Protestant Northern Ireland, but his artistic energy flows from the American films and their iconic heroes he encountered as a boy in Belfast. Branagh's biography reveals that he draws potential rather than paralysis from finding himself placed between rival legacies, traditions and cultures: Protestant and Catholic in Belfast; English and Irish in Reading (where his family moved when he was ten); and Stratford and Hollywood in his Shakespearean career.

Branagh's nerve and intelligence are his most original qualities. His genius as an artist is as a synthesiser; his imagination works like a magpie, stealing good ideas from others but linking them in surprising and original ways. His films, for instance, show obvious debts to Welles, Hitchcock, Kasden, Coppola and Lean. His play, *Public Enemy* (the first work staged by his Renaissance Theatre Company), reaches back to Cagney and the Hollywood gangster films of the 1930s as a prism through which to capture the fantasies of a young lad coming of age in Belfast in the 1960s. When it comes to film, Branagh has the courage of his conventions. He works towards a personal style by studying and appropriating masters (Hitchcock for *Dead Again*) and models (*The Big Chill* for *Peter's Friends*). As his synthesising imagination might suggest, his four most successful films to date are his Shakespeare adaptations: *Henry V* (1989), *Much Ado About Nothing* (1993), *Hamlet* (1996) and *Love's Labour's Lost* (2000).

For the first three, Branagh had strong stage productions as inspiration: Adrian Noble's Royal Shakespeare Company productions of *Henry V* (1984) and *Hamlet* (1992–3) with Branagh as king and prince, and Judi Dench's *Much Ado About Nothing* (1988) for Renaissance with Branagh as Benedick. From each, Branagh took several dominant visual ideas. Dark, sombre, conspiratorial interiors for *Henry V*, distinguished by the use of backlighting to suggest the mystery surrounding the newly crowned king, and rain and mud for the exteriors, with the Battle of Agincourt heavily influenced by Welles's great battle scene in *Chimes at Midnight*. *Much Ado* was all Italian summer sun and heat spilling over in festive energy, with individual moments echoing Hollywood movies as diverse as *The Magnificent Seven* and *Singin' in the Rain*: a bright, fleshy, romantic day in contrast to *Henry V*'s dark night of the king's soul on a risky imperial quest for personal and national identity. For his *Hamlet*, Branagh extended and revised the family focus of Noble's RSC production, which looked back at Shakespeare's play through the Scandinavian eyes of Ibsen, Strindberg and Ingmar Bergman.[1]

In all four films, but particularly in *Much Ado*, Branagh was striving to reach the large popular American film audience dominated by teenagers. This was an audience which had been touched only once before by a Shakespeare film: Zeffirelli's *Romeo and Juliet* (and now again, post-*Much Ado*, by Baz Luhrmann's *Romeo+Juliet*). Pauline Kael, in her review of *Henry V*, calls Branagh a 'flamboyant realist', which is one way of saying that he manages to merge Zeffirelli's lush, extravagant style with a cool, intelligent understanding of his Shakespearean material.[2]

Branagh is a product of the postmodern moment dominated by a sense of belatedness; a sense that originality is exhausted and that only parody and pastiche and intertextual echo remain. Rather than finding such a condition enervating, Branagh's work seizes on its possibilities. Branagh is, in Ihab Hassan's term, a reconstructionist; an artist who creates out of the bits and shards of the postmodern moment.[3] Peter Donaldson has brilliantly demonstrated how the gritty strenuousness of Branagh's *Henry V* was inspired not only by Noble's post-Falklands/Vietnam stage production, but by a powerful aesthetic struggle with Laurence Olivier's 1944 film which had been prompted by Olivier's desire to bring Shakespeare – and the English cultural tradition he represents – to the service of the nation as the Allies launched the invasion to reclaim Europe from Hitler.[4] Branagh's *Henry V* insisted, in its historical moment, that coming home was as important as going over.

Again in his 1996 film of *Hamlet*, Branagh offers us a bright, bold mirror in stunning contrast to Olivier's dark impressionist maze, and seeks to synthesise the Freudian operatic romance of Zeffirelli's *Hamlet* with the cold politics of Kozintsev's great Russian film of the play. Many reviewers have stressed the film's debts to David Lean, noting that Branagh's cinematographer, Alex Thompson, worked as a focus-puller on Lean's *Lawrence of Arabia*. My own students have found cinematic intertextual echoes in the film, ranging from Kubrick's *The Shining* to Franklin Schaffner's *Patton*, Wes Craven's *Friday the 13th* and Bergman's *Fanny and Alexander*.

Branagh's route beyond Olivier, as a British-trained Shakespearean who makes films, lies in his infatuation with popular film culture, with what we have come to call 'Hollywood'. Branagh is, in fact, the first director of Shakespeare films to mix Olivier's attention to the spoken text with Welles's fascination with camera angle and editing and Zeffirelli's visual and musical romanticism. Branagh's Shakespeare speaks *and* moves, something of a rarity in the genre where word and image often jostle one another for dominance; his Shakespeare films are distinguished by their bold life and robust energy. He is a director willing to take chances, particularly by not treating his Shakespearean material, even in his full-text *Hamlet*, as sacred.

This bravura quality is apparent from the opening frames of *Henry V*, where he first introduces Derek Jacobi's Chorus striking a match ('O, for a muse of *fire*') on a darkened sound stage and then throwing on the full lamps ('To ascend the *brightest* heavens of invention') as he manages to suggest that film requires the same imaginative participation by the audience as does the theatre. Here Branagh also is subtly evoking and revising Olivier's famous opening of his *Henry V* in a replica of Shakespeare's Globe. In that film Olivier gave himself a sly double entrance: first, backstage, sliding into the frame from the left and clearing his throat before making his move out on the Globe stage to be greeted (as Burbage) by the 'Elizabethan' audience's enthusiastic applause.

Branagh was equally audacious by introducing his Henry, back-lit and in long shot, framed in a huge door and looming mysteriously like some medieval version of Darth Vader. Branagh, cleverly, then shoots Henry from the back as he moves down a row of his courtiers and finally turns to settle himself on the throne. Here we get the first close-up of the king, in stunning contrast to the camera's initial elevation of his power and mystery, for what we now see is the face and body of a tousle-headed boy – Luke Skywalker rather than Darth Vader – swamped by the size of the throne on which he sits. Each actor-director, then, gives himself a double entrance: Olivier invites our shock of recognition of his status as both international star of stage and film and dynastic heir to a four-hundred-year-old tradition of Shakespearean acting; Branagh invokes the shock of the vernacular unknown: not the Shakespearean actor-king but the cheeky pretender.

His film of *Much Ado About Nothing* (1993) also announces its intentions from its opening sequence. Here he plucks Balthazar's song ('Sigh no more, ladies') from Act 2 scene 3 to use as a framing device. We first hear Emma Thompson's voice reciting the opening words of the lyric as the words themselves pop up on the blank screen, inviting us – as in the singalongs which preceded silent films where a bouncing ball appeared above the words of the song – to murmur the words with her and register wry amusement at the way in which the song's description of male inconstancy and deception speaks not only to Shakespeare's comic concerns with the worlds of war and wooing but also to Branagh's delicate balancing of one foot on the verbal shore of the play and one in the visual sea of the film.

Branagh's camera then moves from word to painted image as it focuses on a painting (in progress) of a Tuscan landscape and then slides – in a single pan shot lasting over a minute – from the canvas to the landscape itself, peopled with tanned picnickers responding to Emma Thompson's Beatrice, perched in a tree, nibbling on an apple and reading Shakespeare's song to her fellow revellers as a bee buzzes about her face and birds chirp in the soundtrack. Here, with a masterful film economy, Branagh manages to move from printed text, to scenic representation as we might find it in a stage production, to his 'on location' film landscape. In a flash, the film cuts from the hillside picnickers, most of them women, down into the valley where we see the men, with a humorous nod to *The Magnificent Seven*, thundering home on horseback. Branagh has suddenly transformed his Shakespearean narrative into the language and history of film. As in his opening of *Henry V*, but now with more confidence and sophistication, Branagh here is placing his stylistic mark on his way of translating Shakespeare into film.

Branagh's route to his full-text film version of *Hamlet* followed the pattern he established previously of linking stage Shakespeare with film Hollywood. In 1992 he returned to the Royal Shakespeare Company and his artistic collaboration with its director Adrian Noble to perform his fourth Hamlet, this time in a full-text version.[5] Noble's approach was intensely domestic, suggesting the play's affinities with Ibsen and Strindberg, and Bob Crowley's set designs were influenced by Ingmar Bergman's *Fanny and Alexander*. During the production's run from December 1992 to March 1993, Branagh was busy with developing his next film, *Mary Shelley's Frankenstein*. Once again Branagh was merging and min- gling the two traditions of stage and film as preparation for his most ambitious Shakespearean film project. *Frankenstein* was his first experience of working in the big-budget commercial American film tradition, this time following the model of Francis Ford Coppola, who had most recently directed another classic nineteenth-century novel often raided by the movies, *Bram Stoker's Dracula*. Coppola's film company, Zoetrope, was producing Branagh's film.

It is indicative of Branagh's fascination with commercial films that while Noble and Crowley were looking to Bergman as inspiration for their stage *Hamlet*, Branagh had mastering more epic film models in mind as he laid the groundwork for his own screen version of *Hamlet*. *Mary Shelley's Frankenstein* gave Branagh the experience of dealing with a $40 million budget and provided him the technical resources to shoot on an epic scale. The film was not a critical success but, contrary to common assumption, it more than recovered its costs in its world-wide distribution and video sales and rentals. Most importantly it allowed Branagh the opportunity to expand his cinematic vocabulary as he approached his ambitious plan to film a four-hour *Hamlet*. It should be noted that after completing *Frankenstein* Branagh also wrote and directed its cinematic antithesis, *In the Bleak Midwinter* (1995: released as *A Midwinter's Tale* in North America), before tackling *Hamlet*. This quiet, clever, low-budget, black and white film (shot in twenty-one days) tells the story of a troop of English actors as they struggle to mount a production of *Hamlet* as a Christmas benefit to help save a dilapidated church in the fictional English village of Hope. If *Frankenstein* allowed Branagh to extend his film craft, *In the Bleak Midwinter* provided him with the opportunity to cherish humorously his stage roots and the Ealing Studios film comedies of the 1940s and 1950s. The film is a wonderful compendium of backstage stories and loving tributes to the eccentricities of the acting profession – 'a Christmas card from Branagh to his public' – as H. R. Coursen has generously suggested.[6]

A year later Branagh sent out a very different sort of Christmas message when his epic film of *Hamlet* opened in America on December 25th. In his earlier films Branagh had demonstrated two crucial qualities: he had found a substantial audience for Shakespeare and he could make films on time and within budget, precisely the qualities lacking in one of his great predecessors, Orson Welles. What Branagh learned from Welles, however, beyond the perils of treating cava- lierly the engine (money) of a commercial art form, was how to hold a film audi- ence's attention with images as well as words. Though Branagh does not rival Welles's pure cinematic dazzle, he does have an uncanny ability to give us word and image without being dull. Nothing approaches the achievement of his *Hamlet* in this regard in the Shakespeare on film canon. Branagh's *Hamlet* stretches and challenges our assumptions about what is possible in a Shakespeare film. The very idea of a four-hour Shakespeare film is Wellesian in its extravagance, but only Branagh had created the commercial track record which allowed him to secure financing for such an enterprise, and only Branagh had the creative and organisational skills to deliver on a scheme as potentially mad as Dr Frankenstein's.

Branagh's intentions are signalled from the film's opening moments, which revise his practice in *Henry V* and *Much Ado About Nothing* where, as we have seen, he was determined immediately to translate Shakespeare's narrative into the language of film. Here, in contrast, he begins quietly with a word, HAMLET, chiselled in the base of a giant statue of the old king, and the solitary figure of Francisco on patrol in front of Elsinore's gates. In order to squeeze all of Shakespeare's text into four hours of film, Branagh's camera rarely has the liberty to silently explore and establish landscape. His challenge is to use the camera inventively to keep our eyes absorbed as the verbal narrative hurries on uninterrupted.

The film is at its best when it moves inside Elsinore and presents us with the red, white and gold glitter of Claudius's court. In another radical departure from previous *Hamlet* films – even Zeffirelli's operatic psychoanalytic romance – Branagh gives us an interior Elsinore which positively sparkles. This is *film noir* with all the lights on. Its key physical image is a series of mirrored doors which line the walls of Claudius's court. This world appears open, rich and inviting as Derek Jacobi's vigorous, attractive Claudius and his bride, still in her wedding dress, sweep down the great hall through lines of applauding courtiers to take their place on the throne. But the camera quickly discovers a still, solitary figure all in black who, in league with the camera, will expose the black and grained spots which lie just beneath the surface of this lavish world.

Each of Branagh's Shakespeare films quickly establishes its atmosphere, landscape and cinematic style. One of his trademarks is to make his Shakespearean material visually inviting; his films are bold and vivid. Several other stylistic and aesthetic traits distinguish Branagh's Shakespeare films. They have all grown out of stage productions and feature a core group of actors (including Branagh himself, Brian Blessed, Richard Briers, Derek Jacobi, Gerard Horan, Judi Dench, Michael Maloney and Emma Thompson) augmented by international stars drawn from a wide range of stage and film experiences: Paul Scofield and Robbie Coltrane in *Henry V*, Michael Keaton and Denzel Washington in *Much Ado About Nothing*, John Gielgud and Billy Crystal in *Hamlet*, and Alicia Silverstone and Nathan Lane in *Love's Labour's Lost*. *Hamlet* features actors from Russia, Africa and France as well as from England and America. Only Orson Welles, in his *Chimes at Midnight*, has attempted to accommodate such an international flavour to an English-language Shakespeare film.[7] Branagh wants 'different accents, different looks' to produce Shakespeare films that 'belong to the world'.[8]

Branagh is not shy in his desire to entertain, to bring Shakespeare to a wider audience by 'telling the story with the utmost clarity and simplicity'.[9] His films seek, as the medium demands, a naturalistic style for speaking and acting Shakespeare. Branagh's Shakespeare films are unique in their attention to language, as Geoffrey O'Brien has pointed out in writing about Branagh's *Henry V*: 'The job of the actor was to clarify, line by line and word by word, not just the general purport of what the character was feeling, but the exact function of every remark . . . The result was a more pointed, even jabbing style, a tendency to deflate sonority in favor of exact meaning, while at the same time giving the meter of the verse a musician's respect, and the rhetorical substructure of the lawyer's questioning eye.'[10] Branagh's visual style is dynamic and direct with signature moments in each film establishing its tone, atmosphere, camera style and interpretive approach: murky interiors and muddy exteriors in *Henry V* capped by the four-minute tracking shot of Henry carrying Falstaff's dead page across the Agincourt battlefield; the highly charged festive opening in the sun-drenched Tuscan landscape of *Much Ado* and the three crane shots spaced throughout the film, of the initial encounter between the men and women in Leonardo's courtyard, of Benedick splashing in the fountain superimposed on Beatrice in the swing after the mutual gulling scenes, and the final swirling dance through the villa and into the garden to celebrate the new harmony; the epic 70mm. scope of *Hamlet* coupled with mirrored and *trompe-l'oeil* doors reflecting one version of reality while hiding several layers of another. And finally lush original film scores from Patrick Doyle.

Doyle's scores are emblematic of Branagh's desire to employ an extravagant film vocabulary. In his *Henry V*, for instance, which features such gritty images as Bardolph's hanging (with his feet left to dangle in the top of the frame for the following scenes featuring first Mountjoy and then the Chorus) and a grimy, decidedly unheroic mud-laden battlescene, Doyle's score, at the close of Agincourt, swells from a single voice singing a 'Non Nobis' to a huge choir supported by a full orchestra. The score romanticises the English victory in a way that the battle's images do not, opening the door for Branagh's detractors to accuse such moments in his films of being ideologically unstable and politically pernicious. Such critics are impatient with the contradictions in Branagh's style, contradictions which Branagh's eclectic imagination embraces and, in the case of *Henry V* as Norman Rabkin has elegantly outlined, are built into the very fabric of Shakespeare's play.[11] Is Henry a tyrant or a Christian king? The answer is: both. Michael Manheim's analysis of the film understands the ways in which Branagh's performance of Henry captures that central ambiguity: 'Not glamour but sincerity is the word for [Branagh's] Henry . . . [and] he is the Henry for our time basically because along with his ingenuousness, sincerity, and apparent decency – he is also a ruthless murderer. Branagh's characterization radically divides our sympathies.'[12] This tension drives the film as it has driven the subsequent critical debate about Branagh's achievement.

Henry V, made on a shoestring budget of 4.5 million pounds, brought unexpected audiences and recognition, including Branagh's nomination for Academy Awards as Best Actor and Best Director in 1990. This success allowed him to raise the financing for a second Shakespeare film: *Much Ado About Nothing*. This was an unconventional choice, as no film of a Shakespearean comedy had ever found a large or receptive film audience, not even Franco Zeffirelli's *Taming of the Shrew* (1966), featuring the most famous film couple of the 1960s: Elizabeth Taylor and Richard Burton.

Branagh's approach to *Much Ado* stresses its affinity with Shakespeare's festive comedies and their explorations of gender confusions of love and loyalty prompted by wooing and tested by wedding. Here it is the men, specifically Claudio and Benedick, who are so prompted and tested among the tensions of male bonding, the confusions of wooing and the commitments of wedding.

Branagh's film has its climax and its finest moments where wooing and wedding meet and clash: Claudio's shameful disruption of the ceremony of his marriage to Hero and the genuine union of Beatrice and Benedick that rises from its ashes. Robert Sean Leonard's Claudio is an insecure boy whose face is flushed by confusion and embarrassment as quickly as it is coloured by the blush of romance. Setting the wedding outside the villa's small chapel gives Branagh's camera ample scope to record Claudio's petulant tantrum. He savagely shoves his bride to the ground and makes a triumphant circuit of the scene, overturning benches and ripping away decorations before nestling in next to Denzel Washington's elegant Don Pedro to re-establish what he smugly believes to be the primacy of the male order. By contrast, Branagh's Benedick goes to his knees to join Beatrice at Hero's side and looks on in amazement as Leonato, with an ugly violence, makes the opposite move to join the male club by condemning his own child. The father is restored to his senses only by Benedick's pledge to honour the Friar's plan.

Then Beatrice and Benedick move into the chapel, where, first through her tears and anger and then through his commitment to her passion, they create a ceremony and construct a vow issuing not from social practice and tradition but from their own imaginative response to Hero's crisis. Branagh shoots a kneeling Beatrice in profile over Benedick's left shoulder so that we see and react to her through his perspective. They aren't squared to the camera because they aren't yet square with each other. Beatrice's anger, and her frustration with her gender's limitations when it comes to acting on that anger, lead her to kick over the communion bench she has been kneeling on, as she cries out: 'O that I were a man for his sake, or that I had any friend would be a man for my sake!'

Branagh's Benedick is transformed by her passion. Earlier we had seen his nervous cocky jester melt into the explosive comic romantic in the gulling scene. Now both of those excessive portraits are clipped, darkened and matured as we watch his mind absorb and understand the issue that spurs Beatrice's fury. For the first time in the film, Branagh allows his Benedick to look directly into the camera's eye as he honestly confronts his emotional commitment to Beatrice. Branagh underscores 'soul' in his quiet query, 'Think you in your *soul* that Count Claudio hath wronged Hero?' because it is a word Claudio himself has flung about recklessly. Thompson chooses to underline 'thought' in her reply, 'Yea, as sure as I have a *thought* or a soul', completing the marriage of mind and heart between them, which is then sealed by the vow the entire scene has moved towards: 'Enough. I am engaged; I will challenge him.'

Benedick's commitment to action completes Beatrice's outrage and creates a surprise: a constant man. The words that lead man to woo and to wed will now be as consequential as those that lead him to war. This intelligent moment, like Thompson's performance throughout, is what allows us to release our critical, sceptical selves to enjoy the film's exuberant excesses – Branagh's Gene Kelly-like splashing in the fountain superimposed on Thompson's high flying in a swing to complete the neatly segued scenes of the unmaskings of their true affections.

Branagh's film makes us laugh (a rarity in even the best films of Shakespeare's comedies) in moments that range from Thompson's wry reading of 'Sigh no more' to the men pounding home, lifting in and out of their saddles in slow motion, to Branagh's struggle with a lawn chair as he positions himself for his own gulling, to Thompson's fiercely reluctant march down one of the garden's hedge-lined corridors to call Benedick to dinner, to the way each reads, admires and seeks to improve upon the sonnets each has written to the other demonstrating 'our hands against our hearts'.

Branagh is here merging Shakespeare's comic tradition with an equally robust form of Hollywood comedy which has come popularly to be known as 'screwball' but has been more appropriately described by Stanley Cavell as the Hollywood comedy of remarriage.[13] Cavell sees that the intelligent play of wits which distinguishes the romantic commerce between the heroes and heroines in these films – most often played by Cary Grant and Katharine Hepburn – represents a movement towards a mutual recognition of freedom and equality between the sexes in which each freely rechooses the other after the relationship has been ruptured, strained or divorced. Thus Cavell's decision to classify such films as *The Philadelphia Story*, *The Awful Truth* and *Bringing Up Baby* as comedies of remarriage. The witty bickering and confusion of gender roles in these comedies leads, Cavell argues, 'to acknowledgement; to the reconciliation of a genuine forgiveness; a reconciliation so profound as to require the metamorphosis of death and revival; the achievement of a new perspective on existence; a perspective that presents itself as a place, one removed from the city of confusion and divorce'.[14] Shakespeareans, of course, can hear echoes of Northrop Frye and C. L. Barber in Cavell's language here as he rediscovers the structure and romantic energy of Shakespearean comedy buried in the heart of these remarkable films.

Beatrice and Benedick are surely the prototypes for the bantering pairs who distinguish Cavell's Hollywood comedies. The movement of the contrasting romantic plots in *Much Ado* is to bring each pair of lovers, in very different fashions, through the metamorphosis of separation and divorce into the revival of forgiveness and reconciliation. Beatrice and Benedick's progress through this pattern is self-created and unique while Hero and Claudio's is socially generated and conventional.

Branagh's film demonstrates visually how Shakespeare's two plots are intimately linked, in Cavellian terms, because it takes Claudio's immature and cruel disruption of the socially sanctioned ritual of marriage to spur the creation of Beatrice and Benedick's privately conceived and imagined ceremony of reconciliation and re-engagement. Rather than seeing his film – as many stage productions do – as solely a vehicle for Beatrice and Benedick, Branagh makes visually vivid the shy, bashful and conventional relationship between Claudio and Hero.

Though, as I have already indicated, Branagh and Leonard do make Claudio's wedding tantrum properly ugly and savage, the power of the moment's impact has been decidedly lessened. Rather than revealing Claudio's insecure and immature male malice (in contrast to Benedick's immediate move to support Hero's innocence) based on his superficial acceptance of the assumptions of the patriarchal order, Branagh's film asks the audience to understand the wounded lover's anger and to sympathise with Claudio rather than to judge him. This has the effect of making Claudio and Hero's reconciliation as romantically inviting and welcome as that of Beatrice and Benedick, allowing them a less problematical place in the concluding moments of Branagh's film than the one they occupy in Shakespeare's text.

Only in his handling of Claudio does Branagh's desire to be lushly cinematic conflict with his otherwise sure and intelligent translation of Shakespeare's comic energies into film rhythms and images. Branagh can infuse his film with so much ripe romantic energy without destroying the more subtle and less conventional elements in Shakespeare's tale because of Thompson's remarkable performance as Beatrice. She is the film's radiant, sentient centre. Intelligence and wit illuminate every moment of her exquisite performance. Thompson's Beatrice can register emotion, underline irony, change mood, raise alarm, deflect attention, suppress sorrow and enhance wit by the mere tilt of her head, the cock of an eyebrow, the flick of an eyelid or the purse of her lips. She can also capture just the right inflection for Shakespeare's muscular prose and deliver it in a rhythm properly suited to the camera, an ability sometimes absent in Branagh's own performance. The economy with which she allows us to understand her previous romantic entanglement with Benedick and her embarrassment at unintentionally encouraging Don Pedro's marriage proposal is film acting at its most subtle.

Much Ado is a solid technical advance on *Henry V*. The later film makes appropriately playful use of the Steadicam (particularly in the circular shot of Don Pedro and the men situated around the garden's fountain in the scene where they gull Benedick) and the crane (in the three overhead shots previously noted). The editing is quicker and surer, especially in the sequence leading through Claudio's explosion at the wedding to Benedick's commitment, in the chapel, to enact Beatrice's desire for revenge.

Branagh extended and tested those technical skills, developed and refined in his work on *Frankenstein*, as he moved to film Shakespeare's monumental exploration of revenge, *Hamlet*. Each of Branagh's Shakespeare's films to date had been larger, longer and more expensive than its predecessors, and in *Hamlet* he moved to the epic canvas by shooting in 70mm.: the film stock associated with David Lean's great epics, *Dr Zhivago*, *Lawrence of Arabia* and *Ryan's Daughter*. Branagh's *Hamlet*, at just under four hours, is the longest commercial film released since Joseph Mankiewicz's *Cleopatra* (1964) and certainly takes top honours for the film with the most dialogue. In fact, in what is perhaps an insider's joke, Branagh's Hamlet speaks text unspoken by any previous Hamlet, as the film depicts him whispering his love poem to Ophelia as she recalls their love-making in a flashback while Polonius announces his discovery of their romance to Claudius and Gertrude.[15]

In his two previous Shakespeare films, Branagh followed the atmospheric suggestions that dominated the stage productions they grew from, but here he breaks free from those stage roots to reimagine the play completely in the language of film. Branagh's camera is in constant motion: it tracks, pans, cranes, zooms in and out, flashes back and circles.[16] Then, startlingly, it will hold an immense close-up on a tiny physical detail like a mouth or a pair of eyes (most notably in the encounter between Hamlet and the Ghost) to allow full attention to the word and its reception. In stark contrast to the intimacy of such close-ups is the film's most hyperbolic scene, which works as a homage to Olivier's discovery of how to handle the Shakespearean soliloquy on film (reverse the normal camera movement, which is from long shot to close-up) and as a visual reminder of Branagh's own *Frankenstein* as well (tiny figure dwarfed by frozen landscape). Branagh shoots 'How all occasions' against a vast expanse of snow and ice and rock. He starts in close and gradually pulls the camera back as the soliloquy builds to reveal Fortinbras's huge army marching off to Poland in the valley below. As the camera cranes up and away, it captures Hamlet with arms stretched out wide crying: 'O, from this time forth / My thoughts be bloody or be nothing worth.' Though this moment seems hyperbolic, it works here because it externalises Hamlet's internal landscape: he's been isolated, cut off, frozen out and reduced in filmic terms to making grand gestures of impotent frustration while Fortinbras gets on with the business of doing.

Branagh frames his tale with a word and a statue. The first shot of the film is the word HAMLET chiselled in stone. Then, as the camera pans to capture a long shot of the palace (actually Blenheim) through its iron gates, we realise the word we have read is chiselled on the base of a huge statue of Hamlet's father, which then appears to clank into life on the first appearance of the Ghost. The film's final shot is of that statue's being toppled and hammered into rubble by Fortinbras's army. Between these two moments, the use of the full text, as well as the resources of film to cut away from the text to view silent action, allows Branagh to assign an importance to Fortinbras at radical odds with any other production of the play I have encountered. Fortinbras looms; he's always in the background and on the move, closing in on a world crumbling from within. It's as though he and Hamlet were two sides of the same revengeful son: one pale and precise moving against the establishment from within, the other dark and intense closing in from without.[17]

The external world in the film is cold, snow-covered, and, in Hamlet's encounters with the Ghost and later with the Gravedigger, starkly wooded: a wasteland. By contrast, the interior world appears bright and bold and open, but, once Hamlet and the camera begin prying behind the mirrored doors which line the great hall of Claudius's court, they uncover a host of *trompe-l'oeil* doors built into everything from bookcases to Tiepolo-inspired wall paintings to the mirrored doors themselves. Nothing in this world, we come to discover through text and image, is what it seems. The soiled beauty which Hamlet's fervid imagination associates with Gertrude and then Ophelia is brilliantly mirrored in the film's design of the Elsinore court. For Hamlet, all the doors have spies behind them; all the mirrors held up to nature reflect Claudius's corrupt decadence.

This is made most painfully apparent in the film's segue from the 'To be or not to be' soliloquy into the nunnery scene. Branagh delivers Hamlet's famous meditation while staring at himself in one of the great hall's mirrored doors (behind which Claudius and Polonius peer back at him through a two-way mirror), as if trying to discover in his reflection some clue to his recent discovery of the disparity between inner and outer, for it is this disjunction that has disjointed his world. Once he spies Kate Winslet's Ophelia – standing some distance away at the entrance to the great room – he moves to her across the expanse of white and black checkered marble floor and delivers 'Soft you now, / The fair Ophelia' directly to her in hushed and tender tones. Their exchange about beauty and honesty continues in this mood, until a noise at their backs prompts Hamlet's query 'Where's your father?' and sets him off dragging Ophelia behind him on a furious move down the line of mirrored doors, opening and slamming each, searching for the spies. Branagh's editing here gives us a complicated series of point-of-view shots cutting between Hamlet's intense search, Polonius's shocked reaction to Ophelia's face being pushed by Hamlet against the two-way mirror, and Claudius's decision to retreat before being directly discovered. Finally, even when discovering the ghost of Claudius's traces, Branagh's Hamlet can see only his own reflection.

This sequence is the film's most stunning merger of text and technique and was perhaps inspired by Orson Welles's great fun-house mirror scene at the conclusion of a very different *noir* masterpiece, *The Lady From Shanghai*. Filming in a mirrored room is remarkably tricky, but Branagh and his cinematographer, Alex Thompson, make it work. The device of shooting the 'To be or not to be' soliloquy with the camera peering over Hamlet's right shoulder capturing the famous words in multiple layers of reflection is inspired. Hamlet is fragmented and fractured; his psyche is troubled by the way in which he not only opposes, but reflects Claudius; and while he keeps trying to hold the mirror up to both Gertrude's and Claudius's natures it keeps throwing back more images of his turmoil than of their transgression. Two other moments in the film create an interesting parallel in the ways in which Claudius and Ophelia get triangulated in Hamlet's mind. Richard Briers as Polonius delivers his parting advice to Laertes in Claudius's private chapel, and he then pins Ophelia in the chapel's confessional to squeeze out of her the details of her romantic relationship with Hamlet. As Polonius angrily warns her to be something scanter of her maiden presence, Ophelia's memory is overwhelmed with images of her love-making with Hamlet. We watch the pleasure of her memory turn to guilt as Polonius insists that Hamlet's vows are meant only to beguile. This is the beginning of Ophelia's unravelling. Later, Claudius will slip into the same confessional after 'The Mousetrap' to try to salve his guilty conscience, and it will be Hamlet as scourge if not ministering priest who hears his confession on the other side of the screen, darting his dagger at Claudius's ear only to withdraw it when he realises (as a flashforward shows the anticipated blow) that such a thrust will send his enemy to heaven. Branagh's use of the flashback/flashforward devices and the images of the mirror and confessional grill are tantalising in their subtle translation of the multiple layers of Shakespeare's text into film vocabulary.

Though Branagh resists giving us pictures of narrated events that other films of the play have made standard – Hamlet's appearance in Ophelia's closet, Ophelia's drowning, Hamlet's sea voyage and escape – he does give us a host of other flashbacks: two instances of Ophelia remembering her love-making with Hamlet; a visualisation of the First Player's evocation of Priam and Hecuba in distress; Fortinbras's negotiating with Old Norway; Claudius, Gertrude and Old

Hamlet engaged in playing an indoors version of curling; Claudius's poisoning of Old Hamlet; and a buck-toothed Yorick cavorting with a young Hamlet. The shots of Hamlet and Ophelia's trysts make an important point about his interpretive approach to the character and play.

Branagh's psychological approach to Hamlet is centred on the Ghost and Claudius rather than his mother. There's not a trace of the Oedipal subtext in his relationship with Gertrude; the famous closet scene is remarkably chaste. Glenn Close's Gertrude is the central figure in Zeffirelli's *Hamlet* and the central object of Mel Gibson's attention. Not so here. Christie is but a handsome sideshow; Jacobi's Claudius is the main event. The struggles of Branagh's Hamlet, and the artistic energies they release, echo Harold Bloom in their focus on fathers rather than on mothers and are intensified by the remarkable physical resemblance of the 'son' to his 'uncle-father'. Branagh here wrestles with the tradition of filmed *Hamlet*s as that line passes from Gade to Olivier to Kozintsev to Richardson to Zeffirelli. His Hamlet's eventual dispatching of Claudius takes Olivier's famous leap even deeper into film past as Branagh whistles his sword through the air to make a dead strike into Claudius and then follows it by pinning Jacobi on the throne with an Errol Flynn-like swing of the giant chandelier that hangs over the great hall. Actor and director and movie tradition all converge in evoking and finally getting even with all the dominating fathers who haunt Branagh's keen awareness of the Shakespearean tradition on stage and film.

This film, like its central character, is excessive but never dull. Branagh, as actor and director, rivets attention. He handles Shakespeare's language with a pace, clarity and intelligence unique to his generation, and hits consonants with the touch of an expert jazz drummer striking the cymbals.[18] His film Hamlet retains the generous nature of his RSC stage performance but with darker shadings which extend throughout the film. The experience of playing Iago, as well as Frankenstein, in the interim undoubtedly helped to bring anger and danger to his previously idealised portrait. Branagh's film emphasises what Maynard Mack's famous essay on the world of *Hamlet* established years ago: the multiple possible alternative versions of Hamlet that the play presents in the figures of Horatio, Laertes, Rosencrantz and Guildenstern, and Fortinbras.[19] They are his alter-egos, but lack his depth and complexity. Horatio is too steady, Laertes too heady, Rosencrantz and Guildenstern too dim and Fortinbras too single-minded, but it is intriguing to consider that Branagh's film gives Fortinbras more significance in its visual narrative than does Shakespeare's text. Fortinbras is the monster Branagh's Hamlet creates and the image of Rufus Sewell's smug self-satisfaction at the film's close lingers even more powerfully in the memory than Hamlet's sacrificial body being carried off. So much so that the film might be called *Dr Hamlet and Mr Fortinbras*.

Branagh followed the unrelenting length and seriousness of his *Hamlet* with *Love's Labour's Lost*, his most quick and giddy Shakespearean adaptation, filmed in 1999 and released in early 2000. Here again Branagh acknowledges his infatuation with the Hollywood films of the 1930s, 1940s and 1950s by recreating Shakespeare's first festive comedy in the tradition of the American movie musical from Busby Berkeley to Fred Astaire and Gene Kelly. The romantic leads in such musicals break into song as naturally as Shakespeare's characters break into sonnet, and Branagh sees that dancing works as an implied metaphor throughout *Love's Labour's Lost* from Berowne's opening query to Rosaline – 'Did I not dance with you in Brabant once?' – to the ultimate refusal of the women to dance out the answer to the men's wooing in the final scene. When Branagh's Berowne breaks into tap to beat out the rhythm of 'Have at you then, affection's men-at-arms', his film does add a precious seeing to the eye (and ear).

Branagh's film becomes so infatuated with its Hollywood sources that it risks being regarded as *Love's Labour's Lite*, but its energy and charm ultimately derive from the clever linkage of Shakespeare's dizzy poetic flights of fancy with the brilliant melodies and lyrics of master American songwriters like Cole Porter and Irving Berlin. The film moves seamlessly from Shakespeare to song, especially in the two great dance numbers 'I Won't Dance, Don't Ask Me' and 'Dancing Cheek to Cheek', which frame the wooing games, and 'There's No Business Like Show Business' and 'They Can't Take That Away From Me', which capture the way Shakespeare, in *Love's Labour's Lost*, explodes the conventional comic ending. Branagh strings his confection together by another long-abandoned movie staple: the news reel, where his own voice (echoes of Olivier and Welles) serves as that of the rapid-fire narrator. The local villagers suffer the greatest compression (and transformation – Holofernes becomes Holofernia) in Branagh's trimming of the text. Nathan Lane as Costard is perhaps the most successful of all the American comedians, from Michael Keaton to Billy Crystal, whom Branagh has cast in clown roles, and Timothy Spall's Don Armado does a wonderful turn on Cole Porter's 'I Get a Kick Out Of You'. The relationship between Hollywood and Shakespeare which was echoed in certain visual moments in Branagh's *Much Ado About Nothing* and *Hamlet* becomes more than a hint or echo in his *Love's Labour's Lost*: it is the creative energy which drives the film and provides its comic pleasures.

The particular flamboyance and populism of Branagh's Shakespeare films have provoked controversy. Some academic Shakespeareans and film critics are uneasy with Branagh's attempt to straddle the worlds of stage and film, of Stratford and Hollywood, and feel that he is too comfortable in uncritically accepting Shakespeare as a cultural icon. His *Henry V* is faulted for presenting an emotional and sympathetic portrait of the king in the film's anti-war landscape, while *Much Ado* is censured for its exuberant commercialism. His *Hamlet* received respectful treatment from the leading American film reviewers, but was hammered by many of their British counterparts, who were almost universally dismissive in their responses to Branagh's direction and performance.[20] Such disputes over the nature of Branagh's achievement are likely to be a lasting part of his Shakespeare on film legacy because his films have appeared at a particularly anxious moment in the history of Shakespeare studies and have found themselves caught up in a vigorous end-of-century debate about Shakespeare's place and role in contemporary politics and culture.

Branagh's Shakespeare films, however controversial, have revitalised the genre even as they have extended its limits. His films have created a unique synthesis of competing elements, often seen as mutually exclusive, between text and screen and between canonical and commercial values. Branagh has been able successfully to translate Shakespeare, for his cultural moment, into the language of film without sacrificing the poetry those moving images are meant to capture and serve and even transcend. Branagh is not bashful about wanting his films to entertain; his ambition is all wrapped up with his fascination with the heyday of Hollywood in the 1930s and 1940s and with the great Shakespeare films of the 1950s and 1960s. His films represent an unconventional marriage, something like that we might imagine for Beatrice and Benedick, between Shakespeare and Hollywood, and have sparked a renaissance in the twentieth-century's sporadic fascination with Shakespeare as material for film.

NOTES

1 See my interview with Noble about the production in *Shakespeare and the Classroom*, 3 (Spring 1995), 7–10.
2 Pauline Kael, *Movie Love* (New York, 1991), p. 216.
3 See Hassan's 'Pluralism in Postmodern Perspective', *Critical Inquiry*, 12 (1986), and 'Making Sense: The Trials of Postmodern Discourse', *New Literary History* (1987).
4 Peter S. Donaldson, 'Taking on Shakespeare: Kenneth Branagh's *Henry V*', *Shakespeare Quarterly*, 42 (Spring 1991), 60–71; p. 61.
5 Branagh first performed the role at RADA in 1981, then for his Renaissance Company in 1988, and then a full-text BBC radio version in 1992.
6 H. R. Coursen, '*A Midwinter's Tale*', *Shakespeare Bulletin* (Summer 1996), 38.
7 Welles's cast included actors from England (John Gielgud, Keith Baxter, Alan Webb and Margaret Rutherford), Ireland (Norman Rodway), France (Jeanne Moreau and Marina Vlady), Italy (Walter Chiari) and Spain (Fernando Rey).
8 *Much Ado About Nothing: Screenplay, Introduction, and Notes on the Making of the Movie* (New York and London, 1993), p. x.
9 *Ibid.*, p. ix.
10 Geoffrey O'Brien, *The New York Review of Books*, 44, 2 (6 February 1997), 12.
11 Norman Rabkin's chapter, 'Either/Or: Responding to *Henry V*', is in his *Shakespeare and the Problem of Meaning* (Chicago, 1981). See Chris Fitter, 'A Tale of Two Branaghs: *Henry V*, Ideology and the Mekong Agincourt', in Ivo Kamps, ed.,

Shakespeare Left and Right (New York and London, 1991), pp. 259–75; Curtis Breight, 'Branagh and the Prince, or a "royal fellowship of death"', *Critical Quarterly*, 33, 4 (1991), pp. 95–111; and Donald K. Hedrick, 'War is Mud: Branagh's Dirty Harry V and the Types of Political Ambiguity', in Lynda E. Boose and Richard Burt, eds., *Shakespeare, the Movie. Popularising the Plays on Film, TV and Video* (London and New York, 1997), pp. 45–66.

12 Michael Manheim, 'The English History Plays on Screen', in Anthony Davies and Stanley Wells, eds., *Shakespeare and the Moving Image* (Cambridge, 1994), p. 130.

13 See Davies and Wells, *Shakespeare and the Moving Image*, p. 117, for Russell Jackson's association of Branagh's film with screwball comedy.

14 Stanley Cavell, *Pursuits of Happiness: The Hollywood Comedy of Remarriage* (Cambridge, MA, 1981), pp. 17–18.

15 In a wonderful irony the film's only Academy Award nomination was for Best Screenplay. See Russell Jackson's 'Kenneth Branagh's Film of *Hamlet*: The Textual Choices', *Shakespeare Bulletin* (Spring 1997), 37–8, for an explanation of the screenplay's adoption of elements from the First Folio and First Quarto and Second Quarto texts.

16 For a discussion of the ways in which Branagh replaces textual editing with film editing to shape his interpretation of the play, see Laurie E. Osborne's 'Shakespearean Short Cuts: Fragmentation and Coherence in Branagh's *Hamlet*', paper presented to the Shakespeare on Film session at the 1997 Modern Language Association meeting.

17 For a fuller exploration of Branagh's treatment of Fortinbras, see Robert F. Willson, 'Kenneth Branagh's *Hamlet*, or The Revenge of Fortinbras', *The Shakespeare Newsletter* (Spring 1997), 7–9.

18 For Branagh's approach to language, see his interview with Paul Meier, 'Kenneth Branagh: With Utter Clarity', *The Drama Review*, 41, 2 (Summer 1997), 82–9.

19 Maynard Mack, 'The World of *Hamlet*', *The Yale Review*, 41 (1952), 502–23.

20 For negative reaction to Branagh's *Henry V* see Fitter 'A Tale of Two Branaghs' and Breight 'Branagh and the Prince'; for *Much Ado About Nothing* see Courtney Lehman, '*Much Ado About Nothing*? Shakespeare, Branagh, and the "national-popular" in the age of Multinational Capital', *Textual Practice*, 12, 1 (1998), 1–22; and for *Hamlet* see Nigel Andrews, 'Variety Night at Elsinore Palace', *The Financial Times* (13 February 1997); Geoff Brown, 'Ken's Lust Action Hero', *The Times* (13 February 1997); Jonathan Coe, 'Hamlet', *New Statesman* (14 February 1997); and John Mullen, 'Ken, Al and Will, Too', *Times Literary Supplement* (21 February 1997). For more positive initial reactions to *Hamlet*, see Terrence Rafferty, 'Solid Flesh', *New Yorker* (13 January 1997); Geoffrey O'Brien, 'The Ghost at the Feast', *New York Review of Books* (6 February 1997); Janet Maslin, 'William Shakespeare's *Hamlet*', *New York Times* (25 December 1996); and Stanley Kaufman, 'At Elsinore', *The New Republic* (27 January 1997). For a comprehensive survey of *Hamlet*'s reception in the popular press see H. R. Coursen, 'The Critical Reception of Branagh's Complete *Hamlet* in the U. S. Popular Press', *Shakespeare and the Classroom*, 5, 2 (Fall 1997), 29–39; and Nina da Vinci Nichols, 'Branagh's *Hamlet* Redux', *Shakespeare Bulletin*, 15, 3 (Summer 1997), 38–41.

PART IV

Critical issues

14

CAROL CHILLINGTON RUTTER

Looking at Shakespeare's women on film

Cinema is a 'looking' medium that writes its texts in visual language, and cinema has always been interested in looking at women. My account of Shakespeare's women on film wants to signal this interest from the beginning by remembering Bogart's 'Here's lookin' at you kid' in *Casablanca*, not just because that line, which cues the film's repeated instances of lingering focus on Bergman's face, defines a whole genre of cinematic looking, but also because it has achieved epigrammatic status independent of the film. It's become a slogan for much wider cultural habits that may have originated in films like *Casablanca* but now circulate in culture at large, reproducing cinema's looking practices in real life. The movies, in short, have taught us how to look at each other. To see how cinema has looked at Shakespeare's women, I want to begin with an instance of subversive looking: a wink, the one Mary Pickford's Kate aims sideways out of the frame at the end of *The Taming of the Shrew*, caught, in the next shot, by her sullen sister Bianca, whom it instantly transforms into a smiling conspirator. That wink rewrites Shakespeare's ending. But more importantly, it inserts into this *Shrew* a way of looking that is going to signify for the future of Shakespeare's women on film.

Pickford's 1929 *Shrew*, directed by Sam Taylor, was the first 'talkie' Shakespeare, a production gamble she financed with both her money and celebrity as 'America's Sweetheart': she was the most famous and highly paid face in the world and half of an internationally recognised 'star couple'.[1] For movie-goers, Pickford was also a palimpsest of dozens of earlier silent film roles available to be read as powerfully legible trace memories or residues through the surface of this *Shrew*: the saccharine-sweet, main-chancer Pollyanna; the truly awful Rebecca of Sunnybrook Farm; countless mettlesome underdogs who, in reel after reel and in Pickford's famous curls managed to win through in spite of Petruchio-style swaggerers.

Running only sixty-eight minutes, this *Shrew* was cut to the bone. Christopher Sly, Lucentio, Tranio, most of Bianca and nearly all of Shakespeare's fifth act, including the wager, were axed, but a new framing device was inserted, a knockabout puppet show that has Judy spurning the suitor she clobbers for the one who clobbers her, obviously predicting the taming-to-come where furniture, cats and suitors will fly but where, too, a rain-sodden Kate, pitched knee-deep into the mire that swamps Petruchio's front door, will stagger through a *pas de deux* with a mother pig that elevates slapstick into heart-rending tragicomedy. This film *Shrew* gives Kate significant costumes and props – a man-sized whip, a black riding habit to glower in, a miserable wrecked wedding dress to shiver in. The camera records looks that long takes make meaningful: withering, knowing, come-hithering. And Kate has business on and off the text. Her howl, when Petruchio stamps on her foot at the wedding, is taken for 'I will.'

Then at the end comes the wink. In narrative terms, its effect is to invert the conclusions the 'submission' speech seems just to have settled in Shakespeare's text. That text told one story; now this wink, another, making Kate's submission a ploy and patriarchal authority – the authority to tame a shrew – a male fantasy, merely tolerated by knowing women who turn out to be *shrewd* while men are just dopes. But the wink works on a technical level as well, and it is here that it signals the difference film is going to make to the future interpretation of Shakespeare's women's roles. To go back one step: Kate's final speech issues from its origins in the theatre. It is 'theatre sized': rhetorical, histrionic, written for delivery in a speaking-place where the images are *in the lines*, in the 'words, words, words'. Words, though, are a liability in film; as Peter Holland has observed, film is antagonistic to the density of Shakespeare's language.[2] Film, says Ingmar Bergman, 'begins with the face'.[3] By contrast, the wink belongs to the new medium. The language it depends on is visual – what the camera records *between the lines* and *instead of the lines* – and its exclusionary meaning can only be read cinematically, across the sequence of shot/reverse shot that cuts between Kate and Bianca. The camera, then, constructs two gendered endings for this *Shrew* while Pickford's wink cuts the movie *Shrew* free from the theatre *Shrew*, ironically asserting the superior authority of film's visual language over the playwright's theatre language at the very moment when the 'talkie' movie is speaking Shakespeare's lines for the first time. In the movies, as the wink signals, meanings are going to reside in the extra-textual narratives the camera constructs by its looking.

In what follows I survey a number of women's narratives – both textual and extra-textual – to think about how film constructs those narratives technically: the way it photographs women, in close-up, in mid or long shot, in tracking shots; by turns intensifying concentration on a face, an eye, a foot, or impassively observing, or drawing back, marooning women in compositions that register isolation and them as objects.[4] I am interested in the way film uses *mise-en-scène*, placing women against poetically expressionistic or densely realised social backgrounds that inform their roles; the way it assembles women's narratives through editing; the way it uses that definitively filmic technique, the flashback, to invent prehistories, to call the past into the present, or to realise fantasies. Film returns again and again to certain motifs: women running; women framed (in doorways, windows, wimples, hats: all reiterative of the larger framing the shot is doing); dressing up and dressing down; women seeing themselves in mirrors, both literal and figurative; women confined: put into corsetted costumes and claustrophobic rooms, walled gardens, curtained beds, narrow labyrinths; women released into open landscapes. Film's historic interest in female bodies – in beauty and its wreck, in the monstrous, the regulated, the stereotyped – constantly exceeds the specifications of Shakespeare's theatre texts: on film, female bodies proliferate, women's roles multiply, filling in the *mise-en-scène* with supplementary extra-texts that are there to be read with – or against – the dominant narrative. As film deprivileges Shakespeare's words, so it coincidentally redistributes the balance of power between men's and women's roles: not only are there more women in Shakespeare films than playtexts but they have much more to perform.[5]

Pickford's *Shrew* anticipates all these issues, and in the seventy years since its release, as popular culture has absorbed feminism and internalised pop-versions of its discourses, so have the movies: Baz Luhrmann's *Romeo + Juliet* (1996) brilliantly delivers 'Shakespeare' to a post-feminist age. Just how radically women's roles have been repositioned in the movies can be observed in four films of the history plays: these remakes, across five decades, of Shakespeare's most resolutely masculine narratives might collectively be retitled 'you've come a long way, baby'.

In *Richard III*, the harridan Queen Margaret, remaindered from the previous regime, worms her way through the play like conscience. If Richard is the play's gargoyle, Margaret is its caryatid, her prophetic curses paradoxically fissuring the building of his warped Machiavellian ingenuity.[6] In *Henry V*, Katherine fraternises with the enemy fourteen scenes before her country's rout at Agincourt: she studies the invader's language. And, blazoning her own body – so that body parts produce parts of speech: '*de hand*', '*de fingres*' – she learns to name the material that is going to be demanded in exchange for peace.

Both plays interrogate excessive masculinity – call it heroism or megalomania, men are 'jolly, thriving wooer[s]' for whom rape is the ready alternative. And in the plays, women are central to this interrogation which they conduct as much personally as politically. But not in Laurence Olivier's films. His design inspiration for *Henry V* (1944), the Duc de Berri's *Book of Hours*, seems to locate women in his directorial imagination as occupying the same space as medieval illuminations, decorative marginal glosses to the main matter. (Renée Asherson's Katherine doesn't get a mention in Olivier's autobiography; a horse blinded in the Agincourt sequence gets two paragraphs.[7]) Olivier sets Katherine's

English lesson in a walled garden, conspicuously built of studio flats to achieve a deliberately distorted scale and false perspective, an artificial space, more like the backstage of the Globe in the film's opening sequence, where boy players become women by shoving oranges down their fronts, than like the 'real' spaces covered by Henry's military progress. Indeed, there is a sense in which Olivier's Henry calls Katherine imaginatively into being: having devastated Harfleur, Henry gazes over the battlements into the distance; the marching drumbeat resolves into a plaintive clarinet while the camera pans across a painted land-scape that dissolves into a long shot of an Oz-like city that further dissolves into a door opening as Katherine appears. Asherson's performance is as flattened as the tableau background, her lovely face framed in an 'authentic' coif that empha-sises the way her eyes are constantly lowered, averted, never meeting the camera's gaze.[8] Photographed in mid-shot, she is a compositional figure in a picture, demure and passive, inscrutable even in the potentially political extra-text written around her appearance in the garden: entering, she pauses to look over the battlements to watch five noblemen ride for Harfleur; later, only one returns. Seeing him, she raises her eyes from the courtyard to the horizon. Is she count-ing the cost of war in male bodies? Answering Henry's beckoning gaze?

In the wooing scene, she repeats that same look when she replies to Henry's 'simply-the-most-active-gentleman-of-France' courtship antics with a single line: 'Is it possible dat I should love de *ennemi* of France?' She gazes out over vasty fields, but they are picturesque, not scarred, and an enigmatic smile is already playing about her lips. She is stalling, not resisting, and she yields to the kiss that cuts to the close-up on their hands, Henry's lion signet clasping her *fleur de lys*, firmly '*le possession de moi*'. This film performance does not admit any real inkling of Katherine's political significance, the way she collects up and focuses the playtext's troublesome moves between interchangeable 'batteries' that make both cities *and* virgins targets of 'hot and forcing violation'. Indeed, the female claim to political seriousness is trivialised throughout this film, the original '*law Salique*' debate registering the 'female question' ludicrous as cod-clerics (antic-ipating Monty Python) fall all over each other, law scrolls unravelling around them. But at least Asherson's Kate is no fool, like her podgy, pampered brother, clearly his father's son: France here is kinged out of A.A. Milne, not Holinshed. Unusually, since the part is habitually cut, France is also queened, and by the only clued-up aristocrat in this papier mâché court: Janet Burnell's no-nonsense Isabel even elbows France in the ribs to prompt his response to Henry's terms. Some hope then for 'claiming from the female'.

Ten years later Olivier cut Margaret from *Richard III* (1955). Lady Anne – an achingly young Claire Bloom: another face out of Renaissance saints' portrai-ture – is mesmerised like a rabbit when she stares into Richard's eyes and doomed when, wrapped in his black spider embrace as he slides his ring down her finger, she yields to his kiss, not once but twice.[9] Thereafter, Anne – not Margaret – is this film's ghost. Her ruin is written in her moves, though never on her face, as she is dragged to the steps of Richard's throne, watches him ascend, then faints. The camera cuts between Richard fixing reptile eyes upon Anne as if measuring striking distance, and Anne herself, supported by women, raising delicate fingers to her lips – remembering 'honey words', or recognising the truth she cannot speak? – then turning, walking away into the dark of the long shot, her final exit framed by Richard's throne.[10]

Of course, with Margaret cut, there is no one in this film to play mongoose to Richard's cobra. Instead, the most pervasive female presence is an entirely extra-textual one, Jane Shore, King Edward's mistress, only mentioned in the playtext. She gestures to the new-crowned king as she cuts a diagonal through his corona-tion procession, and while it moves, massed, in one direction, she alone moves in another, finally taking up a (power?) position just behind the throne. Such visual disruptiveness connects her to the scene's other dissident: earlier, as cries saluted Edward, Richard, recognisable suddenly in profile when his head swivels sharply, snatched the close-up away from his brother. This connection is not coincidental: in scene after scene associative editing twins the hunchback and the whore, evi-dently proposing – perhaps interchangeably – two usurpations. One way to read this visual subtext is to see Shore's body projecting a crude politics of misogyny, her mute strumpet/witch figure registering that there are more devils afoot – more potent, more ancient – than Richard's ancestor Machiavel. Women in this film have no apparatus to contest Richard's malevolence, but at the level of archetype, Shore simply snookers him by issuing an unspoken prior claim to damnation.

Some decades on, these same roles on film are not just bigger, more complex, nuanced; they are also more intelligent. And actors, not just directors, are clearly agents of these performances. Emma Thompson (*Henry V*, 1989) playing Katherine's English lesson against a white aviary of fluttering doves – a vision of paradise after the hell-slaughter of Harfleur – shows a Kate whose hands may be occupied with the tools of female vanity but whose mind is elsewhere. While her hair is brushed, she gazes into a mirror self-critically, registering that she knows Henry's terms of exchange and is calculating her beauty's worth. '*Il faut que j'apprenne à parler*' is a flat statement of political necessity. But this sober, polit-icised Kate is also playful. She 'performs' her English lesson from behind her bed curtains, one hand emerging like an actor taking the stage to impersonate '*de fingres*'. Full of laughter, she's clearly more than a match for any player king (though her laughter dies when she opens the door on to her father's haunted face). It's this laughter that later places the implacable countenance Kate holds aloof from Henry in a wooing that is an encounter between maladroit victor and unbending vanquished. Kenneth Branagh's Henry is never so callow as when, having devastated her country, he proposes – with no sense of irony – 'to plead his love-suit to her gentle heart'. '*O bon Dieu! Les langues des hommes sont pleines de tromperies*' is a withering dismissal of his political crassness (a million miles from Asherson's coquetry). Thompson's Kate *is* genuinely amused by Henry – Branagh's French, unlike Olivier's, is unbelievably awful: and the laughter that bursts out of her may be hopeful for the future – but at the end, she is unsmiling, a Kate given, not yet won.

In Branagh's film, claiming from the female is a tensely serious business that returns at the end, reconfigured as a self-critiquing counter-text to the film's most famous shot, the one that tracks Henry across the battlefield of Agincourt carrying the dead boy over his shoulder as 'Non Nobis' builds from a single tentative voice to a wall of sound constructed to make Englishmen throw themselves off it, persuading them, in the very sight of child-slaughter, 'Dulce et decorum est . . .' The repulsive sentimentality of this heroising sequence is undercut by women: from the background, wading through mud and blood directly into the camera's line of vision come a mob of French women clamouring to tear Henry to pieces.

It is this sort of extra-textual narrativity that Richard Loncraine constructs so brilliantly for women in *Richard III* (1996), set in a 1930s Britain in which fascism – Hitler-style – is on the rise. But while the Yorks at war are grotesquely phallic (in the pre-title sequence a tank bursts, gun-turret first, through the walls of the Lancastrian bunker; Richard mows down the prince in a gas mask that, bizarrely, looks like an anatomical drawing of scrotum and penis), and while the architecture of Yorkist hegemony is aggressively masculine (brutalism assaults the eye in buildings, machines, uniforms, even haircuts), Yorkist society is glamorously feminised. As the royal family dresses for its victory ball, a nanny holding a towel chases the little, shrieking princes; a nurse in a starched cap administers pills to the king; an airline hostess points the sozzled playboy-aristo, just off a transatlantic flight, in the right direction; a chanteuse croons a theme song for the victorious house of York – 'Come live with me and be my love' – in a swinging two-step. In this world, women dress like 1930s movie stars but don't imagine their parts in 'real life' will look like ones they've seen in the movies – spurned lovers, romantic dead-beats, gangsters' molls. Then they do.

Anne (Kristin Scott Thomas) is seduced over the naked corpse of her husband in a grey hospital morgue among autopsy tables, soiled sheets and plumbing pipes by a Richard (Ian McKellen) who plays the scene's staggering misogyny for near-comic cliché. Down on one knee, he uses his one good hand to hold Anne's hand to his lips, tugs at his ring with his teeth and slips it from his mouth on to her finger. The gesture reads like an obscene act of oral sex.[11] Married to him, Anne travels on addiction: pills, then harder stuff whose ravages shadow her hollow eyes with dark circles. *En route* to Richard's coronation in the back seat of a black Bentley she raises her chic skirt over her stocking top, finds a space among the bruises on her thigh and injects.

This coronation is one of the bleakest sequences in the film because of the way Loncraine uses it to construct a complicated riff on power, gender and represent-ation, exploiting filmic clichés of beauty to critique that exploitation and cutting between film registers – the glamour photo, *film noir*, documentary – to inter-rogate the medium's complicity.[12] He writes the coronation on Anne's face, dis-solving from her morphine black-out in the Bentley to a procession of ecclesiastics elevating the crown over Richard's head: a drug induced nightmare? No. The camera cuts to a close-up on Anne. The surface of her face is a flawless cosmetic mask, but the blue eyes staring out so startlingly from above the rouged cheeks and scarlet lips are vacant, and the neck is stacked with so many rows of diamonds that the head looks decapitated. As the camera travels into extreme close-up on this face we are looking at the front cover of *Vogue* as imagined by Salvador Dali, then we seem – the move is surreal – to travel *through* the face into a shot of the crown descending on to Richard's head. The next shot bizarrely dis-solves back into Anne's face, the camera repeating that move of travelling into her empty eyes while the coronation fanfare is drowned by the insane music in her head, Westminster Abbey's bells pealing in slow motion out of sequence. Then another dissolve produces a repeat of the first coronation shot: the Archbishop, the diadem. Richard is being crowned all over again. Only now the image is grainy and grey, an image from nightmare. Or film.

As the camera pulls back, we see Anne: disconcertingly, jewels gone, cigarette drooping from a corner of her mouth, sitting behind Richard in the blue haze of a projection room, staring fixedly at a screen. She is watching a black and white news reel, the coronation nightmare mechanically and endlessly repeated as her permanent present; for her, the filmic equivalent of Lady Macbeth's sleepwalk-ing. Here is life as instant history, graphic archive, memory written mechanically on to narrative; more appallingly for Anne, film footage is what remains of her when, shortly, she's assassinated.

Loncraine's film graphically understands the consequences of Richard's evil in female terms and locates in women's voices the only source of moral opposition to his nihilistic agency. Annette Bening's Queen Elizabeth is a Wallis Simpson upstart but also a hickory-hard Yankee; Maggie Smith, a formidable Dowager Duchess who reanimates Shakespeare's Margaret, but also brings his Volumnia, Lawrence's Gertrude and Cagney's Ma Jarrett into play with her.[13] When Bening's American accent and arhythmic delivery of the 'proper' English pen-tameter find a voice to out-wisecrack the demon king, she can out-manoeuvre him. When Maggie's Smith's matriarch, with her farewell speech, pins Richard under the Darwinian scrutiny of his own history like an arachnid specimen, power-driving the crippling lines, 'To war take with you my most grievous curse', he never recovers. In Loncraine's film, science and the gods are marshalled against Richard, but it's a woman who issues the call-up, and it's a woman the film remembers at the end. As Richard plunges to his death swathed in flames like Cody Jarret ('On top of the world, Ma') in *White Heat*, the soundtrack glosses the visual allusion with an ironic theme tune, Al Jolson belting out 'I'm sitting on top of the world.'[14]

What marks the shift from Olivier to Loncraine is not just how Loncraine reads women's roles off Shakespeare's playtext but how he reads those roles off contemporary culture, finding an immediately decipherable visual language for the 1990s to reproduce something like the potency women project in the original script, *circa* 1590. The fact that he recognises that power as requiring representation (for Olivier certainly did not) is a cultural indicator. But equally, Loncraine doesn't disguise the fact that 1990s men are still nervous of powerful women: *inter alia* his film comically and ironically documents contemporary male culture's self-regarding anxieties and the moves it makes to displace them on to women.

Of course, plenty of male anxiety circulates in Shakespeare's comedies – where a politics of desire reconfigures the politics of power – but in films of these comedies anxiety is dispersed by frank celebration of the female sexual body. (Sometimes, utterly mindlessly: Branagh's *Much Ado About Nothing* never recovers from the pre-adolescent hysteria of its opening sequence which can't decide whether Emma Thompson's Beatrice is Dorothy Parker, Miss Jean Brodie or Lolita.) In Shakespeare, the object of comedy is, by the end, to assemble the right number of bodies in the right ratio of sexes (1:1); but the problem is the regulation of women's bodies, trying to confine within patriarchal structures what evades containment not least because it defies both social and physical definition: women in Shakespeare exceed the limits. Tasked with managing female desire: what a nightmare! Shakespeare's comic men might as well set themselves to herding cats.

No film proposes the question about how we read the gendered body so wonderfully – and disconcertingly – as Trevor Nunn's *Twelfth Night* (1995) with its teasing opening sequence. The camera pans across a scene below deck on a sailing ship where the passengers, outlandish in late-Victorian fancy dress, are ignoring a rising gale. The camera settles on identical twins, at the piano to do their 'turn', stunningly got-up in harem costume, veils covering their lower faces, a concealment that only emphasises their seductive eyes. From the shadows, Antonio, in mariner's uniform, gazes hungrily. We read them as women. Until mid-way through the soprano chorus of 'O mistress mine' they 'sing both high and low', and 'low' booms out in a bass voice! Which of them is the man? Which of them does Antonio desire? Eyes narrowing, the piano-playing twin moves to unmask the impersonator, pulling aside the first twin's veil to expose what's underneath. A moustache! Frowning, that former 'she' (now written 'he') reciprocates, pulls aside the second twin's veil, and discloses – another moustache.

These 'monster' androgynes – women's kohled eyes over men's hirsute lips – appeal helplessly to their audience who roar delight at each disclosure. Again, the first twin reaches out. S/he tugs the corner of the opposite moustache – and pulls it off! So *that's* the sister! But there's still another moustache. And just as the bare-faced twin grimly reaches for it – the comic rhythm of the sequence working to make us project the next step, imagine *it* ripping off, leaving us where we started – the ship runs aground.

There's chaos: rigging falls, the piano slides across the deck, the twins stagger below, Sebastian pulling off his wig – but not his moustache – as they throw belongings into the trunk that is going to wash ashore with Viola: clothes, a sepia photograph, a wooden box of theatrical make-up. That close-up on the possessions that make the twins what they are (skirts vs. shirts, a child of each sex flanking the father in the photograph) literalises the common terms of gender differentiation but also suggests gender erasure, for the box of greasepaint significantly remembers what the masquerade so disconcertingly taught us: gender is what we 'read', nothing more, perhaps, than a performance slapped on with the Leichner no. 5. If so, farewell difference; farewell differentiating claims to what men and women 'owe' in love.

It is this idea that Nunn's mellow, elegiac film – its nostalgia intensified by its period setting in a National Trust country house – proceeds to explore as shipwrecked Viola (Imogen Stubbs) transforms herself into her brother across a sequence of short takes that closes in on body parts: the chest bound flat, the folded handkerchief shoved down the trousers, the voice deepened by seal-barking, the final metamorphosis matched against the brother in the photograph. Memorably, this film anatomises first melancholy then madness by looking into shadows, peering into the moribund gloom of Olivia's house or the self-indulgent half-light of Orsino's, pursuing shadows across autumnal lawns and into midnight kitchens, interrogating mad Malvolio in half-darkness. Shadow is a metaphor for death but paradoxically a metaphor also for what can be recuperated from death: the shadow of Viola's grief disperses as she memorialises her brother by becoming his shadow-self. Reanimating Sebastian, Viola embodies a committtedness to life that reanimates Illyria: here, Olivia falls in love with Viola/Cesario not for his person but for his energy, for the way he throws back her curtains to flood her house with light and shouts 'Olivia!' so exuberantly that rooks fly startled from a copse and Malvolio, indoors, plucks off his pince-nez in alarm. Shadow, though, is a way of figuring gender as well: profoundly, Nunn's photographic strategies work to suggest for every body a shadow twin of the other sex, opposite, but somehow attached. Comedy triumphs in this *Twelfth Night* when bodies stand face to face and Sebastian completes the action interrupted by the storm, gently peeling off Cesario's moustache to reveal Viola underneath.

The comic body that interests Franco Zeffirelli is not the opposite self but the exaggerated self, and he explores it in a Rabelaisian Renaissance *Taming of the Shrew* (1966) with a larger-than-life Kate – Liz Taylor – poured into costumes she overflows, the bosom several sizes bigger than the bodice. For Zeffirelli, comedy is social and normative – located in crowded streets and stuffed houses; balconies, galleries, windows packed with neighbours-as-spectators – and it is occupied with archetypal patterns of human behaviour: men make journeys, women get chased. So Lucentio, Petruchio, the pedant, the duped father are all Padua *arrivistes*; love-stricken Lucentio pursues Bianca through the streets of Padua; mercenary Petruchio pursues Kate through doors, rooms, corridors, on to the ridge tiles and through the collapsing roof on to the family wool fortune piled in a barn below. After her submission speech Kate hot-foots it again, out of a closing door, leaving Petruchio to fight his way through a scrum of female bodies.

But most significantly for Zeffirelli, comedy is about excess, not just saturnalian reversal but monstrous carnival abundance – 'too much' Kate – and the problem she poses of how to get a grip on her. To this end, he announces his film's rules of engagement in spectacular fashion in the opening sequence: Lucentio and Tranio, newly arrived in teeming Padua, unpack their saddlebags and discuss their agenda for serious academic life. (The camera cuts to a street-level window opposite where a courtesan, her Venetian crimped hair brushed by her female minder, glances up and spots the newcomers.) Philosophy is fine, says Tranio, but let not 'love [be] an outcast . . .' He stops dead. He's seen the courtesan. She smiles and slowly stands, expanding into a mountain of female flesh. She fills the window! Another reverse shot (there are fourteen of them in this sequence) registers Tranio's speechlessness before cutting back, past the wrinkled face of the crone next door who's watching him, laughing, then travelling up the giant's body, from the chopines to the swelling bosom, the *décolletage* adjusted lower by the minder. 'No profit grows where is no pleasure ta'en,' grins Tranio, but 'profit' and 'pleasure' in his text, put against the supplementary text in the window, are suddenly *double entendres*.

This 'woman on display' is one kind of 'household stuff', and as the sequence plays upon stereotypes of female beauty – the hag, the crone, the painted woman – it predicts future attractions. Kate, too, is 'household stuff' who first appears as a single menacing eye pressed against a crack in a window, and the way Tranio stares at the courtesan anticipates Lucentio's first transfixed sight of Bianca. But this sequence does more. It plays with agency. The giant courtesan looks first, and it's clear that she is the one managing the gestures that manage the answering gaze: when Tranio falls all over himself out of the scene, she gives him the fig. Most wonderfully, her reaction to Tranio's sheepish astonishment registers that she knows what he's thinking: this woman – all women? – are much too much for mere men to handle.

In her supplementary narrative, Zeffirelli's fat madonna frames *Shrew*'s action and provides the key text for reading the other 'excessive' body this film puts on display, Taylor's Kate. She's there at the beginning, leading the carnival procession that explodes out of academic sobriety into the heaving streets of Padua as emaciated Death, carried out on a stretcher, is replaced with her inexhaustible carnality. She's there at the end, packed into the gallery with the rest of Padua. The whole city attends the feast, and just as laughter has always been directed at men in this film, so civic laughter finally normalises, and neutralises, the husbands' discomfitures. She weeps (perhaps with sentimental joy?) into her handkerchief as Kate speaks of husbands and lords, big hearts and love. There is little anxiety and no neurosis attached to the sexual female body in this film, for by setting this *Shrew* in a carnivalised peasant culture, Zeffirelli finds a way of disarming the sexual politics that get tangled up with modern productions of Shakespeare's play. Kate's outrageousness occasions carnival 'paroxysm'[15] and the 'taming' is understood not as the end of a line; rather, as a constantly receding destination on a continuous cultural cycle.

In tragedy, Shakespeare habitually uses the woman's body to proxy the crisis of masculine self-representation that is the play's narrative focus. What Hamlet or Lear or Othello finally understands about himself is achieved through his catastrophic misunderstanding, misconstruction of Ophelia, Cordelia, Gertrude, Juliet, Desdemona. Eleven major films of these four plays over the past fifty years have produced significant reassessments of the parts women play in tragedy, both in terms of their performative stature and their narrative function. Some of these performances have literally reinvented roles by their reinterpretations; others have provided more local insights which, nevertheless, alter our understanding of the role for ever.[16]

Irene Worth's Goneril in Peter Brook's bleakly primitive black and white *King Lear* (1971) belongs in the first category. Patiently, grimly, schooling the father who has retired into self-willed childishness; standing among splintering furniture as the king and his hundred knights, 'men of choice and rarest parts', wreck her house; taking Lear's appalling curse of her womb full on the face without legitimating his wrath with any reaction that might absorb the damage Lear is doing: this performance makes us understand Lear's daughters anew, not as Ugly Sisters but abused children whose father is responsible for inventing the metaphors that turn them, one by one, into monsters: 'barbarous Scythian', 'marble-hearted fiend', 'riotous appetites'. Brook shoots the cursing sequence ('Hear, Nature, hear! . . . Into her womb convey sterility') as a series of reverse shot close-ups that fill the frame with Paul Scofield's terrible eyes and Worth's mask-like countenance, her illegible face functioning as an alienation device to make us hear Lear's terrible imagery stripped of aesthetic shelter. In this sequence, Brook's camera technique reconfigures the audience's understanding of the king by the way he photographs the woman's face, and he does so again at the end, this time photographing women's bodies. Quick edits fuse the sisters' deaths – Regan's skull is smashed; Goneril brains herself on a stone; Cordelia drops from a gibbet. Then, in long shot, the camera watches Lear stagger across the wasteland battlefield carrying Cordelia's corpse, a doll with a noose around her neck. As Lear kneels, lays out the body and speaks to her, the camera puts dead Cordelia just out of shot, just out of reach. When Lear bids 'Cordelia! stay a little' the camera projects his fantasy: 'What is't thou say'st?' sees Cordelia standing in the frame, very much alive, turning her head towards her father. But the next shot exposes the hallucination as delusion. The camera cuts; Cordelia is gone. The tricks of photography duplicate the tricks of Lear's mind, but more profoundly duplicate the faulty looking, the tampering with images that plague Lear's view of Cordelia (and her sisters) from the beginning.

Read as celluloid intertexts, four *Hamlet*s document a history of roles in performance but also what John Styan would call their 'spectrum' and 'tolerance'.[17] In Olivier's 1948 film, Jean Simmons's Ophelia is a sensual child in a mock-Tudor Elsinore of eerily empty corridors, blond plaits framing her face, artlessly unaware of her erotic appeal but also ambiguously sexualised: as Polonius intones 'Neither a borrower', she toys with the purse hanging from Laertes's belt and looks like she's fondling him.[18] Opposite this Ophelia, Eileen Herlie's buxom Gertrude is a queen cut from a deck of playing cards, an utterly improbable occupant of the sensationally vulgar – and vaginal – Oedipal bed this film constructs to locate Hamlet's psychosis.[19] In 1964, Elsinore in Kozintsev's black and white *Hamlet* is situated somewhere in the Gulag, and Anastasia Vertinskaia's Ophelia is a Soviet functionary whose body is a site of state repression: first, taught a dance that makes her a puppet; later, forced into tortured physical constructions, her hair stiffened over increasingly bizarre metal forms; her body weighed down by jewels, laced breathless into bodices, distorted by farthingales. Elza Radzin's peroxided Gertrude is a superannuated Ophelia, her sexual habits intimated by the dance of centaurs that attends Claudius's debauched revels; her vacuousness represented by the empty dress, laid out like a corpse, which two mincing lackeys carry away from her bed. In 1990, Helena Bonham-Carter is the true intellectual in a pre-Raphaelite action-man Elsinore where Glenn Close's flushed, adolescent Gertrude is discovering the 'hey day in the blood'. Bonham-Carter's brooding, twitchy face, set incongruously beneath an infantile bonnet, maps the collision of ideas that finally drives her mad: 'Fear it'; 'Do not believe his vows'; 'I did love you once'; 'I loved you not'; 'Believe none of us.' Simmons, mad, was prettily disordered; Bonham-Carter is filthy, repulsive, lewd: her assault upon a boyish sentry who must stand to attention even as she masturbates his sword belt is a displaced, cruder version of Hamlet's assault on her. In 1996 Kate Winslet is a dumbed-down Ophelia-for-our-times, disastrously disabled by flashbacks that make nonsense of her narrative by inventing an extra-text that presents her as the obligatory tits-and-bum in a mass market 'erotic thriller'.[20] When Polonius shoves her into a confession box to interrogate her about Hamlet ('What is between you?'), a flashback covers – and contradicts – her answer ('He hath importun'd me with love / In honourable fashion'.) While she says so, the flash-back shows Hamlet in bed with her, grappling her in sweaty love-making. This Ophelia is not 'honest': neither virgin nor candid. Sexually practised, and a prac-tised liar who, *post mortem*, makes a credulous ninny of her brother who buries her as a virgin, she ceases to represent any value alternative to Gertrude's. Here, 'Frailty, thy name is woman' is confirmed in Ophelia's 'polluted' flesh.

All of these *Hamlet*s produce unforgettable images and sequences. Simmons materialises into the nunnery scene like a ghost out of a receding perspective of arches, an effect of the deep-focus photography Olivier used so stunningly in this film; Bonham-Carter – first in long shot, then close-up, and shot from below at an odd angle that distorts her – sits cross-legged on Gertrude's high throne arranging memory-posies out of bits of bone. Vertinskaia, after Polonius's murder, is dressed in mourning: outside, we see her shadow play like a surreal phantom upon a torch-lit window before the camera cuts to an interior to watch her fastened into an iron bodice, a cage loaded with a dress it takes four servants to lift. Winslet, wearing an institutional gown, stands in a padded cell obediently facing the wall, the camera's surveillance looking in from the warden's peep-hole. Close, watching the duel that is meant to be a 'play' of swords, mops her unexpectedly sweaty brow then puts tentative fingers to her ear as her delight in Hamlet's joke-violence turns to slow, horrified recognition and her stricken face stares from the poisoned chalice to Claudius, this whole fatal 'history' a series of quick intercuts 'behind' the main action.

Where Kozintsev rarely moves into close-up – tragedy for him is a social event and his camera is placed where mid-shots frame social content – other directors of *Hamlet* close in on women's faces to exploit the contradiction between their 'essential' unknowability and the conscious – or even unconscious – recognitions they achieve. Women stand before mirrors that figure their distortions (this, perhaps a way of prefiguring the devastating recognitions to come): Simmons's mad Ophelia, reaching for a water lily, breaks into a million fragments her image on the water's surface; Close confronts her raddled Other in the garish, trans-vestite Player Queen who stares out boldly from the play-within-the-play; Winslet, her face violently slammed by Hamlet against a glass door that is also a two-way mirror, wears on her twisted, discoloured flesh the punishment of the two men – Hamlet on one side of the mirror, Polonius on the other – she is trapped between; Vertinskaia, drowned, lies under six inches of water that scrutinise her like a microscope lens.

When Kozintsev produces that final photograph of Ophelia as an object he is stating tragic consequence: this thing is what *Hamlet* has made of her. By contrast, the objectification of Desdemona's body in Orson Welles's *film noir* *Othello* (1952) is the premise enabling the film's narrative strategy: Iago's project depends not upon turning Desdemona into a thing, but in turning one kind of thing into another, Madonna into gargoyle. Suzanne Cloutier's Desdemona is an icon, frequently immobile, nearly speechless, the emblematic 'white' against which male psychotic activity – this film's real subject – is darkly displayed. Only when she elopes, running down a stairway that looks like a twisted thicket, does this Desdemona possess agency. Elsewhere she is the passive muse of Othello's horrible imaginings, photographed in nightmarish, poetically expressionist shots constructed to represent his sexual neurosis with her body. (Significantly, perhaps, Cloutier's 'performance' is as much a male invention as Desdemona's: Welles-as-*auteur* constructed it in the cutting room.[21])

Welles's camera looks at Desdemona through barred windows and grillework. It tracks her through her domestic quarters on Cyprus, a labyrinth of columns in vaulted catacombs that seem to map female unknowability or perhaps male anxiety, and it watches her from the parapets as, far below, reduced in estimate to that 'cunning whore of Venice', her diminished figure moves across a terrace whose fish-scale mosaic pattern becomes in extreme long shot a sheet of tears. This *Othello* feels like a stalker film; the love story is perverted. When Othello dresses in white, it is to 'marry' Iago, and sex is written in the film language of the thriller. Othello's phallic presence, consummating first marriage then murder, is a shadow looming upon bed curtains, spreading across a wall, reaching out shadow arms to engulf Desdemona, advancing upon the camera to fill the entire screen with blackness, the soundtrack palpitating like heartbeats and rising to vocal crescendos that end like screams. On her wedding night, Desdemona lies motionless in headshot as black hands rip apart the bed curtains – her hymen? – and Othello looms over her, a sequence later repeated when, suspecting her, he returns to their bed, rips back the curtains and tries to read the sheets. On her deathbed, she again lies motionless – unaware that Othello's shadow has watched her undress and is now moving implacably towards her. But suddenly she squeezes her eyes shut, feigning sleep, as she hears a heavy door banging shut, a candle, extinguished, fizzling, a dense blackness approaching, filling the blank screen that is also her imagination. Again, curtains rip apart. And when Desdemona, her profile in extreme close-up, finally speaks Othello's name, his face, part of the dark, horribly materialises out of the dark, his lips nearly touching her cheek, only a whisper away. Produced throughout as object, this Desdemona is likewise produced as victim, the flawless beauty of her face finally registering not as innocence but as fatal ignorance – ignorance of dirt. It is this face that, sickeningly, Othello preserves even as he kills it, covering it with what looks like a handkerchief – and works like a death mask. Through it, Othello kisses Desdemona, a kiss that gags, and finally suffocates her.

Oliver Parker's *Othello* (1995) covers much of this same ground; indeed, seems frequently to quote Welles directly, but, in colour, without grit or grain (but with some menace: Laurence Fishburne's bald, hooded-eyed, tattooed Othello is dangerously violent from the beginning). So Parker's camera tracks through Venice, shooting through grilles and lattices; it follows the muffled figure who, landed from a gondola, runs through the early morning Rialto marketplace where cats forage in piles of garbage and courtesans pass with clients: image associations for Desdemona's elopement. Irène Jacob's stunning, open-faced beauty is the object of the camera's gaze, but where Welles shot Desdemona from Othello's obsessive point of view, Parker makes her common property, 'popular'. (Indeed, popularising this story, making it 'as accessible as *Fatal Attraction*',[22] was Parker's stated project for this film.) When Desdemona dances for Othello at their wedding feast, reverse shots interlock their pleasured looking; then the camera moves back to show Cyprus society 'grossly gaping' too; then cuts to the 'common' revels out-of-doors: on the back of an army wagon a soldier mounts a whore; underneath, Iago tauntingly gropes Roderigo's groin.

The price of accessibility is paid for in this film by a Desdemona it collapses into cliché with predictably explicit sex scenes and an eroticised, sentimentalised death – as her ugly struggle fails, Jacob's Desdemona dies caressing Othello's face. Even more disastrously, Parker uses filmed sequences to literalise Othello's imaginary, his Iago-induced 'thoughts unnatural', that produce sick seizures which dissolve into nightmare fantasies. In one, a return to the wedding feast, Cassio dances in lascivious slow motion with Desdemona; in another, a return to the wedding night, Othello approaches his bed, sees a shadow-body moving behind the gauze curtains, parts the drapes with his sword and discovers, as naked bodies roll apart, Cassio coupling Desdemona. The problem with this second sequence is that nothing keys it as fantasy: the line between 'the real' and 'the imaginary' appears seamless. (Compare Stanley's dream in Loncraine's *Richard III*. When the body rolls over in *that* sequence, nightmare has transformed Richard with boar's snout and tusks.) Parker's sensationalising literalism requires spectators to experience Othello's point of view, to see what Othello sees, the fantasy-become-reality, so it makes Fishburne an Othello who has ingested, incorporated Iago's suggestions which his imagination then literally writes on to Desdemona's body in a series of images that work, perversely and reductively, to instantiate and validate the misogynistic stereotypes ('she must have change, she must') that Shakespeare's play circulates. This Othello sees Desdemona in bed with Michael Cassio – and so do we. At the level of cinematic representation, then, the woman's body is recruited and exploited to literalise male fantasy in this film, a move that inverts Shakespeare's performance narrative where male fantasy is written on *male* bodies as men victimise men by exchanging male cultural 'knowledge' about women ('I know our country disposition well'), so that, as Iago seduces Othello, we see the Moor's body acted upon, turned, twisted, finally felled by a seizure. What happens in Parker derails Shakespeare's interrogation of masculinity by making women somehow at fault for male fantasy. Moreover, a 'real' woman is made to cooperate with this fantasy: Jacob's naked body performs the very pornographic work – even, one might say, the very commercial work – in the film that the film is bound to resist for Desdemona in the narrative. And because the film, throughout, so resolutely feeds the fantasy that all women are whores, this sequence raises 'real' doubts about Desdemona which the role-according-to-Shakespeare has a near-impossible time recuperating. The 'sex scandal murders' of this *Othello* would register death on Cyprus as merely the stuff of daily tabloid headlines, domestic tragedy at its most accessible, if it weren't for Emilia.

Parker's film mostly ignores Emilia: her relationship with Desdemona is left unexplored; her troubling and troublesome soliloquy ('I am glad I have found this napkin') is cut; her own handkerchief scene more than humiliates her: it makes her abject. She enters to Iago (who is bored to death of her and faking sleep: a parodic echo of Welles?), tries to tease him into love with the token, then is thrust on to her front and brutally sodomised by him. He instantly recovers, sits astride her in a headshot that – staggeringly – simply cuts her and her reaction out of the frame, and delivers to the camera a cheeky comment about 'trifles light as air'.[23] But something extraordinary takes over. Emilia seizes the film's ending. Momentarily, she gives Desdemona back a voice. (Othello thinks Emilia's 'My lord, my lord!' whispered at the door is coming from Desdemona's suffocated corpse and pushes the pillow down harder on her dead face.) Defying Othello, Emilia doesn't even flinch when he puts his sword to her throat but stretches away from the blade as if she were going to spit, then knocks it aside: 'Oh gull, oh dolt! As ignorant as dirt.' And as, wonderingly, she begins to understand Iago's villainy – 'You told a lie; an odious, damned lie' – she makes a decision: 'Be wise,' he advises her, quietly, seductively; 'get thee home.' For a split second, the true report of Desdemona's story hangs in the balance. Emilia in headshot looks into Iago's eyes. 'I will not' declares her divorce.

In these final moments, Anna Patrick's performance trades on a marital history that Parker's 'erotic thriller' leaves largely unwritten. What, one wonders, was the fatal attraction between Emilia and Iago (as between Othello and Iago, Roderigo and Iago) that only she has the courage to rethink and repudiate? It is precisely this marital history that Zoë Wanamaker writes – and painfully anatomises – in Trevor Nunn's *Othello* (1990). This is a television film, shot in a studio, so it can afford to be a much more actorly film than Parker's: there are no exteriors, no location settings; a theatrically full Shakespeare text generates the film's images while the camera concentrates on actors' bodies in their domestic relationships. I refer to it because this is the one *Othello* where the women's stories get fully told. Imogen Stubbs's girlish, impulsive, incandescent Desdemona is set against Wanamaker's watchful, damaged Emilia, the veteran military wife who, woken in the middle of the night and told she's to accompany a woman she doesn't know to the ends of the earth, packs her bags. Handing over the handkerchief, she is attempting, pathetically, to buy momentary approval from her sadistic husband, wearily opening up the black hole that is her marriage: 'I nothing, but to please his fantasy.' Her nuanced playing, especially here and in Act 4 scene 3, the 'willow' scene, where the women share contraband – a box of chocolates locked in the one drawer Othello couldn't open when he ransacked the room – and gossip – more contraband: 'O, these men, these men!' – establishes Emilia as one of Shakespeare's great tragic roles. When, roaring, Wanamaker defies Othello – 'Do thy worst!' – and breaks free of her collusion with Iago's lies – 'Perchance, Iago, I will ne'er go home' – the voice Emilia acquires seems to be the voice of women's history. Here is a role that claims the agency that eludes Ophelia, Gertrude, Desdemona.

As one of Shakespeare's latest film collaborators, Baz Luhrmann might be read as taking the notion this chapter started with to its meta-filmic limit: in *William Shakespeare's Romeo + Juliet* (1996) 'looking' is a master metaphor whose conventional economies he knowingly constructs and anarchically deconstructs. There are classic 'Hollywood' shots in this film that could come straight from Bogart and Bergman; others spoof the tradition and look like MTV send-ups. But Luhrmann begins and ends by reversing the metaphor: this is a film which seems to be looking at us.

Luhrmann puts *Romeo + Juliet* in a postmodern cityscape (Mexico City's cathedral is set in downtown Los Angeles; the cops' chopper swoops through Miami), a world saturated with Shakespeare but also with his women: the pool hall on Verona Beach is called The Globe; Montague construction is 'retail'd to posterity'; Capulet oil will 'add more fuel to your fire'. 'Gloria' Capulet is also Cleopatra, and Juliet, when she first appears, underwater, is Ophelia; in her wings, she's a teen angel but also one of Titania's fairies; in her convent school uniform, Isabella. In this Verona, media culture *is* culture: images (enhanced, manipulated, accelerated, spliced; from photographs, newspapers, film footage) construct a pastiche reality; people watch television even on the beach and actions are immediately converted from life to film, replayed as media events. No one lives in 'real' time. The tragedy of the 'star cross'd lovers' is already retrospective, an item on the nine o'clock news, where the (female) news presenter, framed inside a television screen, looks out at us and delivers the Prologue as reportage.[24]

This is a fragmenting world of conspicuous wealth, kitsch consumption, urban dereliction, ubiquitous violence and nostalgia: the beach is an *ubi sunt* location, with its abandoned Sycamore Grove bandstand staring out to sea, its tawdry ferris wheel, its carnival-colony of down-and-out boardwalk entertainers. 'The boys' own the streets and speak Shakespeare like some crazy gang-rap; Juliet is the film's still centre: her precise 'I'll look to like, if looking liking move' exasperates her pill-popping *Dallas* socialite mother who, on speeded-up film, is whipped into her Cleopatra costume like a cartoon character. Juliet is such a square! But she's also sane. Her element is water (against the conflagration on the streets), and Romeo surfaces from his Ecstasy trip – 'Queen Mab' here is slang for class-A drugs – to fall in love with her through a wall of floating angelfish.

Luhrmann's women do not repair, rather they register, postmodern fragmentation. Gloria Capulet first appears on screen as a gaping, lipsticked mouth; the Nurse presents a screen-filling bottom; convent girls are black-stockinged legs; a car hostage, her handbag; Juliet, a face, and eyes. These images play off popculture's self-assured feminist inversions: fashion is grunge and glamour, iconoclastic parody (so Gloria, grotesque in her stocking cap before her Cleopatra wig is yanked on). And Luhrmann parodies the script's great moments: Romeo leaps on to the balcony as 'light through yonder window breaks' to find he's staring at the Nurse; Juliet enters by the lift, beside his dangling feet. 'Dead', she wakes on her high altar of flowers and candles in the kitsched-up cathedral, reaches out and touches Romeo, whose hand, holding the phial, is at his lips. He looks, gasps – and knocks back the poison.

The camera leaves this scene when Juliet blows her brains out: cutting away to Christ's point of view on the altar, then craning higher and higher to regard this scene as a feast of light, then cutting to out-takes that reprise the lovers' history before returning to a low-angle shot that surrounds them in star-burst patterns of candlelight, recalling the fireworks at the Capulets' ball. Fire dissolves into water: once again, Romeo and Juliet are falling into the swimming pool, kissing, bubbles rushing around them. The image freezes. But just as the woman's body, for Luhrmann, does not figure societal integration or repair, so the death of the beautiful woman is neither redemptive nor a glorious apotheosis: Luhrmann cuts to grainy, low-resolution film footage as TV cameras watch bodybags loaded into an ambulance. The studio presenter ends the news; the screen resolves to snow.[25]

What Luhrmann gives us is a film that foregrounds looking, not just in the conceit of watching-the-news that frames the tragedy or in the dazzling manipulation of film technology that simultaneously constructs and deconstructs the story, but in the multiplication of spectator positions. This is a film that watches watchers, frequently children, literally 'innocent bystanders', mute onlookers to these events: grubby chicano children, fingers clutching a chain-link fence, a little girl looking out from a caravan window. Blank-faced, they monitor our looking, ask questions about how we look, how we react, how we relate to the images we're seeing. But while these mutes are eloquent in Luhrmann, they remain marginal.

In *Titus* (1999), Julie Taymor makes the silent 'extra' central. The film's opening sequence, an extra-textual riff proleptic of things to come, establishes a boy's own world where violence has been naturalised to domestic interiors. An eight-year-old kid, home alone, sits at a 1950s American kitchen table that's covered with after-school food and toys, a miniature military arsenal in plastic: tanks and aeroplanes, gladiators, GI Joes, futuristic robots. The scene frames a continuity between history, consumption, violence and play. When play tips into frenzy and the child begins trashing the table, he triggers (somehow) apocalypse: a huge explosion. A protector – or abductor – dressed bizarrely like a last-century circus strongman, drags him from hiding, carries him down burning stairs, through a door – and into the past, a Roman coliseum where his toys are not just life-sized, but on the move, and where he's been captured to play young Lucius, Titus Andronicus's grandson, and to watch, in silence, the appalling family history – Rome's history – that ensues.[26]

This is a play about masculinity, about warriors, politicians, fathers, brothers: the twenty-five sons of Titus Andronicus, twenty-one of them corpses; the two sons of the dead Caesar, competing for empery; the captive sons of the vanquished Goths, marked for sacrifice; the senators and men of Rome, trying to make the best of things. The first ten minutes of Taymor's film focus almost exclusively on male bodies: mud-daubed, helmeted, like clock-work toys in triumphal procession; wounded, amputated, like monumental statues brought back to life in the baths as water pours over them; obsolete, their tomb-swaddled bodies shoved into wall vaults as if into bread ovens; their empty boots, lined up as if on parade, ritually strewn with sand. The only two women who figure in Titus's Rome anchor either end of the city's self-regarding value system – civilisation/anarchy, culture/barbarism, city/wilderness, chastity/impudence. They're Beauty and the Beast, whose bodies, functioning as metonyms, as 'dream-images of the collective' (to wrench Walter Benjamin's term from a very different context[27]), bear the brunt – symbolically, actually – of the extravagant violence released in this film.

When she first appears, Tamora (Jessica Lange) looks like a wild animal; Lavinia (Laura Fraser), like Grace Kelly stepped out of some futurist issue of *Vogue*. Presented to the emperor as a war-trophy, the captive Goth, scrubbed up and powerfully sensuous, is an exotic primitive, curiously tattooed, in a solid gold bustier and gold-tipped corn-row plaits. Promoted to trophy-wife, she gains a body double, the massive inflatable sex toy – big-boobed, glaze-eyed, pucker-mouthed – that floats languidly on the indoor pool while the wedding orgy seethes. In the forest in red jodhpurs she spreads her legs to Aaron – offering a 'dark hole' that tropes the dark pit the Moor has dug nearby for Titus's sons. In the revenge fantasy she plays to grief-maddened Titus, she bristles with daggers. At the reconciliation lunch, she tucks daintily into the slab of rare-cooked pie Titus slams onto her plate. Tamora, in Taymor, is the monstrous mother, playing nurse to her hysteric epicene husband, romping with her glam-rock Clockwork Orange sons, producing a 'devil' baby, and finally, in a monstrous gastronomic parody of civility, consuming her own issue – Titus's banquet wittily arranging the literalisation of metaphor, Tamora's womb ultimately her children's tomb.

She epitomises perverse nurture, and Lavinia, in Taymor, perverse culture: for Lavinia (fragile in silk against her brother's armour, a Roman doll), is male property, the object of male custom, male rivalry, male violence – first, the idealised object, then trashed. Raped, she's a monstrous joke. Seen in long-shot, stripped to her petticoat, she stands on a stump in a blighted swamp. Up close, her lopped wrists sprout dry sticks instead of hands. She's a macabre toy – and Chiron and Demetrius laugh dementedly, mooning at their life-sized play-thing. (Later, in the 'penny arcade' sequence that recalls the rape and mutilation, she's Marilyn Monroe in that iconic movie still from *The Seven Year Itch*, holding her skirts down as her assailants, turned to tigers, lunge and slash at her.[28]) But returned home, she's a thing that forces Titus to suffer and to re-think Rome, a mangled 'map of woe' inscribed with Tamora's maternal revenge, the excessive product of the original barbarism, the 'cruel, irreligious piety' practised by 'civilised' Rome – the human sacrifice of Tamora's son.

Throughout, Taymor situates the Boy as witness, indeed, films the story through his eyes. An apprentice to male violence, inducted to its practices, he's nevertheless not yet a man, still something of a girl – and as beautiful as Mercutio in Luhrmann. (Like Luhrmann, Taymor sees the androgynous male body as a kind of 'space between' where culture rehearses different gender scenarios that offer human history 'saving' alternatives.) As the child's looking registers, blow by blow, the dismemberment of his family, so his action works to repair the damage. In one hauntingly poetic sequence, the Boy finds in a woodworker's shop which specialises in restoring church ornaments – broken madonnas, disciples, pilgrims, angels – a pair of open, carved hands to give Lavinia. And in the film's final sequence, the 'captured' Boy captures Aaron's doomed baby, carrying him out of the coliseum killing-field – where 'history' lies wasted. As the camera follows their long exit – a reprise of the film's opening – what spectators are left with is the face of Aaron's baby looking back. Challenging our looking, Taymor's ending reframes the citation I began with – 'Here's lookin' at you kid'.

But it challenges us, too, to re-think our spectator positions – on this film, on its histories, and on ours. Because when we look at the movies, we look at ourselves.

NOTES

1 Mary Pickford, *Sunshine and Shadow* (London, 1956), esp. pp. 311–12. Her husband was Douglas Fairbanks. See also Barbara Hodgdon, 'Katherina Bound; *or*, Play(K)ating the Strictures of Everyday Life', in *The Shakespeare Trade. Performances and Appropriations* (Philadelphia, 1998), pp. 12–15.

2 Peter Holland, 'Two Dimensional Shakespeare: *King Lear* on Film', in Anthony Davies and Stanley Wells, eds., *Shakespeare and the Moving Image* (Cambridge, 1994), p. 64.

3 Quoted in Jack J. Jorgens, *Shakespeare on Film* (Bloomington, IN, 1977), p. 23.

4 I am drawing on Laura Mulvey's seminal theorisation of gendered spectatorship, 'the gaze' and '*to-be-looked-at-ness*', 'Visual Pleasure and Narrative Cinema', *Screen*, 16, 3 (Autumn 1975), rpt. in Gerald Mast et al., eds., *Film Theory and Criticism* (Oxford, 1992), pp. 746–57. Mulvey's formulations have been critiqued and rethought: see particularly *The Spectatrix*, a special issue of *Camera Obscura*, 20–1 (1989).

5 For example, Ophelia in Shakespeare's playtext has six scenes; in Branagh's film, fourteen.

6 Jorgens, *Shakespeare on Film*, p. 136.

7 Laurence Olivier, *Confessions of an Actor* (London, 1982), p. 103.

8 Some of these 'effects' were forced upon the film by technical constraints. See *ibid.*, pp. 105, 104.

9 Here, as in Loncraine's *Richard III*, Anne is wooed over the body of her husband, not, as in Shakespeare's playtext, the body of her father-in-law, King Henry VI. In this wooing, Olivier breaks one scene into two, perhaps for plausibility. See Jorgens, *Shakespeare on Film*, p. 139.

10 When Anne exits, there is no further female presence in the film until she returns as a ghost.

11 But this is one of his joke deceptions. McKellen's Richard gets his sexual kicks in murder. See for example the surprise 'erection' that kills Rivers; the porn-photo voyeurism of Hastings's death; the peeping-tom garrotting of Buckingham. 'Straight' sex doesn't interest him. He approaches Anne – she's in a négligé, standing invitingly at the foot of the stairs – but only to turn off the lights and exit down the hall.

12 Loncraine's directorial background in television advertisements and commercial films is certainly in play here. See Ian McKellen, *William Shakespeare's Richard III: A Screenplay* (London, 1996), pp. 26–7.

13 For the connection between Richard and Cagney see James N. Loehlin, ' "Top of the World, Ma": *Richard III* and Cinematic Convention', in Lynda E. Boose and Richard Burt, eds., *Shakespeare the Movie. Popularising the Plays on Film, TV and Video* (London and New York, 1997), pp. 67–79.

14 *Ibid.*, pp. 74–5.

15 I am thinking here of Michael Bristol's comments on festival, violence and transgression in *Carnival and Theater* (London, 1989), where he quotes Roger Caillois from *Man and the Sacred*: 'in its pure form, the festival must be defined as the paroxysm of society . . . The paroxysm is not only its climax from a religious but also from an economic point of view. It is the occasion for the circulation of wealth . . .' (p. 34).

16 Two *King Lear*s (Brook, Kozintsev); four *Hamlet*s (Olivier, Kozintsev, Zeffirelli, Branagh); three *Othello*s (Welles, Nunn, Parker); two *Romeo and Juliet*s (Zeffirelli, Luhrmann).

17 John Styan, 'Changeable Taffeta: Shakespeare's Characters in Performance', in Philip C. McGuire and David A. Samuelson, eds., *Shakespeare: The Theatrical Dimension* (New York, 1979), pp. 136–7.

18 On Ophelias in film performance see my 'Snatched Bodies: Ophelia in the Grave', *Shakespeare Quarterly*, 49/3 (Fall 1998), 299–319.

19 For a brilliant psychoanalytic reading of this film see Peter S. Donaldson, *Shakespearean Films/Shakespearean Directors* (Boston, MA, 1990), pp. 31–67, esp. p. 34.

20 This marketing tag, used by Columbia Pictures in print advertisements for Oliver Parker's *Othello*, equally describes *Hamlet*. In a BBC Radio 3 interview in advance of the film's UK release on 14 February 1996, Branagh described the flashbacks as necessary for 'explaining' the relationship between Hamlet and Ophelia.

21 See Tony Howard, 'When Peter Met Orson', in Boose and Burt, *Shakespeare, the Movie*, p. 131, and Micheál MacLiammóir, *Put Money in Thy Purse* (London, 1976), esp. pp. 35–9, 134–6, 140–1, 225, 227.

22 Quoted in Loehlin, ' "Top of the World, Ma" ', p. 67. Profiled in the *Sunday Times* magazine before shooting began (29 May 1995), Parker commented: 'We are keen to make [*Othello*] youthful and passionate. Passion is the driving force of the whole piece. I'd call it an "erotic thriller". It will be two hours of steamy twists and turns.'

23 For me, this is the most seriously miscalculated moment of the film; alternatively, the most cynically misogynistic moment.

24 In Zeffirelli's *Romeo and Juliet* (1968) the Prologue was spoken in voice-over by the most 'authentic' voice of contemporary Shakespeare theatre – the voice, almost, of 'Shakespeare' himself: Laurence Olivier.

25 On Luhrmann's film as a 'chick flick' see Barbara Hodgdon, '*William Shakespeare's Romeo+Juliet*: "Everything's Nice in America?" ', *Shakespeare Survey*, 52 (2000), 25–6.

26 On this film see also Peter S. Donaldson, 'Game Space / Tragic Space: Julie Taymor's Titus', in Barbara Hodgdon and W. B. Worthen, eds., *A Companion to Shakespeare and Performance* (London, 2005), 457–77, and Carol Chillington Rutter, 'Looking like a Child – or – *Titus*: The Comedy', *Shakespeare Survey*, 56 (Cambridge: Cambridge University Press), 1–26.

27 Quoted in Rachel O. Moore, *Savage Theory: Cinema as Modern Magic* (Durham, 2000), p. 76.

28 *Titus* abounds in inter-filmic citation – Fellini's *La Strada*, *8½*, *Amarcord*, *Satyricon*, *Edward Scissorhands*, *Rosemary's Baby*, *The Omen*, *The Piano*, *Velvet Goldmine*, *The Silence of the Lambs* – but also quotes Jane Howells's BBC *Titus Andronicus* (1985) and Deborah Warner's 1987 RSC stage production.

15

NEIL TAYLOR

National and racial stereotypes in Shakespeare films

We all object to stereotypes. They are oversimplified preconceptions, involving those who trade in them in lazy thinking and prejudice. They don't derive from direct experience. They are subject to fashion. And they tend to come into conflict with one another. But however objectionable they may be, on intellectual or moral grounds, we can't avoid them in our own, as well as other people's, thinking.

When, in Kenneth Branagh's film of *Hamlet* (1996), the Gravedigger (Billy Crystal) remarks that in England the men are as mad as Hamlet, we laugh. Not exactly uproariously, but in the way, no doubt, that the line has raised a laugh for four hundred years. We laugh at the complexity of the dramatic irony in the situation – the Gravedigger's subject is his Prince, he is his Prince's subject, and yet here he is literally addressing his Prince on the subject. However, we also laugh at the English playwright giving the Danish character a stereotypical characterisation of the English. And if we're English we laugh, slightly awkwardly, at the joke at our expense (not sure whether or not we recognise ourselves in it, not sure whether we're particularly proud of our great English playwright's laboured handling of it). But when the actor saying the line is Billy Crystal, we laugh in a new way, too. Now the joke is not just a joke delivered by those traditional Shakespearean stereotypes the Common Man and the Clown, but a joke delivered by another set of stereotypes – the comic, the film star and the American. Even the nationality of the joke itself seems somehow to have changed a little.

But what does 'nationality' mean? It is all very well objecting to national and racial stereotypes on the grounds that nations and races are maligned by their use. But what is it that is being maligned? What is a nation and what is a race, and are we sure we know who belongs to which nation and to which race? (Are we not all ethnic-hybrids?) The nation state is a comparatively recent invention, and a 'nation' is self-evidently a human construct, subject to continuous revision as wars or changes in government redraw maps. As for 'race', in the early modern period the word was sometimes used interchangeably with 'nation' to refer to a people (e.g. the French), but usually it referred to a person's lineage (e.g. the descendants of Ham). Then, in the nineteenth century, it began to be used to mean a permanent category of humans, a type or sub-species.[1] However, as Tzvetan Todorov has pointed out, the term is scientifically useless, for 'we obtain completely divergent subdivisions of the human species according to whether we base our description of the "races" on an analysis of their epidermis or their blood types, their genetic heritages or their bone structures'.[2]

We have to recognise, therefore, that 'race', like 'nation', is a word used for the purpose of classifiying ourselves or other people and that its usage arises out of beliefs about self-identity and Otherness rather than out of scientific realities. Michael Banton has written that the question which generates all racial theories is simply 'Why are they not like us?'[3] The same question seems to arise immediately one 'nation' contemplates another.

Shakespeare was born and lived in England, and wrote plays in English which were performed in England. While some of his material is English, too – English stories, English history, English characters living in England – a lot of it, indeed the overwhelming majority, is not. The lists of his *dramatis personae* are dominated by the non-English. Of his plays, only fifteen have English settings (these figures include *Cymbeline* and *Macbeth*, which involve some scenes in England and some in other countries) while twenty-seven have non-English settings. His representations of Englishness and non-Englishness inevitably engage with Elizabethan national sterotypes.

When we turn to productions of Shakespeare, on stage or in the cinema, we are no longer dealing exclusively with Shakespeare's view of things. Actors, designers, directors, screenplay writers, producers – even audiences – they all have their own ideas and their own cultural perspectives. And Shakespeare is a global commodity, performed and read, produced and consumed around the world. He may have been English, but 79 per cent of the films of his plays have been made outside England,[4] and much of the money that has gone into the production even of those films made in England comes from non-English sources. But whoever makes the films, and whether or not the characters or setting are English, the films themselves are obliged to negotiate the fact that the plays were originally designed for consumption by the English.

One response is to try to forget that fact. The Shakespeare films of the great Japanese director, Akira Kurosawa, set out deliberately to assimilate Shakespeare into Japanese culture. For example, his *Kumonosu-djo* (1957: generally known in English as *Throne of Blood*) tries to recreate *Macbeth* through Noh. American directors cannot really take this route, since the English language binds them to at least some dimensions of Shakespeare's playtext. When Joseph Mankiewicz made his *Julius Caesar* (1953) in Hollywood with a cast of English and American actors, all of them – even Marlon Brando – tried to speak with impeccable English accents. On the other hand, when Orson Welles made his *Macbeth* (1948), despite the fact that Macbeth and his fellow-countrymen were dressed to suggest they inhabit Mongolia after the Martians have landed, Welles obliged his cast to try to speak with Scottish accents. The dialogue was pre-recorded, and the actors then mimed along while the film was shot. But the producers, Republic, were dismayed by the test screenings and would not release the film until the Scottish accent had been replaced by an American one.

Shakespeare rarely provides his foreign characters with any language other than English, and when he does it is usually to make them seem fools. The Princess of France in *Henry V* is there to be laughed at for her ignorance of English vocabulary and her unconscious propensity for a French figure, *double entendre*. A complementary English stereotype is a reluctance (at the very least) of the English to speak foreign tongues, certainly with a foreign accent. In Laurence Olivier's film of *Henry V* (1944) he (or is it Henry?) 'decimates the French language'.[5] Olivier doesn't seem to be holding up the English king for ridicule, his accent is proudly English and he clearly cannot be bothered to try to speak French properly.

Philip Edwards claims that 'The idea of "Britain" was one of the major enthusiasms of Englishmen',[6] but G. K. Hunter describes the English Elizabethans as looking on the Irish, the Welsh and the Scots as 'absurd deviations from an English norm'.[7] Indeed, Shakespeare seems to be mocking Fluellen, Jamie and MacMorris in *Henry V* for their inability to speak English the way the English regard as properly – a stereotyping preserved in Olivier's film, where their accents and, to some extent, dialects are emphasised for comic effect.[8]

However much financial constraints encourage them to shoot in studios, the naturalistic conventions of film encourage directors to shoot on location. Ian McKellen has explained that the production designer on Richard Loncraine's *Richard III* (1996) automatically started out planning to use an English stately home as the opening set.[9] He then changed his mind but, even though some of them are unconventional choices, he shot later scenes in such emphatically English locations as Strawberry Hill House, Lambeth Bridge, St Pancras Chambers and Battersea Power Station. In the making of Olivier's *Henry V*, the war inhibited his ability to shoot on location in such 'Heritage' space, so England was characterised by a model of London, a studio mock-up of the Globe Theatre and an interruption in play for rain. Over there in France the weather was beautiful. When Peter Hall made his *A Midsummer Night's Dream* (1968), he ignored the fact that Shakespeare's play is set in Greece, and moved it to England (in and around an English country house called 'Athens') because it is 'quite clearly a play about an English summer in which the seasons have gone wrong. It is winter when it should be summer; everywhere is wet and muddy. This is described by Titania in a central speech. This is why I shot so much of the film in the rain, during a bad-weather period lasting about six weeks.'[10]

Kenneth Branagh's *Henry V* (1989) challenges this and other stereotypes of Britishness. Now, rather than standing out in the open landscape of France amidst bright sunshine, proudly bearing the respective emblems of their different countries, the non-English British crouch in the dark of the trenches amidst torrential rain and, while Ian Holm's uncannily unmuddied Welshman creates a kind of comedy, the accents of the muddy Scots and Irish and their differences from him and each other are suppressed. Similarly, in the last scenes Branagh's Henry struggles with French when he woos Katherine, but it isn't his accent or knowledge that are at fault, it's just that he's out of practice – give him time and he'll be fluent.

But however much Branagh's Shakespeare films may challenge certain stereotypes, Britishness is alive and kicking. In Sarah Street's analysis, the revival of British cinema in the early 1980s was characterised by nostalgic period films drawing on classic literature about upper-class life, precise and loving photography of sites of national heritage, and a focus on male rivalry and bonding.[11] That sounds a reasonable description of *Henry V* (where the Chorus paces the white cliffs of Dover[12] and the band of brothers bond with their king). For all that it was shot on location in Tuscany against scenes of Italian heritage, it will do well enough for *Much Ado About Nothing* (1993) too. And as for Branagh's *In the Bleak Midwinter* (1995), a lightweight comedy about some actors mounting a production of *Hamlet* on a shoestring, it is more about Ealing comedy Britishness than it is about Shakespeare's play.

Branagh's own subsequent *Hamlet* was heavily marketed for its British associations. While his then wife, Emma Thompson, was picking up plaudits, dollars and even Oscars, for classic Britishness films like *The Remains of the Day* (1993) and Jane Austen's *Sense and Sensibility* (1995), *Hamlet*'s trailers and credits emphasised the British names in its cast – names which included Ken Dodd as Yorick, Sir John Gielgud as Priam, Sir John Mills as the King of Norway, Lord Attenborough as the English ambassador and the Duke of Marlborough as Fortinbras's General! (Shepperton Studios may not have been recognisable as the setting of the interior shots of Elsinore, but American tourists would surely recognise the Castle's exterior as being the Duke of Marlborough's seat, Blenheim Palace.)

At the same time, Branagh manages to assemble international 'names', particularly Americans. Just as the non-British English-speaking film industry has always had to cope with Shakespeare's Englishness, the British film industry has always had to cope with the dominance of Hollywood in the industry as a whole. John Collick has described how, in the early years of cinema 'Many English officials felt that the movie industry of the United States, seemingly obsessed with criminal life, violence and unholy passions, undermined the influence of traditional English values throughout the colonies.'[13] The Americans responded by making films of Shakespeare, which enabled them to claim that they were producing instructive and improving material. The British responded in turn with their own Shakespeare films, an indigenous high-art product to boost British claims to be resisting Americanism.

The British may not have seen off the American film industry in those early skirmishes, but the cultural war was not lost. Even in as recent a film as *Looking for Richard* (1996), Al Pacino is complaining that the problem with being an American in Shakespeare is a feeling of inferiority 'to the way it has been done by the British'. Pacino goes on to interview Sir John Gielgud, who patronisingly explains that American actors are at a disadvantage in comparison with British actors when it comes to playing Shakespeare because they lack a feeling for the Elizabethan period: 'Perhaps they don't go to picture galleries and read books as much as we do.'

The world is divided stereotypically into Us and Them. But there are different kinds of Them. In his classic essay on 'Elizabethans and Foreigners', G. K. Hunter mapped out the two sets of stereotypes informing all Elizabethan attitudes to foreigners.[14] The medieval world which they inherited was divided into the Christian world and the non-Christian world: the further you got from the Holy Land, the more pagan and the less fully human were the people you came across. But the Reformation had ensured that Elizabethans also divided the world into England and the Rest. (This meant that there was an automatic ambiguity built into that section of the world which was inhabited by the Christian Rest, e.g. Italy.)

Shakespeare's foreigners can be divided into those who are close enough to provide a threat, and those who are harmlessly remote. The French fall into the first camp, the ancient Romans into the second and the Italians occupy an ambiguous territory between. But once we turn to the film industry the picture complicates: the threat for twentieth-century Britons comes not from the French, but from the Germans, the Russians and the Americans. So one set of national stereotypes is pretty well bound to interfere with the other. At the same time, the Germans, the Russians and the Americans are themselves making films of Shakespeare.

For representations of the French, the obvious text is *Henry V*. Raymond Durgnat's allegorical reading of Olivier's film was that 'Agincourt is D-Day, where the French are the Germans, until Henry courts Katherine, whereupon the French are probably the French',[15] while Jack Jorgens saw in 'the killing of the boys in the English camp . . . the Nazi slaughter of the Jews'.[16] However, a note written by an official to the French Foreign Minister, Georges Bidault, in September 1947, objected to the stereotyping of the French: with 'Shakespearean violence and cruelty' the film seemed to portray the moral faults and weaknesses of the French knights – 'their lack of restraint, their heedlessness, their inability to bother themselves with what matters' – as if these were 'the permanent traits of our character'.[17]

In the late 1980s and early 1990s, a period in British history when the 'real' enemy might be said to have been the Argentinians, Iranians or Iraqis, the stereotype of the enemy still seemed to be the Germans. Branagh's *Henry V* treats the ostensible enemy, the French, with no less seriousness than the British, but the battle of Harfleur is being fought in the trenches of World War I. And in Loncraine's *Richard III*, while stereotypical 1930s English aristocrats and royals jostle with American interlopers (Annette Bening as a kind of Mrs Simpson), Ian McKellen is got up to look like Hitler and addresses his people at what feels like a Nuremberg Rally.

Films of Shakespeare's Roman plays have inevitably been affected by the Hollywood biblical and classical epic, which ultimately derives from the nineteenth-century theatrical tradition of solemn, stirring grandeur, with large casts and large-scale stage spectacle. Epic tends to mean expensive, and in his *Julius Caesar* Mankiewicz was obliged to keep costs down by shooting in black and white and using scenery and costumes from the recently-released *Quo Vadis?* (1951). Directors who challenge the epic Roman stereotype can fall foul of their audiences. Samuel Crowl complains of Charlton Heston's *Antony and Cleopatra* (1972) that it domesticates Cleopatra and the lifestyle of her palace which, 'complete with a coffee table containing a miniature pool filled with gold fish and model ships, is imagined as a version of tasteless Hollywood opulence'.[18] Jack Jorgens seems approving when he finds in Mankiewicz's *Julius Caesar* that 'The night storm scene in the square, echoing the dark, rain-slicked streets and menacing shadows of *film noir*, establishes a sinister atmosphere and evokes Hollywood gangster films', but then protests that the battle at Philippi 'unfortunately resembles a stock Indian ambush'.[19]

Meanwhile, like the French the Romans can sometimes turn out to be other nationalities in disguise. Even in Mankiewicz's *Julius Caesar*, according to producer John Houseman, 'we were prepared to evoke . . . Hitler at Nuremberg . . . Mussolini on his balcony'.[20] They genuinely believed that black and white would also evoke the audience's experience of contemporary political events as communicated by newspaper photographs, cinema news reels and television. Thus, the medium and the director's style can operate as a stereotype-trigger: Samuel Crowl wonders if Mankiewicz is processing American political anxieties about an internal enemy, the threat to the film industry posed by Senator Joe McCarthy.[21] One is reminded of the allegorical uses to which Shakespeare was put in Eastern Europe and the USSR under communism, a tradition reflected in Grigori Kozintsev's film of *Hamlet* (1964), where Claudius's court is used to evoke the oppressive tyranny of Stalinism.

Shakespeare's two plays with a Venetian setting, *The Merchant of Venice* and *Othello, the Moor of Venice*, occupy the ambiguous territory of the Christian Rest. But their central characters are obliged, by virtue of their racial identities, to fulfil Elizabethan stereotypes of the Other – the Jew and the Moor. As G. K. Hunter explains, in *The Merchant of Venice* Shakespeare 'focuses his Venice . . . not by pointing it back to England, but by pointing it out to the remoter world of "blaspheming Jews", whose non-Christianity, like that of pagans, infidels, Moors, and Turks gave depth of meaning to "foreignness" that mere difference of European race could hardly do'.[22]

'Shylock', so John Gross asserts, 'would not have held the stage for four hundred years if he were a mere stereotype.'[23] But Marlowe's Jew of Malta is a grotesque with a bottle-nose (3.3.10) and the stage history of Shylock reveals the persistence of the same stereotyping, however much individual actors have resisted it. Edmund Kean's decision to wear a black, rather than red, wig was a deliberate attempt to break for the first time with the traditional representation of Shylock as an equivalent to the Judas of medieval drama. Even in the 1930s, according to Pierre Solin, the conventional representation of Jews in the French cinema involved large noses, fawning behaviour, clumsy hopping around and Germanic accents,[24] and when he appeared in Jonathan Miller's stage production of *The Merchant of Venice* (1970, later filmed for television in 1973), despite Kean and all those actors, including Henry Irving, who had attempted to humanise and dignify Shylock over the years, Laurence Olivier felt he had to fight against the same stereotype: 'I was determined to maintain dignity and not stoop physically and mentally to Victorian villainy. Not for me the long, matted hair, invariably red, the hooked nose and the bent back.'[25]

The invention of cinema did little to modify the stage stereotype of Shylock. In Gerolamo Lo Savio's Italian silent *Il Mercante di Venezia* (1910), a bearded Ermetti Novelli grins, curtsies, fawns and bobs. Henri Desfontaines's *Shylock* (France, 1913) begins with a preliminary sequence in which Harry Baur in white tie and tails is transformed by means of a dissolve into a bearded Shylock, with a large wallet at his waist, clowning to the camera. In the street, and later in the courtroom, he is pushed and poked, laughed and jeered at and reviled by the Venetian citizenry – he gesticulates and scowls in retaliation. Seated on cushions on the floor, he has a sensual, almost sexual, relationship with his money bags, caressing them with his cheek. He kisses the hands and robes of the Christians, and grovels to them, and when thwarted he creeps on the floor. A contemporary reviewer complained that Baur had 'gone back to earlier traditions for his impersonation of Shylock, reviving memories of the time when the Jew was regarded more or less as an object of ridicule and mirth rather than sympathy'.[26]

The Jew of Mestri (Germany, 1923), Peter Paul Felner's adaptation of *The Merchant of Venice*, starred Werner Krauss as Mordecai (Shylock). Krauss is impressive and dignified early on, and his hatred of Christians is understandably fuelled by a scene in which they drive his wife to her death. The film closes with a scene designed, at least to an extent, to command sympathy: after a subtitle, 'Desolation', the camera lingers in close-up on Mordecai's wild staring eyes and open mouth, then the eyes shut and there is a fade. But in court, sharpening his knife on his boot, Krauss plays histrionically to the crowd in triumphalist mode, milking the situation through an incredibly long build-up to plunging the knife into Antonio's breast. Krauss later appeared as all the Jews except Süss in the Nazi propaganda film *Jew Süss* (1940), and then re-emerged on stage as Shylock in a production at the Burgtheater in Vienna by the Nazi, Lothar Muthel.[27] In 1943, the Nazis tortured the Jewish Harry Baur to death.

Michael Radford's *The Merchant of Venice* (2004) attempts a serious engagement with many of the cultural issues raised by the play, and successfully embeds Al Pacino's sobering, naturalistic portrayal of Shylock's ordeal in a city poisoned by ethnic division and shamed by the presence of the Ghetto. Within the Antonio plot, Gobbo grotesquery is effectively erased in the interests of unity of feeling; unfortunately, once Radford turns to Belmont and the casket plot, he also turns to old-style comic racial stereotyping of the Prince of Morocco.

Most, but not all Moors on the Elizabethan stage were villains, and Hunter argues that *Othello* is 'the most magnificent specimen of the dramatic "inversion of racial values" '.[28] Even so, as John Gillies points out,

> all Shakespearean Moors combine a generic exoticism or exteriority with an inherent transgressiveness . . . all are imagined in terms of polluting sexual contact with European partners [he cites Aaron, Morocco, Gobbo's Moor, Othello, Cleopatra, Claribel's Ethiope of Tunis, all conceived as being involved in miscegenation] . . . None has any real existence independent of their transgressiveness of those margins (geographic and marital) whose purpose it is to exclude them.[29]

They have, in other words, an in-built 'structural' stereotypicality, a threat to society which is ultimately sexual.

Any production of *Othello* automatically raises the issue of casting by stereotype: will the actor who plays Othello be black or white? Werner Krauss was angered by the opinion of Max Reinhardt (himself Jewish) that Shylock could not be played empathetically by a non-Jew. But the ethnic origins of the actor playing Shylock have never seemed as significant as the colour of the actor playing Othello – or, indeed, any black character in any film. When, for example, a black character is represented by a white actor or a white company or production team, the black spectator may well be caught between an automatic *identification* with that black character and an *alienation* from the particular representation of black identity and experience. The US opening of Steven Spielberg's *The Color Purple* (1985), a white man's film of a black author's text, was boycotted by the National Association for the Advancement of Colored People even though most of the cast and crew were black or third-world people.[30]

Although there were black Othellos on the American stage before Paul Robeson appeared in a 1943 New York production (and Robeson had himself played Othello in London in 1930), the overwhelming majority of stage Othellos have been played by white actors. Indeed, it was 8 July 1958 before a black actor, Edric Connor, appeared in Shakespeare at Stratford-upon-Avon, and then it was to sing (Gower in *Pericles*). Even when Elizabeth Welch appears in Derek Jarman's film of *The Tempest* (1979), it is only as a cabaret turn, singing 'Stormy Weather'.

In silent films, black actors were restricted to stereotypes established by D. W. Griffith, such as 'the ghost-frightened eye-rolling teeth-clattering "coon"'.[31] Manthia Diawara has described his *The Birth of a Nation* (1915), as 'grammar book for Hollywood's . . . obsession with miscegenation, and its fixing of Black people within certain spaces, such as kitchens, and in certain supporting roles, such as criminals'.[32] We think of film as a naturalistic medium but in the silent era it was entirely acceptable to have black actors acting alongside blacked-up actors. In *The Birth of a Nation*, the black rapist was played by a white actor, because he had to touch Lillian Gish, and thirteen years later Topsy in *Uncle Tom's Cabin* (1928) was played by the white Rosetta Duncan in blackface alongside the black Noble Johnson as Tom.

It is no surprise, therefore, that as recently as 1952 and 1965 Orson Welles and Laurence Olivier should have been appearing in films of *Othello* in blackface. Indeed, up until the 1980s, any white Shakespearean stage actor would normally have aspired to play the part. But now, blackface no longer convinces. The mask has ceased to be a convention and become an outrage. Laurence Olivier strove 'to be black . . . to look out from a black man's world' but racial stereotyping contaminates the whole enterprise. First, his director, John Dexter, was telling him to be a 'pompous, word-spinning, arrogant black general'[33] (surely the word 'black' is redundant?). Then, his own conception of 'being black' required him to 'be beautiful', to develop a deep sensuous voice ('dark violet – velvet stuff'), to speak with an accent and to walk 'like a soft black leopard'.[34] Finally, despite Olivier's own disappointment in what he achieved in Stuart Burge's later film,[35] Jack Jorgens could praise it for reeking of the magnificence of the stage – but add the racist qualification, 'despite a West Indian veneer'.[36]

Similar conflicts inform other *Othellos* where the main actor is white – for example, Dmitiri Buchowetski's silent version with the English title of *The Moor* (Germany, 1922), and the much stronger *Othello* directed by Sergei Yutkevich (1955). An opening subtitle of Buchowetski's film describes Othello (Emil Jannings) as 'intellectual, tender, lofty; warlike, heroic, impetuous'. It soon turns out that these are not the expected qualities of a black man but derive from his unusual parentage, an Egyptian prince and a Spanish princess – his blood is 'as fair as hers'. For all that, Jannings plays him as (in René Clair's opinion) 'a stupid child'.[37] Only when he is still and in close-up can he be taken seriously. Otherwise he is a ponderous, overweight, waddling clown: at one point, tossing and turning in his sleep because of dreams of Cassio and Desdemona together, he falls out of bed and on to the floor; at another, he stuffs the handkerchief in his mouth and tears it to shreds with his teeth. Yutkevich's good-looking film is organised, in Anthony Davies's opinion, around Othello's trust in Iago. Because that trust is part of his faith in mankind, his discovery of Iago's treachery is the climax of the tragedy.[38] This is encapsulated in the moment when Othello (Sergei Bondarchuk) asks quietly 'Are there no stones in heaven but what serve for the thunder?' When he exclaims, 'O precious villain', the camera zooms in to concentrate in extreme close-up on his huge goggle eyes – violently white not only against the black (black-face) face but highlighted by a narrow shaft of light – and the Moor is suddenly transformed into the stereotypical stupid negro from the earliest days of film.

Of the blackface film Othellos, Orson Welles is the most resistant to stereo-type and the most at ease with the camera and the role. But since the 1980s and 1990s, black actors have regularly played black roles, and while the stereotyping of the black man as, for example, the agent of miscegenation is still present in Shakespeare's storyline, the removal of the blackface mask seems like an act of liberation. Laurence Fishburne, who plays Othello in Oliver Parker's film (1995), seems to operate almost literally as himself, a black man who has succeeded in a world which is not only competitive but structurally opposed to his success. What was once a taboo against the representation of the physical relationship between a black man and a white woman is broken by Parker's decision to show Othello and Desdemona consummating their marriage. This, along with Fishburne's own image as Hollywood star, reinforces what Jacqui Jones believes is the mainstream film stereotype of the black male as a sexual being while chal-lenging the stereotype that the black male is merely a sexual being.[39] In the film's final scene Fishburne's cool withheldness moves convincingly into suffering, and there is a mutuality in the relationship which he and Desdemona establish as, while she still caresses him and he weeps, he kills first her and then himself.

Tim Blake Nelson's film entitled O (2000) is an intelligent and compelling adap-tation of Othello set in an all-white prep school in South Carolina, where a lone black student, Odin James, has been recruited to be the star of the basketball team. 'O' is for Odin, 'O' is also for Other, but 'OJ' inevitably recalls a star from the class of, 94. The film cleverly sophisticates the play's racial stereotyping by (a) invoking conflicting media stereotypes in its portrait of O (Mekhi Phifer) as a black sports star who is young, cool and winning, but who nevertheless has drugs in his history and a capacity for sudden violence; and (b) O and his white girlfriend Desi (Julia Stiles, star of those other Shakespearean teen-flicks, *10 Things I Hate About You* and *Hamlet*) discussing the politics of political correctness. Ironically, at the time of its intended release in 1999, the school setting allowed a new kind of stereotyping to override issues of race. And this revealed the fact that the film is not ultimately organised around O – nor even the intrigue initiated and partly controlled by the Iago figure, Hugo (Josh Hartnett). It is presented as the story of Hugo himself. His voice-over narration introduces, occasionally comments on, and finally closes the action; it is his face we watch as his schoolmates die around him, and the closing shots are of his removal from school under police escort. The film's release was delayed for almost two years because of the intensity of the media coverage of Columbine and its threat to a nation's self-stereotype.

Thirty years earlier, Liz White's film of *Othello* (USA, made 1962–6, first shown 1980) not only had an all black cast and production team but, as described and analysed by Peter Donaldson in his book *Shakespearean Films/Shakespearean Directors*, rejected the racial stereotypes which the play traditionally evokes. It eliminated all white characters: Othello is African, the 'Venetians' are lighter-skinned black New Yorkers and Iago is an American black servant whose self-alienation is not understood by an affectionate but paternalistic Othello. The murder of Desdemona is shot in dim blue light, which has the effect, in Donaldson's opinion, of making us aware that the image of 'the featureless black devil or racist projection' is a stereotype, the consequence of 'a skewed vision'.[40]

It has now become possible, on stage and on film, to cut across racial and national stereotypes almost at will. In November 1997 Jude Kelly's stage production at the Lansburgh Theatre, Washington D.C., departed from the conventional *Othello* by casting black actors in most of the white roles but a white actor (Patrick Stewart) as Othello. The text was unchanged, so Othello was referred to as being black despite being patently white.[41]

In Kenneth Branagh's *Hamlet* the first actor on screen is black (Ray Fearon, playing Francisco) and his *Much Ado About Nothing* has a black, American Hollywood star (Denzil Washington) as Don Pedro. Here is a statement about colour blindness, but it is also an attempt to move into a world where, if there are stereotypes, they are neither national nor racial. The published screenplay reads 'DON PEDRO and his men. Riding through a mist of dust and heat haze, they look like a combination of Omar Sharif riding into *Lawrence of Arabia* and *The Magnificent Seven*.'[42] Branagh explains 'I was determined . . . not to cast only British actors . . . this film would be seen mostly by people coming fresh to Shakespeare in movie form. Different accents, different looks. An excitement borne out of complementary styles and approaches would produce a Shakespeare film that belonged to the world.'[43]

Baz Luhrmann would seem to share that vision. His version of *William Shakespeare's Romeo + Juliet* (1996), like Robert Wise and Jerome Robbins's *West Side Story* (1961), actually introduces national and racial stereotypes where there were none before – the Capulets and Montagues are racially distinct 'households' in the Cuban-American community of 'Verona Beach', and Mercutio is a black drug-peddler. But Luhrmann's directorial style mimics the TV commercial and pop-video. The camera is always frenetically on the move and there is much use of fade-in, fade-out, zoom-in, zoom-out, along with intercut or superimposed written phrases, and a full pop music score. The most striking feature is the bewilderingly rapid cutting between shots: over the film as a whole the average length of a shot is only 3.1 seconds, and in Act 1 scene 1 it is down to 1.8!

Romeo + Juliet is best read as multi-ethnic and supra-national, not because the corporate bodies (Montagues and Capulets) are multi-nationals – that's left unstated – but because the world of MTV is global. Luhrmann's film is wittily self-aware of the interconnectedness of the wealth of media-discourses involved in its production, publication and promotion. What was once a theatre piece has now become a film to be seen in a cinema, on television or, most likely of all, on video. The Chorus is a newscaster on a television screen, and Luhrmann's *mise-en-scène* involves his actors in working round and within, and bringing back into play, a redundant piece of architecture stranded on the beach at Verona Beach – a large proscenium arch, left over from a derelict theatre or cinema called The Globe.

NOTES

1 Michael Banton, *Racial Theories* (1987; second edn, Cambridge, 1998), p. 6.
2 Tzvetan Todorov, ' "Race", Writing and Culture' in Henry Louis Gates, Jr., ed., *'Race,' Writing and Difference* (Chicago, 1985), pp. 370–1, quoted by James R. Andreas, 'Othello's African American progeny', in Ivo Kamps, ed., *Materialist Shakespeare: A History* (London, 1995), p. 195.
3 Banton, *Racial Theories* p. 233.
4 Kenneth S. Rothwell and Annabelle Henkin Melzer, eds., *Shakespeare on Screen: an International Filmography and Videography* (London, 1990), updated with my own information, together reveal that 28 have been made in Britain (the concept of 'English' is hard to maintain at this level!) while 132 have been made outside Britain.
5 Jack J. Jorgens, *Shakespeare on Film* (Bloomington, IN, 1977), p. 130.
6 Philip Edwards, *Threshold of a Nation: a Study in English and Irish Drama* (Cambridge, 1979), p. 74.
7 G. K. Hunter, 'Elizabethans and Foreigners', first published in *Shakespeare Survey*, 17 (1964), reprinted in *Dramatic Identities and Cultural Tradition* (Liverpool, 1978), pp. 3–30, p. 18.
8 It must be admitted that there is a little comedy in Michael Shepley's bluff, slightly dim, public school Gower.
9 Ian McKellen, *William Shakespeare's Richard III* (London, 1996), p. 44.
10 Peter Hall, quoted in Roger Manvell, *Shakespeare and the Film* (New York, 1971), p. 123.
11 Sarah Street, *British National Cinema* (London, 1997), p. 103.
12 Or, rather, Beachy Head. For a discussion of the significance of this setting, see Graham Holderness, ' "What ish my nation": Shakespeare and National Identities', in Ivo Kamps, ed., *Materialist Shakespeare*, pp. 218–38.

13 John Collick, *Shakespeare, Cinema and Society* (Manchester and New York, 1989), p. 39.

14 Hunter, 'Elizabethans and Foreigners', esp. pp. 13–30.

15 Raymond Durgnat, *Films and Feelings* (Cambridge, MA, 1971), p. 261, quoted in Jorgens, *Shakespeare on Film*, p. 126.

16 Jorgens, *Shakespeare on Film*, p. 126.

17 John W. Young, 'Henry V, the Quai d'Orsay, and the Well-being of the Franco-British Alliance, 1947', *Historical Journal of Film, Radio and Television*, 7, 3 (1987), 319–21; p. 320.

18 Samuel Crowl, 'A World Elsewhere: the Roman Plays on Film and Television', in Anthony Davies and Stanley Wells, eds., *Shakespeare and the Moving Image* (Cambridge, 1994), pp. 146–62; p. 159.

19 Jorgens, *Shakespeare on Film*, pp. 102, 105.

20 *Ibid.*, p. 96, citing John Houseman, quoted in Roy Walker, 'Look upon Caesar', *Twentieth Century*, 154 (1953), 472; the same ideas are recorded in Houseman's *Unfinished Business: Memoirs 1902–1988* (New York, 1989), p. 324.

21 Crowl, 'A World Elsewhere', p. 149.

22 Hunter, 'Elizabethans and Foreigners', p. 24.

23 John Gross, *Shylock* (London, 1992), p. 5.

24 Pierre Solin, 'Jewish Images in the French Cinema of the 1930s', *Historical Journal of Film, Radio and Television*, 1, 2 (October 1981), 139–50.

25 Laurence Olivier, *On Acting* (London, 1986), p. 123.

26 Writing in *Bioscope* (12 June 1913).

27 Gross, *Shylock*, pp. 218, 295–6.

28 Hunter, 'Elizabethans and Foreigners', p. 29.

29 John Gillies, *Shakespeare and the Geography of Difference* (Cambridge, 1994), p. 25.

30 See Joan Rigby's discussion of the issues involved: 'From Walker to Spielberg', in Peter Reynolds, ed., *Novel Images: Literature in Performance* (London and New York, 1993), p. 172.

31 Jim Pines, *Blacks in Films: a Survey of Racial Themes and Images in the American Film* (London, 1975), p. 12.

32 Manthia Diawara, 'Black American Cinema: the New Realism', in Manthia Diawara, ed., *Black American Cinema* (London, 1993), p. 3.

33 Jorgens, *Shakespeare on Film*, p. 203.

34 Olivier, *On Acting*, p. 106.

35 *Ibid.*, p. 220.

36 Jorgens, *Shakespeare on Film*, p. 194.

37 René Clair, *Réflexion Faite* (Paris, 1951), p. 55.

38 Anthony Davies, 'Filming *Othello*', in Davies and Wells, *Shakespeare and the Moving Image*, p. 207, citing Yutkevich, '*Othello*', *Cinema 56*, 2, 10 (1956), 13.

39 Jacqui Jones, 'The Construction of Black Sexuality: Towards Normalizing the Black Cinematic Experience', in Diawara, *Black American Cinema*, p. 250.

40 Peter S. Donaldson, ' "Haply for I am black": Liz White's *Othello*', in his *Shakespearean Films/Shakespearean Directors* (Boston, MA, 1990), pp. 140–1.

41 Reviewed in *Shakespeare Bulletin*, 16, 2 (Spring 1998), 913.

42 *Much Ado about Nothing by William Shakespeare. Screenplay, Introduction and Notes on the Making of the Film by Kenneth Branagh* (London, 1993), p. 10.

43 *Ibid.*, pp. ix–x.

16

NEIL FORSYTH

Shakespeare the illusionist: filming the supernatural

Reginald Scot's 1584 treatise *The Discovery of Witchcraft* has a section entitled 'To cut off one's head, and lay it in a platter, &c, which the jugglers call the decollation of John the Baptist'. Scot explains how the Elizabethan playhouses worked this particular conjuring trick by means of a stage-device that looked like a pillory, and which showed one actor's head as if it belonged to another body. Other contemporary documents describe many similar illusions, which seem to have been common on the stage as well as on street-corners. Opinion was divided about their value: Ben Jonson despised their vulgarity in the Induction to *Bartholemew Fair*, some denounced them as witchcraft, others felt that 'if these things be done for recreation and mirth, and not to the hurt of our neighbour, nor to the profaning and abusing of God's holy name, then sure they are neither impious nor altogether unlawful, though herein or hereby a natural thing be made to seem supernatural'.[1] It would be a mistake therefore to assume that members of Shakespeare's audience automatically suspected that such 'jugglers' were in league with the devil, even though several contemporary plays, from *Doctor Faustus* to *Friar Bacon* to *Volpone* exploit that idea – for fear, for laughs, for satire. The inherent theatricality of Shakespeare's plays (disbelief only partially suspended) means there is room for lots of stage-tricks in the midst of the ordinary pretences of his theatre (costumes, stage-voices, boys as women). Both depend on illusion, but there is also a complex relationship, often a necessary conflict, between the representation of the mundane and the marvellous.

From its beginnings, the art of film has also pulled in two different directions, towards realism and towards magic.[2] One tendency derives from the Lumière brothers, who came to film from photography, and who at first simply tried to reproduce time and event accurately – a train arriving at the station or the famous shot of workers leaving the Lumière factory. The other is the tradition of Georges Méliès, a stage magician turned *cinéaste*, many of whose films had the words 'nightmare' or 'dream' in their titles. The Lumières recorded reality: Méliès transformed it. What began with Méliès continued in the *grand guignol* ideas of Eisenstein and his 'montage of attractions', in Cocteau's Surrealism, in experiments like James Stewart's dream of falling in Hitchcock's *Vertigo* and the final sequences of Kubrick's *2001*; it is manifest in animation, in the Spielberg-style special effects which have so outdistanced what Méliès could manage, and it survives especially in the immensely popular horror-movie genre, where ghosts and witches and diabolical possession are six-a-penny. But these two contradictory traditions come together, as in Shakespeare's theatre, in the idea of illusion: stage- or film-magic depends on visual illusion, but then so does the representation in still cinematic shots on celluloid of moving images in familiar, recognisable settings – exploiting the tendency of the eye to perceive a sequence of still shots as moving when projected at the right speed. Indeed Méliès's reaction to the first Lumière showing brings the two explicitly together: he was at first dismissive to see merely a still photo of a street scene, but then it started to move, and he was enchanted. He writes:

> a still shot of the Place Bellecour in Lyon was shown. Somewhat surprised, I just had time to say to my neighbour, 'They got us all here for projections like this? I've been doing them for over ten years', when a horse pulling a wagon began to walk towards us, followed by other vehicles and then pedestrians, in a word all the animation of the street. Before this spectacle we sat open-mouthed, stupefied, astonished beyond all expression.[3]

And almost immediately Méliès started to adapt stage magic to film.[4]

This kind of *trucage* was part of a wider phenomenon in the days of the nascent cinema. Spiritualism and table-tapping were frequently practised by stage-magicians turned charlatans as a more lucrative source of income. Hypnotism or Mesmerism was a common theatrical spectacle. The distinction is really between the art that conceals its own artifice beneath the pretence of quotidian realism, the kind of illusionism that developed in the nineteenth century and that we see in wax museums and photography or in George Eliot's homages to Dutch realist painting in *Adam Bede* or Constable in *The Mill on the Floss*, and that which celebrates its own artifice even though it may, like a conjuror (an 'illusionist'), deliberately mystify the spectator about how its magic is performed. And apart from the enormously popular stage-conjuring as practised by Méliès at the Théâtre Robert Houdin, and by his English mentor John Neville Maskleyne at London's Egyptian Hall, another ingredient in the background of early film is that popular genre, Victorian fairy paintings, some of which were actually illustrations for Shakespeare plays such as *A Midsummer Night's Dream* or *The Tempest*. Recall too those famous late Victorian photographs of fairies taken by children that Conan Doyle believed in, but which were admitted as fakes in 1983, when the children had become very old women. Méliès and his followers were adapting a powerful tradition to a new art-form.

They were not, though, working only for an audience of credulous bumpkins. Their shows depended on a double sense of belief and incredulity, as Méliès's own theatre of magic depended on a decline in belief in the supernatural. We admire the magician's skill, and in film we admire the power of the apparatus itself. Successful illusion is still understood as illusion, even if we cannot see exactly how it is done. Furthermore, the prevalence of images of machines such as the train directs our attention (or reflection) towards the mechanical power of the means of reproduction.[5]

The basic argument of this chapter, then, is that Shakespeare films can be read according to how they exploit this informing doubleness of film, and in particular how they use the Méliès dimension, the magic and the *trucage*, to represent the Shakespearean supernatural – fiends, fairies, ghosts and witches. 'Illusionist' thus retains its double meaning: film itself is illusionist, but within it there is the doubled illusionism of Méliès, illusion within illusion.

Three aspects of what Méliès did for film are important for this approach. First, more generally, *le septième art* was permanently marked by his infusion of stage-magic into the screen tradition, to the point that it could never be simply a realist medium. Second, Méliès makes things happen in front of a static camera, since the early cameras were large and heavy and difficult to move. This means that the point of view given to the film viewer is essentially that of the theatre audience, out front, so that we look at the screen as we look at the stage through its proscenium arch, aware (more or less) that we are attending a show. This point of view is familiar to anyone who has seen one of those early Méliès films, and it was seriously modified as further techniques were invented. It remains, nonetheless, a key element of cinematic allusions to Méliès. Third, Méliès very early on liberated screen time from real time by simply stopping the camera while he made an adjustment to the staged show: the disappearing lady trick, one of his most popular, he effected on film simply by stopping the camera while the lady gets out from inside the frame that supports the cloth covering her, such that when the camera starts up again, the cloth can be removed . . . and the lady has vanished. This simple trick is at the origin of all the ways film-makers extend the possibilities of illusion.[6]

Nevertheless one soon notices a certain unease about spectacle and illusion in the style of Shakespeare films and in the discussion of them. There are several reasons for this. One is no doubt the long-standing suspicion of theatre itself in Anglo-Saxon, Puritan-based culture, connected with suspicions about dressing-up, pretending to be someone else, sexual licence and in its more extreme forms the denunciation of theatre as a tool of the devil. In the case of the Shakespearean tradition, there is a further ingredient: the late Victorian and Edwardian theatres had fully developed the tendency that began in the Restoration theatres towards pictorial representation within the frame of grandiose West End proscenium arches, but the influential William Poel had begun a counter-trend to get away from the splendid spectacles and to recon-struct a supposedly pure and unscenic theatre such as Shakespeare himself was imagined to have worked in.[7] Many modern Shakespeareans, still influenced by Poel and what he stood for, will have wanted anything but a return to complex stage 'devices'[8] and the discredited elaboration of costume and spectacle, even in the new medium of film. This discomfort with pictorial illusion also has some-thing to do with the fact that film art grew up with Modernism, in which high and low art-forms were fiercely separated, so that 'special effects' are for children or certain subgenres, horror and sci-fi, not the serious mainstream.

All this suspicion makes it especially difficult when what is being presented cannot but be supernatural, like the ghost of Hamlet senior. In Tony Richardson's 1969 film of *Hamlet*, Nicol Williamson has a strong light shining in his face whenever the ghost is 'present'. But we see nothing. Olivier (1948), who managed well the midnight darkness for the battlement scenes that the afternoon Globe could not aspire to, was famously dissatisfied with his misty, dry-ice ghost, to the point that he dubbed in the voice himself. And he makes much of Horatio's rational scepticism. As the ghost leaves at the sudden cock-crow, we cut back to the watching soldiers in a long shot and way below, as if the camera is now where the ghost was, looking back down as it floats off up into the cloud. Then Horatio guarantees the truth of the experience by 'the sensible and true avouch of my own eyes' – a line which in this context refers to the cine-matic experience, to the magical vision. The motif of the sceptic convinced guar-antees not simply the reality of the ghost but the authenticity of what might otherwise seem to the audience, and certainly to Olivier, like a hokey ghostie film, not high classic art. And Zeffirelli too (1990) has trouble with the ghost, so that Paul Scofield seems merely to have dropped in for a serious talk with his son, but hardly to come from a different dimension.

Only the Russian Kozintsev (1964), following in the steps of Eisenstein, makes intelligent use of the 'cinema of attractions', confining the ghost to his own sequences, misty and vast, and never allowing shots with ghost and human together: one result is to make the ghost seem huge and especially imposing against the beauty of the open sky. And Shostakovitch lends him his most dis-turbing and powerful music. The film-language created for the early ghost per-vades other scenes of this widescreen film: we soon see Ophelia already weirdly moving in an inappropriate space for a dance, wind blowing clouds across the dark sky, curtains billowing, flames wavering, everything, in short, that is other than the world of Claudius's earthbound and imprisoning court. Just as the ghost is to appear, horses burst loose, disturbed in some way by the night or the elements, by their extra sense of danger or the supernatural.[9] Men emerge into the night, but the camera focuses on the aurora borealis, a vast sign in the heavens, as the soundtrack says 'Look where it comes again.'[10] We see a ruin, castle walls, and the camera leads Hamlet to the seashore, from where he looks up to see the uncertain figure on the battlements. As the long scene develops (five minutes) and the ghost tells his story, he becomes more and more distinct as a figure in full armour, and thus unrecognisable as any particular human being. The up/down relation is maintained between father and son and the wind blows his cloak throughout. Finally, as he says he must go because of the coming dawn, and cries 'Remember me', the camera shows Hamlet looking for him, and then itself searches, sweeping down and around as the clock strikes five, and reinforcing the power of the ghost even in his absence.

Kozintsev's background was in the Constructivism of the revolutionary period. In particular, he founded FEKS, the Factory of the Eccentric Actor, in 1922, the main goal of which was to undermine bourgeois expectations of realism by new techniques, by reassembling images, as in that disturbing horsemen sequence, and above all by following Eisenstein and other founders of Russian cinema to make the new public see the provocative, mysterious, otherness of this filmic world.[11] Hence he was well prepared to construct his strange and compelling ghost, not because he believed in the supernatural but because he knew about film and what it could do.

Kozintsev's ghost scene is given extra prominence as the only one: the first scene of the play is missing entirely. This makes the ghost appear in the development of the film only once we have experienced the full impact of the public style of the new regime – oily, showy, superficial. The ghost, insistent and implacable in his demands, gets extra credibility from this transposition, almost as if he appears in response to our distaste at Claudius, as if he comes as much to set right the politics of this corrupt court as to avenge his own murder. And the result is that, in the absence of the first scene, the ghost appears especially and indeed only for Hamlet, who receives its message as a political challenge as well as a psychologically disturbing appeal to his dynastic and family loyalty.

Branagh's 1996 ghost, in the person of that substantial actor Brian Blessed, harks back to the Russian ghost in some respects, but the main scene, Act 1 scene 4, like the film in general, has little sureness of touch. This ghost too is shown only in separate frames, with actors looking fearfully up into the sky when he speaks to them. But most of the symbolic motifs that suggest the ongoing impact of the supernatural in Kozintzev are missing. Instead the watching soldiers (including a Jack Lemmon hopelessly out of his depth) react to the ghost through the solid bars of an earth-bound fence, like the Manet girl gazing at a train. And the ghost looks first like the statue of King Hamlet, on which the camera has dwelt before, now come to life and gesticulating as if he/it were still a bit stiff in the joints. The film then whisks us suddenly outside into the surrounding woods and blue-grey coloured night, to a place insistently and facilely

Avernian, where the ground cracks mysteriously to release smoke (updated dry ice) and noise. In a sudden silence the ghost speaks in close-up, always in a stage whisper that becomes increasingly tedious as the long speech about the murder unfolds. The film here uses one of its several flashback sequences (brightly coloured in contrast to the night-time grey) to illuminate the Blessed narration, until the speech ends on close-ups of the eyes of father and son as those windows of the soul are penetrated. The two try to link hands, like a Sistine God and Adam, but the ghostly hand disappears without touching Branagh's and the musical overlay becomes heavily sentimental and destroys the potentially impressive mood. The banality of the soundtrack here is typical of the uncertainty of most filmed *Hamlets*.

Michael Almereyda's New York *Hamlet* of 2000 is remarkable for several reasons, the least outlandish of which is an extra appearance by the Ghost. A gloomy Sam Shepard looks on, leaning on a door-frame, at the end of the scene in which Hamlet agrees to fight with Laertes. Hamlet's line 'Let be' (5.11.170), which closes the 'we defy augury' speech, is delivered to the watching ghost. Apart from this, the representation of the ghost has two interesting ideas. For the play's first scene, told in flashback, the ghost first appears on a surveillance monitor in the Denmark Corporation building. This obviously picks up on all the spying going on in the play, but it also links the ghost with the elaborate use of video monitors, cameras and television throughout the film. The play-within-the-play, for example, turns out to be a video called *The Mousetrap* made by Hamlet, and most of the soliloquies are video sequences Hamlet has composed. Video technology, indeed the already old-fashioned Pixelvision technology, is the film's way to represent, or invent, interiority – which is thus linked, as in Saint Augustine's *Confessions* Book X, to memory, and so to the ghost's 'Remember me.'[12] Hamlet's first attempt at the 'To be or not to be' speech is on a video screen as we see him (and he sees himself) trying out various ways of shooting himself, a rather unfunny visual pun. The film is in fact so interested in playing with self-reflexivity that it risks disappearing up its own lens.

The second interesting aspect of the ghost is that, as he walks away down the corridor, refusing to speak to the guards and unstayed by Horatio's 'Stay, illusion', he disappears into the Pepsi machine. The machine bears the logo 'One', a Pepsi brand in 1999. The contrast between a ghost, even one dressed in an elegant New York coat and looking as serious as Shepard does, and a back-corridor, let alone a Pepsi machine, is very bizarre. That may indeed be the only point. But like many of the inventive visual ideas in the film, it certainly provokes speculation: does corporate culture control us in the way the ghost controls Hamlet? Is the Pepsi machine the way back to Purgatory for a ghost who has lost his fizz? Is Pepsi thereby acknowledged as the ultimate representative of a *passé* corporatism?

Otherwise, for his second appearance, his meeting with Hamlet (1.iv) the ghost is seen - first on the guard's monitor, but then by Hamlet – on the balcony. The only bizarre thing about this is that we are on the fifty-ninth floor. The ghost leaves the same way, but is still seen leaning on the balcony, carrying his coat as Hamlet tells Horatio of the visit. In the next shot of the balcony, the ghost has gone. But there is nothing at all magical or supernatural – or even insubstantial – about him, and indeed he gives Hamlet a strong fatherly hug at one point. Had we not already seen him absorbed by the Pepsi machine we would not know from his appearance that he is a ghost. He has to identify himself to Hamlet as his 'father's spirit', which is no doubt why he looks a bit grey. At two moments at least he is replaced by the camera looking back, as if with his point of view, at Hamlet, but this idea is not at all pointed: it is simply the reverse shot so common in filmed dialogue.

It is perhaps curious that a film so interested in itself *as film* should not manage to make anything more of the ghost, even if the director wanted to avoid the film-as-celluloid-ghost idea we find elsewhere. (For examples, see the discussion of Welles's *Macbeth*, below.) None of the sheer oddity of the ghost is exploited: it comes as a surprise to find that Gertrude can't see him in the closet scene and so calls him 'the very coinage of [Hamlet's] brain'. After all, he is sitting quite comfortably in a chair at the time. The film's failure to link the ghost with its own technology may arguably have the effect of shifting the status of the ghost within the terms of the cinematic history I have been outlining. If the unreliability of the past is what the constant use of video technology emphasises (Hamlet is shown frequently manipulating images, pausing, rewinding, freezing), then the association of the ghost with all this Méliès-based trickery must somehow be severed if he is to be believed. Thus, when he actually visits Hamlet personally, although he appears on the balcony he walks into the room through a door Hamlet opens for him, he wears a coat and a tie, he is filmed at the same level as Hamlet, he touches a handkerchief to his poisoned ear and then touches his son in the same place, their dialogue uses the ordinary naturalistic conventions for conversation of shot / reverse shot, and they hug. All of this has the effect, oddly enough, of solidifying the ghost once he speaks to his son. This is perhaps why Almereyda offers him an extra appearance at the moment of decision, leaning not on the edge of the film, but prosaically and credibly on a door frame.

Macbeth is a different case from *Hamlet*. There is less diffidence about filming the supernatural, which is obviously central to the play, and this encourages film directors to cross the divide between high and low culture. Banquo's ghost is usually fully represented and marvellously horrifying: both Welles and Polanski borrow directly from horror traditions, Polanski explicitly using its bloody violence as well, while Kurosawa has his own clear cultural sense of how a ghost will appear, and how others will react. Indeed the artistic (though not commercial)[13] success of these *Macbeth* films is due partly to the eery power of these supernatural visitations. Their very presence makes stage or screen *Macbeth*s fun to watch. And, as Nicholas Brooke argued in his 1990 Oxford edition, *Macbeth* is all about illusion. Thus the transfer to screen- from stage-illusion can heighten the focus of the play rather than distract us with too much dry ice or other chemical magic. Already in *Hamlet* the status of the ghost is problematic ('Be thou a spirit of health or goblin damned?'), but in *Macbeth* the question of the supernatural and its status is central: are these village women or supernatural, hellish visitants, devilish minions? Is the dagger I see before me really there? Is Banquo's ghost?

That illusion is central to *Macbeth* is announced by the non-naturalistic prologue suggesting reversals of what we see ('fair is foul and foul is fair', and later, that definitive 'nothing is but what is not'). Illusions of various kinds then dot the play. The sleepwalking scene is representative of the role of delusion (caused by psychological disturbance, and recognised as such on stage by doctor and nurse, and so by the whole audience). But the Birnam wood scene is more ambiguous. Macbeth is tricked by the prophecy, and though the event itself is explained beforehand as a military tactic, it is not so understood by its first observers: the Messenger says he saw it but knows not how to say it, and finally admits that 'Anon methought the wood began to move', 5.5.33. Thus the characters (or some of them), but not the audience, are deceived, and the scene is a good example of purely naturalistic illusion, supposedly at work in the ordinary world. The head of Macbeth, on the other hand, brought on at the end, is a characteristic stage illusion and obviously intended, at least momentarily, to horrify. But the main ingredients of this pattern of illusion are as follows:

(1) *Weird Sisters*. They are visible to all, but ambiguous. Are they village witches (a word only used once in dialogue, though regular in the stage-directions of the Folio) or supernatural beings ('weird' means 'fate': its loose modern meaning begins only in the nineteenth century)? They can foresee, but what can they actually do? In their own words, 'Though his bark cannot be lost / Yet it shall be tempest-tossed', 1.3.23–4, which suggests their power is limited. They vanish into air as Macbeth says, 'as breath into wind' (1.3.79), and Banquo wonders if they were there or 'have we eaten on the insane root / That takes the reason prisoner?' (1.3.83–5).

(2) *The dagger*. This is the opposite case. It has a definite form, but is seen only by Macbeth, and he seems to realise it is not there:

> Art thou not, fatal vision, sensible
> To feeling as to sight? Or art thou but
> A dagger of the mind, a false creation
> Proceeding from the heat-oppressèd brain?   (2.1.37–40)

Macbeth confuses the matter further by drawing his actual dagger and then seeing the illusory one as more vivid, now with 'gouts of blood / Which was not so before' (2.1.47–8). Words create the dagger, plus the actor's gestures, which focus on the place where the dagger is not.

(3) Banquo's ghost is again a different case: it is seen by Macbeth but not by others on stage. It was also seen by a witness (Simon Forman) at the 1610 Globe performance, yet Lady Macbeth says to her husband 'You look but on a stool' (3.4.68). The Folio (1623) has an entrance for the ghost, yet the stage-history of the scene shows it can be done with or without: bring the ghost on stage and the spectator sees what Macbeth sees, but with an empty chair, the reactions of the others predominate, we are outside the hallucination, and Macbeth has gone (temporarily) mad.[14] The scene is similar to the last appearance of the ghost in the Hamlet closet-scene, when he is seen by Hamlet (and usually the audience too), but not by Gertrude. Was there in fact a convention, understood by the audience, in which at this structural slot in the play the ghost may appear only to the main character? Yet the scene is different from the parallel Hamlet scene in that the ghost neither speaks nor acts, nor requires action: Shakespeare's focus is on the reactions of Macbeth and the others present. The objective status of the ghost is unclear.

(4) *Apparitions*. The climax of these scenes comes with the apparitions of Act 4 scene 1, which is the fullest Weird Sister scene and the last. It does not mystify, but simply amazes, and it can be done with simple stage-devices: cauldron, smoke, trap or less.

There is a clear distinction in each of these cases between realism and supernatural phenomena, but the relation between them is shifting, and neither the mundane nor the supernatural is uncomplicated. Brooke may be right[15] to propose that no clear answer is possible to the question of the role of illusion in the play, but in that case the result of any given production may be merely confusing. Polanski's film is just that.

Polanski's 1971 *Macbeth* is an odd mixture: it gets some things right and a lot wrong. Essentially Polanski was working within the naturalistic conventions of Hollywood, which left him rather lost when it came to the supernatural bits. Rather like his Macbeth (Jon Finch), who tries and fails, with accompanying eery sounds, to grasp the floating image of a dagger (obvious enough to the eye of the audience, indeed sparkling with a Disney or washing-powder radiance), Polanski lacks any context, inherited or invented, within which to represent the sheer strangeness of the play. He sets the film in a pre-Christian Scotland given over to a demonic cult, yet visually his witches are no 'secret, black and midnight hags'. Though they are certainly not attractive, Polanski chooses to present these ambivalent creatures as rural women, not devilish spirits: they keep goats, they live in daylight (indeed much of the film, curiously, takes place in bright daylight), they are apparently worshippers of the earth-goddess, at least as such creatures might be imagined in California, and they function as a modern coven, living in caves and eating raw food because it is good for you.

An illustration of this uncertainty is Polanski's treatment of Act 4 scene 1, the last visit to the witches, including the apparitions. At the beginning Macbeth and Lady Macbeth mount the stairs to bed, which indicates that this is to be partly a dream sequence. But it quickly escapes from dream status, and takes on a kind of hallucinogenic quality. While he lies in bed, Jon Finch recites his remarkable lines from Act 3 scene 4 about going to the Weird Sisters again ('I am in blood / Stepped in so far, that should I wade no more, / Returning were as tedious as go o'er[16] . . . *Strange things I have in head*, that will to hand / That must be acted ere they may be scanned', my italics). Francesca Annis sleeps beside him. But then suddenly we see her from below, standing outdoors, a commanding Hecate-like figure, as if she is the spur to his intent, and he is up and away on horseback to a strange powerful music in an eery but bright light.

On the heath he meets the women and the scene's problems begin. The woman who greets him takes him literally by the sword and leads him down into the earth, underground, obviously into 'Hell', or Avernus. In general the women are done up like Breughel peasants, not a bad idea in itself (all *cinéastes* need to find a visual reference of some kind in which to locate the world of the play), but here it jars with the supernatural implications of Hell and of these witches and their 'masters'. In order to prepare for the vision of these masters, Jon Finch drinks the liquid from the cauldron, for all the world as if he is anxiously determined to get high (in the terms of contemporary California drug culture: in spite of various stage imitations, please note that this drinking of the witches' brew is not in Shakespeare's text). The visions that follow are rather bewildering (as perhaps they should be) in their styles and points of reference, but the real problem, cinematically and thematically speaking, is when Finch draws his sword and violates the border of the vision world by beheading Macduff (who is himself, it seems, dressed as a reference to a knight in Eisenstein's famous *Alexander Nevsky* battle on the ice, and so to film ghosts in Polanski's head, but ghosts who have no business in *Macbeth*). When Malcolm and Donalbain appear as Polanski's version of the third apparition (in Shakespeare a child crowned with a tree branch), we are inevitably reminded of a California LSD experience in magical daylight, and the parallel may have a certain period interest for 1960s reference to and discussion of the sources of the supernatural. But the real significance, within the film's own terms, of this use of the Duncan sons in the vision is to prepare us for Polanski's addition to the plot, the return of Donalbain at the end of the film, and to remind us of the actor's characteristic limp (the last shot of the film shows him going back to visit these underground witches in this same dream/heath landscape: is the cycle of violence to be renewed, this time by a civil war between the brothers?). At the end of this whole 'masters' sequence, Jon Finch wakes up in the forest, or on the heath (the landscape is not clear), but certainly not in his bed (which would have been unforgivable bathos), and denounces the women who guided this bizarre acid trip as 'infernal', using Macbeth's line from 4.1.155.

Undoubtedly Polanski is interested in making something horrific of the witches, but he is caught between conflicting ideologies. He wants to suggest, it seems, that the witches could be seen from a political and feminist perspective as earthy and rebellious, healthily disrespectful of masculine and royal authority, but he cannot go very far along those lines without overbalancing the meaning of the whole film, which remains a serious and tragic engagement with evil. And at the same time, he has an irremediably adolescent attitude to the supernatural and horror in cinema, as witness that tediously unfunny version of the Dracula plot, *The Fearless Vampire Killers* (1967). So the last thing Macbeth sees as he dies is a confused, swirling vision of the surrounding soldiers, but we then realise that we are being shown all this from inside the severed head: these are the terminal spasms after the beheading.

It is Orson Welles, perhaps, who most fully exploited the magic tradition, but in characteristically original ways, for his own 1948 *Macbeth*. The film was withdrawn from the Venice Film Festival in favour of Olivier's *Hamlet* in that year, an event with which Wellesians and serious film-buffs (as opposed to Shakespeareans) have never really made their peace. Indeed Anthony Davies argues that, in spite of all its flaws, and they are many, this is the film which separates mere Shakespeareans from those who take cinema seriously as high art.[17] In the history of Shakespeare films, this is the one that, for many, authorises the cinematic assertion of one's right to revise Shakespeare in the terms of cinema's own spatial and imaginative possibilities.

In this high claim Welles's *Macbeth* is, I think, largely unsuccessful, partly because of the minuscule budget with which Welles had to work, and partly because the vision Welles imposes on the film as a whole (symbolised by that peculiar invention, the 'Holy Father') risks trivialising its politics and making a mere allegory out of the opposition between these dark primitive forces and the uncertain and tentative reaching of the film's world towards Christianity.[18] These allusions to a supposedly pre-Christian Scotland are everywhere in the visual images of the film, in the stark structures of the already ancient castles, the bizarre caves and spaces we enter through a combination of skilful camera work and papier mâché, the spiky, deliberately un-Christian crosses on the long staffs like divining rods the witches carry (to contrast with the infrequent occasions where the Celtic cross itself is represented), and also in the values of all the main characters' speeches, or such lines as they have left to them from the truncated and rearranged script. And those lines, unpardonably, laughably, the actors speak in fake stage-Scots (although not if you have only seen the 1950 retake ordered by the RKO studio when someone told them how bad the language sounded, which mixed in often unsynched voices). The film is nonetheless filled with moments of genius, and some of them have to do with how Welles thought out the supernatural dimension.

A fine German–French–Swiss TV programme entitled 'The Lost Films of Orson Welles' (1995) begins with a delicious clip which shows a youngish Welles marching imperiously on-stage and performing a magic trick, for all the world as if he were a reborn Méliès, bringing out of a magician's bucket not a flock of doves but a lovely white fowl. Merely by staring at it intently Welles subdues and even frightens this poor bird till its head draws back and its neck curves like a swan of Avon. Welles then discusses for his TV audience 'The illusionists, the stage illusionists, [whose] last great days came to an end with the last great days of the stage and theatre magicians. There were giants in those days. That was when theatre was theatre, still beglamoured and bedazzled with theatricality', and he goes on to talk about 'those grand old wonder workers' and 'illusion in the high old style'. He is apparently talking partly about the late nineteenth century, partly about his own childhood ('Magic has an innocence that appeals to me, it's a return to childhood, it's like playing with toys, it's pure play, and a little more than that, it can have a kind of second-rate poetry that I find attractive, when you suspend disbelief and it becomes a very good kind of theatre'), and partly imagining a mythical past ('giants in those days'), imbued with Poel's ideas of Shakespeare's stage. Welles was often driven to hold an audience with his rhetoric at the expense of truth, and this was the same Welles who was fascinated by stage-magic.

Arguably it is this Welles who reveals the true Shakespearean possibilities in the art of film, the magic swan often hidden in the folds of Lumière realism. Like Shakespeare, Welles knew that the art he worked with needs often to present its own forms not only as the vehicle but as the tenor of its meanings. In Shakespeare this takes the form of those ubiquitous stagings of theatrical shows, from the straightforward plays-within-plays to the more complex scenes in which, say, a shrew is induced to play the obedient wife or a Malvolio is tricked into playing the kind of theatrical role he apparently despises. In Welles, we see it in those moments in which he shows film as being not simply representational but fundamentally about itself. At one point, for example, Welles allows the camera to stand in the place of Banquo's ghost in order to look back at Macbeth – which can be read as a reminder that film is itself merely a ghost, light passing through a strip of celluloid and projected on to our present from some past when the shooting took place.[19] In this complex scene with Banquo's ghost Welles shows himself fully in command of the art of cinema: on stage you have to choose whether you want a ghost or an empty chair, but Welles gives us both, cutting between the horrified Macbeth's deep-focus vision of the ghost sitting at an empty table, and the increasingly bewildered guests who see, like Lady Macbeth, only an empty chair.[20] Is Macbeth's vision hallucination or reality? Méliès or Lumière? There is no way to tell.

Long before he made the film, Welles had staged the play in 1936 at the Lafayette, a Harlem theatre, and he set it in 'the rank and fever-stricken jungles of Haiti', using drums and voodoo references to produce 'a witches' scene that is logical and stunning and a triumph of the theatre art . . . If it is witches you want, Harlem knows how to overwhelm you with their fury and phantom splendour.'[21] The production risked trouble in view of the recent Harlem riots, about which Welles was pretty naive. Word got about that, in what was quickly known as 'the voodoo Macbeth', black culture was being made fun of, 'a campaign to burlesque negroes'. Welles, or so he thought, was able to convince the angry crowds that it was not so, and that on the contrary he was making use of black actors and voodoo for important cultural statements.[22] And indeed he was doing something radically new and different – putting on Shakespeare with the Negro Theater Unit, using Roosevelt's New Deal funds from the Federal Theater Project.

For his film, though, made more than ten years later, Welles abandoned Haiti and black actors and returned the imagined setting to Scotland, but retained the important idea of the voodoo doll. The image instantly makes the witches dominant, and this dominance Welles manages spatially in the first scene, even before the credits. A small crowned effigy is seen at the level of the witches' feet, indeed we see the witches themselves constructing the clay form of the doll. It is the doll rather than the man himself that is decorated with Macbeth's sequence of honours, Glamis, Cawdor, king, and then finally beheaded at the end of the film. Thus, rather than use any *trucage* for Macbeth's own head, Welles invests this local Americanised black magic with most of the film's import.[23]

The result is a strange, compelling but somehow constrained and even zombie-like Macbeth; Welles plays the role himself, with great fatigue at times, as if he is weary of the role he is being asked to play by these tyrannical directors. Perhaps in this respect the witches represent the role of Republic Pictures' boss Herbert Yates, who had insisted on a low budget (less than $900,000) and a three-week shooting schedule. But from another point of view they are a version of Welles himself as the film's director, getting as much as he can out of his exhausted cast. These witches are their own 'masters', not merely representative of that pre-Christian primitive world, if not actually running it. So the sequence in which the weird sisters summon their satanic 'masters' is omitted: Macbeth himself sees the future visions of 4.1, his body lit and centrally positioned on the screen as if at the bottom of a pit, but we don't. (Perhaps Tony Richardson recalled this idea of Welles, forced on him by the minimal budget, as the solution for his own supernatural problem: how to render the ghost of Hamlet's father, which appears as a white light on the main character's face.) Yet through the power they thus acquire, the world of the film created by Welles resembles nothing so much as Dorian Gray's. The Macbeth world is taken over at the end by the strange voodoo double – so intense is Welles's fascination with what makes the play, and the film, magical – as the beheaded doll comes to represent, but also to substitute for, the human world of murdered kings and bloody battle.

In various ways, Welles makes film and magic traditions overlap. His aim is to show the forces of darkness taking over, even in power already, and to do so he uses melodrama and horror-movie techniques rather than more traditional theatre. The original Lafayette Theatre production turned on what Richard France calls 'stagey responses which make horror movies both ridiculous and yet exhilarating'. This can be very wearying, he adds, as some of the film acting also shows, but it quite deliberately links Welles's picture with the techniques we associate with early, silent film. Spectacle predominates over dialogue, as in the nineteenth-century melodrama with which the stage-magic tradition is closely linked.[24]

Voodoo drums were present on stage in Harlem, and Welles retains them for the screen, as in the transition from the banquet to the witches' scene of Act 4 scene 1. And these drums produce a splendid instance of horror-melodrama by ceasing at the exact moment when the axe falls on Cawdor's neck. Each film episode is thus linked with the underlying theme of the dark powers which both prepare the way for, and then gradually entrap, Macbeth. Indeed the whole film is shot in a kind of recurrent and encircling gloom, occasionally lifted for the important light–dark and open–closed contrasts. This, together with the violently disjunctive editing, sharp vertiginous angles and turbulent weather, make for an expressionist style, clearly developed in homage to films like Murnau's 1926 *Faust*.

To all this Welles deliberately adds a sense of helpless desperation, of the kind we feel in nightmare, thus making the spectator personally conscious of his inability to intervene on the screen. And Welles's own acting of Macbeth, as if sleepwalking at times, or even drunk like the porter, underlines this experience of conscious helplessness: indeed he puts himself into his wife's sleepwalking scene as a silent but obvious spectator, much closer to the audience and larger on screen than the doctor or nurse, and like us as we watch Lady Macbeth rush away to her suicidal leap off the cliff on to the rocks and sea below. In Shakespeare, this death is simply reported to Macbeth: Welles's decision to link it to the sleepwalking scene and to include Macbeth as spectator is an attempt to render in cinematic terms the odd detachment of Macbeth's famous reaction, 'She should have died hereafter. / There would have been a time for such a word. / Tomorrow and tomorrow . . .' (5.5.17–19).

For most of these points, the opening sequence of the film can serve as an example, in particular of how cinematic and thematic reference overlap. Welles mixes several uses of dissolve with this (supposedly) Scotch mist as it swirls and then clears for the image of the Celtic cross, then obscures again and reveals the witches up on their precarious papier mâché rock, then closes and opens for the surface of their cauldron, then for the clay doll. The bubbling cauldron in fact takes over the whole screen, sucking us in, to the point that it becomes a self-referential image of the film itself, deliberately evoking the magical side of film tradition, and requiring the spectator to pass through that surface into the worlds of both the film and the witches. Thus both the witches and the ghost evoke in Welles specific techniques of the art of film and suggest with which tendency, Méliès or Lumière, he has most artistic sympathy. But these recurring representations of instability also evoke dream or nightmare and produce in some spectators the need to escape or awake: indeed when I have watched Welles's *Macbeth* in the cinema, I sense a pervasive restlessness around me, linked, I am sure, to his sense of the darkness of this pre-Christian, sinister nightmare as akin to the darkness of the cinema where we are required to sit patiently and watch.

Nightmare is important also for what is certainly the most original version of *Macbeth*. All critics who have reflected on Shakespeare films recognise that *Kumonosou-djo* (*Throne of Blood*, 1957) is a key film, acknowledged by many as the greatest. When he adapted *Macbeth* to Japanese traditions Akira Kurosawa had not only to choose an appropriate historical context which allowed the basic issues of fealty and treachery to have their starkest meanings, but also to find cinematic styles which could render the peculiar mixture of power and helplessness essential to Shakespeare's play, in particular to its use of the supernatural.

Of all the scenes in the film, the first forest scene is the one that has been most thoroughly analysed, since it shows the peculiar qualities of the film so clearly. Commentators note the way the rain is picked up in the verticality of the trees, stress the symbolic use of the horses, praise the vigour of the tracking shots which move the two actors through and ever deeper into this forest as labyrinth and pore over every detail of the encounter with the single spirit who substitutes for the Shakespearean witches. It is hard to add much to this mass of commentary, but the film will respond well to our basic premise about the importance of the double tradition within film language.

First we need to acknowledge that the two actors who play Washizu and Miki (the Macbeth and Banquo figures) are two of the finest in Japanese cinema, and in the case of Toshiro Mifune, of world renown. The vigour and anxious bravery with which he plays the role of a loyal, stolid, somewhat unreflective samurai gradually tempted by prophecy and wife to murder his lord is exemplary of a whole style of realistic cinema acting (though it may look stylised now to

Western eyes unfamiliar with Japanese conventions). The contrast between the powerful physical presence of these two warriors in their dark clothes and the slightness of the androgynous white spirit is one of the most striking aspects of the scene. And indeed the contrast embodies the opposing moods and styles that are here brought into contact: speed and stillness (both of actors and of camera), dialogue and solitary song, noise and quiet, dark and light, physical and spiritual power, life and death, nature and the supernatural.

The scene occurs relatively early in the film, though not so early as its equivalent in Shakespeare, since the whole historical and political setting has first been established – the troubled civil strife at the end of feudalism in the sixteenth century. Then, even as the two horsemen enter the forest they pause and comment on the strangeness of the terrible storm of lightning and rain, and allow the audience to notice the oddity of the lighting: already through backlighting and a mist-effect whiteness is beginning to infect the screen. Initially the two riders canter about in this dark wet place, shot through the tangled branches of the undergrowth, alternately in still and then fast tracking shots. Gradually we realise from the reversals of direction and camera angle that they are in fact lost: they notice this by recognising that they have doubled back over their own hoofprints, but obtusely and ironically they congratulate each other on knowing the terrain, unlike the enemy, who will certainly get lost in this Spider's Web Forest. Then Washizu (Macbeth) rather pointlessly fires an arrow up into the tall tops of the backlit trees and immediately we hear on the sound track an uncanny laugh, and the horses whinny: the sense of oddity, at the very least, is jolting, but the action of firing the arrow preserves the ambiguity about who causes what. The two men determine to cut their way out, but another sequence of fast horseriding brings them still deeper into the forest. A mist is slowly rising. (In all the medium shots of fast horseriding, instead of tracking the camera remains stationary, simply turning rapidly on its stand as the horsemen ride in a circle around, through the bushes and trees of the forest: the position of the camera locates and anticipates for us the focus of the scene which follows, the white spirit of the forest. Camera and supernatural are again one.)

Now comes, suddenly, the strange sight of a white bamboo cage-like structure, behind a large tree: we perceive it from behind the two men on horseback, who have now stopped moving but whose horses still stir restlessly. Cut back to them for a powerful reaction shot. 'My horse has never been so frightened', says Washizu, sure that an evil spirit is blocking their way. Courageously he controls his horse and forces it towards the camera, and so, in the narration, towards the spirit. The two men now say they see the spirit, and in one of several extraordinary film-moments Washizu (Toshiro Mifune) makes to shoot the spirit (is it a him/her?) with his bow. But just at this moment on the soundtrack begins a strange song or chant, and so, unlike Polanski's Jon Finch, Washizu desists, allowing the spirit world to remain, at least for the present, separate, inviolate, not penetrated by a human weapon. Cut back to the two men whom we watch dismount, still looking towards the source of the sound, and they then move forwards, the camera following them till they stop, then continuing till it shows the spirit in medium shot, white, utterly other, spinning thread from one reel to another as it sings. Reaction shots show the two men transfixed, peering through the undergrowth and into the white-lit scene.

Finally they move sideways and the camera comes in round behind them till it shows us the full scene framed by the two warriors, light framed within the dark forest, a film within a film. The two warriors quickly become spectators of a magic show, frontally presented as in the Méliès films, rather than from a constantly shifting viewing position in what became the classical style, to absorb the spectator into the film-space. Indeed, arguably the scene combines Lumière and Méliès traditions but keeps them distinct: the watching warriors framing the screen still belong to the outside or Lumière world of history – battle, horses, rushing messengers and feudal hierarchies – even though they are momentarily lost in this strange forest which is now revealing its secret soul. But the scene they look in at, the camera now still, is pure Méliès.

Japanese legends about androgynous seers make Kurosawa's witch-substitute exactly right for the world of the film, which is successful because of its total adaptation to 'Shakespeare without the words'.[25] There on screen is this unutterably strange spirit, chanting and spinning, mesmerising us as we watch the thread cross from reel to reel. Unmistakably this is destiny, and indeed the thread is near its end already. But even more clearly than in the case of the cauldron's surface in Welles, the spinning reels also refer to the magic art of film itself.[26]

The two warriors now step forward and open the door of the cage and ask the spirit what it is and whether it can speak. The scene is then framed again, a clear Méliès reference, as the two warriors look in from outside the frame while the spirit prophecies the equivalent of Macbeth's three promotions, including that Washizu will eventually be boss of the Castle of the Spider's Web (the French chose this more exact term for the title of the Film, *Le Château de l'Araignée*). Miki too (Banquo) gets his own prophecy. At the end of the sequence we suddenly and for the first time see the scene from the back, reversing the Méliès position, putting us backstage as the spirit answers Miki's questions. But the vision is still there, and no less mysterious. After one reaction shot, we see it from behind as it rises and with a sudden gust of wind disappears, blown away or simply taken back into the spirit world, magicked away like the disappearing lady of Méliès. As in Kozintsev's *Hamlet,* ghost and spirit and wind are aligned thematically, reinforcing a folk idea and one that in many languages also links them etymologically.

The forest scene concludes with two key images. First we watch as Washizu, then Miki, react to the disappearance of the spirit, look around them, and then deliberately step forward into the white space vacated by the spirit. Here perhaps lies the meaning of the film, for they never really leave that space, or at least what it represents, again: they are *magicked*. And what this means is in one sense that they have become entirely creatures of the film, existing only in the space that was previously identified with the screen. They look back in surprise, behind them but at the camera, reacting to the fact that the frame through which they stepped is no longer there: they have crossed over into the Méliès world.[27] Then comes the second key image, as the camera moves away and reveals in the contiguous space of the forest a pile of bones, and military hardware. So this was a death-place too, we now realise, and there too the heroes are for ever stuck, doomed. The film now represents this by a long, almost tediously long sequence of the two men once again lost in the mist, galloping hither and yon until finally Kurosawa allows them, and us, to emerge and rest.

The spirit returns in a later scene when Washizu goes back to the forest after the death of Miki-Banquo, but we no longer have the same framing possibility, since there is only one warrior. This time the visions evoked by the witch-spirit force Washizu to turn around to look at them, implying that he is now surrounded by this magic and evil world. And the forest prophecy he hears has even more resonance than in Shakespeare, since it is this same Tangled Web Forest itself which will move towards the Castle of the Spider's Web it has always till now protected with its deceptive and labyrinthine trails.

In Shakespeare's play a link is built up in several ways between the witches and Lady Macbeth. In Kurosawa, the visual images attached to the spirit since the first scene in the forest also establish a deliberate cinematic parallel with Washizu's wife: they have similar white Noh-theatre make-up, and both use a still and undemonstrative style of acting, making a very strong contrast with the vigorous Toshiro Mifune. And indeed that contrast of the two styles enacts the two aspects of film tradition that we associate with Méliès and Lumière.

Banquo's ghost scene is also managed with great skill. Two points are especially notable, first that when the ghost appears on screen it occupies the same position as that in which we first saw Washizu's wife, and it too is white. This links it back to the chain of imagery associated with the supernatural and the strange throughout the film. Second, we the cinema audience see the ghost only through Washizu's eyes, i.e. when the camera substitutes for his viewpoint. At the end, when we watch Washizu attack the ghost with his sword, his place is simply empty: Washizu can see it, but no one else can, and nor can we. The contrast with the forest scene, when Washizu refrained from firing his arrow, is clear and important for the film's meaning. Illusion has now become delusion.

The largely successful use of film tradition for the supernatural in *Macbeth* films may also be used to point an important contrast between film and television. In April 1997 BBC television showed *Macbeth on the Estate*, a modern-dress version of the play set on the Ladywood estate in Birmingham, directed by documentary maker Penny Woolcock. This is a provocative and in many ways exemplary effort to get the best of both contemporary and Shakespearean worlds, but it is rather bizarre in its adaptation of the witches and what they represent. They become simply three very strange children, who sit in an inside space, a crowded living room adapted to childish fantasy and entered through hangings and low openings rather than doors. These 'weird children', as Macbeth calls them, but apparently in the modern not the Shakespearean sense of 'weird', prophesy in television close-up, with fantasy ingredients like cloth picture dolls and a candle-lit *mise-en-scène* – passing strange, it is true, but manifestly not evil. Much evil there is in this teleplay, but its source is not mysterious at all: it resides quite clearly in the drug-driven underworld of gang rivalry in which the characters all live. It is inherent in their social context, not in the supernatural, which has been – apart from these odd children – eliminated.

The same reticence is clear in the way television deals with Banquo's ghost. Whereas Orson Welles exploited the cinema and its fundamental technique of montage or cross-cutting precisely to give us both possibilities, a deluded Macbeth and a horrifying presence, in TV that chance is usually missed. The ghost is simply a delusion of the disturbed Macbeth's drug-crazed psyche in Woolcock's sociological, documentary-style version. In the fine 1978 Thames TV adaptation of Trevor Nunn's RSC production, as in the 1983 Jack Gold BBC/Time-Life version, he is not visible to the audience. Perhaps it was felt the scene would be too hard to accept in one's living room (even though many American horror or sci-fi films like *The X-Files*, made for TV, do bring ghosts and other frights into that cosy space). Perhaps it was even the fear of being thought too 'American' that prompted the omissions, or perhaps the fear of ridicule in the highbrow Shakespeare culture with its persistent English reticence towards the supernatural. Even the BBC witches are simply dirty and bedraggled, distasteful but not especially demonic women. In all these cases where the supernatural is suppressed, the rationale is obviously that the psychological has replaced the supernatural just as psychoanalysts have replaced priests. Only the *hoi polloi*, it is thought, those benighted masses who turn out for those contemporary Stephens – Spielbergs and Kings – continue to accept screen magic of the Méliès kind. But TV Shakespeare thus aims at a very restricted idea of what the respectable middle class will buy.

This TV discomfort with the supernatural is palpable, and not only in *Macbeth*. In the often admirable[28] sequence directed by Jane Howell in 1982 for the BBC / Time-Life series, the on-stage fiends of *1 Henry VI* are simply omitted and Joan merely looks at the camera. Even the ghosts who appear before the Battle of Bosworth in *Richard III* are incorporated into dreams, reproducing that common retreat from the supernatural into the psychological. A close-up takes us inside the head of sleeping Richard, a voice-over repeats his mother's curse from Act 4 scene 3, then a nightmare sequence brings back the murdered victims who mock Richard and revere Richmond.[29]

These examples show that television (or at least the naturalism that dominates TV drama) is a less appropriate medium than film for presenting Shakespeare, who was himself, it seems, always fascinated with stage devices for presenting the supernatural. Early in his career, in *1 Henry VI*, Joan la Pucelle, as we just noted, talks to fiends who (in the Folio direction) 'walk and speak not', 'hang their heads', 'shake their heads' and eventually 'depart'; the Duchess of Gloucester and Margery Jourdain summon spirits which appear on-stage and utter prophecies that come true in *2 Henry VI*. And in his last plays, Cerimon in *Pericles* resurrects Thaïsa with the help of spells, napkins and fire, while in *Henry VIII* there is (in Folio Act 4 scene 2) 'The Vision', in which a sleeping Queen Katherine is visited by six white-robed figures wearing golden vizards who bow, dance and hold a garland over her head. (Again the BBC version eliminates the supernatural, keying the scene instead to a religious mural seen by the queen as she starts to doze: then in dream she imagines a younger self rising and dancing with those figures.[30]) Indeed in the later plays, especially the romances which could use the new (1610–11) indoor artificially lighted Blackfriars theatre as well as the Globe, Shakespeare exploited the contemporary popularity of magic for the miracles of *The Winter's Tale* and *The Tempest,* and used masque effects for the supernatural, as in the harpy's intervention to remove the banquet, or the descent of Jupiter on an eagle in *Cymbeline.* (Perhaps, as Nicholas Brooke proposes, the intrusive Hecate dance-scenes in *Macbeth* were added for Blackfriars performances.) All of this suggests, along with the presence of both high and low culture within his plays, that Shakespeare might have been happy to learn from the tradition of Méliès, from *trucage*, from horror movies, even from melodrama, just as Orson Welles or Kurosawa did. Prospero, who also alludes to Ovid's witch Medea, would then be his final version not only of the Renaissance magus in all his ambivalence, but also of the playwright as illusionist. Peter Greenaway's 'spell-stopped' film *Prospero's Books,* with its frames within frames, its 'high charms', its rendering of the tempest-tossed ship as a child's toy galleon and the water world as a boy's fantasy of omnipotence as he pisses, is a baroque, dense, claustrophobically rich tribute to the connection of magician and playmaker, though it probably 'reads' better on video than in the cinema, and might have made more use of popular magic and less of the austere and constantly writing magus.

Prospero–Shakespeare is comparable with the famous John Dee, Elizabeth's astrologer and magician. He was a highly ambivalent figure, both medieval and modern, using pure mathematics but often for superstitious or occult purposes. He had trouble with the authorities at various times, but Dee was first indicted,

NEIL FORSYTH

not for some egregious use of alchemical magic, nor even for using incomprehensible mathematical symbols, but for his role in a student play. At Cambridge, as a future magician would, he invented a special effect for a student production of a classical play, Aristophanes' *Peace*.[31] It is not clear whether the authorities regarded Dee's stage-trick as physically or spiritually dangerous, but arrest him they did. Add now to this composite image of the Elizabethan magus those 'jugglers' of the street-corner and popular stage, and we can begin to imagine how the Shakespeare who invented both Prospero the masque-maker and Autolycus the trickster might have enjoyed making movies.

NOTES

1 Samuel Rid, *The Art of Jugling or Legerdemaine*, London, 1612: B2v, quoted in Michael Mangan, ' ". . . and so shall you seem to have cut your nose in sunder": Illusions of Power on the Elizabethan Stage and in the Elizabethan Marketplace', *On Illusion: Performance Research*, 1.3 (1996), 53. The text is reprinted in *Rogues, Vagabonds and Sturdy Beggars*, ed. Arthur Kinney (Amherst, MA, 1990). More generally see Linda Woodbridge, *The Scythe of Saturn: Shakespeare and Magical Thinking* (Urbana, IL, 1994), pp. 1–11.
2 A brief restatement of this common view of film aesthetics will be found in James Monaco, *How to Read a Film* (London, 1981), p. 236. David Bordwell, *On The History of Film Style* (Cambridge, MA 1998), p. 44, regards it as too rigid a distinction.
3 George Sadoul, *Histoire Général du Cinéma*, vol. I, *L'Invention du cinéma 1832–1897* (Paris: Denoël, 1948), p. 279, my translation. On Méliès, see Madeleine Maltete-Méliès, ed., *Méliès et la naissance du spectacle cinématographique* (Paris, 1984), pp. 53–8. For a review of some relevant films, see Maïté Vienne, *La Figure de l'ange au cinéma* (Paris; 1995); see also Marina Warner, 'The Uses of Enchantment', in Duncan Petrie, ed., *Cinema and the Realms of Enchantment* (London, 1993), pp. 13–35.
4 See Tom Gunning's argument for early cinemagoers as sensation-hungry and astonished by attractions in a series of articles: 'The Cinema of Attraction[s]', in Thomas Elsaesser and Adam Barker, eds., *Early Cinema: Space, Frame, Narrative* (London, 1990), pp. 56–62, 'Primitive Cinema: A Frame-Up? or The Trick's On Us', *Cinema Journal*, 29 (Winter 1988–9), and 'An Aesthetic of Astonishment: Early Film and the (In)Credulous Spectator', in Linda Williams, ed., *Viewing Positions* (New Brunswick, NJ, 1995), pp. 114–33.
5 cf. Gorky's account of a 1896 showing at an exhibition in Moscow: 'It speeds right at you – watch out! It seems as though it will plunge into the darkness in which you sit, turning you into a ripped sack full of lacerated flesh and splintered bones . . . but this too is but a train of shadows. Belief and terror are larded with awareness of illusion, even bleak disappointment of the ungraspable phantom of life itself', quoted by Gunning in 'An Aesthetic of Astonishment', p. 118.
6 These early shows have been widely copied and reproduced on video. See for example, *Georges Méliès: Cinema Magician*, a film by Patrick Montgomery and Luciano Martinengo, 1978/1994, or *Camera – Moving Pictures: no. 2, Georges Méliès*, Granada Television/Educational Film Services, 1981/1991.

7 Marion O'Connor, *William Poel and the Elizabethan Stage Society* (Cambridge, 1987, with slides).

8 'Devices' translates literally the Greek word *mechane*, from which derives English 'machine': the word occurs most famously in the phrase 'deus ex machina', a common scene in Greek drama but one of which Aristotle is famously suspicious as a way to solve the complexities of the plot. Even the author of a book on Shakespearean magic like Linda Woodbridge can still write of 'certain superficial and flashy theatrical effects like Joan of Arc's spooky demons or Margaret's flesh-creeping curses' (*The Scythe of Saturn*, p. 11): she is more interested in the 'deep structure of what happens in the plays'.

9 Shots, pp. 57–65; see *Grigori Kosinzew: 'Hamlet'*, the transcript by Gerhard Müller-Schwefe published in German by Gunter Narr Verlag of Tübingen, 1981, pp. 30–1. Kozintsev's horses are also a cinematic allusion to the scene in Kurosawa's *Throne of Blood*, based on 2.4.14–19, when Banquo and Fleance discuss whether to go to the banquet since the horses patently don't want to. On that film, see below.

10 Or I suppose it does: Pasternak's Russian translation is frustratingly and confusingly rendered back into Shakespeare by the English subtitles. I discuss these *Hamlet* films at greater length in 'Ghosts and Courts', *Filming Hamlet: Shakespeare Yearbook 1998* (Lampeter, 1998), pp. 1–17.

11 John Collick, *Shakespeare, Cinema and Society* (Manchester, 1989), pp. 127–40, makes a case for Bakhtinian carnival as the dominant idea, but surely the Méliès tradition of spectacular illusion in film is more important.

12 See Katherine Rowe, '"Remember me": Technologies of Memory in Michael Almereyda's *Hamlet*', in Richard Burt and Lynda E. Boose, eds., *Shakespeare, the Movie, II* (London: Routledge, 2003), p. 34.

13 See Samuel Crowl on the deadening legacy of the Polanski film in *Shakespeare Observed* (Athens, OH, 1992), pp. 19–34.

14 Marvin Rosenberg, *The Masks of Macbeth* (Berkeley, CA, 1978), pp. 441–50.

15 Nicholas Brooke, Introduction to *Macbeth* (Oxford, 1990), p. 23.

16 Polanski's notorious and gratuitous violence makes these lines, according to E. Pearlman, the film's 'text'. See '*Macbeth* on Film: Politics', in Anthony Davies and Stanley Wells, eds., *Shakespeare and the Moving Image* (Cambridge, 1994), p. 254. One may question, though, whether the violence of this Polanski film, at least, is 'gratuitous' in any serious sense, in spite of its tangential relation to the clearly gratuitous Charles Manson murders of Polanski's wife, Sharon Tate, and friends.

17 Anthony Davies, *Filming Shakespeare's Plays* (Cambridge, 1988), pp. 83–4.

18 Welles imposed a similar but inverted allegory on Falstaff, who, he claimed in several interviews, stands for the 'old England' being lost in the drive towards the mechanical modernity of Henry V.

19 Welles's Banquo banquet had been entirely different in the stage version, with dance music by Virgil Thompson forming part of a genuine melodrama (musical play). The film scene, by contrast, exploits candle-light in darkness, depth of field and bizarre devices like a close-up of Macbeth's pointing finger and shadow which leads the camera and the viewer inexorably towards our first view of the ghost.
    The idea of film as ghost is startlingly clear (through contrast) when a film is used as a part of theatrical staging: in the RSC's 1997 production of *Hamlet*, the opening scene had Alex Jennings silently scattering his father's ashes to the backdrop of a flickering home-movie showing father and small son playing in the snow. Colourful staging

set off and framed this quiet and old-fashioned black and white film-as-ghost. The film of Hamlet's past in fact *was* the ghost.

20 See Lorne Buchman's analysis of this scene in *Still in Movement* (Oxford, 1991), pp. 21–2.

21 Brooks Atkinson, the *New York Times* reviewer, quoted in Simon Callow, *Orson Welles: the Road to Xanadu* (London, 1995), pp. 237–8.

22 So at least he tells Professor Richard Marienstras, in an unpublished videotaped interview. But beware: what Simon Callow says of newspapers is just as true of interviews, that Welles 'was unable to resist a fix of publicity; merely to see a reporter's notebook was to unleash his powers of invention' (*ibid.*, p. xii).

23 Polanski's (1971) opening scene drew from Welles's (1948) in this as in other respects: his witches bury emblems of despair in the sand, a noose and a dagger in a severed hand, and immediately we hear the sounds of battle on the soundtrack as the credits roll: the witches, as powerful here as in Welles, have produced their first example of ordinary evil, war. See Norman Berlin, '*Macbeth*: Polanski and Shakespeare', *Literature/Film Quarterly*, 1, 4 (Fall 1973), and Buchman, *Still in Movement*, p. 70.

24 Richard France, 'The Voodoo *Macbeth* of Orson Welles', *Yale/Theatre*, 5 (1974), 66–78.

25 See Dennis Kennedy, 'Shakespeare Without His Language', in James C. Bulman, ed., *Shakespeare, Theory and Performance* (London, 1996), pp. 133–48, on performances of Shakespeare in translation.

26 Jack J. Jorgens, 'Kurosawa's *Throne of Blood:* Washizu and Miki Meet the Forest Spirit', *Literature/Film Quarterly*, 11 (1983), 167–73, first suggested that the reels were a metaphor for the projector or the editing table. Peter S. Donaldson, *Shakespearean Films/Shakespearean Directors* (Boston, MA, 1990), p. 76, adds other meta-cinematic references.

27 See Donaldson, *Shakespearean Films*, p. 77. He reproduces two stills, before and after, to show the visual continuity between the stepping through the frame and noticing its absence.

28 Graham Holderness praises this sequence for its refusal to accede to the series director Jonathan Miller's programme for resolute television naturalism: 'Radical Potentiality and Institutional Closure', in Jonathan Dollimore and Alan Sinfield, eds., *Political Shakespeare* (Manchester, 1985), pp. 192–3. Holderness's argument resembles mine in that he distinguishes 'illusionistic' and its opposite as a basic contrast in film theory, but 'opposite' for him means a Brechtian awareness of the medium, not magic tricks.

29 See Alan Dessen, 'The Supernatural on Television', *Shakespeare on Film Newsletter*, 11 (December 1986), 1–8.

30 *Ibid.*, p. 1.

31 Barbara H. Traister, *Heavenly Necromancers: The Magician in English Renaissance Drama* (Columbia, MO, 1984), p. 18.

17

TONY HOWARD

Shakespeare's cinematic offshoots

In the year 2000, King Lear walked into the Namibian desert. In 2002, his Fool was murdered in Liverpool's post-industrial docks. Meanwhile Richard III clawed his way to the top of East Los Angeles's drugs gangs, the Macbeths took over a fast-food restaurant, Othello became Commissioner of the Metropolitan Police, and Hamlet learned to trust her uncle. Shakespeare, that is, provided the narrative spine for the Dogme experimental film *The King is Alive* (dir. Kristian Levring, Denmark, 2002), the bleak British social allegory *My Kingdom* (dir. Don Boyd, UK, 2002), the Hollywood exploitation movie *The Street King* (dir. James Gavin Bedford, USA, 2002), the comedy *Scotland PA* (dir. Billy Morrissette, USA, 2001), Geoffrey Sax and Andrew Davies's t.v. *Othello* (2001) exploring contemporary race and gender problems, and the teen thriller *The Glass House* (dir. Daniel Sackheim, USA, 2001). Diverse in form, technique, audience and achievement, these updatings represented a practice as old and intriguing as Shakespearean cinema itself.

In 1911 the British trade press welcomed the Danish silent film *Desdemona*, where a jealous modern actor murders his wife on-stage during a performance of *Othello*. The producers were congratulated for understanding the public, for providing not 'unadulterated Shakespeare' but 'a good modern play with a plot not too deep but just deep enough for mental exercise without effort, while interest and excitement are sustained throughout'. There were 'countless hordes to whom the Bard's plays do not appeal in the remotest degree', but making a film 'so to speak, around the tragedy of Othello' should suit and satisfy and perhaps improve this mass audience.[1] There were many such modernisations and adaptations in the silent era – Asta Nielsen's cross-dressed *Hamlet*, perhaps the greatest silent Shakespeare film, plays fast and loose with the original – and when in the late 1930s Warner Brothers' *A Midsummer Night's Dream*, MGM's *Romeo and Juliet* and in England Twentieth Century Fox's *As You Like It* [2] were all critical and commercial failures and the studios abruptly lost faith in the plays' box-office potential, screen Shakespeare did not simply disappear. Just as 'Shakespeare' permeates our culture iconographically from cheque cards to cigars, so in mainstream film culture the plays have functioned as myths and sources; they materialise repeatedly and often unnoticed on cinema screens through allusions and variations, remakes, adaptations and parodies. In this broader, culturally important, sense 'Shakespearean film' is not only populated by Olivier, Welles, Branagh and company – Jean-Luc Godard, Jean-Paul Sartre and James T. Kirk are also there, alongside Cole Porter, Katherine Hepburn, Arnold Schwarzenegger, Mel Brooks and Sid James. Here we can only point to a vast terrain of cinematic appropriation, and suggest some historical implications of 'free' Shakespearean film.

Some of these were careful close reworkings of the original, some merely alluded to the tale or tapped into it as dramatic shorthand; some tried to popularise Shakespeare and some derided 'Shakespeare' as symbolic of whole structures of class privilege, cultural inequality or social control. Thus the history of Shakespearean adaptations mirrors the cultural and political history of the societies that made them much more overtly than orthodox Shakespearean film, where until recently directors strained to recreate history or evoke 'timelessness'. Orson Welles's versions were originally attacked because he refused to subordinate his creativity to Shakespeare's. He used the Falstaff plays to denounce modern political hypocrisy and militarism (*Chimes at Midnight*'s horrific battle evokes the Somme, Korea and Vietnam) and tried to find backing for a modern-dress news reel *Julius Caesar* and an anti-racist *Merchant*; like Welles, but usually with greater commercial acumen, the adaptors have a contradictory relationship with the plays, longing to borrow their dramatic power and mythic resonance yet rebelliously asserting their own freedom. This almost Oedipal relationship is important for an understanding of the ways both the industry (popular cinema) and the independent *auteur* (art films) have recycled Shakespeare.

During World War II, Shakespeare in Anglo-American cinema symbolised the survival of values. Scenes of the Blitz were intercut with air-raid wardens quoting 'Be not afeared, the isle is full of noises' in the spy thriller *The Yellow Canary* (dir. Herbert Wilcox, 1943) and with John Gielgud's Hamlet in the documentary *A Letter to Timothy* (dir. Humphrey Jennings, released 1946), a meditation on wartime Britain's legacy to the young. (We shall see that generational themes became central to Shakespearean film adaptations.) In Ernst Lubitsch's great black comedy *To Be or Not to Be*, set in occupied Warsaw (USA, 1942), two familiar speeches become leitmotifs. In a brilliantly underplayed running joke, whenever the pompous actor Joseph Tura (Jack Benny) speaks Hamlet's Soliloquy, someone walks noisily out (usually to make love to Tura's wife); but meanwhile a Jewish spear-carrier dreams of playing Shylock and saying 'Hath not a Jew eyes . . .' He quotes it amidst the bombed city's rubble where his eloquence reproves a montage of brutal Nazi posters – 'CONCENTRATION CAMP' . . . 'EXECUTED' – and finally he speaks the speech straight into the face of Hitler himself (or seems to – this is a film about illusions). This crystallised contradictory popular attitudes: 'Shakespeare' could signify stagey pretentiousness and yet Shylock's words preserve fundamental truths and give a voice to the victimised millions.[3]

In post-war Britain, largely thanks to Olivier, Shakespearean film became prestigious and educational (several minor companies vied to make condensed schools versions) but except for Welles's *Macbeth* and Mankiewicz's *Julius Caesar*, Hollywood kept its distance. Instead it used the plots as raw material for mainstream genre films. In 1946 Twentieth Century Fox turned *The Tempest* into the Western *Yellow Sky* (dir. William Wellman) and followed it in 1949 with Mankiewicz's powerful urban melodrama *House of Strangers*, partly based on *King Lear*. This was itself remade as a Western, *Broken Lance* (dir. Edward Dmytryk, 1954), and in 1955 Columbia responded with both a cheap gangster flick filmed in England, *Joe Macbeth* (dir. Ken Hughes), and *Jubal* (dir. Delmer Daves) a cowboy *Othello*. MGM's contribution was the science-fiction *Tempest*, *Forbidden Planet* (dir. Fred McLeod Wilcox, 1956). Most were in the new cinemascope process: Shakespeare meant grandeur and the wide landscape became an existential stage where human actions might be larger than life or dwarfed by nature. And in all these films the dream of creating a new world is central; Shakespeare provided images and fables to help articulate the prosperous optimism of the Truman–Eisenhower years, but in ways that involved a bruised settling of accounts with America's heritage.

Romeo and Juliet: 'There's a place for us' (*West Side Story*)

Such adaptations work differently for three kinds of spectator – those who compare them knowingly to the original, those for whom the films are introductions to Shakespeare's plots and those who are simply guaranteed 'interest and excitement' because of the source material's proven strength. In the case of Romeo and Juliet, synonyms for young love, film-makers can rely on universal recognition: we inherit so many of our images of romance, generational discord and social hatred from the play that it's impossible to list all its cinematic reincarnations. For instance, the musical comedy *Romeo and Julie/Romeo i Julcia* (Poland, 1937) mocked the contradictory aspirations of inter-war Poland – the hero patriotically loves a rustic but his ambitious father wants him to marry an American – whereas in the heat of World War II neutral Switzerland made *Romeo and Juliet in the Village/Romeo und Julia auf dem Dorfe* (1941), an escapist fantasy of love in idyllic scenery and petty feuds over farmland.[4] After the war, the romantic tragedy *The Lovers of Verona/Les Amants de Vérone* (dir. André Cayatte, France, 1949) told of the doomed love of two stand-ins who meet during a Shakespearean film-shoot. Their passion unlocks violent family memories of the Occupation – her father was a fascist – and they die on Romeo and Juliet's tomb. Then the Cold War revivified the myth. In 1960 versions appeared on both sides of the Iron Curtain: Jiri Weiss's *Romeo, Juliet and Darkness/Romeo, Julie a Tma* recalled the plight of Czech Jews during the Holocaust while Peter Ustinov's diplomatic satire *Romanoff and Juliet* (USA) showed romance undermining America and Russia's efforts to control tiny Concordia. By 1966 in *Romeo and Juliet of Today/Kuko su se Voleli Rome i Julija* (Yugoslavia), the lovers were divided by status and money in a Communist society trying to embrace Western values. The list extended to subcultures, from *West Side Story*'s Sharks and Jets fighting in New York's Latin American community (dir. Robert Wise and Jerome Robbins, USA, 1961[5]), to *The Punk* (dir. Mike Sarne, UK, 1993), where Rockers hunt Punks in Notting Hill and an unemployed teenager falls for an heiress (American again) playing Juliet in a pub theatre – after poolroom duels and apparent death by heroin, love conquers all.

Alongside these social allegories, other films were more playful – a Belgian *Romeo and Juliet* (1990) featured love-sick talking cats. Many backstage comedies featured actors playing actors playing the lovers (John Barrymore, Bette Davies, Katherine Hepburn, etc.) and of course Shakespeare, as our epitome of Good Taste, is rife for conversion into Bad: from *Panic Button* in the innocent 1960s (dir. George Sherman, USA, 1964) – where the charmingly mismatched Maurice Chevalier and Jayne Mansfield appear in a deliberately dreadful *Romeo and Juliet* – to the emetic teen-flick *Tromeo and Juliet* (dir. Lloyd Kaufman, USA, 1996), in which Juliet and the Nurse have lesbian sex, Romeo masturbates, various body parts are removed, the feud is between rival porn czars and incest rules.[6]

King Lear: 'Let's keep this in the family' (*House of Strangers*)

Though we traditionally see the director as the *auteur,* here the screenwriter is equally important. *House of Strangers, Broken Lance* and *Joe Macbeth* were all credited to the prolific Philip Yordan,[7] who often engaged with epic social breakdown (*The Decline and Fall of the Roman Empire*), the heroic and the subversive (from *El Cid* to *Johnny Guitar*), and personally engaged in the game of illusion and reality by acting as a front for several blacklisted writers. *House of Strangers* and *Broken Lance* star Edward G. Robinson and Spencer Tracy respectively as proud immigrant patriarchs, the creators of modern America: Robinson plays Gino Monetti, an Italian New York banker, Tracy is an Irish rancher, Matt Devereux. But the founding fathers have become America's Lears, bullying and humiliating three grown sons and making them slave for their birthright. As individualists, they refuse to acknowledge the modern community's laws: Monetti despises account-books, treating debtors with arbitrary charity or harshness, and Devereux destroys a government-backed mining operation polluting his water. They give their sons everything in a legal ploy to avoid prison, and are instantly overthrown. Lear's kingdom evolves overnight into a brutally efficient capitalist organisation. There is also an idolised fourth son, Cordelia crossed with Edgar (played by Richard Conte, then Robert Wagner). Whereas Kurosawa's *Ran* changes Lear's daughters into sons on the historical grounds that female inheritance in seventeenth-century Japan would be implausible, the fact that 1950s Hollywood did the same was a striking instance of sexual conservatism.

In *House of Strangers* the *Lear* parallels are unstressed till a brilliantly urbanised storm: Monetti is stripped of dignity ('Go eat peanuts in the park'), and driven from his bank as deafening pneumatic drills rip through the walls and drown his baffled threats. But in *Broken Lance* Yordan strengthens the 'Bardic' tone by stripping away social and psychological detail to expose a mythic structure and by idealising the youngest son, who becomes the half-Indian hero of an anti-racist *Romeo and Juliet* subplot. The setting frees the characters to become larger than life again: Devereux tamed the frontier long ago by single-handedly making peace with the Indians (the broken lance) and married into the tribe. His second wife (Katy Jurado) has some of the Fool's plain-speaking functions, and references to tribal 'superstition' restore an anti-naturalistic dimension: we see Devereux dead but upright in the saddle, and in both films the father's spirit haunts the loyal son's imagination. In *House of Strangers* he refuses to take revenge, but in *Broken Lance* he kills his evil half-brother, the Western's simple conventions reinstating Renaissance codes of masculinity and poetic justice. However, whereas in Shakespeare the young must take control of the state, the youthful heroes and heroines of all the 1950s Hollywood adaptations refuse their tainted inheritance and depart for the unknown.

In *The Godfather* (USA, 1972) the third son is forced to return to the family and a baptism in blood. Here the Shakespearean analogues are probably accidental, but when a decade of financial failures compelled Francis Ford Coppola to make *Godfather III* (1990), he deliberately tried to give it grandeur by copying *King Lear*. At a lavish party evoking the start of both the first *Godfather* and the play, the ageing Michael Corleone (Al Pacino) tries to retire from crime for his children's sake but in the process throws the Mafia network into primal anarchy. As in *Lear*, 'legitimacy' is a key theme and Coppola introduces Michael's illegitimate nephew Vincent (Andy Garcia) whose loyalty is in question until the end – is he Edgar or Edmund? *Lear* gave Coppola three structural high points: the opening, the storm – Michael goes into hiding and is struck down not by madness but a diabetes attack (the medical realism of Pacino's acting makes this work) – and the catastrophe. Echoing real-life scandals, Corleone forges an alliance with corrupt papal bankers and in the bravura cross-cut finale we see an eye pierced and a body hanging (not Cordelia but a banker, based on Roberto Calvi, who died mysteriously at Blackfriars Bridge near Shakespeare's Globe). Moments later a sniper kills Michael's daughter on the steps of an opera house. He holds her and howls. Coppola also copied *Ran*, dropping the vengeful daughters but building up another woman, in this case Michael's sister (Talia Shire), into a scheming monster. The film's weakest element is Corleone's daughter – at best an innocent sacrificial symbol, at worst a sexual pawn – and Coppola muddied the sexual politics further by casting his own inexperienced daughter Sophia, insisting she *was* the character.

Whereas the theatre has used *King Lear* to test dominant gender attitudes ever since the early 1970s, it was not until Jocelyn Moorhouse filmed Jane Smiley's feminist novel *A Thousand Acres* (USA, 1997) that popular cinema finally confronted *Lear*'s disturbing sexual dimensions. This time Latty Creek (Jason Robardes) means to split his Iowa farm between his three daughters Ginny (Jessica Lange), Rose (Michelle Pfeiffer) and Caroline (Jennifer Jason Leigh) until Caroline, a lawyer, expresses doubts and her enraged father cuts her out. Though his sanity deteriorates, the real psychological journey is Rose and Ginny's: they begin to remember a buried history of sexual abuse. Creek – and implicitly Shakespeare – pits the sisters against each other, yet they start to communicate. Moorhouse removes the blinding scene (still in the novel) but Rose herself is mutilated (a mastectomy) as Shakespeare's 'unnatural hags' become complicated survivors played by three of the decade's leading actresses. Whereas Coppola's *Lear* echoes were tactics to dignify an unnecessary sequel, *A Thousand Acres* insists on the disturbing psychological implications of the myth itself.

Hamlet: 'People always confuse things with their appearance' (*Ophélia*)

In 1968 Enzo Castellari directed a spaghetti Western, *Johnny Hamlet*.[8] This genre thrived by pushing conventions to the point of self-parodic excess, frequently as a disguise for Marxist critiques, and here Johnny 'Hamlet' Hamilton returns home after the Civil War, finds his murderous uncle Claude has taken over the ranch, and meets a gallery of familiar characters – Gertrude, Horace, Ross. The villains crucify him. But such exoticism was rare. *Hamlet*'s specific appeal to film-makers lay in its familiarity, its potential for social realism. On-screen, Elsinore became the post-war capitalist *status quo*.

In 1959 a British B-picture, *An Honourable Murder* (dir. Godfrey Grayson) turned *Julius Caesar* into a tale of boardroom coups, with Antony delivering his speech to the investors – it was released in a double-bill with a documentary about the territorial behaviour of gorillas – but *Hamlet*'s psychological and family dimensions and its exploration of guilt offered richer possibilities: Claudius's *realpolitik*, Polonius's prying bureaucracy, Elsinore's 'normality' based on lies – here was compelling material for film-makers determined to confront their own inheritance and survey the society their parents had built on the ruins of war. Also, Helmut Käulner directed Hardy Kruger in a contemporary West German *Hamlet – The Rest is Silence (Der Rest ist Schweigen)* – where Claudius was a Rhine-Ruhr industrialist, and in Japan a year later Akira Kurosawa abandoned samurai cinema for his *Hamlet, The Bad Sleep Well (Warui Yatsu Hodo Yoku Nemeru)*. Launching his production company – 'I wanted to make a film of some social significance' – it attacked civic corruption, 'the worst crime that there is'.[9]

The Bad Sleep Well opens with an astonishing twenty-minute wedding breakfast. When a corporation executive marries his daughter to his secretary Nishi (Toshiro Mifune), a chorus of journalists gate-crash the party, tipped off that the fraud squad will arrest powerful guests. We are forced to work out who's who in an incomprehensible closed community while the wedding party try to ignore the disaster. This is not only the first court scene of *Hamlet* but also 'The Mousetrap': a giant cake shaped like an office-block is wheeled in with a rose marking the window from which an executive fell to his death. Only later will we understand that one guest's shocked response reveals his guilt. Without much exaggeration, a reporter describes this sequence as 'the greatest one-act play I've ever seen', only to be told, 'No, it's only the Prologue.' The *Hamlet* parallel comes into focus slowly. Nishi is the dead man's son, come to take revenge. Gertrude and Claudius are cut, because Kurosawa presents modern corporate Japan as the world according to Polonius, and Hamlet infiltrates it by marrying Ophelia (it's her playboy brother who disrupts the wedding with sarcastic speeches). The corporations conceal their crimes through a culture of subservience and shame – murder is hardly necessary when terrified lackeys commit suicide to save their superiors – until the stone-faced, virtually silent Nishi stops one conspirator from jumping into a volcano and makes him play the Ghost to scare his masters. Such baroque black-comic details make *The Bad Sleep Well* resemble *The Revenger's Tragedy* rather than *Hamlet* until Nishi drops his guard. He despises himself for not hating enough. Kurosawa gives him one accomplice, a Horatio, and sets the graveyard scene in a vast ashen bombsite where in 1945 they were child-conscript factory workers. Their Wittenberg was the firestorm. Fifteen years later Kurosawa depicts a society where no one accepts responsibility. Nor will they, for the end is shocking. Hamlet unbends, confides in Ophelia and is murdered. Another 'accident' preserves the system.

Claude Chabrol's *Ophélia* (France, 1962) pretends to be the same film. It also begins brilliantly, with a coffin lid shutting on us. An industrialist's widow marries his brother Adrien, who lives in a country château where a gang of neo-fascist thugs protect him from strikers. Whereas Kurosawa makes *Hamlet* emerge gradually into his world, Chabrol introduces it centrally and meta-cinematically.

Olivier's *Hamlet*, showing at the local fleapit, convinces the highly strung son Yvan (unsympathetically acted by André Jocelyn) that life repeats art: his uncle is a murderer, his girlfriend Lucie is Ophelia and he's Hamlet. Feigning (?) madness, he lectures the crows on mortality, insults everybody and disrupts dinner by claiming the servants spit in the soup. He denounces the murderers in a film-within-the-film; Lucie's spying father has a heart-attack up a tree; and Adrien tries to kill Yvan, fails and commits suicide. Whereupon, in a Hitchcockian transfer of guilt, Yvan learns there was no murder. He is not Hamlet: 'People always confuse things with their appearance.' Indeed most of the characters live fantasy lives (do the revolutionary strikers only exist in the boss's conscience?) and though Chabrol's grotesque bourgeoisie are corrupt, he denies that their crimes – still less the solutions – are as melodramatically clear-cut and domestic as in *Hamlet*. The self-dramatising Yvan represents the egotism of artists, intellectuals and youth, and Chabrol provides no reassuring points of identification for the audience. Yvan is not the objective observer he supposes, and cinema itself is exposed as a medium at the mercy of spectators: it's the thugs who recommend *Hamlet* ('It's got fighting in it') and though we probably read the locale – 'Erneles' – as an anagram of 'Elseneur', it isn't.

By 1987 irony ruled. In Aki Kaurismäki's *Hamlet Goes Business* (*Hamlet Liikemaailmassa*) – a Finnish 'black-and-white, underground B-movie classical drama' – a powerful sawmill-owner is poisoned and his brother plans to close the mills and buy up the Swedish rubber-duck industry. Life is so hermetically shrunk and privatised now that Ophelia drowns herself in the bath and Hamlet (the comedian Pikka-Pekka Petelius), who keeps failing to seduce her, makes her brother work in a toilet. The bizarre has become the norm. Whereas adaptors normally invoke classical literature to remind us of enduring ethical certainties, these characters have the Shakespearean names because this is what Shakespeare's characters have become: today's Hamlet stages *The Importance of Being Earnest* (with interpolated homicide), escapes death by poisoned chicken and then turns out to have killed his father. In a pseudo-Marxist finale Hamlet's chauffeur kills him, saves the millworkers, runs off into the sunset with the maid and leaves us to decide how ludicrous this is. Kaurismäki's lugubriously funny *film noir* is a post-industrial epitaph for a dying system doomed indefinitely to repeat its tragedies as farce.[10]

Macbeth: 'Which one of you guys done this?' (*Joe Macbeth*)

Different plays have inspired different adapting strategies. *Macbeth* and *Othello* have been seen as studies of the relationship between marriage, eroticism – in *Macbeth* strangely cementing the lovers, in *Othello* destroying them – and violence. Of all the plays, *Macbeth* has been adapted most directly, indeed almost naively. *Joe Macbeth* is a cheap transatlantic gangster film where fading American actors (Paul Douglas and Ruth Roman) rub shoulders with Sid James (Banky). This is the most 'loyal' of Philip Yordan's Shakespeare adaptations, and for that very reason the worst; though it has deliberately ironic overtones for 'sophisticated' viewers, this is simplified Shakespeare – consider *Macbeth*'s popularity in Victorian melodrama houses – where Lily and the stolid hitman Mac rub out 'the Duke' and Mac becomes 'kingpin', only to shoot Lily at the end by accident. Yordan cuts Malcolm and Macduff so that Fleance (Lennie) is the victor, but otherwise paraphrases plot and dialogue closely:

> *'It's done. I won't go out there again!'* . . . *'Nobody says nothing. We all know what's going on, but nobody says nothing.'* . . . *'Put the finger on Banky.'* . . . *'You saw yourself in a yellow mirror.'*

Gang wars provided a modern context for the play's tribal codes of violence and though the odd casting and tiny budget – only three major sets and two locations – suggest amateur dramatics, it is impossible to dislike the film. Poverty creates a weird somnambulist tone: as Mac climbs the stairs to commit the murder his boss suddenly appears downstairs and invites Lily for a swim in the lake. The gently insistent ringing of a bell on a buoy effectively builds tension and the killing is half-suggested, half-shown as Mac drags his victim underwater. The climax exemplifies its economical virtues – as Mac becomes more isolated, darkness embraces him and he shoots desperately into total blackness – and it wasn't surprising when *Joe Macbeth* was remade in 1990 as the more upmarket *Men of Respect* (US, William Reilly).[11] As before, the protagonists (John Torturro and Katherine Borowitz as Michael and Ruthie Battaglia) run a restaurant as a front ('Pleasant!', says Rod Steiger, the new Duncan-figure) but this time, following Roman Polanski, they are a young charismatic couple, vulnerable as well as ambitious (she will commit suicide).

The Shakespearean parallels are still lumbering – enter Duffy and Mal – but Reilly tries to modernise the supernatural factor. *Joe Macbeth* gave the prophecies to a pair of street eccentrics, Rosie the hot-chestnut-seller and 'Prince Charles', a sandwich-board-man, and dismissed their influence: 'Maybe what happened happened not because Rosie said it would, but because you did what she said.' Michael Battaglia, however, falls in with a group of decadent occultists out of *Rosemary's Baby* and begins to see visions. They promise him invulnerability till the stars fall from heaven – he's killed during a firework display and, though literally dazzling, the end is morally darker: Banky's son rejects the keys to *Joe Macbeth*'s mansion and walks away, but Reilly's film ends with the same character ritually welcomed by the Mafia elders as a 'man of respect'. Again following Polanski, the future promises only more bloody seizures of power.

Othello: 'Desdemona will not die tonight' (*Men Are Not Gods*)

Delmer Daves's psychological Western *Jubal* (USA, 1955) also paraphrased Shakespeare simply – 'Haply for I am black / And am declined into the vale of years, but that's not much' becomes 'I can't change this ugly face none', – but Daves reworked *Othello* from the moral viewpoint of the innocent bystander, Cassio. He becomes the drifter Jubal Troop (Glen Ford) who meets a mismatched couple, Shep, a genial but slobbish rancher, and Mae, his Canadian wife (Ernest Borgnine and Valerie French). The *Othello* parallels are precise: Shep wooed Mae with tales that he was a Wyoming cattle king come to waft her to his castle; his herd is besieged (by mountain lions), and when he makes Jubal foreman a jealous ranch-hand (Rod Steiger) claims Mae is Jubal's mistress. But Daves reverses one pivotal assumption: Mae really *is* unfaithful. She tries to seduce Jubal, has had an affair with Steiger and falsely confesses in the bedroom scene, frantically hoping Jubal will kill Shep in self-defence. He does. Steiger's character murders her and whips up a lynch mob with a Mark Antony speech.

Demonised female sexuality is the heart of *Jubal*. Though Mae is partly Madame Bovary ('For a woman it's 10,000 acres of loneliness') she's also a stock *film noir femme fatale*. In the second half, Daves sidelines her potential tragedy and introduces his own symbol of female purity – a chaste young woman ('I've not been kissed') from a wagon train of Christians seeking the Promised Land. She and Jubal fall in love, so Bianca and Desdemona are reversed – or rather Daves creates two Desdemonas, one voracious and one virginal, and Desdemona II gives Jubal a handkerchief after he haltingly reveals the origin of his restless wanderings: the Mother. Jubal's mother (cf. Clarence's dream) watched uncaringly as his father died saving him from drowning. *Jubal* tries to turn *Othello* into a hymn to decency, but its force derives from Mae's doomed longings and from Steiger's acting, for though the script simplifies Iago's envy, Steiger makes him a whinnying psychotic mystery and darkens an escapist genre.[12]

Iago also dominates *All Night Long* (dir. Michael Relph and Basil Dearden, UK, 1961). This is set in a London jazz club where an embittered drummer (played by Patrick McGoohan) convinces the black American trumpeter Aurelius Rex [13] (Paul Harris) that his wife Delia (Marti Stevens) is unfaithful. Again the villain's motive is one-dimensional – Delia refused to join his band – but unlike Daves, Relph and Dearden strain to make *Othello* modern – McGoohan fabricates evidence on session tapes – and match its claustrophobia by trapping everyone in an all-night party. They use dizzying crane and tracking shots and a strong jazz score from John Dankworth, Dave Brubeck and others who appear as themselves, 'authenticating' Shakespeare. This time tragedy is averted and McGoohan ends the film alone and shunned, drumming madly. Ever since Verdi's *Otello* (filmed by Zeffirelli in 1986) this play's passion has invited musical expression, and in 1973 McGoohan directed *Catch My Soul,* the film of Jack Good's rock opera *Othello.* He outdid *All Night Long* with pyrotechnic camera-work and echoed *Jubal* by using American landscapes (the Rio Grande). Although Good's stage show had retained the original plot and the film still used Shakespeare's language, it tried to exploit a vogue for rock religiosity (cf. *Jesus Christ Superstar* and *Godspell*) by turning Othello (Richie Havens) into a modern evangelist trying to build a new church. Iago (Launce le Gault) is a redneck satanist backed vocally by the 'Tribe of Hell'. Yet again, he is the film's one great success: evil fascinates us. The hippy Desdemona dies by the altar before being welcomed into Heaven by a half-black, half-white Christ.[14]

However poorly, *Catch My Soul* did respond to *Othello*'s metaphysical symbols. Normally the play has attracted producers because of its accessibility and the tight focus on sexuality – Oliver Parker's 1995 *Othello* was marketed as an 'erotic thriller' – but, paradoxically, it has also been used throughout cinema history as a Pirandellan vehicle to explore the psychology of performance.

Desdemona (Denmark, 1911), *A Modern Othello* (UK, 1917) and *Carnival* (UK, 1921) all told of performers becoming entangled with the monstrous emotions they enact. They established a subgenre: usually a husband and wife are starring in Shakespeare's play and he, consumed by jealously, tries to kill her on-stage. Arbitrarily, it may end in murder, suicide or reconciliation: 'A comedy, a farce . . . Or call it a tragedy if you prefer . . . why not? It's exactly the same', says a cynic in *Les Enfants du Paradis* (dir. Marcel Carné, France, 1945) which plays rich variations on the interplay of theatre and life. In this romantic epic, filmed as the Occupation ended, two nineteenth-century actors, the ebullient tragedian Frédérick Lemaître (played by Pierre Brasseur)[15] and the doomed pierrot Debureau (Jean-Louis Barrault) spend their lives pursuing Garance (Arletty) – a living symbol of the Feminine and Truth. Lemaître projects his jealousy into his acting: 'Thanks to you I shall be able to play Othello! . . . I didn't feel him. He was a stranger. There it is, now he's a friend, he's a brother, now I know him, I have him in my grasp!' For Lemaître performance is therapy ('Othello is cured!') but Debureau sees Othello as a 'sad and ridiculous' victim of love ('Like me') and would turn the play into mime, denying him language, self-expression and release. Later Jean-Paul Sartre wrote *Kean* for Brasseur (filmed Italy 1956, starring Vittorio Gassman) and extended such contradictions into a philosophical game. Sartre's hero disrupts his own *Othello* by meditating wildly on the chinese-box of falsity/authenticity he inhabits. 'Listen, I am going to tell you something – I'm not alive, I only pretend.' And yet 'Real emotions are the same as stage emotions, just worse acted.'

Hollywood and England have been interested in psychology, not philosophy. They have used the Othello actor to explore madness and tentatively touch on sexual violence. In *Men Are Not Gods* (dir. Walter Reisch, UK, 1936) an actor

sees life as a repertoire of roles and uses Shakespeare as shorthand to justify adultery: the first thing Edmund Davey (Sebastian Shaw) tells the heroine Ann
(Miriam Hopkins) is, 'In private life the parts are reversed. Desdemona is the
jealous one; Othello is the victim' (i.e., 'My wife doesn't understand me').
Shakespeare was shorthand for the film-makers too: after an hour of social
comedy and subtle emotional work by Miriam Hopkins, Ann tells Davey to stay
with his wife for 'as long as she lives' and there is a creaking shift of genres. He
interprets it as incitement to murder; rushes to the theatre and tries to strangle
Desdemona, transformed from a cosseted near-invalid into a maniac. The
Shakespearean parallels substitute for plausibility, and they work to the extent
that male emotions are rendered infantile. In the psychological thriller *A Double
Life* (dir. George Cukor, USA, 1947) Ronald Coleman plays an actor who sub-
merges himself in his roles so intensely that they take him over. Inevitably, a
homicidal self is released when he plays *Othello* on Broadway with his ex-wife
and he strangles the Bianca-figure, a lonely waitress, as if rehearsing. Like
Men Are Not Gods, this film mingles backstage banter with wild melodrama –
incidentally both Othellos act better when insane – but their climaxes diverge.
In the English film the husband and wife are reunited, in *A Double Life*
Coleman/Othello stabs himself.

There is a racial factor here. Othello used to be envisaged as a savage sexual
underself waiting to consume the most sophisticated of men, the classical actor,
who dons black make-up and is tainted by pitch. The Othello motif still haunts
films set as far apart as Montreal's artists' quarter (*An Imaginary Tale/Une
Histoire Inventée*, France, 1990) and 1950s rural Ireland (*The Playboys*, UK,
1992) – in both cases the Desdemona figure finally escapes from an insular
microsociety – but the most historically significant variant was also the most
light-hearted, Touchstone/Disney's *True Identity* (dir. Charles Lane, USA, 1991).
Lenny Henry plays a frustrated black American actor longing to fulfil himself by
playing Othello. He becomes embroiled in a crime plot and survives by reversing
conventions and disguising himself in whiteface. In Disney, dreams come true:
he understudies James Earl Jones's Othello – Jones, as an icon of black cultural
achievement, plays himself – and takes over. For all its superficiality, *True
Identity* confronted the black actor's right to play Othello four years before
Laurence Fishburne actually did so. Soon afterwards, Tim Blake Nelson's *O*
(USA, 1999) and Geoffrey Sax's 2001 ITV *Othello* used the play to discuss racial
and sexual tensions in enclosed contemporary communities: London's embat-
tled police force and an elite American college. John Othello is promoted by New
Labour to allay charges of 'institutionalised racism' and win the black urban
vote; in *O* the fallen sports star Odin (cf. O. J. Simpson) insists he be judged as
himself, not as a victim of the ghetto. In the British version, Christopher
Ecclestone gleefully survives to win Othello's place; Nelson makes his young

Iago sympathetic, driven by a need to win his father's love and 'fly': the result was that again Iago dominated the films, raising the question why, when everything else in Shakespeare could be rewritten, the authors decided that the black protagonist must still succomb, rage, kill and perish. The liberal *All Night Long* had been more positive forty years before.

The Tempest: the return of the father

If *Othello* films focus on the performer as a sacrificial gladiator, many *Tempest* films are about the director and the fusion of opposites in art. In the wartime romance *Love Story* (UK, 1944) a dying pianist and a half-blind war hero are brought together by an industrialist financing a *Tempest* production on a Cornish clifftop. Love and hope survive when nature, art and science (an operation saves the hero) come together, exactly as they do in Powell and Pressburger's *A Matter of Life and Death* (UK, 1946) where the benign older man surveys the world in a camera obscura while American troops rehearse *A Midsummer Night's Dream*. After such romantic optimism, William Wellman's *Yellow Sky* (USA, 1948) turned *The Tempest* into a harsh post-war Western where a gang of criminals (bankrobbers replacing aristocrats) stumble on an isolated old man and a girl. The elemental metaphors are reversed. Shakespeare's sea gives way to thirst: fleeing across a desert, on the brink of death they discover no magic island but a ghost town where a prospector and his granddaughter guard water and gold. Wellman focuses on the girl, who is constantly threatened by rape but protects herself with tough talk and a rifle, and on the Caliban question: can any of these degenerates be redeemed? This is not an issue in the most famous *Tempest* offshoot, *Forbidden Planet* (USA, 1956): here American manhood is represented as a brave crew of astronauts who find Professor Morbius (Walter Pidgeon) and his daughter Altaira (Anne Francis), sole survivors of an expedition to Altair 4. Their polite servant Robby the Robot is a compound of Ariel, the Michelin Man and the play's *commedia* elements. For once the superimposed film genre fits exactly because *The Tempest* itself was proto-science-fiction, a response to the utopian possibility of literally finding/founding new worlds in America, of using accumulated human knowledge to start anew. In both play and film human nature is the problem. The spaceship is attacked by an invisible beast, 'a monster from the id' – Morbius's primeval subconscious unleashed by alien technology. Prospero *is* Caliban and so 'the great globe itself' literally explodes into a point of light. This kitsch, beautiful, film is politically reactionary – the intellectual must be distrusted and military force is benign ('We're all part monster in our unconscious: that's why we have laws and religion'), but it profoundly influenced later *Tempest* interpretations because, confronting two new sciences, Einstein's and Freud's, it warned that the real forbidden planet is the mind.

The Fall occurs on Altair 4 when Commander Adams kisses Altaira. Most *Tempest* films focus problematically on Miranda's sexual awakening. In *Yellow Sky* and *Forbidden Planet* there's no Ferdinand: she's won by an 'experienced' older man, and other films actually eroticise her relationship with Prospero, the director's surrogate. Michael Powell planned to film Shakespeare's play (seeing cinema as the fusion of science and art, he included a scene with Galileo) but after his career collapsed when *Peeping Tom* (1959) was denounced as pornography, like Prospero Powell went into exile, working for the embryonic Australian film industry. In his *Age of Consent* (Australia, 1968) James Mason plays a disillusioned New York painter who rediscovers inspiration by isolating himself on the Great Barrier Reef. Bright sand and extraordinarily beautiful undersea photography dominate this film, but there is a Sycorax nearby, a drunk woman with a beachcombing daughter (Helen Mirren) who predictably becomes the painter's naked Muse, Miranda-Ariel. *Age of Consent* is a benign comedy which at least handles its menopausal male fantasy of sexual/artistic renewal with tact – there's no intimacy till the very last frame – but *The Tempest*'s allure for ageing male directors is obvious. In Paul Mazursky's *Tempest* (USA, 1982) another visual artist flees the cultural court of New York to find lost Arcadia. John Cassavetes and Gina Rowlands play the architect Philip Dimitriou and his estranged actress-wife Antonia, who is having an affair with a tycoon, Alonso. Philip takes his teenage daughter Miranda (Molly Ringwald) to a Greek island, where he has an affair with a singer and Miranda is drooled over by Kalibanos the goatherd (Raul Julia) who, stealing science to suit his needs, lives in a cave watching TV. When Antonia and Alonso cruise by, an elaborate encounter-group session begins. Caught between sophistication and primitivism, the film is awkwardly self-conscious, so lumbering psychodrama – Kalibanos accuses Philip of incestuous desires and they try to drown each other – jostles self-parody: the truth-seekers trip over Japanese tourists and, knowing what hostile critics would say, Mazursky writes in a 'Woody Allen Lookalike'.[16] Still, Shakespearean therapy works and music sounds as Philip and Antonia go home: 'We'll turn Manhattan into an isle of joy.'

'I can't stop crying': recycling Shakespeare in the nineties

But home had changed. In John Boorman's *Lear* offshoot *Where the Heart Is* (USA, 1990), Stewart McBain, a tyrannical property developer in love with the 'poetry' of destruction, drives out his three spoilt children – Chloe (art student), Jimmy (computer freak) and Daphne (aimless) – and makes them fend for themselves in an old Brooklyn house environmentalists stopped him destroying. The trio turn it into a palatial haven for a new extended family, including a gay dress designer, an occultist, and a tramp (Christopher Plummer), who proves to be a

Fool/Merlin, their guide into magical possibilities. Jimmy uses his computer-hacker skills to ruin his father, who wanders the streets, where the homeless charge him $5 for a cardboard box.

This was one of several early 1990s films which used Shakespeare to condemn the social savagery of the Thatcher–Reagan era, the new jungle capitalism. Shakespeare was made homeless, claimed for those on the hungry margins and made a voice of protest. In Christine Edzard's *As You Like It* the court became a London bank foyer and Arden the wastes of Docklands; actors doubled (e.g. the two Dukes) to show the rich becoming redeemed through dispossession. Gus Van Sant's fascinating *My Own Private Idaho* (USA, 1991) modernised the *Henry IV* plays, turning Hal into Scott (Keanu Reeves), a politician's rebel son who escapes into the underclass as a rent-boy, hanging out with the Falstaffian Bob. His flight from the family is counterpointed with the story of a young narcoleptic (River Phoenix) haunted by idyllic rural memories of a lost mother, whom he finds, only to discover a web of incest. Character differences are expressed through contrasted, semi-improvisational acting styles: Phoenix – intuitive, focused and unpredictable – suggests helpless honesty whereas Reeves is mannered. (Unfortunately Van Sant experimented by making his embarrassed cast paraphrase their *Henry IV*-based scenes in pseudo-Elizabethan dialogue; this is the worst of both worlds.) There are repeated quotations from *Chimes at Midnight*, though the grimy and dangerous Bob bears none of the promised resemblance to Welles's Falstaff ('Here comes Father Christmas') and whereas *Chimes* ends with elegiac sorrow, Bob's gang erupt into a carnivalesque orgy on top of his coffin, disrupting Scott's father's funeral. Scott watches, embarrassed, having rejoined his biological family and class. Unlike Henry V, he finally has no loyalties except to himself; he has been a sexual tourist and, rejecting sex as love, is left with nothing but pretence and voyeurism. In total contrast *Where the Heart Is* is a family film. Like *Godfather III*, it was a father–daughter collaboration, co-written with Telsche Boorman, and it glorifies reconciliation, turning *Lear* into a whimsical fantasia. Once McBain remembers what suffering means and his children are forced to be independent, urban hell becomes utopia: they so respect their father that they destroy their home to make way for his building project, he appreciates Chloe's art, love blossoms, their long-lost mother returns and the gay dress designer turns out to be a heterosexual in disguise.

This is not altogether surprising given the fact that Boorman's film was another Touchstone/Disney product (it was originally to have been filmed amongst London's homeless). Disney applied the playing-Shakespeare-brings-self-fulfilment plot to the *Dream* in *Dead Poets' Society* and to *Hamlet* in *Renaissance Man* (sullen recruits become blank-verse-yelling heroes) and to *Hamlet* in *Outrageous Fortune* (Shelley Long plays Hamlet). Disney also turned *Hamlet* into *The Lion King* and politically corrected *The Tempest* in *Pocahontas*. There are too many such recyclings in 1990s cinema to list, from Arnold Schwarzenegger's *Last Action Hero* to Steve Martin's *LA Story*, because they reflect Hollywood's globalisation of film culture – the recycling of certain internationally recognisable cultural icons – and the targeting of high school and college audiences familiar with canonical Great Books[17]. When Baz Lurhmann's *Romeo + Juliet* made unprecedented profits, Shakespearean adapt-ation became so intensely appealing to Hollywood that a new sub-genre emerged, putting the teenagers themselves in the plots. The *Shrew* became *Ten Things I Hate About You* (dir. Gil Junger, USA, 1999); the *Dream* inspired a cheerful musical, *Get Over It* (dir.Tommy O'Haver, USA, 2001); and in *The Glass House* (2001), Hamlet became a bereaved high-school girl whose murderous guardian frames her for plagiarising Harold Bloom on *Hamlet*. Julia Styles, Kirsten Dunst and Leelee Sobieski played charismatic heroines. The popularisation also touched television. American networks wove Shakespeare into baroque re-inventions of national myths: in Jack Bender's creaky *The Tempest* (1998), Peter Fonda played Gideon Prosper, a progressive Mississippi plantation-owner who learns voodoo magic, conquers death and wins the Civil War for freedom; then in *King of Texas* (dir. Uli Edel, 2002), Alamo veteran John Lear (Patrick Stewart) sees the error of his xeno-phobic ways and dies defending the rights of Mexican settlers. More wittily, in 2005 the BBC relocated four plots (*Much Ado*, *Macbeth*, the *Dream* and the *Shrew*) in modern British milieux from newsrooms to Parliament.

Hollywood's embrace of recycled Shakespeare reached its zenith in 1999 when both *The Taming of the Shrew* and *Othello* were remade as high school movies – *10 Things I Hate About You* and *O* – and the romantic comedy *Shakespeare in Love* (directed by John Madden) was awarded the Oscar for Best Picture. The playwright had probably first appeared on screen himself as a major character in the silent short *Shakespeare Writing 'Julius Caesar'* (1907), which begins with him at a loss for ideas, shows his characters take shape before our eyes and ends with him crowned with laurels. Madden's film – written by Marc Norman and Tom Stoppard – adapts this simple inspira-tional pattern and also reworks motifs and jokes familiar from many other biographical fantasies, from Shaw's *Dark Lady of the Sonnets* onwards. The commercial success of Madden's knowing, confidently charming film not only made it a colourful player in the contemporary popularisation of Shakespeare, but also in the marketing of Heritage Britain. Book-of-the-film editions of the sonnets were published, there was a campaign to 'save' the playhouse built for the film, and a member of the Royal Family even renamed himself after one of the characters, Lord Wessex – or at least seemed to have done so. This blurring of fiction and history was apt.

Shakespeare in Love borrows the backstage-drama formula that playing Shakespeare is a gateway to self-fulfilment and neatly applies it to Shakespeare himself. Here an ill-matched crew of Elizabethan theatre people are transformed and united by the process of creating *Romeo and Juliet*. The film is a companion-piece to Stoppard's play *The Real Thing* in its exploration of theatre and love as twin arenas ruled by both lies and truth, and it adheres to his own description of comic drama as dialectical – a way of disagreeing with yourself in public. For it simultaneously debunks the Romantic deification of Shakespeare and takes it in rhapsodic new directions. At first Joseph Fiennes plays him as a mere hack with writer's block, scrounging ideas off Marlowe in a *Carry On* London of mud, blood, chamber-pots and farcical anachronisms. However, when the aristocrat Viola de Lesseps (Gwyneth Paltrow), facing an arranged marriage to the venal (and broke) Lord Wessex, disguises herself as a boy player, another perspective competes with the burlesque. Viola becomes Shakespeare's muse, and for the length of the film the audience may subscribe to the myth that Great Art is the direct product of a Great Writer's extraordinary experience. As he writes *Romeo and Juliet* against the clock, he improvises, steals and picks up unconsidered trifles, but most of all transcribes his and Viola's love-scenes. Passion jolts him into genius.

At times the script is manipulative in its efforts to produce 'Shakespearean' good feeling. Fraught moral situations are regularly contrived, then arbitrarily abandoned. At various points Shakespeare is wracked by guilt because he is a liar, an adulterer, responsible for murder and in love with a boy. He then quickly learns – in the last case within seconds – that half of these aren't true, and that the others don't matter. Thus Stoppard and Norman rethrone a traditional Shakespeare – unproblematic, heterosexual and apolitical. However, the technic-ally brilliant script steers the film – logically, given its emotional sleights-of-hand and Stoppard's love of intellectual paradox – to an intriguing set of multiple endings. Throughout, art is presented as both more and less 'true' than fact. Shakespeare overshadows Viola's fiancé in every way, but though in one scene he out-fences him, he cannot win – Shakespeare's sword is just a prop. At the end, on-stage, he and Viola themselves play Romeo and Juliet and can triumph over every adversity; a *dea ex machinea* Queen Elizabeth (Judi Dench) declares they have proved art can reveal the very soul of love. But outside the theatre's walls, law rules. There Elizabeth commands that Viola must marry and sail with her brute husband to the Americas. The film finally surmounts this contradiction by reshuffling its main plot lines into a different kind of comic pattern. Loss galvanises Shakespeare into writing what will become *Twelfth Night*. We see Viola shipwrecked (which Viola? – Shakespeare's or the 'real' one?) and as the credits roll she crosses a vast tropical beach and disappears into a mysterious forest. The film's last trick is to turn what might be a tragic moment – the writer's defeated withdrawal – into a pastiche of half the comedies at once, an affirmation that it is possible – through art? in life? – to jump from a state of victimisation into worlds of possibility. Shakespeare writes Viola's freedom.

In unpredictable times Shakespeare's survival was once again reassuring. In the post-apocalyptic *The Postman* (1997) Kevin Costner restores civilisation by reintroducing Shakespeare and the US mail, and in *Star Trek VI: The Undiscovered Country,* a pop allegory about the fall of the USSR after Chernobyl, two famous 1960s Hamlets, David Warner and Christopher Plummer disguised as Klingons, discuss the Soliloquy. The film toasts 'the undiscovered country', meaning the future, not death.[17] But ground shifts quickly. Though the t.v. *Tempest* and *King of Texas* were Clintonian, the latter's ending expressed a post-9/11 nervousness: the Edgar character stands on guard scanning the borders, awaiting intruders. Don Boyd's *My Kingdom* and Kristian Levring's *The King is Alive* both used *Lear* to show European society confronting terminal crisis. Boyd's Lear (Richard Harris) was a Liverpool gang boss who had poisoned and demoralised the city's poor through drug trafficking; he watched, bewildered, as his own family perished in scenes of brutal atrocity. In Levring's film, Western tourists, stranded in the desert when their coach breaks down, act out scenes from Shakespeare to pass the time. *King Lear* articulates, accelerates, their disintegration. 'I didn't understand a word they said', an African comments: 'Neither did they.' There can never have been a unified response to Shakespeare, and three final films crystallise the contradictions.

'Life is chaotic but . . .' – waves and particles

Shakespeare intrigued the critic-directors of the French New Wave. Chabrol (*Ophélia*) lent his camera to Jacques Rivette at weekends to help him shoot *Paris Nous Appartient / Paris Belongs to Us* (1959), the story of radical young artists rehearsing *Pericles* in an empty city. The idealistic stage director chooses *Pericles* as the anti-realist antithesis of bourgeois order, and because it means something: 'Life is chaotic but not Absurd.' However, the project degenerates and he commits suicide amidst an escalating sense of global crisis and paranoia. Rivette leaves the heroine unsure whether to return to the rehearsal, whether there are any meanings to be found in art. One of *Paris Nous Appartient*'s untrained cast, the Marxist director Jean-Luc Godard, returned to Shakespearean meta-cinema decades later, but in a spirit suggesting that his generation's optimism was long past. Norman Mailer rewrote *King Lear* for him (USA, 1987) and was to play the lead with his own daughter as Cordelia. Mailer quit after a day (authorial and directoral authority clashed), leaving Godard to create an intricate meditation on cinema and the psycho-political narratives, systems and structures it refracts. Once again 'Shakespeare' is the space where the past meets our uncertain future.

Sometime 'after Chernobyl' when all art has been destroyed, William Shakespeare Jr. V wanders Europe trying to reconstruct fragments of the canon and noting down the Mafia boss Don Learo's words as he recalls the founding fathers of American mass culture, the gangsters who built Las Vegas. Writing, film-making, history, patriarchy, incest – Godard's visual and spoken commentaries allude to a vast atomised exploitative culture until finally dissidents on a beach at the edge of the world encounter a new *écriture feminine*, Woolf's *The Waves*: 'Against you I will fling myself, unvanquished and unyielding, O Death!' Shakespeare's 'secrets' are passed on to the Fool – Woody Allen. There is no more thorough leftist deconstruction of Shakespeare on film, no firmer attempt to write his epitaph.[18]

Yet in 1995 Eric Rohmer, another veteran of the French New Wave, wryly embraced Shakespeare (and the family) in his humanistic *A Winter's Tale / Un Conte d'Hiver*. Rohmer accepts the romance of strange births, separations and reunions as, however improbably, perhaps the best guide to human affairs we have. Félice, a Parisian hairdresser (Charlotte Vary) meets a young man on holiday and becomes pregnant, but accidentally gives him the wrong address. He disappears. Years later she is in emotional limbo unable to choose between a number of suitors, and her infuriating refusal to commit herself may be jeopardising her daughter's future. A librarian boyfriend takes her to Shakespeare's play and Hermione's woodenly acted resurrection shatters her: 'Faith brings her back.' Just as the film is finishing, she meets her lost boyfriend on a train: Rohmer plays magisterially, almost cruelly, on the emotions, first suggesting that he long ago forgot her and then revealing that, yes, they have both been seeking each other always, across the vasts of time. Opposition or reconciliation? Godard or Rohmer? As long as our cultural yearnings are divided, filmmakers will continue to adapt these plays, hacking away at ancient structures in search of truths they have already half-defined.

NOTES

1 Quoted in Robert Hamilton Ball, *Shakespeare on Silent Film* (London, 1968), pp. 132–4. For space reasons, this chapter concentrates on European and American films. For valuable comment on Shakespeare's significance for global and especially Asian cinema, see Linda Boose and Richard Burt (eds.), *Shakespeare, the Movie, II* (London, 2003).

2 A co-production with the director Paul Czinner's company, Inter-Allied.

3 In Mel Brooks's coarser remake the theatre becomes a refuge for hunted Jews. In *Schindler's List* the Nazi villain quotes Shylock's speech during a sexual assault on a concentration camp prisoner. Normally, though, Hollywood uses it as a universal plea

for tolerance: Mel Gibson in *The Man Without a Face* is a disfigured recluse who begins to relate to others by exploring the play.

4 From Gottfried Keller's *novella* of the same title, itself a literary 'offshoot'.

5 Robbins was the choreographer. *Romeo and Juliet* ballets have often been filmed; cf. *Kiss Me Kate*, where the *Shrew*'s Bianca plot is turned into dance.

6 The play has predictably inspired pornographic versions. See Richard Burt, *Unspeakable Shaxxxspeares: Queer Theory and American Kiddie Culture* (New York, 1998). In mainstream cinema the highpoint of bad taste Shakespeare is *Theatre of Blood* (UK, 1973), a black comedy starring Vincent Price as an actor who devises *grand guignol* murders for the critics, all based on Shakespeare scenes. The most extensive study of the recent popularisation of Shakespeare in the mass media is Linda E. Boose and Richard Burt, eds., *Shakespeare the Movie. Popularising the Plays on Film, TV and Video* (London and New York, 1997).

7 Officially, at least, Yordan was often a 'front' for blacklisted writers, and the precise nature of his role was not always clear. Yordan adapted *House of Strangers* from a Jerome Weidman novel. Yordan only wrote the 'original story' of *Broken Lance* but won an Oscar for it: the screenplay was by Richard Murphy. See *Monthly Film Bulletin* (February 1988), pp. 38–9.

8 *Johnny Amleto* – aka *Quella Sporca Storia del West; Uccidere o non Uccidere*. Castellari co-scripted with the political film-maker Sergio Corbucci.

9 See 'Kurosawa on Kurosawa', interview with Donald Ritchie, *Sight and Sound* (Summer/Autumn 1964), 108–13, 200–3.

10 Even a partial catalogue of loose *Hamlet* adaptations and allusions would fill this chapter. See Stoppard's *Rosencrantz and Guildenstern are Dead* (1991), Branagh's *In The Bleak Midwinter* (1996), Gabriel Axel's *The Prince of Jutland* (1993), based on the Amleth saga, and Bergman's *Fanny and Alexander* (1982), which tells the story of two children from a Swedish theatrical family whose father dies while playing the Ghost and whose mother rejects her old life to marry a priest. Bergman's bitter-sweet elegy for a lost community can be placed alongside James Ivory's *Shakespeare Wallah* (1965), where Anglo-Indian actors slowly realise that the culture of the Raj is dead.

11 Both were Columbia pictures.

12 Cf. Steiger's perfomance in *Oklahoma!* (1955).

13 The script was by Paul Jarrico, a blacklisted American forced like his hero to work in Britain; here he called himself 'Peter Achilles'.

14 Shakespearean film musicals had become increasingly sober by this time. *The Boys from Syracuse* (USA, 1940) was the Rogers and Hart version of *The Comedy of Errors* ('After a play by Shakespeare . . . Long, long after!'), a Roman-follies-style extravaganza which revelled in its cheerful unrespectability and celebrated its own anachronisms in the song: 'Thou Swell'. Such musicals were consciously cinematic: Allan Jones played both Antipholi; *Kiss Me Kate* (USA, 1953) was filmed in 3–D, so in this version of *The Shrew* Kate spent much of her time throwing things at the audience; and *West Side Story* began with a famous shot zooming from the cosmos to a city street.

15 Pierre Brasseur also starred in *The Lovers of Verona* and in *Red Stage/Le Rideau Rouge*, aka *Ce Soir, on Joue Macbeth* (France, 1952).

16 Woody Allen played his own variations on this theme in *A Midsummer Night's Sex Comedy* (USA, 1982) where *The Tempest* meets the *Dream* and Bergman and sequences from Reinhardt's film are affectionately parodied.

17 Credits: *Dead Poets' Society* (Peter Weir, 1987); *Outrageous Fortune* (Arthur Hiller, 1987); *Star Trek VI* (Nicholas Meyer, 1991); *LA Story* (Mick Jackson, 1991); *The Last Action Hero* (John McTiernan, 1991); *Renaissance Man* (Penny Marshall, 1994); *The Lion King* (1994); *Pocahontas* (1994).

18 Godard's previous choice for Lear, Orson Welles, had died. One of the film's motifs overlays Cordelia with St Joan.

FURTHER READING

The following lists include (1) reference works; (2) collected essays and special issues of periodicals; (3) general; (4) published scripts and other background material on individual films. It should be noted that these published scipts often include sequences altered or cut in the film as released, although not all make this plain to the reader. In addition to this summary bibliography, readers are referred to the specialised studies cited in the endnotes to each chapter. A fuller bibliography will be found in Kenneth S. Rothwell's *A History of Shakespeare on Screen* (2nd edn, Cambridge, 2004).

1 Reference

McKernan, Luke and Olwen Terris, eds., *Walking Shadows. Shakespeare in the National Film and Television Archives* (London, 1994). (With informative introduction, historical essays and bibliography: only lists films included in the NFTA.)

Parker, Barry M., *The Folger Shakespeare Filmography* (Washington, D.C., 1977).

Rothwell, Kenneth S. and Annabelle Henkin Melzer, eds., *Shakespeare on Screen: an International Filmography and Videography* (London, 1990). (Comprehensive and detailed, with a valuable introduction and notes on each film.)

2 Collected essays, special issues of periodicals

Boose, Lynda E. and Richard Burt, eds., *Shakespeare, the Movie. Popularising the Plays on Film, TV and Video* (London and New York, 1997).

Shakespeare the Movie II. Popularizing the plays on film, TV, video and DVD, (London, 2004).

Burnett, Mark Thomson and Ramona Wray, eds., *Shakespeare, Film, Fin de Siècle* (Basingstoke, 2000).

Cinéaste, 24, 1 (Fall 1998): 'Shakespeare in the Cinema Supplement' (28–67).

Davies, Anthony and Stanley Wells, eds., *Shakespeare and the Moving Image. The Plays on Film and Television* (Cambridge, 1994).

Eckert, Charles W., ed., *Focus on Shakespearean Films* (Englewood Cliffs, NJ, 1972).

Dorval, Patricia, ed., *Shakespeare et le cinéma. Actes du Congrès de 1998 de la Société Française Shakespeare* (Paris, 1998).

Drexler, Peter and Lawrence Guntner, eds., *Negotiations with Hal. Multi-Media Perceptions of (Shakespeare's) Henry the Fifth* (Braunschweig, 1995).

Literature/Film Quarterly, 20, 4 (1992) (issue on Shakespeare on film and television).

Henderson, Diane E., ed., *A Concise Companion to Shakespeare on Screen* (Oxford, 2006).

Klein, Holger and Dimiter Daphinoff, eds., *'Hamlet' on Screen. Shakespeare Yearbook*, 8 (Lampeter, 1997).

Lehmann, Courtney and Lisa Starks, *Spectacular Shakespeare. Critical Theory and Popular Cinema* (Madison and Teaneck, NJ, and London, 2002).

Mast, Gerald and Marshall Cohen, eds., *Film Theory and Criticism* (New York, 1974) (later editions of this valuable anthology have omitted the section on Shakespeare and film).

Shakespeare on Film Newsletter (1976–1992: subsequently incorporated *in Shakespeare Bulletin*) (regular reviews and articles on filmed Shakespeare).

Shaughnessy, Robert, ed., *Shakespeare on Film*, 'New Casebooks' series (Houndmills, Basingstoke and London, 1998).

Starks, Lisa S. and Courtney Lehmann, eds., *The Reel Shakespeare* (Madison and Teaneck, NJ, and London, 2002).

Welsh, James M., Richard Vela and John C. Tibbetts, *Shakespeare into Film* (New York, 2002).

3 General

Aebischer, Pascale, *Shakespeare's Violated Bodies. Stage and Screen Performance* (Cambridge, 2004).

Anderegg, Michael, *Cinematic Shakespeare* (Lanham, Boulder, New York, Toronto, Oxford, 2004).

Ball, Robert Hamilton, *Shakespeare on Silent Film: a Strange Eventful History* (London, 1968).

Buchanan, Judith, *Shakespeare and Film* (London and New York, 2005).

Buchman, Lorne M., *Still in Movement: Shakespeare on Screen* (New York, 1991).

Buhler, Stephen M., *Shakespeare in the Cinema. Ocular Proof* (Albany, NY, 2002).

Burt, Richard, *Unspeakable Shaxxxspeares: Queer Theory and American Kiddie Culture* (New York, 1998).

Collick, John, *Shakespeare, Cinema and Society* (Manchester, 1989).

Crowl, Samuel, *Shakespeare Observed. Studies in Performance on Stage and Screen* (Athens, OH, 1992).

Coursen, H. A., *Shakespearean Performance as Interpretation* (Wilmington, DE, 1990).
  Shakespearean Production. Whose History? (Athens, OH, 1996).

Davies, Anthony, *Filming Shakespeare's Plays* (Cambridge, 1988).

Dawson, Anthony B., *Shakespeare in Performance: 'Hamlet'* (Manchester, 1995).

Donaldson, Peter S., *Shakespearean Films/Shakespearean Directors* (Boston, MA, 1990).

Fuegi, John, 'Explorations in No Man's Land: Shakespeare's Poetry as Theatrical Film', *Shakespeare Quarterly*, 23 (1972), 37–49.

Hatchuel, Sarah, *Shakespeare, from Stage to Screen* (Cambridge, 2004).

Holderness, Graham, 'Shakespeare Rewound', in Stanley Wells, ed., *Shakespeare Survey 45: 'Hamlet' and its Afterlife* (Cambridge, 1982), pp. 63–74.
  Shakespeare in Performance: 'The Taming of the Shrew' (Manchester, 1989).

Howlett, Kathy M., *Framing Shakespeare on Film* (Athens, OH, 2000).

Jorgens, Jack J., *Shakespeare on Film* (Bloomington, IN, 1977).

Kliman, Bernice W., *'Hamlet.' Film, Television and Audio Performance* (Cranbury, NJ, 1988).

Shakespeare in Performance: 'Macbeth' (Manchester, 1995) (chapter on Polanski).

Kozintsev, Grigori, *Shakespeare, Time and Conscience*, translated by Joyce Vining (London, 1967).

King Lear. The Space of Tragedy, translated by Mary Mackintosh (London, 1977).

Leggatt, Alexander, *Shakespeare in Performance: King Lear* (Manchester, 1991).

Lehmann, Courtney, *Shakespeare Remains. Theater to Film, Early Modern to Postmodern* (Ithaca, NY, and London, 2002).

Levenson, Jill L., *Shakespeare in Performance: Romeo and Juliet* (Manchester, 1987).

Manvell, Roger, *Shakespeare and the Film* (1971; revised edn, London, 1979).

Pilkington, Ace. G., *Screening Shakespeare. From Richard II to Henry V* (Newark, DE, and London, 1991).

Potter, Lois, *Shakespeare in Performance: 'Othello'* (Manchester, 2002).

Rosenthal, Daniel, *Shakespeare on Screen* (London, 2000).

Rothwell, Kenneth S., *A History of Shakespeare on Screen. A Century of Film and Television* (2nd edition, Cambridge, 2004).

Sinyard, Neil, *Filming Literature. The Art of Adaptation* (London, 1986).

Uricchio William, and Roberta E. Pearson, *Reframing Culture. The Case of the Vitagraph Quality Films* (Princeton, NJ, 1993).

4 *Published screenplays and other documentation*

Chimes at Midnight (Orson Welles, 1965)

Bridget Gellert Lyons, ed., *Chimes at Midnight* (script as transcribed from the film, with documents, with an introduction) (Brunswick, NJ, 1988).

Hamlet (Laurence Olivier, 1948).

Brenda Cross, ed., *The Film 'Hamlet'. A Record of its Production* (London, 1948).

Alan Dent, ed., *'Hamlet'. The Film and the Play* (London, 1948) (includes script).

Hamlet (Kenneth Branagh, 1996)

'Hamlet' by William Shakespeare. Screenplay and Introduction by Kenneth Branagh. Film Diary by Russell Jackson (London, 1996).

Hamlet (Michael Almereyda, 2000).

William Shakespeare's 'Hamlet', adapted by *Michael Almereyda, with an Introduction by Ethan Hawke* (London, 2000)

Henry V (Laurence Olivier, 1944)

Andrew Sinclair, ed., *'Henry V' by William Shakespeare, Produced and Directed by Laurence Olivier* (London, 1984).

C. Clayton Hutton, *The Making of 'Henry V'* (London, 1944).

Henry V (Kenneth Branagh, 1989)

'Henry V' by William Shakespeare. A Screen Adaptation by Kenneth Branagh (London, 1989).

Kenneth Branagh, *Beginning* (London, 1989) (volume of autobiography: information on filming).

Much Ado About Nothing (Kenneth Branagh, 1994)

'Much Ado about Nothing' by William Shakespeare. Screenplay, Introduction and Notes on the Making of the Film by Kenneth Branagh (London, 1993).

A Midsummer Night's Dream (Michael Hoffman, 1999)

William Shakespeare's 'A Midsummer Night's Dream' Adapted for the Screen and Directed by Michael Hoffman (London, 1999).

Ran (Akira Kurosawa, 1985)

   Le Livre de Ran. Texte de Bertrand Raison avec la collaboration de Serge Toubiana (Paris, 1985) ('making of' book, lavishly illustrated).

'*Ran*' . . . *Screenplay by Akira Kurosawa, Hideo Ogun and Ide Masato*, translated by Tadashi Shishido (Boston, MA, and London, 1986) (script with Kurosawa's storyboards and other artwork).

Richard III (McKellen/Loncraine, 1996)

   Ian McKellen, *William Shakespeare's 'Richard III'. A Screenplay Written by Ian McKellen and Richard Loncraine, Annotated and Introduced by Ian McKellen* (London, 1996).

Romeo and Juliet (George Cukor, 1936)

   Romeo and Juliet: A Motion Picture Edition . . . arranged for the Screen by Talbot Jennings (New York, 1936) (screenplay, with articles on various aspects of production).

Romeo and Juliet (Franco Zeffirelli, 1968)

   Alan Denson, ed., *Franco Zeffirelli's Production of William Shakespeare's 'Romeo and Juliet'* (2nd edn, London, 1968).

Romeo and Juliet (Baz Luhrmann, 1996)

   Baz Luhrmann, *William Shakespeare's 'Romeo and Juliet' . . . The Screenplay by Craig Pearce and Baz Luhrmann and the Text of Shakespeare's Original Play* (London, 1996) (short introduction by the director).

Throne of Blood / Kumonoso-djo (Akira Kurosawa, 1957)

   Translated by Hisae Niki, in *Seven Samurai and Other Screenplays* (London, 1992).

TITUS (Julie Taymor, 2000)

   TITUS. The Illustrated Screenplay, Adapted from the Play by William Shakespeare [by] Julie Taymor (New York, 2000).

Twelfth Night (Trevor Nunn, 1996)

   Twelfth Night. A Screenplay by Trevor Nunn (London, 1996).

FILMOGRAPHY

Section One lists, alphabetically by English title, the feature films of Shakespeare's plays discussed in the *Companion*. The country of production is given in full except for the United Kingdom (UK), The United States (USA) and the former Union of Soviet Socialist Republics (USSR). Many films have a combination of 'nationalities' including the source of finance and the location of the production. In some cases (notably Welles's *Othello* and *Chimes at Midnight*) the ascribed nationality reflects the international nature of the enterprise, but no one would seriously claim the latter film as a contribution to Swiss cinema. The date given is that of the film's release: reference works will be found to differ in this respect, because of the variation in release dates across the distribution regions, particularly where films have been produced in Europe but partly financed and consequently given their first release in North America. The director's name is given, but principal actors are listed only to the extent that these have commonly been used to identify a film.

Section Two gives a more summary list (title, country, date) of 'offshoots' – films derived in part from Shakespearean originals or making substantial allusion to them. Most of these are discussed or referred to by Tony Howard in chapter 17.

Fuller production details and credits of the films listed in both sections will be found in the reference works by Rothwell and Melzer (*Shakespeare on Screen*) and McKernan and Terris (*Walking Shadows*), which also include descriptive notes and bibliographical references. I have not attempted to give distribution or availability details: films move in and out of the DVD and distributors' hire catalogues, and their availability varies from one region to another. Most of the mainstream screen versions made recently or now owned by major distributors are to be found in the shops, but neither Paul Czinner's *As You Like It* nor Peter Hall's *Midsummer Night's Dream*, for example, have yet been distributed in Great Britain, and Kozintsev's *King Lear* and *Hamlet*, after moving in and out of the video catalogue, have only recently become available on (Russian) DVD. Of the silent films only a handful have been distributed on video: the German *Othello* (1922), Warde's 1911 *Richard III* and a few other silent titles are available in North America. The British Film Institute's valuable *Silent Shakespeare*, issued in 1999 and reissued on DVD in 2005, offers eight items, including Herbert Beerbohm Tree in *King John* (1899: the earliest surviving fragment of a Shakespeare film) and F. R. Benson's company in *Richard III* (1911). In some cases, the DVDs (or their 'special editions') carry commentaries and (in some cases) deleted or alternative versions of scenes. Interviews, either specially commissioned or part of the EPK (Electronic Press Kit) produced alongside the film are also sometimes included. To complicate matters, these DVD issues often vary from region to region, those distributed in the USA – Region 1 – being commonly fuller. The best currently available versions of Olivier's and Kurosawa's films are those from Criterion, available only in Region 1 format.

1 Films of Shakespeare's plays

ANTONY AND CLEOPATRA (UK/Spain/Switzerland, 1972)
Dir. Charlton Heston
Charlton Heston (Antony), Hildegarde Neil (Cleopatra)

AS YOU LIKE IT (UK, 1936)
Dir. Paul Czinner
Elisabeth Bergner (Rosalind), Laurence Olivier (Orlando)

AS YOU LIKE IT (UK, 1992)
Dir. Christine Edzard
Emma Croft (Rosalind)

AS YOU LIKE IT (UK/USA, 2006)
Dir. Kenneth Branagh
Bryce Dallas Howard (Rosalind), Kevin Kline (Jacques), David Oleweyo (Orlando), Adrian Lester (Oliver)

CHIMES AT MIDNIGHT (also known as FALSTAFF) (Spain/Switzerland, 1966)
Dir. Orson Welles
Orson Welles (Falstaff), Keith Baxter (Hal), John Gielgud (King Henry)

HAMLET (UK, 1913)
Dir. E. Hay Plumb
Johnston Forbes-Robertson (Hamlet), Gertrude Elliott (Ophelia)

HAMLET (Germany, 1920)
Dir. Svend Gade, Heinz Schall
Asta Nielsen (Hamlet)

HAMLET (UK, 1948)
Dir. Laurence Olivier
Laurence Olivier (Hamlet), Jean Simmons (Ophelia), Eileen Herlie (Queen)

HAMLET (USSR, 1964)
Dir. Grigori Kozintsev
Innokenti Smoktunovski (Hamlet), Anastasia Vertinskaia (Ophelia), Elza Radzin (Queen)

HAMLET (UK, 1969)
Dir. Tony Richardson
Nicol Williamson (Hamlet), Marianne Faithfull (Ophelia), Judy Parfitt (Queen), Anthony Hopkins (King)

HAMLET (UK, 1990)
Dir. Franco Zeffirelli
Mel Gibson (Hamlet), Helena Bonham-Carter (Ophelia), Glenn Close (Queen), Alan Bates (King)

HAMLET (UK, 1996)
Dir. Kenneth Branagh
Kenneth Branagh (Hamlet), Kate Winslet (Ophelia), Julie Christie (Queen), Derek Jacobi (King)

HAMLET (USA, 2000)
Dir. Michael Almereyda
Ethan Hawke (Hamlet), Julia Stiles (Ophelia), Diane Venora (Queen), Bill Murray (King), Sam Shepard (Polonius)

HENRY V (UK, 1944)
Dir. Laurence Olivier ('in close association with . . . Reginald Beck')
Laurence Olivier (King), Renée Asherson (Katherine)

HENRY V (UK, 1989)
Dir. Kenneth Branagh
Kenneth Branagh (King), Emma Thompson (Katherine), Derek Jacobi (Chorus)

JULIUS CAESAR (USA, 1953)
Dir. Joseph L. Mankiewicz
Marlon Brando (Antony), James Mason (Brutus), John Gielgud (Cassius), Louis Calhern (Julius Caesar)

JULIUS CAESAR (UK, 1970)
Dir. Stuart Burge
Charlton Heston (Antony), Jason Robards (Brutus), Richard Johnson (Cassius), John Gielgud (Julius Caesar), Jill Bennett (Calpurnia), Diana Rigg (Portia)

KING LEAR (USSR, 1970)
Dir. Grigori Kozintsev
Yuri Savit (Lear), Oleg Dal (Fool), Elza Radzin (Goneril)

KING LEAR (UK, 1971)
Dir. Peter Brook
Paul Scofield (Lear), Jack McGowran (Fool), Irene Worth (Goneril)

KING LEAR (Japan 1985): see RAN

LOOKING FOR RICHARD (USA, 1996)
Dir. Al Pacino
Al Pacino (Richard), Kevin Spacey (Buckingham), Winona Ryder (Lady Anne)

LOVE'S LABOURS LOST (UK, 1999)
Dir. Kenneth Branagh
Kenneth Branagh (Berowne), Alicia Silverstone (Princess), Natascha McIlhone (Rosaline), Nathan Lane (Costard)

MACBETH (USA, 1948)
Dir. Orson Welles
Orson Welles (Macbeth), Jeanette Nolan (Lady Macbeth)

MACBETH (Japan, 1957): see THRONE OF BLOOD

MACBETH (UK, 1971)
Dir. Roman Polanski
Jon Finch (Macbeth), Francesca Annis (Lady Macbeth)

THE MERCHANT OF VENICE (2004)
Dir. Michael Radford
Al Pacino (Shylock), Jeremy Irons (Antonio)

A MIDSUMMER NIGHT'S DREAM (USA, 1935)
Dir. Max Reinhardt, William Dieterle
James Cagney (Bottom), Victor Jory (Oberon), Veree Teesdale (Titania), Dick Powell (Lysander), Olivia de Havilland (Hermia), Mickey Rooney (Puck)

A MIDSUMMER NIGHT'S DREAM (UK, 1968)
Dir. Peter Hall (from his RSC production)
Paul Hardwick (Bottom), Ian Richardson (Oberon), Judi Dench (Titania), Ian Holm (Puck)

A MIDSUMMER NIGHT'S DREAM (UK, 1996)
Dir. Adrian Noble (from his RSC production)
Desmond Barrit (Bottom), Alex Jennings (Theseus/Oberon), Lindsey Duncan (Hippolyta/Titania), Finnbar Lynch (Philostrate/Puck)

A MIDSUMMER NIGHT'S DREAM (USA, Italy 1999)
Dir. Michael Hoffmann
Kevin Kline (Bottom), Michele Pfeiffer (Titania), Rupert Everett (Oberon), Stanley Tucci (Puck)

MUCH ADO ABOUT NOTHING (UK, Italy, 1993)
Dir. Kenneth Branagh
Kenneth Branagh (Benedick), Emma Thompson (Beatrice)

OTHELLO (Germany, 1922)
Dir. Dmitri Buchowetski
Werner Krauss (Othello), Emil Jannings (Iago), Ica von Lenkeffy (Desdemona)

OTHELLO (Morocco/Italy 1952)
Dir. Orson Welles
Orson Welles (Othello), Suzanne Cloutier (Desdemona), Micheál Macliammóir (Iago)

OTHELLO (USSR, 1956)
Dir. Sergei Yutkevich
Sergei Bondarchuk (Othello), Irina Skobesteva (Desdemona), Andrei Popov (Iago)

OTHELLO (UK, 1965)
Dir. Stuart Burge
Laurence Olivier (Othello), Maggie Smith (Desdemona), Frank Finlay (Iago)

OTHELLO (UK 1995)
Dir. Oliver Parker
Laurence Fishburne (Othello), Irène Jacob (Desdemona), Kenneth Branagh (Iago)

PROSPERO'S BOOKS (UK/ Netherlands/France/Italy, 1991)
Dir. Peter Greenaway
John Gielgud (Prospero), Michael Clark (Caliban), Mark Rylance (Ferdinand), Isabelle Pasco (Miranda)

RAN ('Chaos') (Japan, 1985)
Dir. Akira Kurosawa
Tatsuya Nakadai (Hidetori/Lear), Peter (Kyoami/ Fool)

RICHARD III (USA, 1912, 1913)
Dir. M.B. Dudley
Frederick Warde (Richard)

RICHARD III (UK, 1955)
Dir. Laurence Olivier
Laurence Olivier (Richard), John Gielgud (Clarence), Ralph Richardson (Buckingham), Claire Bloom (Lady Anne)

RICHARD III (UK, 1996)
Dir. Richard Loncraine, Ian McKellen
Ian McKellen (Richard), Nigel Hawthorne (Clarence), Jim Carter (Buckingham), Annette Bening (Lady Anne), Maggie Smith (Queen Margaret)

ROMEO AND JULIET (USA, 1936)
Dir. George Cukor
Leslie Howard (Romeo), Norma Shearer (Juliet), Edna May Oliver (Nurse), John Barrymore (Mercutio), Basil Rathbone (Tybalt)

ROMEO AND JULIET (UK/Italy, 1954)
Dir. Renato Castellani
Laurence Harvey (Romeo), Susan Shentall (Juliet), Flora Robson (Nurse)

ROMEO AND JULIET (Italy/UK 1968)
Dir. Franco Zeffirelli
Leonard Whiting (Romeo), Olivia Hussey (Juliet), John McEnery (Mercutio)

ROMEO+JULIET (USA, 1996)
Dir. Baz Luhrmann
Leonardo DiCaprio (Romeo), Claire Danes (Juliet)

THE TAMING OF THE SHREW (USA, 1929)
Dir. Sam Taylor
Mary Pickford (Katherine), Douglas Fairbanks (Petruchio)

THE TAMING OF THE SHREW (USA/Italy, 1966)
Dir. Franco Zeffirelli
Elizabeth Taylor (Katherine), Richard Burton (Petruchio)

THRONE OF BLOOD (*Kumonosu-djo*) (Japan, 1957)
Dir. Akira Kurosawa
Toshiro Mifune (Washizu/Macbeth), Isuzu Yamada (Asaji/Lady Macbeth)

THE TEMPEST (UK, 1979)
Dir. Derek Jarman
Heathcote Williams (Prospero), Toyah Willcox (Miranda)

THE TEMPEST (1991): see PROSPERO'S BOOKS

TITUS (USA/Italy, 1999)
Dir. Julie Taymor
Anthony Hopkins (Titus), Jessica Lange (Tamora), Harry Lennix (Aaron), Alan Cumming (Saturninus)

TWELFTH NIGHT (USSR, 1955)
Dir. Yakov Fried
Katya Luchko (Viola)

TWELFTH NIGHT (UK, 1995)
Dir. Trevor Nunn
Imogen Stubbs (Viola), Helena Bonham-Carter (Olivia), Nigel Hawthorne (Malvolio), Ben Kingsley (Feste)

2 'Offshoots'

(English titles are given, together with the title of the original play where this is not self-evident)
Age of Consent (Australia, 1968: *The Tempest*)
All Night Long (UK, 1961: *Othello*)
The Bad Sleep Well (Japan, 1960: *Hamlet*)
The Boys from Syracuse (USA, 1940: *The Comedy of Errors*)

Broken Lance (USA, 1954: *King Lear*)
Carnival (UK, 1921; remake USA, 1931: *Othello*)
Catch my Soul (USA, 1973: *Othello*)
Dead Poets' Society (USA, 1987: *A Midsummer Night's Dream*)
Desdemona (Denmark, 1911)
A Double Life (USA, 1947: *Othello*)
Les Enfants du Paradis (France, 1945: *Othello*)
Forbidden Planet (USA, 1956: *The Tempest*)
The Godfather III (USA, 1990: *King Lear*)
Hamlet Goes Business (Finland, 1987)
An Honourable Murder (UK, 1959: *Julius Caesar*)
House of Strangers (USA, 1949: *King Lear*)
An Imaginary Tale (*Une histoire inventée*, France/Canada, 1990: *Othello*)
In the Bleak Midwinter (UK, 1996: *Hamlet*)
Joe Macbeth (UK, 1955)
Johnny Hamlet (Italy, 1968)
Jubal (USA, 1935: *Othello*)
Kean (Italy, 1956: *Othello*)
King Lear (USA, 1987: Jean-Luc Godard)
Kiss me Kate (USA, 1953: *The Taming of the Shrew*)
The Last Action Hero (USA, 1991: *Hamlet*)
A Letter to Timothy (UK, 1946: *Hamlet*)
The Lion King (USA, 1994: *Hamlet*)
Love Story (USA, 1944: *The Tempest*)
The Lovers of Verona (France, 1949: *Romeo and Juliet*)
A Matter of Life and Death (UK, 1946: *A Midsummer Night's Dream*)
Men Are Not Gods (UK, 1936: *Othello*)
Men of Respect (USA, 1990: *Macbeth*)
A Midsummer Night's Sex Comedy (USA, 1982: *The Tempest* and *A Midsummer Night's Dream*)
A Modern Othello (UK, 1917)
My Own Private Idaho (USA 1991: *Henry IV*)
O (USA 2001: *Othello*)
Ophélia (France, 1962)
Outrageous Fortune (USA, 1987: *Hamlet*)
Panic Button (USA, 1964: *Romeo and Juliet*)
The Playboys (UK, 1992: *Othello*)
Pocahontas (USA, 1994: *The Tempest*)
The Postman (USA, 1997: various)
The Punk (UK, 1993: *Romeo and Juliet*)
Renaissance Man (USA, 1994: *Hamlet*)
The Rest is Silence (Germany, 1959: *Hamlet*)
Romanoff and Juliet (USA, 1960)
Romeo and Julie (Poland, 1937)
Romeo and Juliet (Belgium, 1990)
Romeo and Juliet in the Village (Switzerland, 1941: after Gottfried Keller's novella)
Romeo, Juliet and Darkness (Czechoslavkia, 1960)
A Romeo and Juliet of Today (Yugoslavia, 1966)

Rosencrantz and Guildenstern are Dead (UK, 1991: *Hamlet*)
Scotland PA (USA, 2002: *Macbeth*)
Shakespeare in Love (UK, 1998: *Romeo and Juliet*)
Shakespeare Writing 'Julius Caesar' (USA, 1907)
Star Trek VI; the Undiscovered Country (USA, 1991: *Hamlet*)
A Thousand Acres (USA, 1997: *King Lear*)
Tempest (USA, 1982)
Ten Things I Hate About You (USA, 1999: *The Taming of the Shrew*)
Theatre of Blood (UK, 1973: various)
To Be or Not to Be (USA, 1942; remake 1983: *Hamlet*)
Tromeo and Juliet (USA, 1996)
True Identity (USA, 1991: *Othello*)
West Side Story (USA, 1961: *Romeo and Juliet*)
Where the Heart Is (USA, 1990: *King Lear*)
A Winter's Tale (France, 1995)
The Yellow Canary (UK, 1943: *The Tempest*)
Yellow Sky (USA, 1946: *The Tempest*)

INDEX

Films and plays are identified as such. Productions of Shakespeare's plays are identified with their medium (stage, film, TV etc.) and year. The index does not include entries in the *Companion's* filmography or the list of further reading, or direct readers to end-notes that identify sources for references in the body of the text.

Cambridge Companions to Literature

AUTHORS

Edward Albee *edited by Stephen J. Bottoms*

Margaret Atwood *edited by Coral Ann Howells*

W. H. Auden *edited by Stan Smith*

Jane Austen *edited by Edward Copeland and Juliet McMaster*

Beckett *edited by John Pilling*

Aphra Behn *edited by Derek Hughes and Janet Todd*

Walter Benjamin *edited by David S. Ferris*

William Blake *edited by Morris Eaves*

Brecht *edited by Peter Thomson and Glendyr Sacks* (second edition)

The Brontës *edited by Heather Glen*

Frances Burney *edited by Peter Sabor*

Byron *edited by Drummond Bone*

Albert Camus *edited by Edward J. Hughes*

Willa Cather *edited by Marilee Lindemann*

Cervantes *edited by Anthony J. Cascardi*

Chaucer, *second edition edited by Piero Boitani and Jill Mann*

Chekhov *edited by Vera Gottlieb and Paul Allain*

Coleridge *edited by Lucy Newlyn*

Wilkie Collins *edited by Jenny Bourne Taylor*

Joseph Conrad *edited by J. H. Stape*

Dante *edited by Rachel Jacoff* (second edition)

Charles Dickens *edited by John O. Jordan*

Emily Dickinson *edited by Wendy Martin*

John Donne *edited by Achsah Guibbory*

Dostoevskii *edited by W. J. Leatherbarrow*

Theodore Dreiser *edited by Leonard Cassuto and Claire Virginia Eby*

John Dryden *edited by Steven N. Zwicker*

George Eliot *edited by George Levine*

T. S. Eliot *edited by A. David Moody*

Ralph Ellison *edited by Ross Posnock*

Ralph Waldo Emerson *edited by Joel Porte and Saundra Morris*

William Faulkner *edited by Philip M. Weinstein*

Henry Fielding *edited by Claude Rawson*

F. Scott Fitzgerald *edited by Ruth Prigozy*

Flaubert *edited by Timothy Unwin*

E. M. Forster *edited by David Bradshaw*

Brian Friel *edited by Anthony Roche*

Robert Frost *edited by Robert Faggen*

Elizabeth Gaskell *edited by Jill L. Matus*

Goethe *edited by Lesley Sharpe*

Thomas Hardy *edited by Dale Kramer*

Nathaniel Hawthorne *edited by Richard Millington*

Ernest Hemingway *edited by Scott Donaldson*

Homer *edited by Robert Fowler*

Ibsen *edited by James McFarlane*

Henry James *edited by Jonathan Freedman*

Samuel Johnson *edited by Greg Clingham*

Ben Jonson *edited by Richard Harp and Stanley Stewart*

James Joyce *edited by Derek Attridge* (second edition)

Kafka *edited by Julian Preece*

Keats *edited by Susan J. Wolfson*

Lacan *edited by Jean-Michel Rabaté*

D. H. Lawrence *edited by Anne Fernihough*

Primo Levi *edited by Robert Gordon*

David Mamet *edited by Christopher Bigsby*

Thomas Mann *edited by Ritchie Robertson*

Herman Melville *edited by Robert S. Levine*

Christopher Marlowe *edited by Patrick Cheney*

Arthur Miller *edited by Christopher Bigsby*

Milton *edited by Dennis Danielson* (second edition)

Molière *edited by David Bradby and Andrew Calder*

Nabokov *edited by Julian W. Connolly*

Eugene O'Neill *edited by Michael Manheim*

George Orwell *edited by John Rodden*

Ovid *edited by Philip Hardie*

Harold Pinter *edited by Peter Raby*

Sylvia Plath *edited by Jo Gill*

Edgar Allan Poe *edited by Kevin J. Hayes*

Ezra Pound *edited by Ira B. Nadel*

Proust *edited by Richard Bales*

Pushkin *edited by Andrew Kahn*

Philip Roth *edited by Timothy Parrish*

Salman Rushdie *edited by Abdulrazak Gurnah*

Shakespeare *edited by Margareta de Grazia and Stanley Wells*

Shakespeare on Film *edited by Russell Jackson* (second edition)

TOPICS